Toyota Aygo, Citroën C1 & Peugeot 107
Owners Workshop Manual

Peter T Gill

(6334 - 272)

Models covered

Toyota Aygo, Peugeot 107 & Citroën C1 Hatchbacks with 1.0 litre (998cc) petrol engine

Does NOT cover diesel models, or revised model ranges introduced July 2014

© Haynes Group Limited 2016

A book in the **Haynes Owners Workshop Manual Series**

All rights reserved. No part of this book may be reproduced or transmitted in any form or by any means, electronic or mechanical, including photocopying, recording or by any information storage or retrieval system, without permission in writing from the copyright holder.

ABCDE
FGHIJ
KLM

ISBN **978 1 78521 334 2**

British Library Cataloguing in Publication Data
A catalogue record for this book is available from the British Library.

Printed in India

Haynes Group Limited
Sparkford, Yeovil, Somerset BA22 7JJ, England

Haynes North America, Inc
2801 Townsgate Road, Suite 340, Thousand Oaks, CA 91361, USA

Disclaimer

There are risks associated with automotive repairs. The ability to make repairs depends on the individual's skill, experience and proper tools. Individuals should act with due care and acknowledge and assume the risk of performing automotive repairs.

The purpose of this manual is to provide comprehensive, useful and accessible automotive repair information, to help you get the best value from your vehicle. However, this manual is not a substitute for a professional certified technician or mechanic.

This repair manual is produced by a third party and is not associated with an individual vehicle manufacturer. If there is any doubt or discrepancy between this manual and the owner's manual or the factory service manual, please refer to the factory service manual or seek assistance from a professional certified technician or mechanic.

Even though we have prepared this manual with extreme care and every attempt is made to ensure that the information in this manual is correct, neither the publisher nor the author can accept responsibility for loss, damage or injury caused by any errors in, or omissions from, the information given.

Contents

Illegal Copying

It is the policy of the Publisher to actively protect its Copyrights and Trade Marks. Legal action will be taken against anyone who unlawfully copies the cover or contents of this Manual. This includes all forms of unauthorised copying including digital, mechanical, and electronic in any form. Authorisation from the Publisher will only be provided expressly and in writing. Illegal copying will also be reported to the appropriate statutory authorities.

Contents

Toyota Aygo

The Citroën C1, Peugeot 107 and Toyota Aygo were introduced into the UK in June 2005, and were all built in the same factory. Largely designed by Toyota, using the new 1.0 litre, 3-cylinder VVT-i engine in all three vehicles.

Complementing the small yet spacious body is a small-capacity engine, which thanks to multipoint injection, four valves per cylinder and variable valve timing, manages to offer the performance of larger units. The engine is mounted transversely at the front of the car.

As befits a modern supermini, these models offer high levels of passenger safety, with an impact-absorbing bodyshell and highly-rigid cabin, driver and passenger's airbags, and seat belt tensioners. Most of the latest models also have side airbags fitted.

Three- and five-door Hatchback models are available; all models have front-wheel-drive, with a five-speed Manual Transmission (MT) or a five-speed Multi-Mode Transmission

(MMT), which Citroën call 'SensoDrive' and Peugeot call '2-Tronic'. The front suspension is of conventional MacPherson strut type, incorporating lower arms, and an anti-roll bar; at the rear, a semi-independent beam axle is combined with compact under-floor springs to provide a more spacious load area.

There is a high equipment level, on these models, even at the lower end of the model range. The latest models all feature a driver's airbag, anti-lock brakes, trip computer, engine immobiliser, adjustable folding rear seat, radio/CD and electric power steering – central locking, electric windows and air conditioning are among the equipment fitted higher up the range.

For the home mechanic, these models are a straightforward car to maintain and repair, since design features have been incorporated to reduce the actual cost of ownership to a minimum, and most of the items requiring frequent attention are easily accessible.

Your Aygo, C1 & 107 manual

The aim of this manual is to help you get the best value from your car. It can do so in several ways. It can help you decide what work must be done (even should you choose to get it done by a garage). It will also provide information on routine maintenance and servicing, and give a logical course of action and diagnosis when random faults occur. However, it is hoped that you will use the manual by tackling the work yourself. On simpler jobs it may even be quicker than booking the car into a garage and going there twice, to leave and collect it. Perhaps most important, a lot of money can be saved by avoiding the costs a garage must charge to cover its labour and overheads.

The manual has drawings and descriptions to show the function of the various components so that their layout can be understood. Tasks are described and photographed in a clear step-by-step sequence.

References to the 'left' and 'right' of the car are in the sense of a person in the driver's seat, facing forwards.

Acknowledgements

Thanks are due to Draper tools Limited, who provided some of the workshop tools, and to all those people at Sparkford who helped in the production of this manual.

We take great pride in the accuracy of information given in this manual, but car manufacturers make alterations and design changes during the production run of a particular car of which they do not inform us. No liability can be accepted by the authors or publishers for loss, damage or injury caused by any errors in, or omissions from, the information given.

Peugeot 107

Citroën C1

Working on your car can be dangerous. This page shows just some of the potential risks and hazards, with the aim of creating a safety-conscious attitude.

General hazards

Scalding

• Don't remove the radiator or expansion tank cap while the engine is hot.
• Engine oil, transmission fluid or power steering fluid may also be dangerously hot if the engine has recently been running.

Burning

• Beware of burns from the exhaust system and from any part of the engine. Brake discs and drums can also be extremely hot immediately after use.

Crushing

• When working under or near a raised vehicle, always supplement the jack with axle stands, or use drive-on ramps. *Never venture under a car which is only supported by a jack*.
• Take care if loosening or tightening high-torque nuts when the vehicle is on stands. Initial loosening and final tightening should be done with the wheels on the ground.

Fire

• Fuel is highly flammable; fuel vapour is explosive.
• Don't let fuel spill onto a hot engine.
• Do not smoke or allow naked lights (including pilot lights) anywhere near a vehicle being worked on. Also beware of creating sparks (electrically or by use of tools).
• Fuel vapour is heavier than air, so don't work on the fuel system with the vehicle over an inspection pit.
• Another cause of fire is an electrical overload or short-circuit. Take care when repairing or modifying the vehicle wiring.
• Keep a fire extinguisher handy, of a type suitable for use on fuel and electrical fires.

Electric shock

• Ignition HT and Xenon headlight voltages can be dangerous, especially to people with heart problems or a pacemaker. Don't work on or near these systems with the engine running or the ignition switched on.

• Mains voltage is also dangerous. Make sure that any mains-operated equipment is correctly earthed. Mains power points should be protected by a residual current device (RCD) circuit breaker.

Fume or gas intoxication

• Exhaust fumes are poisonous; they can contain carbon monoxide, which is rapidly fatal if inhaled. Never run the engine in a confined space such as a garage with the doors shut.
• Fuel vapour is also poisonous, as are the vapours from some cleaning solvents and paint thinners.

Poisonous or irritant substances

• Avoid skin contact with battery acid and with any fuel, fluid or lubricant, especially antifreeze, brake hydraulic fluid and Diesel fuel. Don't syphon them by mouth. If such a substance is swallowed or gets into the eyes, seek medical advice.
• Prolonged contact with used engine oil can cause skin cancer. Wear gloves or use a barrier cream if necessary. Change out of oil-soaked clothes and do not keep oily rags in your pocket.
• Air conditioning refrigerant forms a poisonous gas if exposed to a naked flame (including a cigarette). It can also cause skin burns on contact.

Asbestos

• Asbestos dust can cause cancer if inhaled or swallowed. Asbestos may be found in gaskets and in brake and clutch linings. When dealing with such components it is safest to assume that they contain asbestos.

Special hazards

Hydrofluoric acid

• This extremely corrosive acid is formed when certain types of synthetic rubber, found in some O-rings, oil seals, fuel hoses etc, are exposed to temperatures above 4000C. The rubber changes into a charred or sticky substance containing the acid. *Once formed, the acid remains dangerous for years. If it gets onto the skin, it may be necessary to amputate the limb concerned.*
• When dealing with a vehicle which has suffered a fire, or with components salvaged from such a vehicle, wear protective gloves and discard them after use.

The battery

• Batteries contain sulphuric acid, which attacks clothing, eyes and skin. Take care when topping-up or carrying the battery.
• The hydrogen gas given off by the battery is highly explosive. Never cause a spark or allow a naked light nearby. Be careful when connecting and disconnecting battery chargers or jump leads.

Air bags

• Air bags can cause injury if they go off accidentally. Take care when removing the steering wheel and trim panels. Special storage instructions may apply.

Diesel injection equipment

• Diesel injection pumps supply fuel at very high pressure. Take care when working on the fuel injectors and fuel pipes.

Warning: Never expose the hands, face or any other part of the body to injector spray; the fuel can penetrate the skin with potentially fatal results.

Remember...

DO

• Do use eye protection when using power tools, and when working under the vehicle.

• Do wear gloves or use barrier cream to protect your hands when necessary.

• Do get someone to check periodically that all is well when working alone on the vehicle.

• Do keep loose clothing and long hair well out of the way of moving mechanical parts.

• Do remove rings, wristwatch etc, before working on the vehicle – especially the electrical system.

• Do ensure that any lifting or jacking equipment has a safe working load rating adequate for the job.

DON'T

• Don't attempt to lift a heavy component which may be beyond your capability – get assistance.

• Don't rush to finish a job, or take unverified short cuts.

• Don't use ill-fitting tools which may slip and cause injury.

• Don't leave tools or parts lying around where someone can trip over them. Mop up oil and fuel spills at once.

• Don't allow children or pets to play in or near a vehicle being worked on.

The following pages are intended to help in dealing with common roadside emergencies and breakdowns. You will find more detailed fault finding information at the back of the manual, and repair information in the main chapters.

If your car won't start and the starter motor doesn't turn

- ☐ Open the bonnet and make sure that the battery terminals are clean and tight.
- ☐ Switch on the headlights and try to start the engine. If the headlights go very dim when you're trying to start, the battery is probably flat. Get out of trouble by jump starting (see next page) using a friend's car.

If your car won't start even though the starter motor turns as normal

- ☐ Is there fuel in the tank?
- ☐ Is there moisture on electrical components under the bonnet? Switch off the ignition, then wipe off any obvious dampness with a dry cloth. Spray a water-repellent aerosol product (WD-40 or equivalent) on ignition and fuel system electrical connectors like those shown in the photos. Pay special attention to the ignition coil wiring connector and HT leads.

A Check the condition and security of the battery connections.

B With the ignition off, check that the wiring connectors are securely connected to the three ignition coils. These are positioned underneath the upper air filter cover.

C Check that the camshaft wiring plug is securely connected, on the left-hand end of the cylinder head.

D Check that the crankshaft wiring plug is securely connected, on the right-hand side, lower part of the timing chain cover.

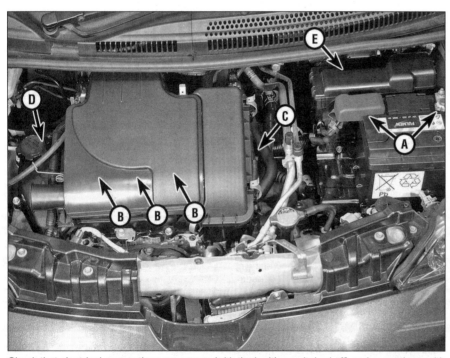

Check that electrical connections are secure (with the ignition switched off) and spray them with a water-dispersant spray like WD-40 if you suspect a problem due to damp.

E With the ignition off, check the fuses and relays in the engine compartment fusebox, behind the battery.

Jump starting will get you out of trouble, but you must correct whatever made the battery go flat in the first place. There are three possibilities:

1 *The battery has been drained by repeated attempts to start, or by leaving the lights on.*

2 *The charging system is not working properly (alternator drivebelt slack or broken, alternator wiring fault or alternator itself faulty).*

3 *The battery itself is at fault (electrolyte low, or battery worn out).*

When jump-starting a car, observe the following precautions:

✓ Before connecting the booster battery, make sure that the ignition is switched off.

Caution: Remove the key in case the central locking engages when the jump leads are connected

✓ Ensure that all electrical equipment (lights, heater, wipers, etc) is switched off.

✓ Take note of any special precautions printed on the battery case.

✓ Make sure that the booster battery is the same voltage as the discharged one in the vehicle.

Jump starting

✓ If the battery is being jump-started from the battery in another vehicle, the two vehicles MUST NOT TOUCH each other.

✓ Make sure that the transmission is in neutral (or PARK, in the case of automatic transmission).

 Budget jump leads can be a false economy, as they often do not pass enough current to start large capacity or diesel engines. They can also get hot.

1 Connect one end of the red jump lead to the positive (+) terminal of the flat battery

2 Connect the other end of the red lead to the positive (+) terminal of the booster battery.

3 Connect one end of the black jump lead to the negative (-) terminal of the booster battery

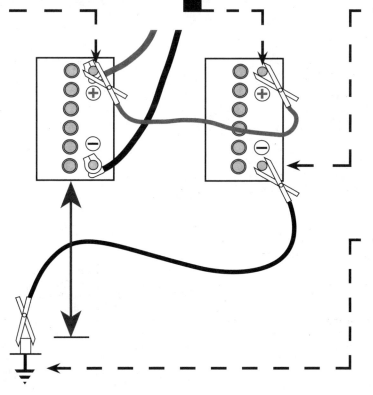

4 Connect the other end of the black jump lead to a bolt or bracket on the engine block, well away from the battery, on the vehicle to be started.

5 Make sure that the jump leads will not come into contact with the fan, drive-belts or other moving parts of the engine.

6 Start the engine using the booster battery and run it at idle speed. Switch on the lights, rear window demister and heater blower motor, then disconnect the jump leads in the reverse order of connection. Turn off the lights etc.

Wheel changing

 Warning: Do not change a wheel in a situation where you risk being hit by other traffic. On busy roads, try to stop in a lay-by or a gateway. Be wary of passing traffic while changing the wheel – it is easy to become distracted by the job in hand.

Preparation

☐ When a puncture occurs, stop as soon as it is safe to do so.

☐ Park on firm level ground, if possible, and well out of the way of other traffic.

☐ Use hazard warning lights if necessary.

☐ If you have one, use a warning triangle to alert other drivers of your presence.

☐ Apply the handbrake and engage first or reverse gear.

☐ Chock the wheel diagonally opposite the one being removed – a couple of large stones will do for this.

☐ If the ground is soft, use a flat piece of wood to spread the load under the jack.

Changing the wheel

1 The spare wheel and tools are located in the luggage compartment, under the boot carpet. Fold back the carpet, and then lift out the plastic wheel cover. Remove the tool tray, which contains the jack, wheelbrace and towing eye.

2 Unscrew the spare wheel retainer anti-clockwise, and then lift out the spare wheel.

3 On models with alloy wheels, one of the wheel bolts may be of the locking type – use the 'key' tool (a special socket usually provided in the glovebox) with the wheelbrace to undo this. On models with steel wheels, prise off the wheel trim from the punctured wheel, using the end of the wheelbrace. Use the wheelbrace to loosen each wheel bolt by half a turn.

4 Locate the jack head below the jacking point nearest the wheel to be changed. The jacking points are between two small indentations in the sill lower edge. Only use the jack on firm, level ground. Ensure that the slot in the jack head engages with the sill flange at the jacking point.

5 Turn the jack handle clockwise until the wheel is raised clear of the ground, then unscrew the wheel bolts and lift the punctured wheel clear. Place the wheel under the vehicle sill in case the jack fails.

6 Fit the spare wheel. Refit the wheel bolts, and tighten moderately with the wheelbrace.

7 Lower the car to the ground, and then finally tighten the wheel nuts in a diagonal sequence. Refit the wheel trim (where applicable). Ideally, the wheel nuts should be slackened and retightened to the specified torque at the earliest opportunity.

Finally . . .

☐ Remove the wheel chocks.

☐ Stow the jack and tools in the correct locations in the car.

☐ Check the tyre pressure on the wheel just fitted. If it is low, or if you don't have a pressure gauge with you, drive slowly to the nearest garage and inflate the tyre to the right pressure.

☐ Have the damaged tyre or wheel repaired at the earliest opportunity.

Identifying leaks

Puddles on the garage floor or drive, or obvious wetness under the bonnet or underneath the car, suggest a leak that needs investigating. It can sometimes be difficult to decide where the leak is coming from, especially if an engine undershield is fitted. Leaking oil or fluid can also be blown rearwards by the passage of air under the car, giving a false impression of where the problem lies.

 Warning: Most automotive oils and fluids are poisonous. Wash them off skin, and change out of contaminated clothing, without delay.

 The smell of a fluid leaking from the car may provide a clue to what's leaking. Some fluids are distinctively coloured. It may help to remove the engine undershield, clean the car carefully and to park it over some clean paper overnight as an aid to locating the source of the leak. Remember that some leaks may only occur while the engine is running.

Sump oil

Engine oil may leak from the drain plug...

Oil from filter

...or from the base of the oil filter.

Gearbox oil

Gearbox oil can leak from the seals at the inboard ends of the driveshafts.

Antifreeze

Leaking antifreeze often leaves a crystalline deposit like this.

Brake fluid

A leak occurring at a wheel is almost certainly brake fluid.

Towing

When all else fails, you may find yourself having to get a tow home – or of course you may be helping somebody else. Long-distance recovery should only be done by a garage or breakdown service. For shorter distances, DIY towing using another car is easy enough, but observe the following points:

☐ Use a proper tow-rope – they are not expensive. The vehicle being towed must display an ON TOW sign in its rear window.
☐ Always turn the ignition key to the 'on' position when the vehicle is being towed, so that the steering lock is released, and the direction indicator and brake lights work.

☐ A front towing eye is located with the jack and wheelbrace in the luggage compartment (see *Wheel changing*). The rear lashing eye (not designed for towing) is a conventional loop under the rear bumper. To fit the front towing eye, prise out the cover on the right-hand side of the front bumper, and remove it. Screw the towing eye in as far as it will go and tighten it with the wheelbrace.
☐ Before being towed, release the handbrake and select neutral on the transmission.
☐ Note that greater-than-usual pedal pressure will be required to operate the brakes, since

the vacuum servo unit is only operational with the engine running.
☐ On models with power steering, greater-than-usual steering effort may also be required.
☐ The driver of the car being towed must keep the tow-rope taut at all times to avoid snatching.
☐ Make sure that both drivers know the route before setting off.
☐ Only drive at moderate speeds and keep the distance towed to a minimum. Drive smoothly and allow plenty of time for slowing down at junctions.

Introduction

There are some very simple checks which need only take a few minutes to carry out, but which could save you a lot of inconvenience and expense.

These *Weekly checks* require no great skill or special tools, and the small amount of time they take to perform could prove to be very well spent, for example:

☐ Keeping an eye on tyre condition and pressures, will not only help to stop them wearing out prematurely, but could also save your life.

☐ Many breakdowns are caused by electrical problems. Battery-related faults are particularly common, and a quick check on a regular basis will often prevent the majority of these.

☐ If your car develops a brake fluid leak, the first time you might know about it is when your brakes don't work properly. Checking the level regularly will give advance warning of this kind of problem.

☐ If the oil or coolant levels run low, the cost of repairing any engine damage will be far greater than fixing the leak, for example.

Underbonnet check points

A *Engine oil level dipstick*

B *Engine oil filler cap*

C *Coolant reservoir (expansion tank)*

D *Brake fluid reservoir*

E *Screen washer fluid reservoir*

F *Battery*

Engine oil level

Before you start

✔ Make sure that the car is on level ground.
✔ Check the oil level before the car is driven, or at least 5 minutes after the engine has been switched off.

 *If the oil is checked immediately after driving the vehicle, some of the oil will remain in the upper engine components, resulting in an inaccurate reading on the dipstick.*

The correct oil

Modern engines place great demands on their oil. It is very important that the correct oil for your car is used (see *Lubricants and fluids*).

Car care

● If you have to add oil frequently, you should check whether you have any oil leaks. Place some clean paper under the car overnight, and check for stains in the morning. If there are no leaks, then the engine may be burning oil.
● Always maintain the level between the upper and lower dipstick marks (see photo 3). If the level is too low, severe engine damage may occur. Oil seal failure may result if the engine is overfilled by adding too much oil.

1 The dipstick is located in a tube at the right-hand rear of the engine; withdraw the dipstick from the tube to check oil level.

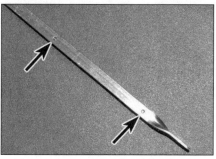

3 Note the oil level on the end of the dipstick, which should be within the upper and the lower marks (dots). If the engine is very hot, the oil level may appear to be above the upper mark. Approximately 1.0 litre of oil will raise the level from the lower to the upper mark.

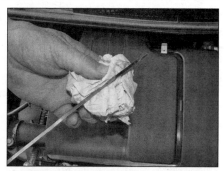

2 Using a clean rag or paper towel, wipe all the oil from the dipstick. Insert the clean dipstick into the tube as far as it will go, then withdraw it again.

4 Oil is added through the filler cap on the top of the engine. Unscrew the filler cap, then top-up the level. If required, use a funnel to reduce spillage. Add the oil slowly, checking the level on the dipstick often. Don't overfill.

Coolant level

 Warning: Do not attempt to remove the expansion tank pressure cap when the engine is hot, as there is a very great risk of scalding. Do not leave open containers of coolant about, as it is poisonous.

Car care

● With a sealed-type cooling system, adding coolant should not be necessary on a regular basis. If frequent topping-up is required, it is likely there is a leak. Check the radiator, all hoses and joint faces for signs of staining or wetness, and rectify as necessary.

● It is important that antifreeze is used in the cooling system all year round, not just during the winter months. Don't top up with water alone, as the antifreeze will become diluted.

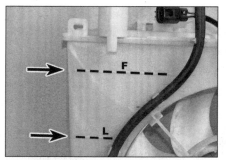

1 The coolant level varies with the temperature of the engine. The see-through expansion tank (located behind the radiator) has F (full) and L (low) level markings. When cold the level should be between the two marks. When the engine is hot, the level may rise slightly above the F mark.

2 If topping-up is necessary, wait until the engine is cold, then remove the cap on the expansion tank.

3 Add a mixture of water and antifreeze to the expansion tank, until the coolant is up to the F mark. Use antifreeze of the same type (and colour) as that which is already in the system. Refit the cap securely.

Brake fluid level

Warning:
• Brake fluid can harm your eyes and damage painted surfaces, so use extreme caution when handling and pouring it.
• Do not use fluid that has been standing open for some time, as it absorbs moisture from the *air, which can cause a dangerous loss of braking effectiveness.*

Safety first!

● If the reservoir requires repeated topping-up this is an indication of a fluid leak somewhere in the system, which should be investigated immediately.

● The fluid level in the reservoir will drop slightly as the brake pads wear down, but the fluid level must never be allowed to drop below the MIN mark.
● If a leak is suspected, the car should not be driven until the braking system has been checked. Never take any risks where brakes are concerned

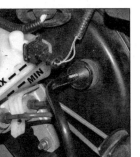

1 The MAX and MIN marks are indicated on the side of the reservoir, which is located right at the back of the engine compartment, on the driver's side. The fluid level must be kept between these two marks.

2 If topping-up is necessary, first wipe the area around the filler cap with a clean rag, then unscrew the cap. When adding fluid, it's a good idea to inspect the reservoir. The fluid should be changed if it appears to be dark, or if dirt is visible.

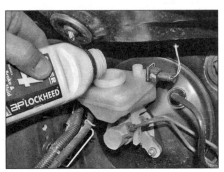

3 Carefully add fluid, avoiding spilling it on surrounding paintwork. Use only the specified hydraulic fluid; mixing different types of fluid can cause damage to the system and/or a loss of braking effectiveness. After filling to the correct level, refit the cap securely. Wipe off any spilt fluid.

Screen washer fluid level

● Screenwash additives not only keep the windscreen clean during bad weather, they also prevent the washer system freezing in cold weather – which is when you are likely to need it most. Don't top-up using plain water, as the screenwash will become diluted, and will freeze in cold weather.

Warning: On no account use engine coolant antifreeze in the screen washer system – this may damage the paintwork.

1 The windscreen/tailgate washer fluid reservoir filler neck is located on the driver's side of the engine compartment, behind the headlight. If topping-up is necessary, open the cap.

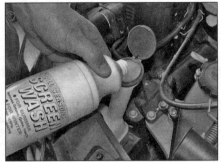

2 When topping-up the reservoir, a screenwash additive should be added in the quantities recommended on the bottle.

Wiper blades

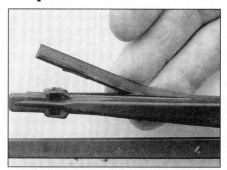

1 Check the condition of the wiper blades, if they are cracked or show any signs of deterioration, or if the glass swept area is smeared, renew them. For maximum clarity of vision, wiper blades should be renewed annually, as a matter of course.

2 To remove a windscreen wiper blade, lift the wiper arm away from the screen and depress the locking clip at the base of the mounting block. With the locking clip depressed, slide the wiper blade out of the hooked end of the wiper arm.

3 Don't forget to check the tailgate wiper blade as well. Unclip the blade from the wiper arm to renew.

Battery

Caution: Before carrying out any work on the vehicle battery, read the precautions given in 'Safety first!' at the start of this manual.

✔ Make sure that the battery tray is in good condition, and that the clamp is tight. Corrosion on the tray, retaining clamp and the battery itself can be removed with a solution of water and baking soda. Thoroughly rinse all cleaned areas with water. Any metal parts damaged by corrosion should be covered with a zinc-based primer, then painted.

✔ Periodically (approximately every three months), check the charge condition of the battery as described in Chapter 5A.

✔ If the battery is flat, and you need to jump start your vehicle, see *Roadside Repairs*.

1 The battery is located on the passenger side of the engine compartment. The exterior of the battery should be inspected periodically for damage such as a cracked case or cover.

2 Check the tightness of the battery cable clamps to ensure good electrical connections. You should not be able to move them. Also check each cable for cracks and frayed conductors.

HAYNES
HiNT

Battery corrosion can be kept to a minimum by applying a layer of petroleum jelly to the clamps and terminals after they are reconnected.

3 If corrosion (white, fluffy deposits) is evident, remove the cables from the battery terminals, clean them with a small wire brush, then refit them. Automotive stores sell a useful tool for cleaning the battery post . . .

4 . . . as well as the battery cable clamps.

Tyre condition and pressure

It is very important that tyres are in good condition, and at the correct pressure - having a tyre failure at any speed is highly dangerous. Tyre wear is influenced by driving style - harsh braking and acceleration, or fast cornering, will all produce more rapid tyre wear. As a general rule, the front tyres wear out faster than the rears. Interchanging the tyres from front to rear ("rotating" the tyres) may result in more even wear. However, if this is completely effective, you may have the expense of replacing all four tyres at once!

Remove any nails or stones embedded in the tread before they penetrate the tyre to cause deflation. If removal of a nail does reveal that the tyre has been punctured, refit the nail so that its point of penetration is marked. Then immediately change the wheel, and have the tyre repaired by a tyre dealer.

Regularly check the tyres for damage in the form of cuts or bulges, especially in the sidewalls. Periodically remove the wheels, and clean any dirt or mud from the inside and outside surfaces. Examine the wheel rims for signs of rusting, corrosion or other damage. Light alloy wheels are easily damaged by "kerbing" whilst parking; steel wheels may also become dented or buckled. A new wheel is very often the only way to overcome severe damage.

New tyres should be balanced when they are fitted, but it may become necessary to re-balance them as they wear, or if the balance weights fitted to the wheel rim should fall off. Unbalanced tyres will wear more quickly, as will the steering and suspension components. Wheel imbalance is normally signified by vibration, particularly at a certain speed (typically around 50 mph). If this vibration is felt only through the steering, then it is likely that just the front wheels need balancing. If, however, the vibration is felt through the whole car, the rear wheels could be out of balance. Wheel balancing should be carried out by a tyre dealer or garage.

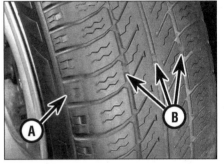

1 Tread Depth - visual check
The original tyres have tread wear safety bands (B), which will appear when the tread depth reaches approximately 1.6 mm. The band positions are indicated by a triangular mark on the tyre sidewall (A).

2 Tread Depth - manual check
Alternatively, tread wear can be monitored with a simple, inexpensive device known as a tread depth indicator gauge.

3 Tyre Pressure Check
Check the tyre pressures regularly with the tyres cold. Do not adjust the tyre pressures immediately after the vehicle has been used, or an inaccurate setting will result.

Tyre tread wear patterns

Shoulder Wear

Underinflation (wear on both sides)
Under-inflation will cause overheating of the tyre, because the tyre will flex too much, and the tread will not sit correctly on the road surface. This will cause a loss of grip and excessive wear, not to mention the danger of sudden tyre failure due to heat build-up.
Check and adjust pressures
Incorrect wheel camber (wear on one side)
Repair or renew suspension parts
Hard cornering
Reduce speed!

Centre Wear

Overinflation
Over-inflation will cause rapid wear of the centre part of the tyre tread, coupled with reduced grip, harsher ride, and the danger of shock damage occurring in the tyre casing.
Check and adjust pressures

If you sometimes have to inflate your car's tyres to the higher pressures specified for maximum load or sustained high speed, don't forget to reduce the pressures to normal afterwards.

Uneven Wear

Front tyres may wear unevenly as a result of wheel misalignment. Most tyre dealers and garages can check and adjust the wheel alignment (or "tracking") for a modest charge.
Incorrect camber or castor
Repair or renew suspension parts
Malfunctioning suspension
Repair or renew suspension parts
Unbalanced wheel
Balance tyres
Incorrect toe setting
Adjust front wheel alignment
Note: *The feathered edge of the tread which typifies toe wear is best checked by feel.*

Electrical systems

✔ Check all external lights and the horn. Refer to the appropriate Sections of Chapter 12 for details if any of the circuits are found to be inoperative.

✔ Visually check all accessible wiring connectors, harnesses and retaining clips for security, and for signs of chafing or damage.

 If you need to check your brake lights and indicators unaided, back up to a wall or garage door and operate the lights. The reflected light should show if they are working properly.

1 If a single indicator light, brake light or headlight has failed, it is likely that a bulb has blown and will need to be renewed. Refer to Chapter 12 for details. If both brake lights have failed, it is possible that the brake light switch operated by the brake pedal has failed. Refer to Chapter 9 for details.

2 If more than one indicator light or headlight has failed, it is likely that either a fuse has blown, or that there is a fault in the circuit (see Chapter 12). The main fuses are mounted behind the battery in the engine compartment. There are also fuses inside the passenger compartment behind the instrument panel.

3 To renew a blown fuse remove it using the plastic tweezer tool provided (where applicable). Fit a new fuse of the same rating, available from car accessory shops. It is important that you find the reason that the fuse blew (see *Electrical fault finding* in Chapter 12).

Lubricants and fluids

Engine . . . . Engine oil, SAE 5W-30 or 10W-30 to specification
API SL or SM

Cooling system. . . . . Ethylene glycol-based antifreeze
suitable for use in mixed-metal engines
Super Long Life Coolant (SLLC) or equivalent

Transmission. . . . . Gear oil to specification API GL-4
Exxon Mobil LV 75 W

Brake systems . . . . Hydraulic fluid to DOT 3 or DOT 4

Tyre pressures

Note: *Pressures given here are a guide only, and apply to original-equipment tyres (155/65 R 14) – the recommended pressures may vary if any other make or type of tyre is fitted; check with the car handbook, or the tyre manufacturer or supplier for latest recommendations. A tyre pressure label is fitted inside the front passenger side door B-pillar* **(see illustration).**

Load	Front	Rear
Normal load (up to 2 people)	2.2 bar (32 psi)	2.2 bar (32 psi)
Full load (more than 2 people)	2.3 bar (34 psi)	2.3 bar (34 psi)

Tyre pressure readings on vehicle B-pillar

Chapter 1
Routine maintenance and servicing

Contents

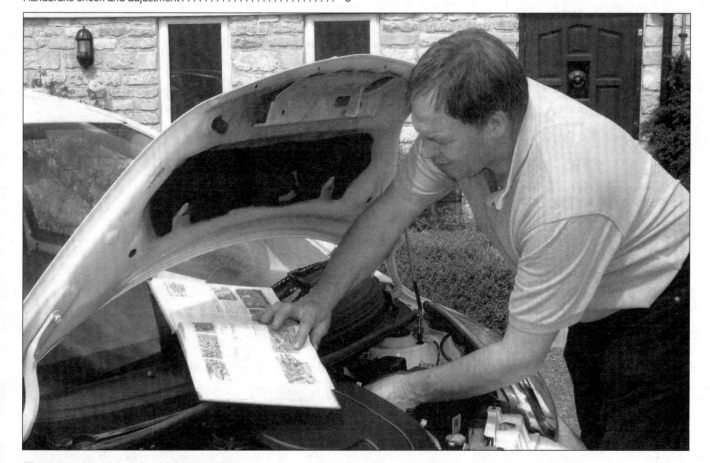

Degrees of difficulty

| Easy, suitable for novice with little experience | Fairly easy, suitable for beginner with some experience | Fairly difficult, suitable for competent DIY mechanic | Difficult, suitable for experienced DIY mechanic | Very difficult, suitable for expert DIY or professional |

Servicing specifications

Lubricants and fluids . . . .   Refer to *Lubricants and fluids* on page 0•16

Capacities

Engine oil (including oil filter) . . . .   3.1 litres
Cooling system (approximate) . . . .   4.0 litres
Transmission (including Multi-Mode) . . . .   1.7 litres
Fuel tank . . . .   35.0 litres

Cooling system

Antifreeze mixture:
   50% antifreeze . . . .   Protection down to -37°C
Note: *Refer to antifreeze manufacturer for latest recommendations.*

Auxiliary drivebelt

Deflection/tension check with 98 N (thumb force) . . . .   9.0 to 11.0 mm

Ignition system

Spark plugs:
   Type   . . . .   Denso KR16HR-U11
   Electrode gap . . . .   1.1 mm
Note: *The spark plug gap quoted is for the plugs listed above. If spark plugs of any other type are to be fitted, refer to their manufacturer's recommendations.*

Brakes

Friction material minimum thickness:
   Front brake pads . . . .   1.0 mm
   Rear brake shoes . . . .   1.0 mm

Tyres

Tyre pressures . . . .   Refer to *Lubricants, fluids and tyre pressures* on page 0•16

Torque wrench settings

	Nm	lbf ft
Alternator:		
Upper bolt.	54	40
Lower adjuster bolts.	34	25
Engine coolant drain plug.	20	15
Engine mounting:		
Right-hand mounting-to-engine support bolts.	24	18
Right-hand mounting-to-body bolts.	52	38
Engine oil drain plug.	30	22
Ignition coils	10	7
Roadwheel bolts.	100	74
Seat belt mounting bolts	42	31
Spark plugs	25	18
Transmission:		
Drain plug	29	21
Filler/level plug	39	29

Maintenance schedule

The maintenance intervals in this manual are provided with the assumption that you, not the dealer, will be carrying out the work. These are the minimum maintenance intervals recommended by us for cars driven daily. If you wish to keep your car in peak condition at all times, you may wish to perform some of these procedures more often. We encourage frequent maintenance, because it enhances the efficiency, performance and resale value of your car.

If the car is driven in dusty areas, used to tow a trailer, or driven frequently at slow speeds (idling in traffic) or on short journeys, more frequent maintenance intervals are recommended.

When the vehicle is new, it should be serviced by a dealer service department (or other workshop recognised by the vehicle manufacturer as providing the same standard of service) in order to preserve the warranty. The vehicle manufacturer may reject warranty claims if you are unable to prove that servicing has been carried out as and when specified, using only original equipment parts or parts certified to be of equivalent quality.

Every 250 miles or weekly
☐ Refer to *Weekly checks*

Every 5000 miles or 6 months, whichever comes first
☐ Renew the engine oil and filter (Section 3)
Note: *The manufacturer recommends that the engine oil and filter are changed every 10 000 miles or 12 months. However, oil and filter changes are good for the engine, and we recommend that the oil and filter be renewed more frequently, especially if the car is used mainly for short journeys.*

Every 10 000 miles or 12 months, whichever comes first
☐ Check the pollen filter (Section 4)
☐ Check all components, pipes and hoses for fluid leaks (Section 5)
☐ Check the exhaust system (Section 6)
☐ Check the condition and tension of the auxiliary drivebelt (Section 7)
☐ Check and if necessary adjust the handbrake (Section 8)
☐ Check and if necessary adjust the clutch and brake pedals (Section 9)
☐ Check the condition and operation of the seat belts (Section 10)
☐ Lubricate all hinges and locks (Section 11)
☐ Check the front brake pads and discs for wear (Section 12)
☐ Check the steering and suspension components for condition and security (Section 13)
☐ Check the condition of the driveshaft gaiters (Section 14)
☐ Check the roadwheel bolts are tightened to the specified torque (Section 15)
☐ Carry out a road test (Section 16)

Every 20 000 miles or 2 years, whichever comes first
☐ Renew the spark plugs (Section 17)
☐ Renew the air filter element (Section 18)
☐ Check the rear brake shoes and drums for wear (Section 19)

Every 40 000 miles or 4 years, whichever comes first
☐ Check the transmission oil level (Section 20)
☐ Renew the auxiliary drivebelt (Section 21)

Every 2 years, regardless of mileage
☐ Renew the brake fluid (Section 22)

Every 4 years, regardless of mileage
☐ Renew the coolant (Section 23)
Note: *If the system is filled with Super Long Life Coolant the renewal interval is 10 years.*

Underbonnet view

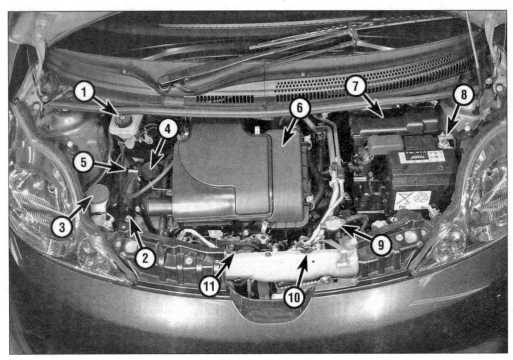

1   Brake fluid reservoir
2   Engine right-hand
    mounting
3   Washer fluid reservoir
4   Engine oil filler cap
5   Engine oil dipstick
6   Air cleaner housing
7   Engine compartment
    fusebox
8   Battery negative terminal
9   Radiator cap
10 Bonnet lock
11 Exhaust manifold

Front underbody view

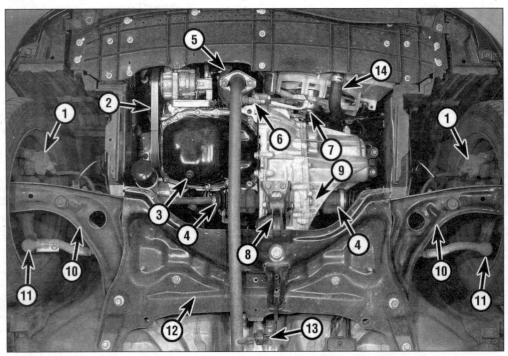

1   Front brake caliper
2   Auxiliary drivebelt
3   Engine oil drain plug
4   Driveshaft
5   Catalytic converter
6   Oxygen sensor
7   Radiator cooling fan
    motor
8   Lower rear mounting
9   Transmission oil drain
    plug
10 Front suspension lower
    arm
11 Track rod
12 Subframe
13 Exhaust front rubber
    mounting
14 Radiator bottom hose

Rear underbody view

1 Rear shock absorber
   mounting
2 Rear axle
3 Rear spring
4 Rear axle pivot/mounting
5 Rear brake hoses
6 Handbrake cable
7 Exhaust rear silencer
8 Exhaust joint
9 Fuel tank
10 Fuel tank filler hose

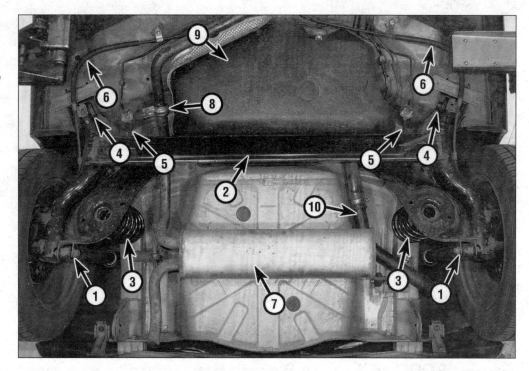

1 General Information

1 This Chapter is designed to help the home mechanic maintain his/her car for safety, economy, long life and peak performance.
2 The Chapter contains a master maintenance schedule, followed by Sections dealing specifically with each task in the schedule. Visual checks, adjustments, component renewal and other helpful items are included. Refer to the accompanying illustrations of the engine compartment and the underside of the car for the locations of the various components.
3 Servicing your car in accordance with the mileage/time maintenance schedule and the following Sections will provide a planned maintenance programme, which should result in a long and reliable service life. This is a comprehensive plan, so maintaining some items but not others at the specified service intervals, will not produce the same results.
4 As you service your car, you will discover that many of the procedures can – and should – be grouped together, because of the particular procedure being performed, or because of the proximity of two otherwise unrelated components to one another. For example, if the car is raised for any reason, the exhaust can be inspected at the same time as the suspension and steering components.
5 The first step in this maintenance

programme is to prepare yourself before the actual work begins. Read through all the Sections relevant to the work to be carried out, then make a list and gather all the parts and tools required. If a problem is encountered, seek advice from a parts specialist, or a dealer service department.

2 Regular maintenance

1 If, from the time the car is new, the routine maintenance schedule is followed closely, and frequent checks are made of fluid levels and high-wear items, as suggested throughout this manual, the engine will be kept in relatively good running condition, and the need for additional work will be minimised.
2 It is possible that there will be times when the engine is running poorly due to the lack of regular maintenance. This is even more likely if a used car, which has not received regular and frequent maintenance checks, is purchased. In such cases, additional work may need to be carried out, outside of the regular maintenance intervals.
3 If engine wear is suspected, a compression test (refer to Chapter 2A Section 2) will provide valuable information regarding the overall performance of the main internal components. Such a test can be used as a basis to decide on the extent of the work to be carried out. If, for example, a compression test indicates

serious internal engine wear, conventional maintenance as described in this Chapter will not greatly improve the performance of the engine, and may prove a waste of time and money, unless extensive overhaul work is carried out first.
4 The following series of operations are those most often required to improve the performance of a generally poor-running engine:

Primary operations

a) Clean, inspect and test the battery (refer to 'Weekly Checks').
b) Check all the engine-related fluids (refer to 'Weekly Checks').
c) Check the condition and tension of the auxiliary drivebelt (Section 7).
d) Renew the spark plugs (Section 17).
e) Check the condition of the air filter, and renew if necessary (Section 18).
f) Check the condition of all hoses, and check for fluid leaks (Section 5).

5 If the above operations do not prove fully effective, carry out the following secondary operations:

Secondary operations

6 All items listed under Primary operations, plus the following:
g) Check the charging system (Chapter 5A Section 5).
h) Check the ignition system (Chapter 5B Section 2).
i) Check the fuel system (Chapter 4A Section 11).

3.4a Pull out the dipstick...

3.4b... and remove the oil filler cap

3.5 Slackening the sump oil drain plug...

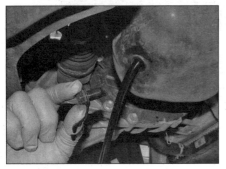

3.6... and draining the engine oil

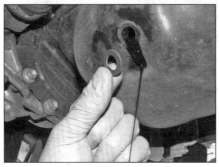

3.7 A new sealing washer will be required for refitting

3.8 Oil filter location on right-hand rear of engine

Every 5000 miles or 6 months, whichever comes first

3 Engine oil and filter renewal

1 Frequent oil and filter changes are the most important preventative maintenance procedures which can be undertaken by the DIY owner. As engine oil ages, it becomes diluted and contaminated, which leads to premature engine wear.

2 Before starting this procedure, gather all the necessary tools and materials. Also make sure that you have plenty of clean rags and newspapers handy, to mop-up any spills. Ideally, the engine oil should be warm, as it will drain easily, and more built-up sludge will be removed with it. Take care, however, not to touch the exhaust or any other hot parts of the engine when working under the

vehicle. To avoid any possibility of scalding, and to protect yourself from possible skin irritants and other harmful contaminants in used engine oils, it is advisable to wear gloves when carrying out this work.

3 Firmly apply the handbrake, and then jack up the front of the car and support it on axle stands (see *Jacking and vehicle support*).

4 Open the bonnet and then pull out the dipstick and remove the oil filler cap **(see illustrations)**.

5 Using a spanner, or preferably a socket and bar, slacken the drain plug about half a turn **(see illustration)**. Position the draining container under the drain plug, and then remove the plug completely.

6 Allow some time for the oil to drain, noting that it may be necessary to reposition the container as the oil flow slows to a trickle **(see illustration)**.

7 After all the oil has drained; wipe the drain plug with a clean rag. Examine the condition of the drain plug seal/washer, and renew it if it shows signs of damage, which may prevent an oil-tight seal **(see illustration)**. Clean the area around the drain plug opening, then refit the plug and tighten it securely.

8 Move the container into position under the oil filter, which is located on the right-hand rear of the cylinder block **(see illustration)**.

9 Use an oil filter removal tool to slacken the filter initially, then unscrew it by hand the rest of the way **(see illustration)**. Empty the oil from the old filter into the container.

10 Use a clean rag to remove all oil, dirt and sludge from the filter sealing area on the engine.

11 Apply a light coating of clean engine oil to the sealing ring on the new filter, then screw the filter into position on the engine **(see illustrations)**.

3.9 Slackening the oil filter using a claw-type removal tool

3.11a Apply a little engine oil to the new filter's sealing ring...

3.11b... then screw it firmly into place by hand only

Tighten the filter firmly by hand only – do not use any tools.

12 Remove the old oil and all tools from under the car, then lower the car to the ground.

13 Fill the engine through the filler hole, using the correct grade and type of oil (refer to Lubricants and fluids for oil specifications) **(see illustration)**. Pour in half the specified quantity of oil first, and then wait a few minutes for the oil to drain into the sump. Continue to add oil, a small quantity at a time, until the level is up to the lower mark on the dipstick. Adding approximately a further 1.0 litre will bring the level up to the upper mark on the dipstick.

14 Start the engine and run it for a few minutes; check for leaks around the oil filter seal and the sump drain plug. Note that there may be a few seconds delay before the oil pressure warning light goes out when the engine is started, as the oil circulates through the engine oil galleries and the new oil filter (where fitted) before the pressure builds-up.

15 Stop the engine, and wait a few minutes for the oil to settle in the sump once more. With the new oil circulated and the filter now completely full, recheck the level on the dipstick, and add more oil as necessary.

16 Dispose of the used engine oil safely, with reference to General repair procedures.

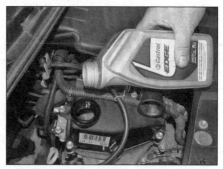

3.13 Fill the engine using the correct grade and quantity of oil

Every 10 000 miles or 12 months, whichever comes first

4 Pollen filter check

1 The filter is located inside the heater housing and can be accessed from the passenger side front footwell.

2 Working up behind the facia panel in the passenger side front footwell, release the retaining clips, by squeezing them together and slide the pollen filter out from the heater housing, noting which way up it is fitted **(see illustrations)**.

3 Check the condition of the filter element – if it is excessively dirty or otherwise contaminated, airflow into the car will be seriously reduced, and a new element should be fitted.

4 Fit the new element (or refit the old one, as applicable), observing any markings indicating its fitted direction, then slide the filter back into the heater housing, and ensure the retaining clips engage.

5 Hose and fluid leak check

Coolant

⚠ **Warning: Refer to the safety information given in Safety first! and Chapter 3 Section 1 before disturbing any of the cooling system components.**

1 Carefully check the radiator and heater coolant hoses along their entire length. Renew any hose which is cracked, swollen or which shows signs of deterioration. Cracks will show up better if the hose is squeezed. Pay close attention to the clips that secure the hoses to the cooling system components. Hose clips that have been overtightened can pinch and puncture hoses, resulting in cooling system leaks.

2 Inspect all the cooling system components (hoses, joint faces, etc.) for leaks **(see illustration)**. Where any problems of this nature are found on system components,

renew the component or gasket with reference to Chapter 3.

3 A leak from the cooling system will usually show up as white or antifreeze-coloured deposits on the area surrounding the leak (see **Haynes Hint**).

 HAYNES HINT *A leak in the cooling system will usually show up as white- or antifreeze coloured deposits on the area adjoining the leak.*

Fuel

⚠ **Warning: Refer to the safety information given in Safety first! and Chapter 4A Section 1**

before disturbing any of the fuel system components.

4 Check all fuel lines at their connections to the fuel rail **(see illustration)**.

5 Examine each fuel hose/pipe along its length for splits or cracks. Check for signs of leakage, which could be anything from a damp hose to an area of bodywork adjacent to the hose which seems especially clean (from being 'washed' by leaking fuel).

6 To identify fuel leaks between the fuel tank and the engine bay, the car should raised and securely supported on axle stands. Inspect the fuel tank and filler neck for punctures, cracks and other damage. The connection between the filler neck and tank is especially critical. Sometimes a rubber filler neck or connecting hose will leak due to loose retaining clamps or deteriorated rubber.

4.2a Release the securing clips at top and bottom...

4.2b... then withdraw the filter out of the housing

5.2 Check the coolant hoses at the left-hand side of the cylinder head

5.4 Check the protective covers on the ends of the fuel lines

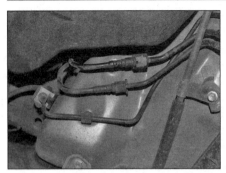

5.7 Check the fuel tank hoses for leaks

7 Carefully check all rubber hoses and metal fuel lines leading away from the fuel tank **(see illustration)**. Check for loose connections, deteriorated hoses, kinked lines, and other damage. Follow the fuel supply line to the front of the car, carefully inspecting it all the way for signs of damage or corrosion. Renew damaged sections as necessary.

Engine oil

8 Inspect the area around the camshaft cover, timing chain cover, cylinder head, oil filter and sump joint faces. Bear in mind that, over a period of time, some very slight seepage from these areas is to be expected – what you are really looking for is any indication of a serious leak caused by gasket failure. Engine oil seeping from the base of the timing chain cover or the transmission bellhousing may be an indication of crankshaft or input shaft oil seal failure. Should a leak be found, renew

5.11 Check the brake pipe unions around the master cylinder for leaks

5.12b... and at the rear (remove the rear wheels for best access)

the failed gasket or oil seal by referring to the appropriate Chapters in this manual.

Air conditioning refrigerant

⚠ **Warning: Refer to the safety information given in Safety first! and Chapter 3 Section 10, regarding the dangers of disturbing any of the air conditioning system components.**

9 The air conditioning system is filled with a liquid refrigerant, which is retained under high pressure. If the air conditioning system is opened and depressurised without the aid of specialised equipment, the refrigerant will immediately turn into gas and escape into the atmosphere. If the liquid comes into contact with your skin, it can cause severe frostbite. In addition, the refrigerant contains substances that are environmentally damaging; for this reason, it should not be allowed to escape into the atmosphere.

10 Any suspected air conditioning system leaks should be immediately referred to a franchised dealer or air conditioning specialist. Leakage will be shown up as a steady drop in the level of refrigerant in the system.
Note: *Water may drip from the condenser drain pipe, underneath the centre of the car, immediately after the air conditioning system has been in use. This is normal, and should not be cause for concern.*

Brake fluid

⚠ **Warning: Refer to the safety information given in Safety first! and Chapter 9 Section 1, regarding the dangers of handling brake fluid.**

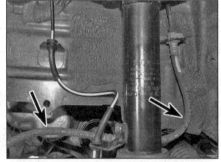

5.12a Check the brake flexible hoses at the front...

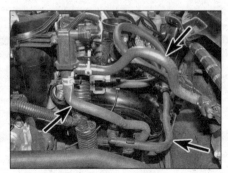

5.17 Vacuum hoses (arrowed) should be checked for signs of damage

11 With reference to Chapter 9 Section 10, examine the area surrounding the brake pipe unions at the master cylinder for signs of leakage **(see illustration)**. Check the area around the base of fluid reservoir, for signs of leakage caused by seal failure. Also examine the brake pipe unions at the ABS hydraulic unit.

12 Inspect the braking system rubber hoses fitted to each front caliper, and above each rear spring **(see illustrations)**. Look for perished, swollen or hardened rubber, and any signs of cracking, especially at the metal end fittings. If there's any doubt as to the condition of any hose, renew it as described in Chapter 9 Section 10.

13 If fluid loss is evident, but the leak cannot be pinpointed in the engine bay, the brake calipers and underbody brake lines and should be carefully checked with the car raised and supported on axle stands. Leakage of fluid from the braking system is serious fault that must be rectified immediately.

14 Brake hydraulic fluid is a toxic substance with a watery consistency. New fluid is almost colourless, but it becomes darker with age and use.

Unidentified fluid leaks

15 If there are signs that a fluid of some description is leaking from the car, but you cannot identify the type of fluid or its exact origin, park the car overnight and slide a large piece of card underneath it. Providing that the card is positioned in roughly in the right location, even the smallest leak will show up on the card. Not only will this help you to pinpoint the exact location of the leak, it should be easier to identify the fluid from its colour. Bear in mind, though, that the leak may only be occurring when the engine is running!

Vacuum hoses

16 Although the braking system is hydraulically-operated, the brake servo unit amplifies the effort you apply at the brake pedal by making use of the vacuum available in the inlet manifold (see Chapter 9 Section 12). Vacuum is ported to the servo by means of a large-bore hose. Any leaks that develop in this hose will reduce the effectiveness of the braking system, and may affect engine running.

17 In addition, many of the underbonnet components, particularly the emission control components, are driven by vacuum via narrow-bore hoses **(see illustration)**.

18 A leak in a vacuum hose means that air is being drawn into the hose (rather than escaping from it) and this makes leakage very difficult to detect.

19 However, if an initial examination of the hoses shows perishing and cracks (especially at the hose ends), or any signs that the hose has become hardened, renewal of that section of hose is advisable.

20 One method for detecting leaks is to use an old length of vacuum hose as a kind of stethoscope – hold one end close to (but not

in) your ear and use the other end to probe the area around the suspected leak. When the end of the hose is directly over a vacuum leak, a hissing sound will be heard clearly through the hose. Care must be taken to avoid contacting hot or moving components, as the engine must be running when testing in this manner. Renew any vacuum hoses that are found to be defective.

6 Exhaust system check

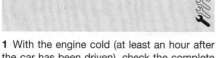

1 With the engine cold (at least an hour after the car has been driven), check the complete exhaust system from the engine to the end of the tailpipe. The exhaust system is most easily checked with the car raised on a hoist, or suitably supported on axle stands, so that the exhaust components are readily visible and accessible.

2 Check the exhaust pipes and connections for evidence of leaks, severe corrosion and damage. Make sure that all brackets and mountings are in good condition, and that all relevant nuts and bolts are tight **(see illustrations)**.

3 Leakage at any of the joints or in other parts of the system will usually show up as a black sooty stain in the vicinity of the leak. To confirm the presence of a leak, with the engine running, briefly block the exhaust tailpipe with a large pad of rag – take care to avoid burning from the hot pipe or hot gases. If the system is sound, there should be a noticeable build-up of pressure – if not, the increased noise should make it possible to pinpoint the source of the leak.

4 Rattles and other noises can often be traced to the exhaust system, especially the brackets and mountings. Try to move the pipes and silencers. If the components are able to come into contact with the body or suspension parts, secure the system with new mountings. Otherwise separate the joints (if

possible) and twist the pipes as necessary to provide additional clearance.

7 Auxiliary drivebelt check

1 A single auxiliary drivebelt is fitted at the right-hand side of the engine. The length of the drivebelt varies according to whether air conditioning is fitted. A manual tensioner is fitted, so the drivebelt tension should be checked at regular intervals (and particularly after fitting a new drivebelt).

2 Due to their function and material makeup, drivebelts are prone to failure after a long period of time, and should therefore be inspected regularly.

3 Since the drivebelt is located very close to the right-hand side of the engine compartment, it is possible to gain better access by jacking up the right-hand front wheel (see *Jacking and vehicle support*) and removing the inner wheel arch liner.

4 With the engine stopped, inspect the full length of the drivebelt for cracks and separation of the belt plies. It will be necessary to turn the engine (using a spanner or socket and bar on the crankshaft pulley bolt) in order to move the belt from the pulleys so that the belt can be inspected thoroughly. Twist the belt between the pulleys so that both sides can be viewed **(see illustration)**. Also check for fraying, and glazing which gives the belt a shiny appearance. Check the pulleys for nicks, cracks, distortion and corrosion.

5 Small cracks in the belt ribs are not usually serious, but look closely to see whether the crack has extended into the belt plies. If the belt is in any way suspect, or is known to have seen long service, renew it as described in Section 21.

6 Check the drivebelt tension by pressing on the belt at a point midway on the longest run between the crankshaft and the alternator

6.2a Check the condition of all exhaust mountings...

pulleys. The belt should be tensioned so that, under firm thumb pressure, there is about 10.0 mm of free movement at the midpoint between the two pulleys. If the drivebelt appears excessively taut or slack, refer to Section 21 and adjust the belt tension.

7 If the belt appears not to be too slack, but has actually been slipping in service, check the belt for any sign of external contamination (eg, by oil or water). If found, cure the source of the leak before fitting a new belt.

8 Handbrake check and adjustment

Checking

1 The handbrake should be fully applied (and capable of holding the car on a slope) after five to eight clicks of the ratchet. The operating cables will stretch over time, and adjustment will be needed.

2 Aside from providing equal braking effort to both rear wheels, for the purposes of the MOT inspection, the handbrake lever must be securely mounted, and the ratchet mechanism should release only by means of the lever's button – if the ratchet releases (for example)

6.2b... and for signs of leaks, especially at the front joint

7.4 Auxiliary drivebelt routing – with air conditioning

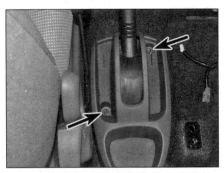

8.3a Undo the retaining bolts...

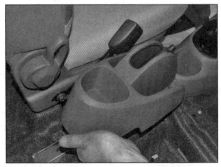

8.3b... and remove the handbrake console...

8.3c... to access the adjusting nut (arrowed)

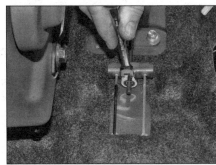

8.6 Adjust the handbrake

when the lever is knocked sideways, the lever assembly should be removed for checking as described in Chapter 9 Section 18.

Adjustment

3 Undo the two retaining bolts and remove the console from around the handbrake lever, to access the adjusting nut **(see illustrations)**.
4 Chock the front wheels and jack up the rear of the car, and support it securely on axle stands (see *Jacking and vehicle support*).
5 Apply and release the handbrake four times to ensure that the self-adjustment mechanism is fully adjusted.
6 With the handbrake set on the seventh notch of the ratchet mechanism, check that both the rear wheels are locked. If not, tighten the handbrake adjusting nut until both rear wheels are locked **(see illustration)**. Once this is so, fully release the handbrake lever, and check that the rear wheels turn freely.
7 Check the adjustment by applying the handbrake fully, counting the clicks from the handbrake ratchet and, if necessary, re-adjust. The handbrake should be fully applied at five to eight notches – do not overadjust, or the handbrake may not release fully.
8 Apply the handbrake by one notch at a time, and check that the rear wheels start to lock up within one or two clicks of each other. Failure to achieve this suggests a problem of some kind with the rear shoes – remove the drums as described in Chapter 9 Section 5 and inspect. Uneven operation could also be due to a seized handbrake cable or linkage (refer to Chapter 9 Section 19).
9 When handbrake operation is satisfactory, refit

the centre console with reference to Chapter 11 Section 25. Lower the car to the ground.
10 Check the operation of the handbrake several times before returning the car to normal service.

9 Clutch and brake pedal adjustment check

Clutch pedal

1 On models with cable-operated clutch (manual transmission), if the clutch is working satisfactorily, further checking is not strictly necessary.
2 Models with a Multi-Mode (2-Tronic/ SensoDrive) transmission, have an electrically-operated clutch, the clutch is self-adjusting, so if working satisfactorily, further checking is not strictly necessary.

12.2 The thickness of the brake pads can be seen through the caliper window

3 Apply the clutch, and check that the pedal operates smoothly and the gears can be selected easily. Uneven operation of the pedal could be due to a faulty cable or linkage (refer to Chapter 6 Section 2). Otherwise, the pedal travel and stroke may be checked and adjusted as described in Chapter 6 Section 3.

Brake pedal

4 As with all modern cars, the braking system on these models are self-adjusting. Provided the brake pedal feels satisfactory (and the brakes work effectively), the chances are that the pedal does not need adjusting.
5 Excessive brake pedal travel may indicate that the brakes need bleeding as described in Chapter 9 Section 11. Otherwise, if the pedal seems set too low, the free play is excessive, or if the history of the car is unknown, the brake pedal can be checked and adjusted as described in Chapter 9 Section 9.

10 Seat belt check

1 Check the seat belts for satisfactory operation and condition. Pull sharply on the belt to check that the locking mechanism engages correctly. Inspect the webbing for fraying and cuts. Check that they retract smoothly and without binding into their reels.
2 Check that the seat belt mounting bolts are tight, and if necessary tighten them to the specified torque see Section 1.

11 Hinge and lock lubrication

1 Work around the car and lubricate the hinges of the bonnet, doors and tailgate with light oil.
2 Lightly lubricate the bonnet release mechanism with a smear of grease.
3 Check carefully the security and operation of all hinges, latches and locks, adjusting them where required. Check the operation of the central locking system, where applicable.
4 Check the condition and operation of the tailgate struts, renewing them if either is leaking or no longer able to support the tailgate securely when raised.

12 Front brake pad and disc wear check

1 Apply the handbrake, then jack up the front of the car and support it securely on axle stands (see *Jacking and vehicle support*). Remove the front roadwheels.
2 The brake pad thickness, and the condition of the disc, can be assessed roughly with just the wheels removed **(see illustration)**. For a

comprehensive check, the brake pads should be removed and cleaned. The operation of the caliper can then also be checked, and the condition of the brake disc itself can be fully examined on both sides. Refer to Chapter 9 Section 3 for further information.

3 On completion, refit the roadwheels and lower the car to the ground.

13 Steering and suspension check

Front suspension and steering

1 Raise the front of the car, and securely support it on axle stands (see *Jacking and vehicle support*).

2 Visually inspect the balljoint dust covers and the steering rack-and-pinion gaiters for splits, chafing or deterioration **(see illustrations)**. Any wear of these components will cause loss of lubricant, together with dirt and water entry, resulting in rapid deterioration of the balljoints or steering gear.

3 Grasp the roadwheel at the 12 o'clock and 6 o'clock positions, and try to rock it **(see illustration)**. Very slight free play may be felt, but if the movement is appreciable, further investigation is necessary to determine the source. Continue rocking the wheel while an assistant depresses the footbrake. If the movement is now eliminated or significantly reduced, it is likely that the hub bearings are at fault. If the free play is still evident with the footbrake depressed, then there is wear in the suspension joints or mountings.

4 Now grasp the wheel at the 9 o'clock and 3 o'clock positions, and try to rock it as before. Any movement felt now may again be caused by wear in the hub bearings or the steering track rod balljoints. If the inner or outer balljoint is worn, the visual movement will be obvious.

5 Using a large screwdriver or flat bar, check for wear in the suspension mounting bushes by levering between the relevant suspension component and its attachment point. Some movement is to be expected as the mountings are made of rubber, but excessive wear should be obvious. Also check the condition of any visible rubber bushes, looking for splits, cracks or contamination of the rubber.

6 With the car standing on its wheels, have an assistant turn the steering wheel back-and-forth, about an eighth of a turn each way. There should be very little, if any, lost movement between the steering wheel and roadwheels. If this is not the case, closely observe the joints and mountings previously described. In addition, check the steering column universal joints for wear, and also check the rack-and-pinion steering gear itself.

Rear suspension

7 Chock the front wheels, then jack up the

13.2a Check the track rod end rubber dust cover...

13.2c... and steering rack rubber gaiter

13.2b... lower balljoint rubber dust cover...

13.3 Check for wear in the hub bearings by grasping the wheel and trying to rock it

rear of the car and support securely on axle stands (see *Jacking and vehicle support*).

8 Working as described previously for the front suspension, check the rear hub bearings, the suspension bushes and the shock absorber mountings for wear **(see illustrations)**.

Shock absorber

9 Check for any signs of fluid leakage around the shock absorber body, or from the rubber gaiter around the piston rod. Should any fluid be noticed, the shock absorber is defective internally, and should be renewed. Note: Shock absorbers should always be renewed in pairs on the same axle.

10 The efficiency of the shock absorber may be checked by bouncing the car at each

corner. Generally speaking, the body will return to its normal position and stop after being depressed. If it rises and returns on a rebound, the shock absorber is probably suspect. Also examine the shock absorber upper and lower mountings for any signs of wear.

14 Driveshaft gaiter check

1 With the car raised and securely supported on stands, turn the steering onto full lock, and then slowly rotate the roadwheel. Inspect the condition of the outer constant velocity (CV) joint rubber gaiters while squeezing the gaiters

13.8a Check for signs of wear in the rear suspension bushes...

13.8b... and the lower shock absorber mounting rubbers

14.1 Check for splits in the driveshaft gaiters

to open out the folds **(see illustration)**. Check for signs of cracking, splits or deterioration of the rubber, which may allow the grease to escape and lead to water and grit entry into the joint. Also check the security and condition of the retaining clips. Repeat these checks on the inner CV joints. If any damage or deterioration is found, the gaiters should be renewed as described in Chapter 8 Section 3, 4.

2 At the same time, check the general condition of the CV joints themselves by first holding the driveshaft and attempting to rotate the wheel. Repeat this check by holding the inner joint and attempting to rotate the driveshaft. Any appreciable movement indicates wear in the joints, wear in the driveshaft splines, or a loose driveshaft retaining nut.

15 Roadwheel bolt tightness check

1 Remove the wheel trims (where fitted), and then slacken the roadwheel bolts slightly.
2 Tighten the bolts to the specified torque (see Section 1) using a torque wrench.

16 Road test

Instruments and electrical equipment

1 Check the operation of all instruments and electrical equipment.
2 Make sure that all instruments read correctly, and switch on all electrical equipment in turn, to check that it functions properly.

Steering and suspension

3 Check for any abnormalities in the steering, suspension, handling or road 'feel'.
4 Drive the car, and check that there are no unusual vibrations or noises.
5 Check that the steering feels positive, with no excessive 'sloppiness', or roughness, and check for any suspension noises when cornering and driving over bumps.

Drivetrain

6 Check the performance of the engine, clutch, transmission and driveshafts.
7 Listen for any unusual noises from the engine, clutch and transmission.
8 Make sure that the engine runs smoothly when idling, and that there is no hesitation when accelerating.
9 Check that, where applicable, the clutch action is smooth and progressive, that the drive is taken up smoothly, and that the pedal travel is not excessive. Also listen for any noises when the clutch pedal is depressed.
10 Check that all gears can be engaged smoothly without noise, and that the gear lever action is smooth and not abnormally vague or 'notchy'.
11 Listen for a metallic clicking sound from the front of the car, as the car is driven slowly in a circle with the steering on full lock. Carry out this check in both directions. If a clicking noise is heard, this indicates wear in a driveshaft joint (see Chapter 8 Section 5).

Braking system

12 Make sure that the car does not pull to one side when braking, and that the wheels do not lock when braking hard.
13 Check that there is no vibration through the steering when braking.
14 Check that the handbrake operates correctly, without excessive movement of the lever, and that it holds the car stationary on a slope.
15 Test the operation of the brake servo unit as follows. Depress the footbrake four or five times to exhaust the vacuum, then start the engine. As the engine starts, there should be a noticeable 'give' in the brake pedal as vacuum builds-up. Allow the engine to run for at least two minutes, and then switch it off. If the brake pedal is now depressed again, it should be possible to detect a hiss from the servo as the pedal is depressed. After about four or five applications, no further hissing should be heard, and the pedal should feel considerably harder.

Exhaust system

16 Listen carefully for any unusual noises from the system, which might indicate that it has started blowing, or that the mountings may be deteriorated, allowing the system to hit the underside of the car.
17 If any noises are detected, inspect the system with the car raised and supported on axle stands (see *Jacking and vehicle support*). Leaks are often accompanied by sooty stains, and are most common at the joints, and at welded sections, where pipes enter silencer boxes. Check the condition of the rubber mountings – if they are cracked or perished, fit new ones.

Every 20 000 miles or 2 years, whichever comes first

17 Spark plug renewal

1 The correct functioning of the spark plugs is vital for the correct running and efficiency of the engine. It is essential that the plugs fitted are appropriate for the engine; suitable types are specified at the beginning of this Chapter. See the label on the top of the cylinder head cover, noting the use of long reach plugs in this engine. If the correct type is used and the engine is in good condition, the spark plugs should not need attention between scheduled intervals. Spark plug cleaning is rarely necessary, and should not be attempted unless specialised equipment is available, as damage can easily be caused to the firing ends.
2 Remove the three ignition coils as described in Chapter 5B Section 3. These models have a direct ignition system (DIS) featuring one ignition coil per spark plug, mounted directly over the plug, with no HT leads.
3 The spark plugs are quite deeply recessed in the top of the engine, and a 16 mm spark plug socket and extension bar will be needed to reach them.

4 It is advisable (if possible) to remove any dirt from the spark plug recesses using a clean brush, vacuum cleaner or compressed air before removing the plugs to prevent dirt dropping into the cylinders. However, the deep recesses on this engine make this an almost-impossible task – just be aware of the danger of anything falling into the spark plug holes when the plugs are removed, and take all possible precautions.
5 Lower the socket and extension into the recesses carefully – if the socket is misaligned and forced in, the ceramic insulator may be broken off. Unscrew each plug in turn, and then carefully withdraw it from the recess so

17.5a Using a spark plug socket and extension...

17.5b... unscrew and remove the spark plugs

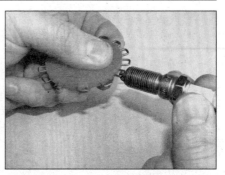

17.10a Using a wire type gauge when checking the gap

that it does not fall out of the socket **(see illustrations)**. As each plug is removed, examine it as follows.

6 Examination of the spark plugs will give a good indication of the condition of the engine. If the insulator nose of the spark plug is clean and white, with no deposits, this is indicative of a weak mixture or too hot a plug (a hot plug transfers heat away from the electrode slowly, a cold plug transfers heat away quickly).

7 If the tip and insulator nose are covered with hard black-looking deposits, then this is indicative that the mixture is too rich. Should the plug be black and oily, and then it is likely that the engine is fairly worn, as well as the mixture being too rich.

8 If the insulator nose is covered with light tan to greyish-brown deposits, then the mixture is correct and it is likely that the engine is in good condition.

9 The spark plug electrode gap is of considerable importance as, if it is too large or too small, the size of the spark and its efficiency will be seriously impaired. The gap should be set to the value given in the specifications in Section 1. Note, however,

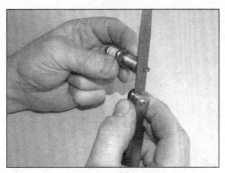

17.10b Measuring a spark plug gap with a feeler blade

17.10c To change the gap, bend the outer electrode only

that modern spark plugs sometimes feature more than one earth electrode – generally, plugs of this type are set at the factory, and their gaps should not be adjusted.

10 To set the gap (on a single earth electrode plug), measure it with a feeler blade and then bend open, or closed, the outer plug electrode until the correct gap is achieved. The centre electrode should never be bent, as this may crack the insulator and cause plug failure, if nothing worse. If using feeler blades, the gap is correct when the appropriate-size blade is a firm sliding fit **(see illustrations)**.

11 Special spark plug electrode gap adjusting tools are available from most motor accessory shops, or from some spark plug manufacturers.

12 Before fitting the spark plugs, check that the threaded connector sleeves are tight, and that the plug exterior surfaces and threads are clean (see **Haynes Hint**).

13 Remove the rubber/plastic hose (if used), and tighten the plug to the specified torque in Section 1 using the spark plug socket and a torque wrench **(see illustration)**. Refit the remaining spark plugs in the same manner.

14 Refit the ignition coils as described in Chapter 5B Section 3, and the air cleaner/inlet duct as described in Chapter 4A Section 5.

18 Air filter element renewal

1 The air cleaner is located on top of the engine. The air cleaner lower housing is part of the cylinder head cover.

2 Release the four spring clips on the side of the air cleaner cover **(see illustration)**.

3 Slacken the two securing clips from the

HAYNES
HiNT

It's often difficult to insert spark plugs into their holes without cross-threading them. To avoid this possibility, fit a short length of rubber or plastic hose over the end of the spark plug. The flexible hose acts as a universal joint, to help align the plug with the plug hole. Should the plug begin to cross-thread, the hose will slip on the spark plug, preventing thread damage to the aluminium cylinder head.

17.13 If available, tighten the spark plugs using a torque wrench

18.2 Release the four spring clips (arrowed)

18.3a Release the retaining spring from the top of the throttle housing...

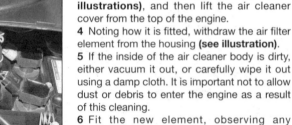

18.3b... and the breather pipe retaining spring (arrowed)

throttle housing and breather pipe **(see illustrations)**, and then lift the air cleaner cover from the top of the engine.

4 Noting how it is fitted, withdraw the air filter element from the housing **(see illustration)**.

5 If the inside of the air cleaner body is dirty, either vacuum it out, or carefully wipe it out using a damp cloth. It is important not to allow dust or debris to enter the engine as a result of this cleaning.

6 Fit the new element, observing any markings indicating correct orientation, then refit the air cleaner cover, making sure all the retaining clips are secure.

19 Rear brake shoe and drum wear check

1 Remove the rear brake drums, and check the brake shoes for signs of wear or contamination. At the same time, also inspect the wheel cylinders for signs of leakage, and the brake drum for signs of wear. Refer to the relevant Sections of Chapter 9 for further information.

2 For a quick check of the brake shoe lining thickness, there is a rubber grommet in the brake drum backplate **(see illustration)**. Apply the handbrake, and then jack up the rear of the car and support it securely on axle stands (see *Jacking and vehicle support*). If required, remove the rear wheel to make access easier.

18.4 Lift the air cleaner cover upwards, and remove the filter element

19.2 Brake shoe thickness access hole in the rear of the drum

Every 40 000 miles or 4 years, whichever comes first

20 Transmission oil level check

1 Position the car over an inspection pit, on car ramps, or jack it up (see *Jacking and vehicle support*), but make sure that the vehicle is level.

20.3 Unscrew and remove the transmission filler/level plug

2 Remove the engine lower cover panels (where fitted) from under the car.

3 Remove all traces of dirt, and then unscrew the filler/level plug from the front face of the transmission **(see illustration)**. A new washer should be fitted to the filler/level plug when refitting.

4 The level must be level with the bottom edge of the filler/level plug hole. If necessary,

20.5 Top-up the oil level if necessary

use a cranked tool such as an Allen key to check the level, but nothing which might break off and fall into the transmission.

5 If necessary, top-up the level with the specified grade of oil (see *Lubricants and fluids*) until the oil just starts to run out **(see illustration)**. Allow any excess oil to flow out until the level stabilises.

 When a transmission oil bottle is more than half-full, squeezing it will force the oil in from below – after that, the bottle will have to be manoeuvred in from above.

6 When the level is correct in the transmission, clean and refit the filler/level plug (with a new washer), and then tighten it to the specified torque.

7 Refit the lower cover panels (where fitted), and lower the car to the ground.

8 Although not part of the manufacturer's

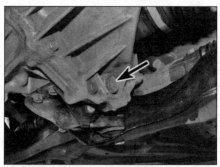

20.8 Transmission oil drain plug (arrowed)

21.2a Slacken the alternator upper pivot bolt...

21.2b... and the two lower securing bolts (arrowed)

21.3 Turn the alternator adjusting bolt (arrowed)

21.4 Remove the belt from around the pulleys

21.5 Auxiliary drivebelt routing – with air conditioning

routine maintenance schedule, it is a good idea to change the transmission oil after a high mileage has been completed, or perhaps periodically on a car which does a lot of stop-start driving. A drain plug is provided at the lower rear of the transmission **(see illustration)** – see Chapter 7A Section 2 for details.

21 Auxiliary drivebelt renewal and adjustment

Removal

1 Jack up the right-hand front wheel, and support the car using an axle stand (see *Jacking and vehicle support*).
2 Salcken the alternator upper pivot bolt (at the top of the alternator), and the securing bolts for the adjuster at the bottom of the alternator **(see illustrations)**.
3 Unscrew the adjuster bolt and push the alternator down towards the engine to release the drivebelt tension enough to free the belt from the alternator pulley **(see illustration)**.
4 Noting how it is routed, remove the belt from

around all the pulleys and withdraw it from the engine compartment **(see illustration)**.

Refitting

5 Fitting the belt is a direct reversal of removal. Feed the belt onto the pulleys **(see illustration)**, ensuring that it is seated properly in the pulley grooves – leave the alternator pulley until last.
6 If necessary, loosen the adjuster bolt even more to allow a new (unstretched) belt to fit, then install the belt onto the alternator pulley, again making sure the belt seats in the grooves.
7 Tighten the adjuster bolt to take up the slack in the belt, but do not try to set the tension at this stage.
8 Using a spanner or socket on the crankshaft pulley bolt, turn the engine through a few turns in the normal direction of travel (clockwise) to settle the belt and ensure that it is running properly in all the pulley grooves.

Tensioning

9 If not already done, salcken the alternator upper pivot bolt (at the top of the alternator), and the lower bolts for the adjuster bolt.
10 Adjust the belt tension by turning the

adjuster bolt in the appropriate direction in small steps at a time.
11 Check the drivebelt tension by pressing on the belt at a point midway on the longest run between the crankshaft and the alternator pulleys. The belt should be tensioned so that, under firm thumb pressure, there is about 10.0 mm of free movement at the midpoint between the two pulleys.
12 To ensure accuracy, each time the belt tension is adjusted, using a spanner or socket on the crankshaft pulley bolt, turn the engine through a few turns in the normal direction of travel (clockwise) to settle the belt.
13 Repeat the procedure in paragraphs 10 to 11 until the belt tension is satisfactory. On completion, tighten the adjuster lock bolt and the alternator lower pivot bolt to the specified torque in Section 1. Lower the car to the ground, then run the engine to check for signs of slipping (noises from the belt).
14 If a new belt has been fitted, do not overtension it to allow for the belt stretching – instead, recheck the tension after (say) a month or 1000 miles. It is quite normal for a new belt to require retensioning after its initial 'running-in' period.

Every 2 years, regardless of mileage

22 Brake fluid renewal

⚠️ *Warning: Brake hydraulic fluid can harm your eyes and damage painted surfaces, so use extreme caution when handling and pouring it. Do not use fluid that has been standing open for some time, as it absorbs moisture from the air. Excess moisture can cause a dangerous loss of braking effectiveness.*

1 The procedure is similar to that for bleeding the hydraulic system as described in Chapter 9 Section 11, except that allowance should be made for the old fluid to be expelled when bleeding each section of the circuit.

2 Working as described in Chapter 9 Section 11, open the first bleed screw in the sequence, and pump the brake pedal gently until nearly all the old fluid has been emptied from the master cylinder reservoir.

3 Top-up to the MAX level with new fluid, and continue pumping until only the new fluid remains in the reservoir, and new fluid can be seen emerging from the bleed screw. Tighten the screw, and top the reservoir level up to the MAX level line.

4 Work through all the remaining bleed screws in the sequence until new fluid can be seen at all of them. Be careful to keep the master cylinder reservoir topped-up above the MIN level at all times, or air may enter the system. If this happens, further bleeding will be required, to remove the air.

> **HAYNES HiNT** *Old hydraulic fluid is invariably much darker in colour than the new, making it easy to distinguish the two.*

5 When the operation is complete, check

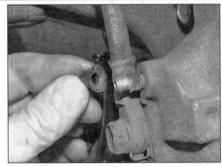
22.5 Make sure the dust caps are fitted

that all bleed screws are securely tightened, and that their dust caps are refitted **(see illustration)**. Wash off all traces of spilt fluid, and recheck the master cylinder reservoir fluid level.

6 Check the operation of the brakes before taking the car on the road.

Every 4 years, regardless of mileage

23 Coolant renewal and pressure cap check

⚠️ *Warning: Wait until the engine is cold before starting this procedure. Do not allow antifreeze to come in contact with your skin, or with the painted surfaces of the car. Rinse off spills immediately with plenty of water. Never leave antifreeze lying around in an open container, or in a puddle in the driveway or on the garage floor. Children and pets are attracted by its sweet smell, but antifreeze can be fatal if ingested.*

Cooling system draining

1 With the engine completely cold, remove the expansion tank filler cap and the radiator cap. Turn the radiator cap anti-clockwise, wait until any pressure remaining in the system is released, then unscrew it and lift it off.

2 Position a suitable container beneath the drain plug, at the right-hand side of the engine compartment, below the coolant pump **(see illustration)**.

3 Slacken the drain plug, and allow the coolant to drain into the container.

4 When the flow of coolant stops, refit and tighten the drain plug and tighten to the specified torque in Section 1. Use a new sealing washer.

5 If the coolant has been drained for a reason other than renewal, then provided it is clean and less than two years old, it can be re-used, though this is not recommended.

6 For complete draining, disconnect the bottom hose from the lower part of the radiator **(see illustration)**.

7 Place a container under the radiator, and then slacken the retaining clip and disconnect the hose. Allow any coolant remaining in the radiator to drain **(see illustration)**.

8 Refit the bottom hose to the radiator, making sure it is fitted correctly and tighten the retaining clip.

Cooling system flushing

9 If coolant renewal has been neglected, or if the antifreeze mixture has become diluted, then in time, the cooling system may gradually lose efficiency, as the coolant passages become restricted due to rust, scale deposits, and other sediment. The cooling system efficiency can be restored by flushing the system clean.

10 The radiator should be flushed independently of the engine, to avoid unnecessary contamination.

Radiator flushing

11 Disconnect the top and bottom hoses and any other relevant hoses from the radiator, with reference to Chapter 3 Section 3.

12 Insert a garden hose into the radiator top inlet. Direct a flow of clean water through the radiator, and continue flushing until clean water emerges from the radiator bottom outlet.

13 If after a reasonable period, the water

23.2 Cooling system engine drain plug (arrowed)

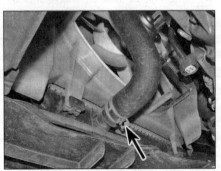
23.6 Remove the bottom hose retaining clip...

23.7... and drain the coolant into a container

still does not run clear, the radiator can be flushed with a good proprietary cleaning agent. It is important that their manufacturer's instructions are followed carefully. If the contamination is particularly bad, insert the hose in the radiator bottom outlet, and reverse-flush the radiator.

Engine flushing

14 Remove the thermostat as described in Chapter 3 Section 4 then, if the radiator top hose has been disconnected from the engine, temporarily reconnect the hose.

15 With the top and bottom hoses disconnected from the radiator, insert a garden hose into the radiator top hose. Direct a clean flow of water through the engine, and continue flushing until clean water emerges from the radiator bottom hose.

16 On completion of flushing, refit the thermostat and reconnect the hoses with reference to Chapter 3 Section 4.

Antifreeze mixture

17 The antifreeze should always be renewed at the specified intervals. This is necessary not only to maintain the antifreeze properties, but also to prevent corrosion, which would otherwise occur as the corrosion inhibitors become progressively less effective.

18 Always use an ethylene-glycol based antifreeze which is suitable for use in mixed-metal cooling systems. The quantity of antifreeze and levels of protection are given in the Specifications.

19 The antifreeze recommended by the manufacturer at the time of writing is their Super Long Life Coolant, which is said to have a 10 year, 100 000 mile life. Owners may still wish to change their antifreeze on a regular basis, especially if the type and quality in the system is unknown.

20 Note that Long Life Coolant should never be mixed with any other type, especially if it is wished to preserve the 'long life' qualities.

21 Remember that a small amount of coolant will always be present in the system, even after draining. Therefore, if coolant of a different type is to be used, the engine and radiator should be thoroughly flushed with

clean water as described previously in this Section.

22 Before adding antifreeze, check all hoses for condition and security.

23 After filling with antifreeze, a label should be attached to the expansion tank, stating the type and concentration of antifreeze used, and the date installed. Any subsequent topping-up should be made with the same type and concentration of antifreeze.

24 Do not use engine antifreeze in the windscreen/tailgate washer system, as it will cause damage to the paintwork. A screenwash additive should be added to the washer system in the quantities stated on the bottle.

Cooling system filling

25 Before attempting to fill the cooling system, make sure that all hoses and clips are in good condition, and that the clips are tight. Note that an antifreeze mixture must be used all year round, to prevent corrosion of the engine components.

26 Remove the radiator filler cap. If a funnel is available for filling the cooling system, use it to reduce the risk of spillage onto the paintwork under the bonnet.

27 Slowly fill the system until the level in the radiator stabilises. Similarly, remove the expansion tank cap, and top-up the level. This process should take several minutes – gently squeeze the radiator hoses to help disperse any trapped air, and keep checking the level in both radiator and the expansion tank.

28 Start the engine; let it run for two minutes, then switch off. Be prepared to top-up the radiator (or expansion tank) as soon as the engine starts – the levels may drop quite quickly.

29 Leave the engine for a few minutes, then recheck the coolant levels in the radiator and expansion tank, and top-up if necessary. Fit the radiator and expansion tank caps once the levels have stabilised.

30 Start the engine once more, and run it at idle until the radiator top hose is fully warm (preferably, wait until the cooling fan cuts in). Keep an eye on the temperature display – if overheating is indicated at any time, switch

the engine off immediately. Once the engine has warmed-up, switch it off, and allow it to cool. When the engine has cooled (preferably overnight), recheck the levels once more, and top-up if necessary.

Airlocks

31 If, after draining and refilling the system, symptoms of overheating are found which did not occur previously, then the fault is almost certainly due to trapped air at some point in the system, causing an airlock and restricting the flow of coolant; usually the air is trapped because the system was refilled too quickly.

32 If an airlock is suspected, first try gently squeezing all visible coolant hoses. A coolant hose that is full of air feels quite different to one full of coolant when squeezed. After refilling the system, most airlocks will clear once the system has cooled, and been topped-up.

33 While the engine is running at operating temperature, switch on the heater and heater fan, and check for heat output. Provided there is sufficient coolant in the system, any lack of heat output could be due to an airlock in the system.

34 Airlocks can have more serious effects than simply reducing heater output – a severe airlock could reduce coolant flow around the engine. Check that the radiator top hose is hot when the engine is at operating temperature – a top hose that stays cold could be the result of an airlock (or a non-opening thermostat).

35 If the problem persists, stop the engine and allow it to cool down completely, before removing the radiator and expansion tank caps, or loosening the hose clips and squeezing the hoses to bleed out the trapped air. In the worst case, the system will have to be at least partially drained (this time, the coolant can be saved for re-use) and flushed to clear the problem.

Radiator cap check

36 Clean the pressure cap, and inspect the seal inside the cap for damage or deterioration. If there is any sign of damage or deterioration to the seal, fit a new pressure cap.

Notes

Chapter 2 Part A
Engine in-car repair procedures

Contents

Degrees of difficulty

Easy, suitable for novice with little experience		**Fairly easy,** suitable for beginner with some experience		**Fairly difficult,** suitable for competent DIY mechanic		**Difficult,** suitable for experienced DIY mechanic		**Very difficult,** suitable for expert DIY or professional	

Specifications

General

Engine type.	Three-cylinder, in-line, twin overhead cam 12-valve, VVT-i (variable valve timing – intelligent). Wedge-shaped combustion chamber with a crossflow cylinder head
Max output	50 kW @ 6000rpm
Max torque	93 Nm @ 3600rpm
Engine codes	384F (CFA, CFB) or 1KR-FE
Capacity	998 cc
Bore	71.0 mm
Stroke	84.0 mm
Compression ratio	10.5: 1
Compression pressure:	
Maximum	13.8 bar
Minimum	10.5 bar
Difference between cylinders	1.5 bar
Firing order.	1-2-3 (No 1 cylinder at timing chain end)
Direction of crankshaft rotation	Clockwise (seen from right-hand side of car)

Lubrication

Oil pressure (at 90°C):	
At 2000 rpm	3.7 bar
At 4000 rpm	5.0 bar

Valves

Valve clearances (cold):	
Checking:	
Inlet	0.15 to 21 mm
Exhaust.	0.28 to 33 mm
Setting:	
Inlet	0.18 mm
Exhaust.	0.31 mm
Valve length:	
Inlet	88.39 mm
Exhaust.	89.11 mm
Valve head diameter:	
Inlet	27.350 to 27.650 mm
Exhaust.	23.450 to 23.750 mm
Valve stem diameter.	3.900 to 4.500 mm
Valve stem-to-guide clearance.	0.010 to 0.065 mm
Valve spring free length	51.63 mm

Cylinder head

Maximum permissible gasket surface distortion	0.05 mm
Maximum cylinder head bolt length (measured from under head).	123.5 mm

Camshafts

Endfloat	0.100 to 0.225 mm
Camshaft operating clearances:	
Inlet camshaft:	
Bearing carrier (No 1)	0.025 to 0.061 mm
Bearing caps (Nos 2, 3 & 4)	0.035 to 0.072 mm
Exhaust camshaft:	
Bearing carrier (No 1)	0.037 to 0.073 mm
Bearing caps (Nos 2, 3 & 4)	0.035 to 0.072 mm

Connecting rods

Big-end bearing journal diameter.	43.000 to 43.024 mm
Radial clearance.	0.016 to 0.040 mm
Axial clearance	0.1 to 0.3 mm

Pistons and piston rings

Piston diameter	70.921 to 70.931 mm
Piston-to-cylinder bore clearance	0.028 mm to 0.052 mm
Piston ring end gap – installed:	
Top compression ring.	0.20 to 0.30 mm
Second compression/sealing ring	0.40 to 0.60 mm
Piston ring-to-groove clearance:	
Top compression ring.	0.030 mm to 0.070 mm
Second compression ring.	0.020 mm to 0.060 mm
Oil control ring	0.070 mm to 0.150 mm

Crankshaft and bearings

Main bearing journal diameter	43.988 to 44.000 mm
Main bearing operating clearance	0.021 to 0.046 mm
Main bearing shell thickness:	
Ref 2	1.983 to 2.013 mm
Ref 3	1.986 to 2.016 mm
Ref 4	1.989 to 2.019 mm
Ref 5	1.992 to 2.022 mm
Big-end crankpin bearing journal diameter	39.992 to 40.000 mm
Big-end bearing operating clearance	0.016 to 0.042 mm
Big-end bearing shell thickness:	
Ref 1	1.492 to 1.495 mm
Ref 2	1.495 to 1.498 mm
Ref 3	1.498 to 1.501 mm
Crankshaft endfloat	0.020 to 0.040 mm
Thrustwasher thickness	1.940 to 1.990 mm

Torque wrench settings

	Nm	lbf ft
Big-end bearing cap bolts: *		
Stage 1	15	11
Stage 2	Angle-tighten a further 90°	
Camshaft bearing caps	13	10
Camshaft bearing 'double' cap	15	11
Camshaft sprocket bolts	47	35
Crankshaft oil seal retainer bolts	10	7
Crankshaft pulley bolt	170	126
Cylinder head cover nuts/bolts	9	7
Cylinder head bolts:		
Stage 1	32	24
Stage 2	Angle-tighten a further 180°	
Engine mountings:		
Left-hand transmission mounting bolts	52	38
Rear mounting bracket-to-transmission bolts	52	38
Rear mounting through-bolt	120	89
Right-hand mounting to engine	24	18
Right-hand mounting to body	52	38
Engine oil drain plug.	30	22
Exhaust manifold	24	18

Torque wrench settings (continued)

	Nm	lbf ft
Flywheel bolts*	78	58
Fuel injection rail-to-cylinder head bolts	27	20
Ignition coil retaining bolts	10	7
Inlet manifold nuts	30	22
Knock sensor	20	15
Main bearing cap bolts: *		
Stage 1	30	22
Stage 2	59	44
Oil filter housing to cylinder block	24	18
Oil pressure switch/sensor	15	11
Oil pump mounting bolts	9	7
Spark plugs	25	18
Sump bolts:		
Large bolts (x9)	24	18
Small bolts (x6)	10	7
Thermostat housing nut/bolt	9	7
Timing chain cover access plug	15	11
Timing chain cover **(see illustration 5.17)**:		
Smaller-headed bolts (1)	24	18
Larger-headed bolts (2)	40	30
Timing chain fixed guide bolts	10	7
Timing chain tensioner guide pivot bolt	19	14
Timing chain tensioner mounting bolts	12	9
Transmission-to-engine bolts	64	47
Transmission-to-engine lower stiffener plate bolts	40	30
VVT-i oil control valve bolt	10	7
Water bypass pipe nuts/bracket bolts	10	7

* Use new bolts

1 General Information

How to use this Chapter

1 This Part of Chapter 2 is devoted to engine in-car repair procedures. All procedures concerning engine removal and refitting, and engine block/cylinder head overhaul, can be found in Chapter 2B.

2 Refer to *Vehicle identification numbers* in the Reference Section at the end of this manual for details of engine code locations.

3 Most of the operations included in this chapter are based on the assumption that the engine is still installed in the car. Therefore, if this information is being used during a complete engine overhaul with the engine already removed, many of the steps included here will not apply.

Engine description

4 The engine is a twin overhead cam, water-cooled, three-cylinder in-line unit, with VVT-i variable valve timing system. The engine is an all-new design, mounted transversely at the front of the car with the transmission to form a combined power unit.

5 The crankshaft is supported in four shell-type main bearings. The connecting rod big-end bearings are also split shell-type, and are attached to the pistons by floating-fit gudgeon pins. Each piston is fitted with two compression rings and one oil control ring.

6 Drive for the overhead camshafts is provided by a spring-tensioned timing chain. The valves are operated by 'solid' tappets, which are directly operated by the cam lobes; no adjustment shims are fitted, so the valve clearances are determined by the thickness of the tappets themselves. This reduces the weight of the valve components, and gives a virtually maintenance-free valve setup. The valves are each closed by a single valve spring, and operate in guides integral in the aluminium alloy cylinder head.

7 The variable valve timing system allows the inlet camshaft timing to be varied under the control of the engine management system, to boost both low-speed torque and top-end power, as well as reducing exhaust emissions. The cylindrical VVT-i controller is fitted directly to the end of the inlet camshaft, and is supplied with two pressurised oil feeds through passages in the camshaft itself. An oil control valve, operated by the engine management system, is fitted to the rear of the cylinder head, and this is used to supply the pressurised oil to the controller through the two oil feeds. The controller contains four vane chambers – depending on which of the two oil feeds is enabled by the control valve, the oil pressure will turn the inlet camshaft clockwise (advance) or anti-clockwise (retard) to adjust the valve timing as required. If pressure is removed from both feeds, this induces a timing 'hold' condition.

8 The oil pump is mounted on the inside of the timing chain cover, and is driven by flats on the end of the crankshaft.

Operations with engine in car

9 The following work can be carried out with the engine in the car:

a) Camshafts and tappets – removal, inspection and refitting.
b) Cylinder head – removal and refitting.
c) Crankshaft oil seals – renewal.
d) Timing chain, sprockets and tensioner – removal, inspection and refitting.
e) Oil pump – removal and refitting.
f) Sump – removal and refitting.
g) Connecting rods and pistons – removal and refitting.*
h) Flywheel – removal, inspection and refitting.
i) Engine/transmission mountings – inspection and renewal.

10 * Although the operation marked with an asterisk can be carried out with the engine in the car after removal of the sump, it is better for the engine to be removed in the interests of cleanliness and improved access. For this reason, the procedure is described in Part B of this Chapter.

2 Compression test – description and interpretation

1 When engine performance is down, or if misfiring occurs which cannot be attributed to the ignition or fuel systems, a compression test can provide diagnostic clues as to the engine's condition. If the test is performed regularly, it can give warning of trouble before any other symptoms become apparent.

3.4 Crankshaft pulley timing mark aligned with timing cover pointer

3.6 At TDC, the timing dot on both camshaft sprockets should be at the top

2 The engine must be fully warmed-up to operating temperature, the oil level must be correct and the battery must be fully-charged. The help of an assistant will also be required.

3 Refer to the wiring diagrams in Chapter 12 and remove the fuel pump fuse from the fusebox. Now start the engine and allow it to run until it stalls.

4 Release the securing clips and remove the air cleaner cover, refer to Chapter 4A Section 5, if required.

5 Disable the ignition system by disconnecting the multiplugs from the coils on top of the engine. Remove all the spark plugs with reference to Chapter 1 Section 17.

6 Fit a compression tester to the No 1 cylinder spark plug hole – the type of tester that screws into the spark plug thread is preferable.

7 Arrange for an assistant to hold the accelerator pedal fully depressed to the floor, while at the same time cranking the engine over for several seconds on the starter motor. Observe the compression gauge reading. The compression will build-up fairly quickly in a healthy engine. Low compression on the first stroke, followed by gradually increasing pressure on successive strokes, indicates worn piston rings. A low compression on the first stroke, which does not rise on successive strokes, indicates leaking valves or a blown head gasket (a cracked cylinder head could also be the cause). Deposits on the underside of the valve heads can also cause low compression. Record the highest gauge reading obtained, and then repeat the procedure for the remaining cylinders.

8 Compare the readings obtained with that

specified at the start of this Chapter. The most important factor is that the compression pressures are uniform in all cylinders, and that is what this test is mainly concerned with.

9 Add some engine oil (about three squirts from a plunger type oil can) to each cylinder through the spark plug holes, and then repeat the test.

10 If the compression increases after the oil is added, the piston rings are probably worn. If the compression does not increase significantly, the leakage is occurring at the valves or the head gasket. Leakage past the valves may be caused by burned valve seats and/or faces, or warped, cracked or bent valves.

11 If two adjacent cylinders have equally low compressions, it is most likely that the head gasket has blown between them. The appearance of coolant in the combustion chambers or on the engine oil dipstick would verify this condition.

12 If one cylinder is about 20 percent lower than the other, and the engine has a slightly rough idle; a worn lobe on the camshaft could be the cause.

13 On completion of the checks, refit the spark plugs, and then reconnect the coil multiplugs. Refit the fuel pump fuse to the fusebox.

3 Top Dead Centre (TDC) for No 1 piston – locating

1 Top dead centre (TDC) is the highest point of the cylinder that each piston reaches as the

crankshaft turns. Each piston reaches its TDC position at the end of its compression stroke, and then again at the end of its exhaust stroke. For the purpose of engine timing, TDC at the end of the compression stroke for No 1 piston is used. No 1 cylinder is at the crankshaft pulley/timing chain end of the engine. Proceed as follows.

2 Ensure that the ignition is switched off (take out the key). Remove the spark plugs as described in Chapter 1.

3 Turn the engine clockwise using a spanner or socket on the crankshaft pulley bolt. If necessary for improved access, apply the handbrake, then jack up the front of the car and support it on axle stands (see *Jacking and vehicle support*). Remove the plastic inner wing cover panel below the engine on the driver's side.

4 Turn the engine to the point where the notch in the outer edge of the crankshaft pulley aligns with the pointer on the timing chain cover above the pulley **(see illustration)**. To ensure that it is on its compression stroke, place a finger over the No 1 cylinder plug hole, and feel to ensure that air pressure exits from the cylinder as the piston reaches the top of its stroke.

5 For further confirmation, remove the cylinder head cover as described in Section 4.

6 If the engine is at TDC on the compression stroke, the marks on the camshaft sprockets should be visible (under the timing chain) at the 12 o'clock position in both cases **(see illustration)** – if not, turn the crankshaft pulley through a full turn and realign the pulley mark with the pointer timing mark.

7 Once No 1 cylinder has been positioned at TDC on the compression stroke, TDC for any of the other cylinders can then be located by rotating the crankshaft clockwise (in its normal direction of rotation), 120° at a time, and following the firing order (see Specifications).

8 On completion, where applicable, refit the cylinder head cover and engine lower cover panel, and then lower the car to the ground. Refit the spark plugs as described in Chapter 1.

4 Cylinder head cover – removal and refitting

Removal

1 The air cleaner lower housing is part of the cylinder head cover. Remove the engine/air filter upper cover, which is secured by four retaining clips and two hose clips. See air filter element renewal as described in Chapter 1, Section 18.

2 Disconnect the wiring plugs from the ignition coils and move the wiring harness clear. Undo the retaining bolts and withdraw the three ignition coils from the top of the cylinder head cover **(see illustrations)**.

4.2a Disconnect the wiring connectors...

4.2b... undo the retaining bolts and withdraw the coils

4.3 Unclip the wiring loom

4.4 Disconnect the breather hose

4.5 Unbolt the purge canister solenoid valve

4.6a Unbolt the wiring loom...

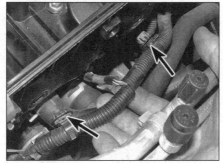

4.6b... and unclip the loom from the side of the cover

4.7 Unbolt the oxygen sensor wiring bracket

3 Unclip the wiring loom from across the top of the cylinder head cover (see illustration), and move it to one side.

4 Release the securing clip and disconnect the crankcase breather hose from the rear of the cylinder head cover (see illustration).

5 Undo the retaining bolt and disconnect the purge canister solenoid valve from the rear of the cylinder head cover/lower filter housing (see illustration).

6 Undo the wiring bracket securing bolt from the rear of the cylinder head cover/lower filter housing, and then unclip the wiring loom from across the left-hand side and move it aside (see illustrations).

7 Undo the retaining bolt and disconnect the oxygen sensor wiring bracket from the front of the cylinder head cover (see illustration).

8 Unscrew and remove the thirteen bolts and two nuts securing the cylinder head cover in the order shown (see illustration).

9 Remove the cover (see illustration), including the rubber gasket, which may well be stuck to the cylinder head – unless the old one can be removed cleanly, a new gasket should be obtained for refitting.

10 With the gasket removed, clean all traces of old sealant from the top of the cylinder head, the cylinder head cover, and the old gasket itself (if it's to be re-used).

Refitting

11 Fit the new (or reclaimed) gasket to the cylinder head cover, making sure it is located fully in the cover groove and around

4.8 Undo the bolts in the sequence shown...

4.9.. and remove the cylinder head cover

4.11 Fit the rubber gasket into the cover groove and around the spark plug apertures

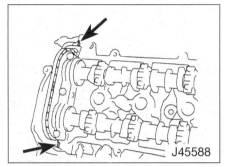

4.12 Apply sealant to the two areas shown

the spark plug apertures at the centre **(see illustration)**.

12 Apply a spot of suitable RTV sealant approx 4 mm diameter to the points on the cylinder head shown **(see illustration)**.

13 Once the sealant has been applied, the cover must be fitted within three minutes. The cover must also be fitted accurately for the sealant to be effective – place a few bolts loosely through the cover before lowering it into position to help with the alignment.

14 Place the cover on top of the engine, making sure the gasket stays in place, and secure it in place with the bolts/nuts. Tighten the bolts/nuts progressively and evenly in the opposite sequence to the removal procedure **(see illustration 4.8)** to the specified torque, and then wipe away any excess sealant.

15 Further refitting is a reversal of removal.

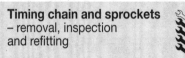

5 Timing chain and sprockets – removal, inspection and refitting

Removal

1 Drain the engine oil and cooling system as described in Chapter 1.

2 Set the engine to TDC on No 1 cylinder as described in Section 3.

3 Disconnect the wiring connector from the crankshaft position sensor on the rear of the timing chain cover **(see illustration)**.

4 Remove the auxiliary drivebelt as described in Chapter 1 Section 21.

5 Remove the cylinder head cover as described in Section 4.

6 Remove the coolant pump as described in Chapter 3.

7 Remove the crankshaft pulley as described in Section 14.

8 Remove the alternator as described in Chapter 5A.

9 Slacken and remove the oil filter from the filter housing on the lower part of the timing chain cover. Undo the three retaining bolts and remove the housing from the timing chain cover **(see illustrations)**. Recover the gasket – a new one must be used when refitting.

10 Remove the sump as described in Section 10.

11 Undo the dipstick tube retaining bolt at the top of the timing chain cover and carefully twist it away from the cover **(see illustrations)**. Note there is an O-ring seal at the base of the dipstick tube into the cylinder block, if required pull out the tube and renew the seal.

12 Disconnect the wiring plug from the VVT-i oil control valve – this is on the rear of the cylinder head. Remove the single mounting bolt, and withdraw the oil control valve from the head **(see illustrations)**.

13 Using a pair of grips, release the securing clip at the rear of the coolant pump housing **(see illustration)**. This will become disconnected as the timing chain cover is removed from the cylinder block.

14 The engine must now be supported, as the right-hand mounting must be unbolted and removed. The best option is to use an engine crane or hoist, and support the engine from above. An engine support bar could be used, but might hamper access to the timing chain area. Though the sump has been

5.3 Disconnect the crankshaft sensor wiring connector

5.9a Remove the oil filter housing...

5.9b... and recover the oil seal

5.11a Move the dipstick tube away from the engine

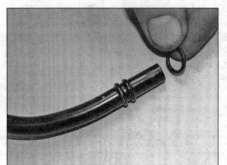

5.11b If removed, renew the oil seal on the lower end of the dipstick tube

5.12a Undo the retaining bolt (arrowed)...

5.12b... and remove the oil control valve

5.13 Release the hose retaining clip

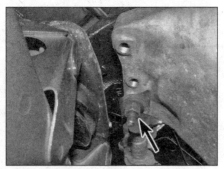

5.15 Engine mounting lower securing nut (arrowed)

5.16 Remove the engine mounting

5.17 Note there are two sizes of bolts

1 Smaller-headed bolts   2 Larger-headed bolts

removed, supporting the engine from below is also an option, providing a large block of wood is used between the jack head and across the crankcase surfaces.

15 Working underneath the engine mounting, remove the nut from the engine mounting stud **(see illustration)**.

16 Remove the four upper bolts securing the engine mounting to the inner wing and timing chain cover, and lift the mounting off the stud to remove it from the engine compartment **(see illustration)**.

17 Remove the remaining eleven bolts securing the timing chain cover – note the positions of the bolts, as they are of different

sizes **(see illustration)**. Note the coolant pump and oil filter housing securing bolts (which have already been removed); also secure the timing chain cover.

18 The cover will need to be prised off, as sealant is used during fitting – take care not to mark the sealing surfaces or damage the cover as it is removed **(see illustration)**. As the cover is removed it will need to be withdrawn from the coolant hose **(see illustration 5.13)**.

19 Once the cover is removed, remove the O-ring seal for the oil pump feed **(see illustration)** which is fitted to the cylinder block, discard – a new one should be used when refitting.

20 Before removing the timing chain tensioner, rotate the lockplate upwards, and then push the tensioner plunger into the body as far as possible (some oil will probably be lost from around the tensioner as this is done). Insert a 3 mm drill bit through the hole in the lockplate to hold it – some 'fiddling' may be required (turning the lockplate and moving the plunger) until the drill bit locks the plunger **(see illustrations)**.

21 Remove the bolts securing the tensioner to the cylinder block, and remove it without disturbing the drill bit.

22 Remove the lower pivot bolt, and take off the timing chain rear guide (which is

5.18 The cover is attached with sealant, and will have to be prised or tapped off

5.19 Oil pump feed oil seal (arrowed)

5.20a Release the pressure on the tensioner...

5.20b... and insert a 3 mm pin (drill bit) to lock the tensioner

5.22 Undo the lower pivot bolt from the guide

5.23 Remove the front guide from the cylinder block

5.24 Slot in crankshaft sprocket (arrowed) for timing mark

5.25a Remove the crankshaft sprocket...

5.25b... and remove the Woodruff key

operated on by the tensioner at the top) **(see illustration)**.

23 Remove the timing chain front guide by undoing the securing bolts (this is only necessary if the cylinder head is being removed later) **(see illustration)**.

24 Before removing the timing chain, check for a mark on the crankshaft sprocket **(see illustration)** – this is used in relation to the yellow timing chain link when refitting.

25 Unhook the timing chain, and remove it from the sprockets. The crankshaft sprocket

just slides off the nose of the crankshaft, over the Woodruff key **(see illustrations)**. Remove the Woodruff key and keep safe for refitting.

26 If the camshaft sprockets are to be removed, hold the relevant camshaft against rotation using a spanner on the hex provided on the shaft. Undo the bolts securing the inlet sprocket and VVT-i controller assembly, or the exhaust sprocket, and remove from their respective camshafts **(see illustrations)**. Do not attempt to separate the VVT-i controller from the inlet sprocket.

Inspection

27 Check the chain rear guide (the one operated by the tensioner) for wear. If the chain has worn a groove deeper then 0.5 mm In the guide, a new guide should be fitted. If the rear guide has worn, it is likely that the other guides will also require renewal.

28 If the chain is known to have seen long service (over 100 000 miles), it's worth considering fitting a new one, if only for peace of mind. No renewal interval is specified by the manufacturer, and although a timing chain is more robust than the rubber 'cambelt' used on other engines, if the chain were to snap the consequences for the engine would be equally serious. If the sprockets show sufficient signs of wear, these too should really be renewed (though this is likely to prove expensive, as the inlet sprocket is not available separately from the VVT-i controller).

29 Remove the drill bit from the chain tensioner to release the plunger. Turn the lockplate clockwise, hold it in this position, and check that the plunger moves freely.

5.26a Hex on camshafts (arrowed) to use spanner...

5.26b... to prevent the camshaft from turning

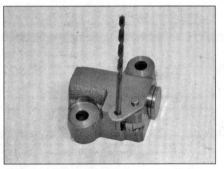

5.29a Tensioner plunger locked in position with 3 mm drill bit

5.29b Push the lockplate up to release the plunger

5.31a Refit the VVT-i controller/inlet sprocket...

5.31b... and fit the securing bolt

5.32a Refit the exhaust sprocket...

5.32b... and fit the securing bolt

5.33 Holding the inlet camshaft using the hex casting

5.34 Align the timing marks to the TDC position

Also check that the plunger locks when the lockplate is released **(see illustrations)**. If a new timing chain or rear guide is being fitted, or if there is any doubt about the tensioner's condition, fit a new one as a matter of course. If the old tensioner is being refitted, compress the plunger and refit the drill bit to hold it.

30 While the timing chain cover is removed, it is recommended that the opportunity be taken to fit a new crankshaft oil seal. See Section 15 in this Chapter for procedure.

Refitting

31 Liberally oil the end of the inlet camshaft, which should be positioned so that the locating peg is at the 12 o'clock position. Hold the VVT-i controller/inlet sprocket with the timing mark at the top, and fit it onto the locating peg on the end of the inlet camshaft.

No particular force should be required – secure the controller with the bolt, hand-tight only at this stage **(see illustrations)**.

32 Hold the exhaust camshaft sprocket with the timing mark upwards, and locate it onto the peg on the end of the camshaft (which should be at the 12 o'clock position) **(see illustrations)**. Again, secure the sprocket with the bolt, hand-tight.

33 As for removal, hold the inlet and exhaust camshafts using a spanner on the shaft's hex, and tighten the sprocket bolts to the specified torque **(see illustration)**.

34 Set the camshaft sprockets to the correct position for TDC on No 1 cylinder – with the markings at 12 o'clock **(see illustration)**. Do not turn the camshafts excessively to achieve this, as there is a danger of the valves hitting the pistons.

35 Refit the Woodruff key back into the end of the crankshaft and fit the sprocket onto the crankshaft **(see illustration)**.

36 Offer up the timing chain. The two gold/ orange links should align with the camshaft sprocket timing marks, with no slack in between the sprockets **(see illustration)**.

37 Similarly, the single yellow link at the base of the chain's run should align with the mark on the crankshaft sprocket **(see illustration)**.

38 Refit the front timing chain guide, and then the rear guide, tightening the bolts to the specified torque.

39 Holding the rear guide against the timing chain, making sure the timing marks are still in line, refit the timing chain tensioner to the cylinder block **(see illustration)**. Tighten the bolts to the specified torque.

5.35 Fit the Woodruff key to the crankshaft

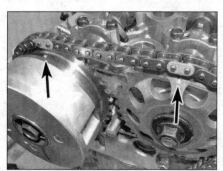

5.36 The two gold/orange links should align with the dot marks on the camshaft sprockets

5.37 The single yellow link should align with the slot in the crankshaft sprocket

5.39 Refit the timing chain tensioner...

5.40... then remove the locking peg

5.42a Apply a bead of sealant to the timing cover mating faces...

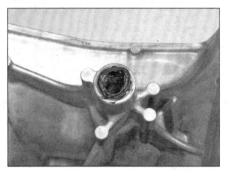

5.42b... around the centre bolt hole...

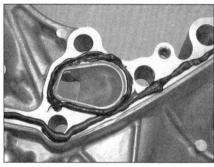

5.42c... and the coolant pump recess

40 Release the tensioner by removing the drill bit (if original tensioner used), ensuring that the plunger engages with the timing chain rear guide **(see illustration)**. Allow the tensioner to take up the slack in the chain. Check the timing marks are still aligned, and then rotate the engine by two complete turns. Check the tension of the chain, and check the timing marks on the sprockets are still aligned. Note: The coloured links will not be aligned with the timing marks now; they are only aligned when the timing is first set up.
41 Fit new O-ring seal to the oil pump feed on the cylinder block **(see illustration 5.19)**.

42 Clean any old sealant from the timing chain cover mating faces. Apply a 3 to 4 mm diameter bead of suitable sealant to the cover, with two further circles of sealant applied around the upper centre retaining bolt hole and the coolant pump recess **(see illustrations)**. Also apply two short lengths of sealant where the cylinder block and head meet. Once the sealant has been applied, the cover should be refitted within three minutes.
43 Offer the cover into position, and then refit the bolts to their previously-noted positions, see paragraph 17.
44 Progressively tighten the bolts in

several stages in the sequence shown **(see illustration)** to pull the cover evenly into place. Finally, tighten the bolts to the specified torque. Note there are two sizes of bolt heads, which require different torque settings.
45 The remainder of refitting is a reversal of removal, noting the following points:
a) Before refitting the cylinder head cover, turn the engine two complete turns clockwise, and check that the crankshaft and camshaft timing marks come back into alignment as described in Section 3
b) Tighten all fasteners to the specified torque.
c) Allow sufficient time for the sealant used on the timing chain and cylinder head covers, and on the sump, to cure before starting the engine.

6 Timing chain tensioner –
removal, inspection and refitting

1 Remove the timing chain cover as described in previous Section. The tensioner can be removed as described in paragraphs 20 and 21, and inspected as described in paragraph 29.

5.42d Apply sealant to the areas shown (arrowed)

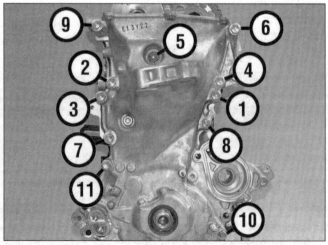

5.44 Timing chain cover tightening sequence

7.2 Access plug for timing chain tensioner

7.4 Insert a screwdriver to release tensioner

7.5 Turn the camshaft slightly if required

7 Camshafts and tappets – removal, inspection and refitting

Note: *The following procedure allows the camshafts to be removed without completely removing the timing chain, which is a time-consuming job. However, if difficulty is experienced with this procedure, removing the timing chain as described in Section 5 is the only alternative.*

Removal

1 Remove the cylinder head cover as described in Section 4.
2 Slacken and remove the cover plug from the timing chain cover, this gives access to the timing chain tensioner **(see illustration)**.
3 Set the engine to TDC on No 1 cylinder as described in Section 3. Paint alignment marks on the timing chain, in line with the timing marks on the sprockets.
4 Insert a screwdriver in through the access hole in the cover and rotate the lockplate upwards **(see illustration)**.
5 It may be necessary to rotate the camshaft slightly clockwise, so that the timing chain pushes the tensioner plunger home **(see illustration)**.

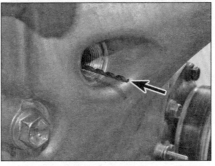

7.6 Insert 3 mm peg (drill bit) to lock the tensioner

6 When the plunger is pushed back, remove the screwdriver and insert a 3 mm drill bit through the hole in the lockplate to hold the plunger in position **(see illustration)**.
7 Hold the relevant camshaft against rotation using a spanner on the hex provided on the shaft. Slacken the bolts securing the inlet sprocket and VVT-i controller assembly, or the exhaust sprocket to their respective camshafts **(see illustration)**.
8 Remove the bolt from the exhaust camshaft sprocket and remove the sprocket from the end of the camshaft, releasing it from the timing chain. Pull the chain upwards and let it

7.7 Using a spanner to prevent the camshaft from turning

down over the top of the inlet sprocket/VVT-i controller assembly.
9 Progressively slacken the camshaft bearing caps across the top of the cylinder head **(see illustration)**.
10 Slide the inlet camshaft sprocket/VVT-i controller assembly from the end of the camshaft slightly, slacken the bolt a few more turns if required. This will allow the No 1 'double' camshaft bearing cap, to be removed from the cylinder head.
11 It is essential that the camshaft bearing caps be refitted to their original locations. Before removing the caps, check that they're

7.9 Slackening sequence for camshaft bearing caps

7.11 This is the No 4 inlet camshaft bearing cap – marked I4, with an arrow pointing to the timing chain

7.12a Loosen the bearing cap bolts...

7.12b... then remove the caps...

7.13... and lift out the camshafts

7.16 Lift out the tappets and store them in their fitted order

7.17 Tappets are numbered (arrowed) for thickness

marked with a letter/number, indicating their fitted position (No 1 is at the timing chain end, inlet and exhaust can be deduced from the manifolds) **(see illustration)**. If no numbers can be seen, make your own with paint or a dot-punch.

12 Remove the securing bolts and carefully withdraw the caps from the camshafts, and store them safely in a clean container **(see illustrations)**.

13 The exhaust camshaft can now be removed from the top of the cylinder head, noting its fitted position **(see illustration)**.

14 Before lifting the timing chain off the inlet sprocket, have ready some wire or string to tie the chain up with – it must not be allowed to fall down (or even go slack), as it may disengage itself from the crankshaft sprocket, which could mean taking off the timing chain cover (Section 5).

15 The inlet camshaft can be removed

complete with camshaft sprocket/VVT-i controller assembly from the top of the cylinder head. Lift the chain from around the sprocket and fasten it to one side. If required, remove the securing bolt and remove the camshaft sprocket/VVT-i controller assembly from the end of the camshaft.

16 Before lifting out the tappets, it's best to have ready a box that's been divided up into twelve sections, or failing that, a piece of clearly marked card, so the tappets can be arranged and kept in their fitted order. The tappets should not be marked in any way (other than perhaps by wrapping a piece of masking tape round, onto which a number can be written). Lift each tappet out, and store it so that it can be refitted in the same location **(see illustration)**.

Inspection

Note: *For complete dismantling of the cylinder*

head (removal of the valves, etc.), refer to Part B of this Chapter.

17 With the camshafts and tappets removed, check each for signs of obvious wear (scoring, pitting, etc.) and for ovality, and renew if necessary. Note the tappets have numbers inside to show their thickness for adjusting valve clearance **(see illustration)**.

18 Measure the outside diameter of each tappet – take measurements at the top and bottom of each tappet, then a second set at right-angles to the first; if any measurement is significantly different from the others, the tappet is tapered or oval (as applicable) and must be renewed. If the top surface of any tappet is worn, check the corresponding lobe on the camshaft.

19 Visually examine the camshaft lobes for score marks, pitting, galling (wear due to rubbing) and evidence of overheating (blue, discoloured areas). Look for flaking away of the hardened surface layer of each lobe. Renew the camshaft if any of these conditions are apparent. Examine the condition of the bearing surfaces, both on the camshaft journals and in the cylinder head. If the head bearing surfaces are worn excessively, the cylinder head will need to be renewed.

Refitting

20 Oil the cylinder head tappets and bores, and carefully refit the tappets to their original positions in the cylinder head – some care will be required to enter the tappets squarely into their bores **(see illustration)**. Check that each tappet rotates freely.

21 Liberally oil the inlet camshaft lobes and the camshaft bearings in the cylinder head. Place the inlet camshaft complete with camshaft sprocket/VVT-i controller assembly back onto the cylinder head. Feed the timing chain around the sprocket, keeping gentle tension on the chain at all times. Make sure the timing mark on the camshaft sprocket aligns with the marks made on the chain on removal.

22 Liberally oil the exhaust camshaft lobes and the camshaft bearings in the cylinder head. Place the exhaust camshaft in place on the cylinder head. Make sure the camshaft is positioned, so that the timing mark on the front of the camshaft sprocket will be in the 12 o'clock position when fitted **(see illustration)**.

7.20 Oil the tappets and their bores before fitting

7.22 Align the timing marks on the exhaust camshaft sprocket to TDC

23 Refit the camshaft bearing caps to their original positions as noted on removal, check the markings on top of the caps, indicating their fitted position.
24 Refit the bearing cap bolts, and tighten the bolts progressively in the opposite sequence of removal **(see illustration 7.9)**, to the specified torque.
25 Refit the sprocket to the end of the exhaust camshaft; fit the sprocket inside the timing chain as it is being fitted. With the chain in position around all sprockets, check that all the timing marks are aligned for TDC on No 1 cylinder.
26 As for removal, hold the inlet and exhaust camshafts using a spanner, and tighten the sprocket bolts to the specified torque **(see illustration)**.
27 Turn the inlet camshaft anti-clockwise slightly, to move any slack in the timing chain onto the rear side. Remove the drill bit from the chain tensioner, and allow the plunger to tension the chain. Check the timing marks are still aligned, and then rotate the engine by two complete turns. Check the tension of the chain, and check the timing marks on the sprockets are still aligned.
28 Coat the threads with sealer and refit the timing chain tensioner access plug to the timing chain cover **(see illustration)**.
29 Refit the cylinder head cover as described in Section 4.

8 Valve clearances – checking and adjustment

Note: *Because the tappets are not fitted with shims, valve clearance adjustment is carried out by fitting new tappets, which requires removing the camshafts.*

Checking

1 Remove the cylinder head cover as described in Section 4.
2 Set the engine to TDC on No 1 cylinder as described in Section 3.
3 With the engine in this position, check the clearances for No 2 cylinder inlet valves, and the exhaust valve clearances for cylinder 3.
4 Insert a feeler blade between the camshaft lobe and the tappet, and record the clearance (C) found for all four valves **(see illustration)**. If

7.26 Using a spanner to prevent the camshaft from turning

the clearances found are within the 'checking' value (refer to the Specifications at the start of this Chapter), no adjustment will be required.
5 Turn the engine, using a spanner or socket on the crankshaft pulley bolt, through one complete turn. The crankshaft pulley mark should now be aligned with the pointer on the timing chain cover, but the camshaft sprocket timing marks should not be visible.
6 With the engine in this position, check the clearances for No 1 and 3 cylinder inlet valves, and the exhaust valve clearances for cylinders 1 and 2.
7 Insert a feeler blade between the camshaft lobe and the tappet, and record the clearance (C) found for the remaining eight valves. If the clearances found are within the 'checking' value (refer to the Specifications at the start of this Chapter), no adjustment will be required.
8 If no adjustment is needed, refit the cylinder head cover as described in Section 4.

Adjustment

9 Remove the camshafts as described in Section 7.
10 Remove each tappet which requires adjustment, and measure the thickness (T) between the top surface and the inner boss, using a micrometer **(see illustration)**. Use the thickness (T) with the valve clearances previously-measured (C) for use in calculating the required thickness of the new tappet (N). For example:
a) Inlet: New (N) = Thickness (T) + Clearance (C) – 0.18 mm.
b) Exhaust: New (N) = Thickness (T) + Clearance (C) – 0.31 mm.

7.28 Refit the access plug to the timing chain cover

11 New tappets are available in 29 sizes from the manufacturer, in increments of 0.020 mm, from 5.120 mm to 5.680 mm **(see illustration)**. Select a new tappet which gives a clearance as close as possible to the setting values given in the Specifications. Mark any new tappets with tape, or store them (with any old tappets) in the correct fitted sequence.
12 Lubricate and fit the tappets, making sure they are all fitted to the correct locations. Check that they are free to turn.
13 Refit the camshafts as described in Section 7, but before refitting the cylinder head cover, turn the engine through two complete turns, and check that the crankshaft and camshaft timing marks come back into align- ment as described in Section 3. Recheck the valve clearances as described in paragraphs 3 to 7.
14 On completion, refit the cylinder head cover as described in Section 4.

9 Cylinder head – removal and refitting

Note: *As the cylinder head, timing chain cover and sump will need to be removed for this procedure, there will need to be some provision made for supporting the cylinder block/transmission in place when the right-hand engine mounting is removed.*

Removal

1 Remove the timing chain and sprockets as described in Section 5.

8.4 Checking a valve clearance

8.10 Checking the tappet thickness

8.11 See the manufacturer with calculated dimensions to check tappet required

9.5 Note the fitted position of the coolant hoses

9.6a Disconnect the earth cable, temp switch and cam sensor wiring connectors

9.6b Undo the bypass pipe retaining nuts (arrowed)...

9.6c... and lower mounting bracket bolt (arrowed)

2 Remove the camshafts as described in Section 7 – this is necessary to gain access to the head bolts. Unless the head is being worked on further, the tappets can stay in place.

3 Remove the exhaust manifold/catalytic converter as described in Chapter 4B Section 5.

4 Remove the fuel injectors and inlet manifold as described in Chapter 4A.

5 Disconnect the coolant hoses from the transmission end of the cylinder head, noting their positions for refitting (see illustration).

6 Work around the cylinder head, and disconnect the wiring plugs, earth leads, wiring harness brackets, etc, as follows:

a) Coolant temperature sensor and camshaft position sensor wiring plugs, at the transmission end of the cylinder head (see illustration).

b) Earth lead above the thermostat housing, also at the transmission end of the cylinder head.

c) Unbolt the water bypass pipe bracket from the transmission end of the head. Renew gasket on refitting (see illustrations).

7 Make sure the engine/transmission unit is supported securely from below before starting to loosen the cylinder head bolts.

8 Loosen the cylinder head bolts (using an 8 mm

splined bit) by a quarter-turn at a time, in sequence (see illustrations). Soak out any oil from the bolt heads before starting and recover the washers from the cylinder head.

9 Remove the eight bolts and washers – it is recommended that they are not re-used, and a complete new set be obtained for refitting. See paragraph 18 for checking procedure for the head bolts.

10 Check round the head that there is nothing still attached, and nothing in the way that will hinder it being lifted away.

11 Carefully lift off the head, and place it on a clean surface – do not allow the lower face to be damaged. If the head is stuck, try rocking it backwards to free it. Do not try and swivel the head on the cylinder block, as it is located by two dowels on the front outer bolt holes (see illustration). When the joint is broken, lift the cylinder head away.

12 Recover the old head gasket, though it cannot be re-used, it may be useful to hold onto for now, to compare with the new one as verification.

13 If the head is to be dismantled for overhaul, remove the tappets as described in Section 7, then refer to Part B of this Chapter.

Preparation for refitting

14 The mating faces of the cylinder head and cylinder block/crankcase must be perfectly clean before refitting the head. If required, remove the two dowels (note their positions) and use a hard plastic or wood scraper to remove all traces of gasket and carbon; also clean the piston crowns.

> **HAYNES HiNT** To prevent carbon entering the gap between the pistons and bores, smear a little grease in the gap. After cleaning each piston, use a small brush to remove all traces of grease and carbon from the gap, and then wipe away the remainder with a clean rag.

9.8a Cylinder head slackening sequence

9.8b Remove the cylinder head bolt bolt including washer

9.11 Locating dowels (arrowed) for cylinder head

9.18 Maximum length of cylinder head should be no more than 123.5 mm

9.23 Ensure that the gasket is fitted the right way up

15 Take particular care during the cleaning operations, as aluminium alloy is easily damaged. Also, make sure that the carbon is not allowed to enter the oil and water passages – this is particularly important for the lubrication system, as carbon could block the oil supply to the engine's components. Using adhesive tape and paper, seal the water, oil and bolt holes in the cylinder block/crankcase.

16 Check the mating surfaces of the cylinder block/crankcase and the cylinder head for nicks, deep scratches and other damage. If slight, they may be removed carefully with a file, but if excessive, machining may be the only alternative to renewal.

17 If warpage of the cylinder head gasket surface is suspected, use a straight-edge to check it for distortion. Refer to Part B of this Chapter if necessary.

18 Check the condition of the old head bolts, and particularly their threads, whenever they are removed. Wash the bolts in suitable solvent, and then wipe them dry. Check each for sign of visible wear or damage, renewing the bolts if necessary. Measure the length of each bolt from the underside of its head to the bolt end, to check for stretching **(see illustration)**. The maximum length for the bolts is 123.5 mm; if any bolts have stretched more than this, renew all the cylinder head bolts as a set. If there is any doubt as to their condition or length, we recommend fitting a complete new set of bolts.

19 Although not essential, if a suitable tap-and-die set is available, it's worth running

the correct-size tap down the bolt threads in the cylinder block. This will clean the threads of any debris, and go some way to restoring any damaged threads. Make absolutely sure the tap is the right size and thread pitch, and lightly oil the tap before starting.

20 If possible, clean out the bolt holes in the block using compressed air (eye protection should be worn), to ensure no oil or water is present. Screwing a bolt into an oil- or water-filled hole can (in extreme cases) cause the block to fracture, due to the hydraulic pressure created.

Refitting

21 To avoid the possibility of valves hitting pistons when the camshafts are refitted and turned, it is advisable to turn the crankshaft a little, so that none of the pistons are at TDC. If required, make your own alignment marks on the crankshaft sprocket and block, so that the crankshaft TDC position can be easily reset before the timing chain is refitted.

22 If removed, ensure the two locating dowels are refitted to their original positions on the block top surface **(see illustration 9.11)**.

23 Check that the new cylinder head gasket is the same type as the original and that any TOP marking is facing upwards, and then locate the gasket onto the top face of the cylinder block and over the dowels. Ensure that it is correctly aligned with the coolant passages and oilways **(see illustration)**.

24 It is helpful to have an assistant on hand as the head is offered into place, as various

items may need to be held clear. Lower the head gently onto the block, making sure the gasket does not move.

25 Lubricate the threads and underside of the heads of the cylinder head bolts lightly with clean engine oil **(see illustration)**.

26 Carefully enter each bolt into its relevant hole, making sure each one has a washer fitted to the cylinder head **(see illustration)**. Screw them in by hand only at this stage, until finger tight.

27 Working progressively and following the opposite sequence of removal **(see illustration 9.8a)** tighten the head bolts to the Stage 1, specified torque.

28 Now the head bolts should be tightened further, to the Stage 2, specified angle. It is strongly recommended that an angle gauge be used for this task **(see illustration)**. Again, follow the tightening sequence.

29 The remainder of refitting is a reversal of removal, noting the following points:

a) Before refitting the cylinder head cover, turn the engine two complete turns clockwise, and check that the crankshaft and camshaft timing marks come back into alignment as described in Section 3.

b) Where applicable, tighten all fasteners to the specified torque.

c) Where used, allow sufficient time for the sealant used on the timing chain and the sump to cure before starting the engine.

d) When the engine is restarted, check for any sign of oil and/or coolant leakage from the various cylinder head joints.

9.25 Lubricate the cylinder head bolts

9.26 Make sure the washers are fitted to the cylinder head

9.28 Angle-tightening the head bolts, using a gauge

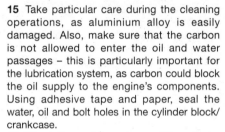

10.5 Remove the lower cover plate

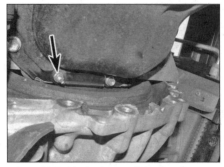

10.6a Undo the retaining nut...

10.6b... and remove the stud

10 Sump –
removal and refitting

Removal

1 Jack up the front of the car, and support it on axle stands (see *Jacking and vehicle support*). Where fitted, remove the engine lower cover panels from under the car.

2 Drain the engine oil as described in Chapter 1. It makes sense to change the oil filter at the same time, but this is not essential.

3 Remove the engine oil dipstick, wipe it clean, and place it to one side.

4 Refer to Chapter 4B Section 6 and remove the exhaust front pipe from the manifold/catalytic converter. We found it was sufficient to disconnect the oxygen sensor

wiring, unbolt the pipe from the manifold/catalytic converter, and move the exhaust to one side.

5 Working under the car, remove the three bolts securing the stiffener plate fitted between the sump and transmission. Lower the plate, and remove it **(see illustration)**.

6 At the transmission end of the sump, remove the sump retaining nut and then remove the stud from the cylinder block **(see illustrations)**. This will need to be removed to allow access for the sump to be removed from the recess in the rear of the flywheel.

7 Unscrew and remove the thirteen bolts and one remaining nut used to secure the sump **(see illustration)**. Note that the three bolts and one nut at the timing chain end, and the one bolt and one nut at the transmission end of the sump are smaller-sized bolts.

8 The sump is further secured in position with

sealant, and some effort may be needed to prise it free.

9 Using a wide-bladed tool, carefully prise off the sump (if a screwdriver is used, take care not to deform the sealing edges of the pan).

10 Keep the sump level as it is lowered, to prevent spillage of any remaining oil in it **(see illustration)**. Also be prepared for oil drips from the crankcase when the sump is removed.

11 Clean any sealant from the sump and engine mating faces – care must be taken not to damage the sealing surfaces. Wipe the mating faces with a suitable solvent, and allow to dry. While the sump is off, check that the oil pick-up pipe/strainer is clear, cleaning it if necessary **(see illustration)**.

Refitting

12 Apply a 3 mm diameter bead of RTV sealant to the sump sealing surface, to the inside of the bolt holes **(see illustration)**. Remember – any excess sealant may find its way into the engine, so use only enough to obtain a good seal. Once the sealant has been applied, the sump should then be fitted within 3 minutes.

13 Offer the sump up to the engine, and locate it on the stud. Secure it hand-tight only at this stage, using all the nuts and bolts – refit the stud and nut to the transmission end of the sump **(see illustrations 10.6a and 10.6b)**.

14 Progressively tighten the sump nuts/bolts to the specified torque, starting at the middle and working your way outwards, then go around and wipe away any excess sealant.

15 Check that the sump drain plug has been refitted and tightened securely – use a new sealing washer.

16 Refit the sump-to-transmission lower stiffener plate, and tighten the bolts to the specified torque.

17 Refit the exhaust front pipe to manifold/catalytic converter as described in Chapter 4B. Reconnect oxygen sensor wiring connector.

18 On completion, lower the car to the ground. Allow time for the sealant to cure before refilling the engine with oil (and refitting the dipstick) as described in Chapter 1 Section 3. Start the engine, and check for signs of leaks from the sump joint.

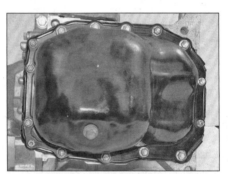

10.7 Sump retaining bolts (x13) and nuts (x2)

10.10 Prise off the sump using a wide-bladed flat tool

10.11 Check the oil pick-up is clear

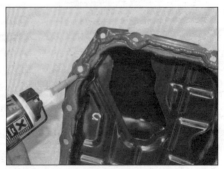

10.12 Apply a bead of sealant to the inside of the holes

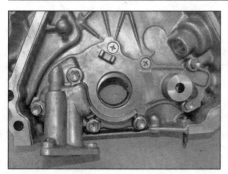

11.3 Oil pump bolted to inside of timing chain cover

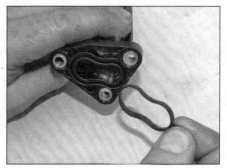

11.8a Fit new seal to oil pick-up pipe...

11.8b... and refit to the lower part of the oil pump

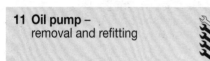

11 Oil pump –
removal and refitting

Removal

1 Remove the timing chain cover as described in paragraphs 1 to 19 in Section 5 of this Chapter.

2 If not already removed, undo the three retaining bolts for the oil pick-up pipe/strainer and remove it from the base of timing chain cover.

3 The oil pump is fitted to the inside of the timing chain cover. Remove the two screws and six bolts, and withdraw the oil pump cover and gears **(see illustration)**. As the pump is removed, note any markings on the driven and drive gears for refitting.

Inspection

4 Blow through the timing chain oil supply jet on the cylinder block, and make sure it's not blocked. Similarly, rinse the oil pick-up pipe and strainer in solvent, and allow to dry.

5 If any of the oil pump clearances appear to be excessive, or if the pump displays any other signs of wear, a complete new pump should be fitted. If the engine is being completely overhauled, fitting a new pump (and an oil pressure relief valve) should almost be a matter of course.

Refitting

6 Liberally oil the pump rotors, and apply some oil to the pump location before fitting.

12.4 Oil pressure switch on rear of cylinder block

Check that the rotors are free of any dirt before fitting.

7 Offer the pump into position. Fit and tighten the mounting bolts/screws to the specified torque, then check that the drive gear turns smoothly.

8 Refit the oil pick-up pipe, together with a new seal, and tighten the nuts and bolt securely **(see illustrations)**.

9 Refit the timing chain cover as described in Section 5.

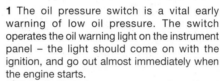

12 Oil pressure switch –
removal and refitting

1 The oil pressure switch is a vital early warning of low oil pressure. The switch operates the oil warning light on the instrument panel – the light should come on with the ignition, and go out almost immediately when the engine starts.

2 If the light does not come on, there could be a fault on the instrument panel, the switch wiring, or the switch itself. If the light does not go out, low oil level, worn oil pump (or sump pick-up blocked), blocked oil filter, or worn main bearings could be to blame – or again, the switch may be faulty.

3 If the light comes on while driving, the best advice is to turn the engine off immediately, and not to drive the car until the problem has been investigated – ignoring the light could mean expensive engine damage.

Removal

4 The oil pressure switch is located on the rear face of the cylinder block, at the timing chain end **(see illustration)**.

5 Disconnect the wiring plug from the switch **(see illustration)**.

6 Unscrew the switch from the block, and remove it. There should only be a very slight loss of oil when this is done.

Inspection

7 Examine the switch for signs of cracking or splits. If the top part of the switch is loose, this is an early indication of impending failure.

8 Check that the wiring terminals at the switch are not loose, then trace the wire from

the switch connector until it enters the main loom – any wiring defects will give rise to apparent oil pressure problems.

Refitting

9 Refitting is the reverse of the removal procedure, noting the following points:

a) *Clean the switch threads, then apply a few drops of thread-locking fluid to them before fitting. Tighten the switch securely.*

b) *Reconnect the switch connector, making sure it clicks home properly. Ensure that the wiring is routed away from any hot or moving parts.*

c) *Check the engine oil level and top-up if necessary (see 'Weekly checks').*

d) *Check for signs of oil leaks once the engine has been restarted and warmed-up to normal operating temperature.*

13 VVT-i system components
– removal and refitting

Note: *For a description of the VVT-i system operation, refer to Section 1.*

VVT-i controller

1 The VVT-i controller is integral with the inlet camshaft sprocket, and can most easily be removed as described in Section 5.

VVT-i oil control valve

2 The oil control valve is fitted at the timing chain end of the cylinder head – at the rear.

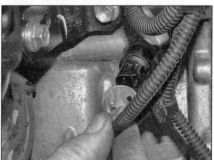

12.5 Disconnect the wiring plug from the oil pressure switch

13.3 Disconnect the VVT-i control valve wiring plug

13.4a Unscrew the bolt...

13.4b... and withdraw the valve from the head – note the O-ring

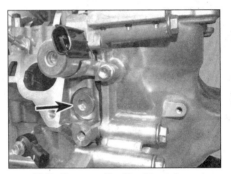

13.9a Remove the blanking plug...

13.9b... and withdraw the filter

14 Crankshaft pulley – removal and refitting

Removal

1 Apply the handbrake, then jack up the front of the car and support it on axle stands (see *Jacking and vehicle support*). Remove the plastic inner wheel trim cover panel from engine on the driver's side.

2 If not already done, remove the auxiliary drivebelt as described in Chapter 1 Section 21.

3 Undo the pulley centre retaining bolt using a socket and bar – make sure the car is securely supported, and that good, close-fitting tools are used, as considerable force will be required.

4 The crankshaft pulley must be held stationary while its retaining bolt is slackened. The first, and easiest, method is to have an assistant sit in the car and engage a gear, then let the clutch pedal up and apply the footbrake hard. There will be considerable 'slack' to take up, but usually this method is sufficient to loosen the bolt.

5 To hold the pulley more directly, a home-made holding tool can be made from two thick, unequal-length, bolted-together strips of metal, with bolts fitted to the ends which can be engaged in the pulley spokes (**see illustration**).

6 Alternatively, remove the starter motor as described in Chapter 5A Section 10, and jam the flywheel ring gear to prevent the engine turning.

7 Loosen and remove the pulley bolt, then take off the pulley (**see illustrations**). The pulley should not be difficult to remove, but may require prising or tapping free.

8 Clean the threads, and examine the pulley bolt carefully once it has been removed, but if there is any doubt about its condition, obtain a new one for refitting.

Refitting

9 Clean the inner side of the pulley, and slide it onto the crankshaft over the Woodruff key.

10 Fit the bolt, and tighten as far as possible until the pulley starts to turn.

3 Disconnect the wiring plug from the valve (**see illustration**).

4 Remove the valve mounting bolt, then carefully withdraw the valve from the head – anticipate a small amount of oil spillage as this is done (**see illustrations**).

5 Recover the O-ring from the valve – a new one should be obtained for refitting.

6 The oil control valve can be checked by using an ohmmeter to check the resistance across the two terminals. The reading should be 6.9 to 7.9 ohms at 20°C. If the reading is not as specified, then the oil control valve will need to be renewed.

7 Refitting is a reversal of removal, noting the following points:

a) Tighten the valve mounting bolt to the specified torque.

b) Check and if necessary top-up the oil level on completion (see 'Weekly checks').

c) Start the engine, and check for signs of oil leaks from the valve.

VVT-i oil control valve filter

8 The filter is fitted below the oil control valve.

9 Remove the filter blanking plug, then carefully withdraw the filter from the head – anticipate a small amount of oil spillage as this is done (**see illustrations**).

10 Recover the sealing washer – a new one should be obtained for refitting.

11 Rinse out the filter in solvent, and allow to dry.

12 Refitting is a reversal of removal, noting the following points:

a) Tighten the filter blanking plug, use new sealing washer.

b) Check and if necessary top-up the oil level on completion (see 'Weekly checks').

c) Start the engine, and check for signs of oil leaks from the filter plug.

14.5 Loosen the crankshaft pulley bolt using a holding tool

14.7a Remove the pulley bolt...

14.7b... and withdraw the crankshaft pulley

15.2 Note the fitted position/depth of the oil seal

15.3 Carefully lever the seal from the cover

11 Using the same method as for loosening to prevent the pulley turning while its bolt is tightened, tighten the pulley bolt to the specified torque.
12 On completion, refit the engine lower panel and lower the car to the ground.

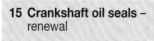

15 Crankshaft oil seals – renewal

Right-hand oil seal

1 Remove the crankshaft pulley as described in Section 14.
2 Before removing the old seal, note its fitted depth, and which way round it is fitted, as a guide to fitting the new seal **(see illustration)**.
3 Using a screwdriver or other suitable lever, prise out the oil seal **(see illustration)**. An alternative method is to drill two small holes in the oil seal, then screw in self-tapping screws and use grips to pull out the oil seal. If this method is used, make sure that all swarf is removed.

 Sometimes, a seal can be loosened by pushing it in on one side – this tilts the seal outwards on the opposite side, and it can then be gripped with pliers and removed.

4 Lightly lubricate the new seal with oil or grease, and offer it into position **(see illustration)**.
5 Carefully fit the seal into the timing chain cover, lips facing inwards, and slide it carefully up to the seat.
6 If a tube (or socket) of the same diameter as the seal is available, this will help to ensure the seal is pressed squarely into place **(see illustration)**. Otherwise, the seal should be pressed in evenly using a blunt instrument.
7 Work equally round the seal, tapping it squarely into place until it is fitted to the same depth as the old one.
8 Refit the crankshaft pulley as described in Section 14.

Left-hand oil seal

9 Remove the flywheel as described in Section 16.

15.4 Offer the seal into position...

10 The oil seal is mounted in a separate carrier, bolted to the end of the cylinder block.
11 Before removing the old seal, note its fitted depth, and which way round it is fitted, as a guide to fitting the new seal.

15.12a Carefully drill a small hole in the seal...

15.12c... and then lever the seal from the housing

15.6... and tap into original position in the cover

12 The seal itself can be prised out of the carrier, or pulled out after a self-tapping screw has been fitted **(see illustrations)**.
13 Lightly lubricate the new seal with oil or grease, and offer it into position **(see illustration)**.

15.12b... fit a self-tapping screw...

15.13 Offer the seal into position...

15.15... and then carefully tap it into position

14 Carefully fit the seal into the carrier, lips facing inwards, and slide it carefully over the end of the crankshaft.

15 Fitting the new seal can be achieved by tapping it in directly, or using a tube of similar diameter **(see illustration)**.

16 Work equally round the seal, tapping it squarely into place until it is fitted to the same depth as the old one, noted on removal.

17 Refit the flywheel as described in Section 16.

16 Flywheel –
removal, inspection
and refitting

Removal

1 Remove the transmission as described in

Chapter 7A or Chapter 7B (as applicable) then remove the clutch as described in Chapter 6 Section 4.

2 Paint an alignment mark between the engine and flywheel before removal **(see illustration)**. This will make sure the flywheel is fitted in the same position as removal.

3 Lock a suitable tool into the ring gear to prevent the crankshaft from rotating as the bolts are removed **(see illustration)**. Take care – considerable effort will be needed to loosen the bolts, and any makeshift tools may slip.

4 Unscrew the six retaining bolts, and remove the flywheel from the rear flange of the crankshaft – take care not to drop it, as it is heavy **(see illustration)**.

Inspection

5 If on removal, the flywheel bolts are found to be in poor condition (damaged threads, etc) they must be renewed.

6 Inspect the starter ring gear for any broken or excessively-worn teeth. If evident, the ring gear must be renewed; this is a task best entrusted to a franchised dealer or a competent garage. Alternatively, obtain a complete new flywheel.

7 The clutch friction surface must be carefully inspected for grooving or hairline cracks (caused by overheating). If these conditions are evident, it may be possible to have the flywheel surface-ground, however this work must be carried out by an engine overhaul specialist. If surface-grinding is not possible, the flywheel must be renewed.

Refitting

8 Check that the mating faces of the flywheel and crankshaft are clean before refitting. Apply a little thread-locking fluid to the bolt threads before they are screwed into position **(see illustration)**. Locate the flywheel onto the crankshaft so that the previously-made mark is aligned, then insert the bolts. Hand-tighten them initially.

9 Prevent the crankshaft from turning as before for loosening, and tighten the bolts in a diagonal sequence to the specified torque.

10 Refit the clutch as described in Chapter 6 Section 4.

11 Refit the transmission as described in Chapter 7A or 7B.

17 Engine/transmission
mountings –
inspection and renewal

Inspection

1 The engine/transmission mountings seldom require attention, but broken or deteriorated mountings should be renewed immediately, or the added strain placed on the driveline components may cause damage or wear.

2 During the check, the engine/transmission must be raised slightly, to remove its weight from the mountings.

3 Apply the handbrake, then jack up the front of the car and support it on axle stands (see *Jacking and vehicle support*). Position a jack under the sump, with a large block of wood between the jack head and the sump, then carefully raise the engine just enough to take the weight off the mountings.

4 Check the mountings to see if the rubber is cracked, hardened or separated from the metal components. Sometimes, the rubber will split right down the centre.

5 Check for relative movement between each mounting's brackets and the engine or body (use a large screwdriver or lever to attempt to move the mountings). If movement is noted, lower the engine and check the mounting nuts and bolts for tightness.

Renewal

6 The right-hand and left-hand engine/transmission mountings can be removed if the weight of the engine is supported by one of the following alternative methods.

7 Either support the weight of the assembly from underneath, using a jack and a suitable piece of wood between the jack and the sump (to prevent damage), or from above by attaching a hoist to the engine. A third method is to use a suitable support bar, with end pieces which will engage in the water channel each side of the bonnet lid aperture; using an adjustable hook and chain connected to the engine, the weight of the engine and transmission can then be taken from the mountings.

8 Once the weight of the engine and transmission is suitably supported, any

16.2 Make alignment marks (arrowed) for refitting

16.3 Home-made locking tool bolted in place to lock the flywheel ring gear

16.4 Unbolt and remove the flywheel

16.8 Use new bolts or thread-lock when refitting

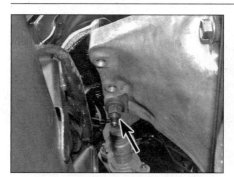

17.9a Remove the mounting nut (arrowed)...

17.9b... from under the engine mounting

17.10a Undo the upper securing bolts (arrowed)...

of the mountings can be unbolted and removed. **Note:** *All references to left and right are as seen from the driver's seat.*

Right-hand mounting

9 Working underneath the engine mounting, remove the nut from the engine mounting stud at the rear of the mounting **(see illustrations)**.
10 Remove the four bolts securing the engine mounting to the inner wing and timing chain cover and lift the mounting off the stud to remove it from the engine compartment **(see illustrations)**.

Left-hand mounting

11 To remove the left-hand (transmission) mounting, remove the battery and battery tray as described in Chapter 5A Section 4.
12 Remove the three bolts securing the transmission mounting to the chassis/inner wing **(see illustration)**.
13 Remove the four bolts securing the mounting to the top of the transmission housing and lift the mounting out from the engine compartment **(see illustrations)**.

Rear mounting connecting arm

14 To remove the engine rear mounting, apply the handbrake, and then jack up the front of the car and support it on axle stands (see *Jacking and vehicle support*).
15 Slacken and remove the two bolts that go through the rear mounting connecting arm **(see illustration)**.
16 The rear mounting connecting arm can now be withdrawn from the subframe **(see illustration)**. If required, the engine can be swung forwards on its remaining mountings, and wedged using a suitable block of wood, to allow better access.
17 If the mounting bracket attached to the transmission is to be removed, undo the three bracket securing bolts, and remove the bracket.

All mountings

18 Refitting of all mountings is a reversal of the removal procedure. Do not fully-tighten the mounting nuts/bolts until all of the mountings are in position. Check that the mounting rubbers do not twist or distort as the mounting bolts and nuts are tightened to their specified torque.

17.10b... and remove the right-hand engine mounting

17.12 Mounting-to-body bolts (arrowed)

17.13a Undo the mounting-to-transmission bolts (arrowed)...

17.13b... and remove the left-hand transmission mounting

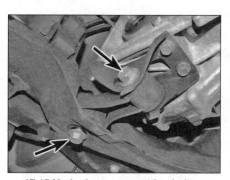

17.15 Undo the two mounting bolts...

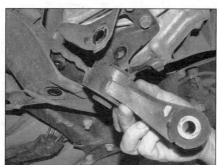

17.16... and remove the lower rear mounting

Notes

Chapter 2 Part B
Engine removal and overhaul procedures

Contents

Degrees of difficulty

Easy, suitable for novice with little experience	Fairly easy, suitable for beginner with some experience	Fairly difficult, suitable for competent DIY mechanic	Difficult, suitable for experienced DIY mechanic	Very difficult, suitable for expert DIY or professional

Specifications

Engine overhaul data and torque wrench settings

Refer to Specifications in Chapter 2A.

1 General Information

1 Included in this part of Chapter 2 are the general overhaul procedures for the cylinder head, cylinder block/crankcase and internal engine components.
2 The information ranges from advice concerning preparation for an overhaul and the purchase of parts, to detailed step-by-step procedures covering removal, inspection, renovation and refitting of internal engine parts.
3 The following Sections have been compiled based on the assumption that the engine has been removed from the car. For information concerning in-car engine repair, as well as the removal and refitting of the external components necessary for the overhaul, refer to Part A, and to Section 5 of this Part.

2 Engine overhaul – general information

1 It is not always easy to determine when, or if, an engine should be completely overhauled, as a number of factors must be considered.
2 High mileage is not necessarily an indication

that an overhaul is needed, while low mileage does not preclude the need for an overhaul. Frequency of servicing is probably the most important consideration. An engine which has had regular and frequent oil and filter changes, as well as other required maintenance, will most likely give many thousands of miles of reliable service. Conversely, a neglected engine may require an overhaul very early in its life.
3 Excessive oil consumption is an indication that piston rings, valve stem oil seals and/ or valves and valve guides are in need of attention. Make sure that oil leaks are not responsible before deciding that the rings and/or guides are to blame. Perform a cylinder compression check to determine the extent of the work required.
4 Check the oil pressure with a gauge fitted in place of the oil pressure switch, and compare it with the value given in the Specifications. If it is extremely low, the main and big-end bearings and/or the oil pump are probably worn out.
5 Loss of power, rough running, knocking or metallic engine noises, excessive valve gear noise and high fuel consumption may also point to the need for an overhaul, especially if they are all present at the same time. If a complete tune-up does not remedy the situation, major mechanical work is the only solution.

6 An engine overhaul involves restoring all internal parts to the specification of a new engine. During an overhaul, the pistons and the piston rings are renewed. New main and big-end bearings are generally fitted (where possible); if necessary, the crankshaft may be renewed to restore the journals. The valves are also serviced as well, since they are usually in less-than-perfect condition at this point. While the engine is being overhauled, other components, such as the starter and alternator, can be overhauled as well. The end result should be an as-new engine that will give many trouble-free miles. Note: Critical cooling system components such as the hoses, thermostat and coolant pump should be renewed when an engine is overhauled. The radiator should be checked carefully, to ensure that it is not clogged or leaking. Also, it is a good idea to renew the oil pump whenever the engine is overhauled.
7 Before beginning the engine overhaul, read through the entire procedure to familiarise yourself with the scope and requirements of the job. Overhauling an engine is not difficult if you follow all of the instructions carefully, have the necessary tools and equipment, and pay close attention to all specifications; however, it can be time-consuming. Plan on the car being tied up for a minimum of two weeks, especially if parts must be taken to an engineering works for repair or reconditioning.

4.7 Remove the plastic tray from the crossmember

4.8 Remove the scuttle panel from the rear of the engine compartment

Check on the availability of parts, and make sure that any necessary special tools and equipment are obtained in advance. Most work can be done with typical hand tools, although a number of precision measuring tools are required for inspecting parts to determine if they must be renewed. Often the engineering works will handle the inspection of parts, and offer advice concerning reconditioning and renewal. **Note:** *Always wait until the engine has been completely dismantled, and all components, especially the engine block, have been inspected before deciding what service and repair operations must be performed by an engineering works. Since the condition of the block will be the major factor to consider when determining whether to overhaul the original engine or buy a reconditioned unit, do not purchase parts or have overhaul work done on other components until the block has been thoroughly inspected. As a general rule, time is the primary cost of an overhaul, so it does not pay to fit worn or sub-standard parts.*

8 As a final note, to ensure maximum life and minimum trouble from a reconditioned engine, everything must be assembled with care, and in a spotlessly-clean environment.

3 Engine removal – methods and precautions

1 If you have decided that an engine must be

removed for overhaul or major repair work, several preliminary steps should be taken.

2 Locating a suitable place to work is extremely important. Adequate workspace, along with storage space for the car, will be needed. If a garage is not available, at the very least a flat, level, clean work surface is required.

3 Cleaning the engine compartment and engine before beginning the removal procedure will help keep tools clean and organised.

4 The engine is removed complete with the transmission by lowering it out of the car. When lowering the assembly, the car's body must be raised and supported securely sufficiently high that the engine/transmission can be unbolted as a single unit and lowered to the ground.

5 An engine hoist or A-frame will be necessary. Make sure the equipment is rated in excess of the combined weight of the engine and transmission. Safety is of primary importance, considering the potential hazards involved in removing the engine out of the car.

6 If the engine is being removed by a novice, an assistant should be available. Advice and aid from someone more experienced would also be helpful. There are many instances when one person cannot simultaneously perform all of the operations required when removing the engine from the car.

7 Plan the operation ahead of time. Arrange for, or obtain, all of the tools and equipment you will need, prior to beginning the job. Some of the equipment necessary to perform

engine removal and installation safely and with relative ease are (in addition to an engine hoist) a heavy-duty trolley jack, complete sets of spanners and sockets as described at the end of this manual, wooden blocks, and plenty of rags and cleaning solvent for mopping-up spilled oil, coolant and fuel. If the hoist must be hired, make sure that you arrange for it in advance, and perform all of the operations possible without it beforehand. This will save you money and time.

8 Plan for the car to be out of use for quite a while. An engineering works will be required to perform some of the work, which the do-it-yourselfer cannot accomplish without special equipment. These places often have a busy schedule, so it would be a good idea to consult them before removing the engine, in order to accurately estimate the amount of time required to rebuild or repair components that may need work.

9 Always be extremely careful when removing and refitting the engine. Serious injury can result from careless actions. Plan ahead, take your time, and you will find that a job of this nature, although major, can be accomplished successfully.

4 Engine – removal, separation and refitting

1 Note: *The engine wiring loom can stay attached to the engine/transmission, so there is no need to disconnect it from most of the engine components. Before removing the engine, check around the engine compartment to make sure everything is disconnected.*

Removal

2 Depressurise the fuel system with reference to Chapter 4A Section 2.

3 Drain the cooling system as described in Chapter 1 Section 23.

4 If the engine is being dismantled, drain the engine oil with reference to Chapter 1 Section 3.

5 Remove the battery and battery tray as described in Chapter 5A Section 4.

6 Remove the air cleaner cover as described in Chapter 4A Section 5.

7 Remove the front bumper as described in Chapter 11 Section 6. Undo the retaining bolts and remove the plastic tray from under the front of the engine crossmember **(see illustration)**.

8 To give better access at the rear of the engine compartment, remove the windscreen motor/wiper linkage and rear scuttle panel, as described in Chapter 12 Section 14 **(see illustration)**.

9 Working at the rear left-hand side of the engine compartment, disconnect the wiring connectors from the fuse/relay box and slide the wiring loom out from the rear of the housing **(see illustrations)**.

10 Undo the securing nut and disconnect

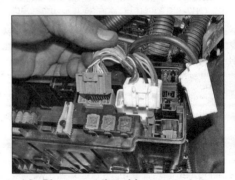

4.9a Disconnect the wiring connectors...

4.9b... and release the loom from the fuse/relay box

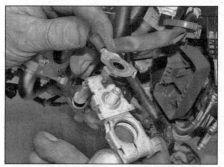

4.10 Disconnect the two positive cables

4.11a Disconnect the earth wires from the bulkhead...

4.11b... and unclip the wiring loom from the bracket (arrowed)

4.12 Unbolt the earth cable from the front of the transmission

4.13 Disconnect the wiring connectors from the engine management control unit

4.14 Disconnect the cable (where fitted) from the throttle housing

the two battery positive connectors from each other **(see illustration)**.

11 Undo the two securing bolts and disconnect the earth wires from the rear bulkhead, then unclip the wiring loom from the mounting bracket **(see illustrations)**.

12 Undo the retaining bolt and disconnect the earth wiring from the front of the transmission casing, then unclip the wiring from the mounting bracket **(see illustration)**.

13 Release the safety catches and disconnect the two wiring block connectors from the top of the engine management ECU on the rear of the bulkhead **(see illustration)**.

14 On models with throttle cable fitted, loosen the adjuster nuts and detach the cable from the throttle body bracket. Disconnect the inner cable from the quadrant on the throttle body and releasing the end fitting **(see illustration)**. Release the cable from the securing clips on and around the engine.

15 Disconnect the vacuum hose from the purge canister solenoid valve at the rear of the cylinder head cover **(see illustration)**.

16 Disconnect the brake vacuum hose from the inlet manifold and unclip it from along the rear of the inlet manifold valve **(see**

4.15 Disconnect the vacuum hose – arrowed

illustrations). Fasten the brake vacuum hose to the rear of the bulkhead.

17 Making sure the fuel system has been depressurised, remove the protective cover and disconnect the quick-release connection from the end of the fuel rail **(see illustrations)**.

4.16a Disconnect the brake vacuum hose...

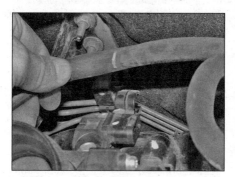

4.16b... and unclip it from the rear of the intake manifold

4.17a Unclip the plastic cover...

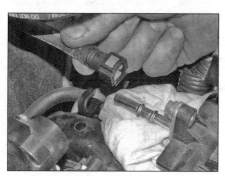

4.17b... and disconnect the fuel pipe from the fuel rail

4.18 Note the position of the coolant hoses for refitting

4.19 Disconnect the coolant hoses (where fitted) to the throttle housing

4.22a Disconnect the wiring connector to the compressor...

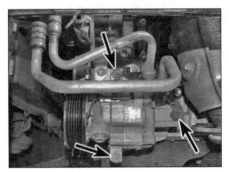

4.22b... undo the mounting bolts...

4.22c... and fasten the compressor to the front crossmember

Plug the ends of the fuel rail and fuel pipe to prevent dirt ingress.

18 Disconnect the four coolant hoses (two radiator and two heater hoses) from the transmission end of the cylinder head, noting their positions for refitting **(see illustration)**.

19 On models with electronic (no throttle cable) throttle housing, disconnect the two coolant hoses from the rear of the throttle housing **(see illustration)**.

20 Jack up the front of the car, and support it on axle stands (see *Jacking and vehicle support*). Although not essential immediately, it would pay at this stage to raise the car sufficiently to allow the engine and transmission to be withdrawn from underneath.

21 Remove the auxiliary drivebelt as described in Chapter 1 Section 21.

22 On models with air conditioning, unbolt the compressor (see Chapter 3 Section 11 for

4.30 Use engine lift to hold the engine...

details). Disconnect the wiring connector and secure it to the front crossmember without disconnecting the refrigerant lines. Unbolt the refrigerant line support brackets as necessary **(see illustrations)**.

23 Unclip and remove the clutch return spring. Release the clutch cable adjuster and then disconnect the end of the cable from the clutch release arm. Unclip the outer cable adjuster from the mounting bracket on the transmission. Move the cable clear of the transmission, taking care not to kink or bend it.

Manual transmission

24 Pull out the spring clips and recover the washers, then unhook the gearchange cable end fittings from the transmission shift/select mechanism, noting their positions (refer to Chapter 7A Section 3).

25 Undo the two retaining bolts and disconnect the cable support bracket from the transmission housing, with the cables still attached. Move the cables clear of the transmission, taking care not to kink or bend them.

Multi-Mode (2-Tronic/SensoDrive) transmission

26 Check the wiring connectors around the transmission with reference to Chapter 7B. Disconnect any wiring, which is not part of the engine wiring loom.

All models

27 Disconnect the exhaust front pipe from the manifold/catalytic converter and remove it from under the vehicle with reference to

Chapter 4B Section 6. Disconnect the oxygen sensor wiring connector before removing the exhaust.

28 Remove both driveshafts as described in Chapter 8 Section 2.

29 Separate the engine rear mounting by removing the through-bolt, referring to Chapter 2A if necessary. Once the rear mounting is disconnected, the engine will be free to swing on its remaining two mountings. To create more room for lowering, it is advisable to unbolt the rear mounting completely and remove it.

30 Make a final check round the engine and transmission, to make sure nothing (apart from the left- and right-hand mountings) remains attached or in the way which will prevent it from being lowered out **(see illustration)**. Also make sure there is enough room under the front of the car for the engine/transmission to be lowered out and withdrawn.

 HAYNES HINT *Lowering the engine/ transmission onto a large board, some strong card, or even an old piece of carpet, will not only protect it from damage, but will make it easier to slide the engine out from under the car.*

31 Securely attach the engine/transmission unit to a suitable engine crane or hoist, and raise it so that the weight is just taken off the two remaining engine mountings. It is helpful at this stage to have an assistant available, either to work the crane or to guide the engine out.

32 With the engine securely supported, remove the right and left-hand engine mountings with reference to Chapter 2A Section 17.

33 With the help of an assistant, carefully lower the assembly from the engine compartment; making sure it clears the surrounding components and bodywork. Be prepared to steady the engine when it touches down, to stop it toppling over **(see illustration)**. Withdraw the assembly from under the car, and remove it to wherever it will be worked on.

Separation

34 To separate the transmission from the engine, first remove the starter motor with reference to Chapter 5A Section 10.

35 Undo the three retaining bolts and remove the lower plate from the sump side of the bellhousing **(see illustration)**.

36 Progressively unscrew and remove the transmission-to-engine bolts.

37 With the help of an assistant, withdraw the transmission directly from the engine, making sure that its weight is not allowed to bear on the clutch friction disc.

Refitting

38 Refitting is a reversal of removal, noting the following additional points:

a) *Make sure that all mating faces are clean, and use new gaskets where necessary.*

b) *Tighten all nuts and bolts to the specified torque setting, where given.*

c) *Apply a smear of high melting-point grease to the splines of the transmission input shaft. Do not apply too much; otherwise there is the possibility of the grease contaminating the clutch friction disc*

d) *On completion, adjust the clutch cable as described in Chapter 6 Section 2.*

e) *Refit the driveshafts as described in Chapter 8 Section 2.*

f) *Refit the exhaust system as described in Chapter 4B Section 6.*

g) *Replenish the transmission oil, and check the level with reference to Chapter 1 Section 20.*

h) *Refill the cooling system as described in Chapter 1 Section 23.*

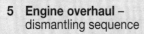

5 Engine overhaul – dismantling sequence

1 It is much easier to dismantle and work on the engine if it is mounted on a portable engine stand. These stands can often be hired from a tool hire shop. Before the engine is mounted on a stand, the flywheel should be removed from the engine, so that the engine stand bolts can be tightened into the end of the cylinder block.

2 If a stand is not available, it is possible to

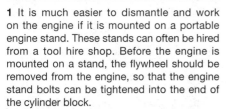

6.4 Using a valve spring compressor...

4.33.. and lower it out from the engine compartment

dismantle the engine with it blocked up on a sturdy workbench or on the floor. Be extra careful not to tip or drop the engine when working without a stand.

3 If you're going to obtain a reconditioned ('recon') engine, all external components must be removed first, to be transferred to the new engine (just as they will if you are doing a complete engine overhaul yourself). Note: When removing the external components from the engine, pay close attention to details that may be helpful or important during refitting. Note the fitted position of gaskets, seals, spacers, pins, washers, bolts and other small items. These external components include the following:

a) *Alternator, air conditioning compressor, etc ('ancillaries').*

b) *Ignition coils and spark plugs.*

c) *Thermostat housing.*

d) *Fuel injection equipment.*

e) *Inlet and exhaust manifolds.*

f) *Oil filter and housing.*

g) *Engine mountings and lifting brackets.*

h) *Coolant pipes and hoses.*

i) *Flywheel.*

4 If you are obtaining a 'short' motor (which consists of the engine cylinder block, crankshaft, pistons and connecting rods all assembled), then the cylinder head, sump, oil pump and timing chain will have to be removed also.

5 If you are planning a complete overhaul, the engine can be disassembled and the internal components removed in the following order:

a) *Engine external components (including inlet and exhaust manifolds).*

6.6... to remove the valve from the cylinder head

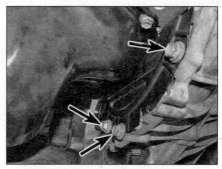

4.35 Undo the three bolts (arrowed) to remove the cover

b) *Sump.*

c) *Timing chain cover (including oil pump)*

d) *Timing sprockets and chain.*

e) *Cylinder head.*

f) *Flywheel.*

g) *Pistons and connecting rods.*

h) *Crankshaft and main bearings.*

6 Before beginning the disassembly and overhaul procedures, make sure that you have all of the correct tools necessary. Refer to the reference section at the end of this manual for further information.

6 Cylinder head – dismantling

Note: *New and reconditioned cylinder heads are available from the manufacturers and from engine overhaul specialists. Due to the fact that some specialist tools are required for the dismantling and inspection procedures, and new components may not be readily available, it may be more practical and economical for the home mechanic to purchase a reconditioned head rather than dismantle, inspect and recondition the original head.*

1 Remove the cylinder head as described in Part A of this Chapter.

2 If not already done, remove all external brackets and elbows.

3 Again, if not already done, remove the tappets as described in Part A of this Chapter, being careful to store the components as described.

4 Using a valve spring compressor, compress each valve spring in turn until the split collets can be removed; compressors are now widely available from most good motor accessory shops. Release the compressor, and lift off the spring upper seat and spring **(see illustration)**.

5 If, when the valve spring compressor is screwed down, the spring upper seat refuses to free and expose the split collets, gently tap the top of the tool, directly over the upper seat, with a light hammer. This will free the seat.

6 Withdraw the valve through the combustion chamber **(see illustration)**. If it binds in the guide (won't pull through), push it back in, and

6.7 Removing the valve stem oil seal

6.9 Keep all the valve components together in labelled containers

de-burr the area around the collet groove with a fine file; take care not to mark the tappet bores.

7 Pull the valve stem seals from the valve guides using a pair of pliers **(see illustration)**. As the seals are removed, note whether they are of different colours for the inlet and exhaust valves – compare with the new parts, and note this for refitting.

8 Remove the valve spring lower seats, and store them with their respective springs.

9 It is essential that the valves are kept together with their collets, spring seats and springs, and in their correct sequence (unless they are so badly worn that they are to be renewed). If they are going to be kept and used again, place them in a labelled polythene bag or similar small container **(see illustration)**. Note that No 1 valve is nearest to the timing chain end of the engine.

---

7 Cylinder head and valves –
cleaning, inspection
and renovation

1 Thorough cleaning of the cylinder head and valve components, followed by a detailed inspection, will enable you to decide how much valve service work must be carried out during the engine overhaul.

Cleaning

2 Scrape away all traces of old gasket material and sealing compound from the cylinder head. Take care not to damage the cylinder head surfaces.

3 Scrape away the carbon from the combustion chambers and ports, then wash the cylinder head thoroughly with paraffin or a suitable solvent.

4 Scrape off any heavy carbon deposits that may have formed on the valves, then use a power-operated wire brush to remove deposits from the valve heads and stems.

5 If the head is extremely dirty, it should be steam-cleaned. On completion, make sure that all oil holes and oil galleries are cleaned.

Inspection and renovation

Note: *Be sure to perform all the following inspection procedures before concluding that the services of an engine overhaul specialist are required. Make a list of all items that require attention.*

Cylinder head

6 Inspect the head very carefully for cracks, evidence of coolant leakage and other damage. If cracks are found, a new cylinder head should be obtained.

7 Use a straight-edge and feeler blade to check that the cylinder head surface is not distorted **(see illustration)**. If the specified distortion limit is exceeded, machining of the gasket face is not recommended by the manufacturers, so the only course of action is to renew the cylinder head.

8 Examine the valve seats in each of the combustion chambers. If they are severely pitted, cracked or burned, then they will need to be renewed or recut by an engine overhaul specialist. If they are only slightly pitted, this can be removed by grinding the valve heads

and seats together with coarse, then fine, grinding paste as described below.

9 If the valve guides are worn, indicated by a side-to-side motion of the valve in the guide, new guides must be fitted. If necessary, insert a new valve in the guides to determine if the wear is on the guide or valve. If new guides are to be fitted, the valves must be renewed as a matter of course. Valve guides may be renewed using a press and a suitable mandrel, however, the work is best carried out by an engine overhaul specialist, since if it is not done skilfully, there is a risk of damaging the cylinder head.

10 Check the tappet bores in the cylinder head for wear. If excessive wear is evident, the cylinder head must be renewed.

11 Examine the camshaft bearing surfaces in the cylinder head as described in Chapter 2A.

Valves

12 Examine the head of each valve for pitting, burning, cracks and general wear, and check the valve stem for scoring and wear ridges. Rotate the valve, and check for any obvious indication that it is bent. Look for pits and excessive wear on the end of each valve stem.

13 If the valve appears satisfactory at this stage, measure the valve stem diameter at several points using a micrometer **(see illustration)**. Any significant difference in the readings obtained indicates wear of the valve stem. Should any of these conditions be apparent, the valve(s) must be renewed.

14 If the valves are in satisfactory condition, or if new valves are being fitted, they should be ground (lapped) into their respective seats to ensure a smooth gas-tight seal.

15 Valve grinding is carried out as follows. Place the cylinder head upside-down on a bench, with a block of wood at each end to give clearance for the valve stems. Take care to protect the camshaft bearing surfaces.

16 Smear a trace of coarse carborundum paste on the seat face, and press a suction grinding tool onto the valve head. With a semi-rotary action, grind the valve head to its seat, lifting the valve occasionally to redistribute the grinding paste **(see illustration)**.

17 When a dull, matt even surface is produced on both the valve seat and the valve, wipe off the paste and repeat the process with fine carborundum paste. A light

7.7 Check the head for warpage using a straight-edge and feeler blades

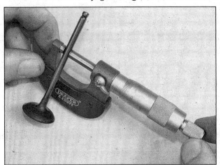

7.13 Measuring the diameter of a valve stem

7.16 Grinding-in a valve seat

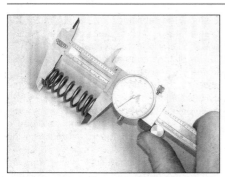

7.19 Checking the valve spring free length

spring placed under the valve head will greatly ease this operation.

18 When a smooth unbroken ring of light grey matt finish is produced on both the valve and seat, the grinding operation is complete. Be sure to remove all traces of grinding paste, using paraffin or a suitable solvent, before reassembly of the cylinder head.

Valve components

19 Examine the valve springs for signs of damage and discoloration, and also measure their free length using vernier calipers or a steel rule, or by comparing the existing spring with a new component **(see illustration)**.

20 Stand each spring on a flat surface, and check it for squareness. If any of the springs are damaged, distorted or have lost their tension, obtain a complete new set of springs. It is normal to renew the springs as a matter of course during a major overhaul.

21 Inspect the tappets for scoring, pitting,

and wear ridges. Renew any components as required – this may be necessary anyway once the valve clearances have been checked (see Chapter 2A Section 8). Note that some scuffing is to be expected, and is acceptable provided that the tappets are not scored.

Valve stem oil seals

22 The valve stem oil seals should be renewed as a matter of course.

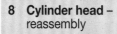
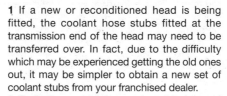

8   Cylinder head –
   reassembly

1 If a new or reconditioned head is being fitted, the coolant hose stubs fitted at the transmission end of the head may need to be transferred over. In fact, due to the difficulty which may be experienced getting the old ones out, it may be simpler to obtain a new set of coolant stubs from your franchised dealer.

2 To fit the new stubs, apply a thin layer of suitable adhesive to the bottom end of each stub. The smaller heater hose stubs are pressed in to a depth of 15 mm, while the larger radiator hose stub goes in 18 mm.

3 Mark a line on each stub, indicating the correct fitted depth. Press each stub in squarely – start it by hand if possible, then tap home using a hammer and block of wood.

4 Fit all twelve valve spring lower seats into their original positions **(see illustration)**.

5 Lubricate the valve stem oil seals with clean engine oil, then fit them by pushing into position in the cylinder head using a suitable

8.4 Fit the valve spring lower seats

socket **(see illustrations)**. Ensure that the seals are fully engaged with the valve guide.

6 Lubricate the valve stems, then insert the valves into their original locations. If new valves are being fitted, insert them into the locations to which they have been ground. Take care not to damage the valve stem oil seal as each valve is fitted.

7 Fit the valve springs and upper seats in their original locations, where applicable **(see illustrations)**.

8 Compress the valve spring and locate the split collets in the recess in the valve stem **(see illustrations)**. Release the compressor, then repeat the procedure on the remaining valves.

9 With all the valves installed, place the cylinder head flat on the bench and, using a hammer and interposed block of wood, tap the end of each valve stem to settle the components.

10 The previously-removed components can now be refitted with reference to Section 6.

8.5a Fit the valve stem seals...

8.5b... and then press them fully onto the guide

8.7a Refit the valve springs...

8.7b... and the upper seats

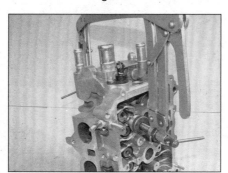

8.8a Fit a valve spring compressor to compress the valve...

8.8b... then locate the collet halves into the valve stem grooves, using grease to 'stick' them in place

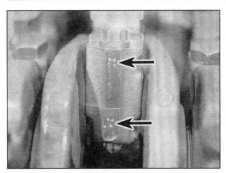

10.6 Mark the connecting rod and cap for position, and store together

9 Timing chain components
– general information

1 Refer to Chapter 2, Part A, Section 5.

10 Piston/connecting rod assemblies –
removal

1 Remove the cylinder head, sump, and oil pump pick-up tube, as applicable, with reference to Chapter 2A.
2 Rotate the crankshaft so that No 1 big-end cap (timing chain end of the engine) is at the lowest point of its travel. If the big-end cap and rod are not already numbered, mark them with a marker pen. Mark both cap and rod to identify the cylinder they operate in.

11.2 Undo the retaining bolts – arrowed

3 Unscrew and remove the big-end bearing cap bolts, and withdraw the cap complete with shell bearing from the connecting rod. Make sure that the shell remains in the cap and if necessary identify it for position. Discard the bolts – they are 'stretch' type, and should not be re-used.
4 If only the bearing shells are being attended to, push the connecting rod up and off the crankpin, and remove the upper bearing shell. Keep the bearing shells and cap together in their correct sequence if they are to be refitted.
5 If the piston is being removed, push the connecting rod up and remove the piston and rod from the top of the bore. Note that if there is a pronounced wear ridge at the top of the bore, there is a risk of damaging the piston as the rings foul the ridge. However, it is reasonable to assume that a rebore and new pistons will be required in any case if the ridge is so pronounced.
6 Repeat the procedure for the remaining piston/connecting rod assemblies. Ensure that the caps and rods are marked before removal, as described previously, and keep all components in order **(see illustration)**.

11 Crankshaft –
removal

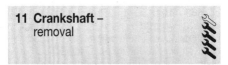

1 Remove the timing chain, crankshaft sprocket, sump, oil pick-up tube and flywheel, with reference to Chapter 2A.

11.5 Checking the crankshaft endfloat with a dial gauge

2 Undo the retaining bolts and remove the crankshaft oil seal carrier from the flywheel end of the cylinder block **(see illustration)**.
3 The pistons/connecting rods must be free of the crankshaft journals, however it is not essential to remove them completely from the cylinder block.
4 Before the crankshaft is removed, check the endfloat. Mount a dial gauge with the probe in line with the crankshaft and just touching the crankshaft.
5 Push the crankshaft fully away from the gauge, and zero it. Next, lever the crankshaft towards the gauge as far as possible, and check the reading obtained **(see illustration)**. The distance that the crankshaft moved is its endfloat; if it is greater than specified, new thrust washers will be required (see Specifications in Chapter 2A).
6 If no dial gauge is available, feeler blades can be used. Gently lever or push the crankshaft in one direction, then insert feeler blades between the crankshaft web and the main bearing with the thrust washers to determine the clearance **(see illustration)**.
7 Check that the main bearing caps have marks to indicate their respective fitted positions in the block. They may also have arrow marks pointing towards the timing end of the engine to indicate correct orientation **(see illustration)**.
8 Unscrew the retaining bolts, and remove the main bearing caps **(see illustration)**. If the caps are reluctant to separate from the block face, lightly tap them free using a plastic- or copper-faced hammer, or loosely refit the just-removed bolts and use them as 'levers'. If the bearing shells are likely to be used again, keep them with their bearing caps for safekeeping. However, unless the engine is known to be of low mileage, it is recommended that they be renewed.
9 Lift the crankshaft out from the crankcase, then extract the upper bearing shells, and the side thrust washers from No 3 bearing. Keep them with their respective caps for correct repositioning If they are to be used again.

11.6 Crankshaft endfloat can also be checked with feeler blades

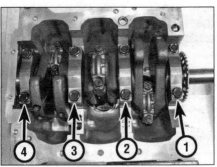

11.7 Check the markings on the main bearing caps

11.8 Main bearing caps, numbered from the timing chain end

12 Cylinder block/ crankcase and bores – cleaning and inspection

Cleaning

Caution: If cleaning the cylinder block with the crankshaft fitted, it is recommended that only the external surfaces are cleaned, as otherwise the internal oil ways and channels may become contaminated, leading to premature wear of the crankshaft and main bearings.

1 For complete cleaning, the core plugs should be removed. Drill a small hole in them, then insert a self-tapping screw and pull out the plugs using pliers or a slide-hammer. Also remove all external components and senders (if not already done), noting their locations.
2 Scrape all traces of gasket or sealant from the cylinder block, taking care not to damage the head and sump mating faces.
3 If the block is extremely dirty, it should be steam-cleaned.
4 After the block has been steam-cleaned, clean all oil holes and oil galleries one more time. Flush all internal passages with warm water until the water runs clear, dry the block thoroughly and wipe all machined surfaces with a light rust-preventive oil. If you have access to compressed air, use it to speed up the drying process and to blow out all the oil holes and galleries.

 Warning: Wear eye protection when using compressed air.

5 If the block is not very dirty, you can do an adequate cleaning job with hot soapy water and a stiff brush. Take plenty of time, and do a thorough job. Regardless of the cleaning method used, be sure to clean all oil holes and galleries very thoroughly, dry the block completely and coat all machined surfaces with light oil.
6 The threaded holes in the block must be clean to ensure accurate torque wrench readings during assembly. Run the correct size tap into each of the holes to remove the rust, corrosion, thread sealant or sludge, and to restore the threads **(see illustration)**. If possible, use compressed air to clear the holes of debris produced by this operation. Also clean the threads on the head bolts and the main bearing cap bolts.
7 Refit the main bearing caps, and tighten the bolts finger-tight.
8 After coating the mating surfaces of the new core plugs with suitable sealant, refit them in the cylinder block. Make sure that they are driven in straight and seated properly, or leakage could result. Special tools are available for this purpose, but a large socket, with an outside diameter that will just slip into the core plug, will work just as well **(see illustration)**.
9 If the engine is not going to be reassembled

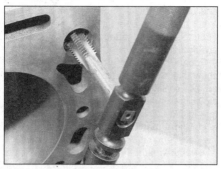

12.6 All the bolt holes in the block should be cleaned and restored with a tap

right away, cover it with a large plastic bag to keep it clean and prevent any corrosion.

Inspection

10 Visually check the block for cracks, rust and corrosion. Look for stripped threads in the threaded holes. If there has been any history of internal water leakage, it may be worthwhile having an engine overhaul specialist check the block with special equipment. If defects are found, have the block repaired, if possible, or renewed.
11 Check the cylinder bores for scuffing and scoring. Normally, bore wear will be evident in the form of a wear ridge at the top of the bore. This ridge marks the limit of piston travel.
12 Measure the diameter of each cylinder at the top (just under the ridge area), centre and base of the cylinder bore, parallel to the crankshaft axis.
13 Next measure each cylinder's diameter at the same three locations across the crankshaft axis. If the difference between any of the measurements is greater than 0.20 mm, indicating that the cylinder is excessively out-of-round or tapered, then remedial action must be considered.
14 Repeat this procedure for the remaining cylinders, then measure the diameter of each piston at right-angles to the gudgeon pin axis, and compare the result with the information given in the Specifications in Chapter 2A **(see illustration)**. By comparing the piston diameters with the bore diameters, an idea can be obtained of the clearances.
15 If the cylinder walls are badly scuffed or scored, or if they are excessively out-of-round or tapered, have the cylinder block rebored (where possible) by an engine overhaul specialist. New pistons (oversize in the case of a rebore) will also be required.
16 If the cylinders are in reasonably good condition, then it may only be necessary to renew the piston rings.
17 If this is the case, the bores should be honed in order to allow the new rings to bed-in correctly and provide the best possible seal. The conventional type of hone has spring-loaded stones, and is used with a power drill. You will also need some paraffin or honing oil and rags. The hone should be moved up-and-down the cylinder bore to

12.8 Core plugs located in the end of the cylinder head and block

produce a crosshatch pattern, and plenty of honing oil should be used.
18 Ideally, the crosshatch lines should intersect at approximately a 60° angle. Do not take off more material than is necessary to produce the required finish. If new pistons are being fitted, the piston manufacturers may specify a finish with a different angle, so their instructions should be followed. Do not withdraw the hone from the cylinder while it is still being turned, but stop it first (keep the hone moving up-and-down the bore while it slows down).
19 After honing a cylinder, wipe out all traces of the honing oil. If equipment of this type is not available, or if you are not sure whether you are competent to undertake the task yourself, an engine overhaul specialist will carry out the work at a moderate cost.
20 Refit all external components and senders in their correct locations, as noted before removal.

13 Piston/connecting rod assemblies – inspection and reassembly

Inspection

1 Before the inspection process can begin, the piston/connecting rod assemblies must be cleaned, and the original piston rings removed from the pistons.
2 Carefully expand the old rings over the top of the pistons. The use of two or three old feeler blades will be helpful in preventing

12.14 Measure the piston diameter at right-angles to the gudgeon pin axis, just above the base of the skirt

13.2 Using feeler blades to remove piston rings

the rings dropping into empty grooves **(see illustration)**. Note that the oil control scraper ring is in three sections.

3 Scrape away all traces of carbon from the top of the piston. A hand-held wire brush or a piece of fine emery cloth can be used once the majority of the deposits have been scraped away.

4 Remove the carbon from the ring grooves in the piston by cleaning them using an old ring. Break the ring in half to do this. Be very careful to remove only the carbon deposits, do not remove any metal, or scratch the sides of the ring grooves. Protect your fingers – piston rings are sharp.

5 Once the deposits have been removed, clean the piston/connecting rod assembly with paraffin or a suitable solvent, and dry thoroughly. Make sure the oil return holes in the ring grooves are clear.

6 If the pistons and cylinder bores are not damaged or worn excessively, and if the cylinder block does not need to be rebored, the original pistons can be re-used. Normal piston wear appears as even vertical wear on the piston thrust surfaces, and slight looseness of the top ring in its groove. New piston rings, however, should always be used when the engine is reassembled.

7 Carefully inspect each piston for cracks around the skirt, at the gudgeon pin bosses, and at the piston ring lands (between the piston ring grooves).

8 Look for scoring and scuffing on the sides of the skirt, holes in the piston crown, and burned areas at the edge of the crown. If the skirt is scored or scuffed, the engine may have been suffering from overheating

and/or abnormal combustion, which caused excessively high operating temperatures. The cooling and lubricating systems should be checked thoroughly.

9 Scorch marks on the sides of the pistons show that blow-by has occurred and the rings are not sealing correctly. A hole in the piston crown is an indication that abnormal combustion (pre-ignition, knocking or detonation) has been occurring. If any of the above problems exist, the causes must be corrected, or the damage will occur again. Typically, the causes may include inlet air leaks, incorrect fuel/air mixture or incorrect ignition timing.

10 Corrosion of the piston, in the form of small pits, indicates that coolant is leaking into the combustion chamber and/or the crankcase. Again, the cause must be corrected, or the problem may persist in the rebuilt engine.

11 If new rings are being fitted to old pistons, measure the piston ring-to-groove clearance by placing a new piston ring in each ring groove and measuring the clearance with a feeler blade. Check the clearance at three or four places around each groove. If the new ring is excessively tight, the most likely cause is dirt remaining in the groove.

12 Check the piston-to-bore clearance by measuring the cylinder bore (see Section 12) and the piston diameter. Measure the piston across the skirt, at a 90° angle to the gudgeon pin, approximately halfway down the skirt. Subtract the piston diameter from the bore diameter to obtain the clearance. If this is greater than the figures given in the Specifications, the block will have to be rebored, and new pistons and rings fitted.

13 Check the fit of the gudgeon pin by twisting the piston and connecting rod in opposite directions. Any noticeable play indicates excessive wear, which must be corrected. The gudgeon pins are secured by circlips, so the pistons and connecting rods can be separated without difficulty. Note the position of the piston relative to the rod before dismantling, and use new circlips on reassembly.

14 Before refitting the rings to the pistons, check their end gaps by inserting each of them in their cylinder bores. Use the piston to make sure that they are square. Using feeler blades, check that the gaps are within the tolerances

given in the Specifications. Genuine rings are supplied pre-gapped; no attempt should be made to adjust the gaps by filing.

Reassembly

15 Install the new rings by fitting them over the top of the piston, starting with the oil control scraper ring sections. Use feeler blades in the same way as when removing the old rings. New rings generally have their top surfaces identified, and must be fitted the correct way round. Note that the first and second compression rings have different sections. Be careful when handling the compression rings; they will break if they are handled roughly or expanded too far.

16 With all the rings in position, space the two top ring gaps at 180° to each other (on opposite sides of the piston). The oil control ring top and bottom rails must be positioned at 90° to the first and second ring gaps – ie, so that none of the end gaps align directly above or below each other.

14 Crankshaft – inspection

1 Clean the crankshaft using paraffin or a suitable solvent, and dry it, preferably with compressed air if available. Be sure to clean the oil holes with a pipe cleaner or similar probe, to ensure that they are not obstructed.

⚠️ *Warning: Wear eye protection when using compressed air.*

2 Check the main and big-end bearing journals for uneven wear, scoring, pitting and cracking.

3 If the crankshaft has been reground, check for burrs around the crankshaft oil holes (the holes are usually chamfered, so burrs should not be a problem unless regrinding has been carried out carelessly). Remove any burrs with a fine file or scraper, and thoroughly clean the oil holes as described previously.

4 Using a micrometer, measure the diameter of the main bearing and connecting rod journals, and compare the results with the Specifications (Chapter 2A). By measuring the diameter at a number of points around each journal's circumference, you will be able to determine whether or not the journal is out-of-round **(see illustration)**. Take the measurement at each end of the journal, near the webs, to determine if the journal is tapered. If any of the measurements vary by more than 0.02 mm, the crankshaft will have to be reground, and undersize bearings fitted.

5 Check the oil seal contact surfaces at each end of the crankshaft for wear and damage. If an excessive groove is evident in the surface of the crankshaft, consult an engine overhaul specialist who will be able to advise whether a repair is possible or if a new crankshaft is necessary.

14.4 Measure the diameter of each crankshaft journal at several points

14.6 Flat area (arrowed) on crankshaft position sensor rotor

6 Check the condition of the crankshaft position sensor rotor (which looks like a thin sprocket). The rotor is a press-fit on the crankshaft. Check that the rotor is not distorted or damaged – it should have a flat area, which is used as a reference by the crankshaft position sensor **(see illustration)**.

15 Main and big-end bearings – inspection

1 Even though the main and big-end bearings should be renewed during the engine overhaul, the old bearings should be retained for close examination, as they may reveal valuable information about the condition of the engine. The size of the bearing shells is stamped on the back, and this information should be given to the supplier of the new shells.

2 Bearing failure occurs because of lack of lubrication, the presence of dirt or other foreign particles, overloading the engine, and corrosion **(see illustration)**. Regardless of the cause of bearing failure, it must be corrected before the engine is reassembled, to prevent it from happening again.

3 When examining the bearings, remove them from the engine block, the main bearing caps, the connecting rods and the rod caps, and lay them out on a clean surface in the same general position as their location in the engine. This will enable you to match any bearing problems with the corresponding crankshaft journal.

4 Dirt and other foreign particles get into the engine in a variety of ways. Dirt may be left in the engine during assembly, or it may pass through filters or the crankcase ventilation system. It may get into the oil, and from there into the bearings. Metal chips from machining operations and normal engine wear are often present. Abrasives are sometimes left in engine components after reconditioning, especially when parts are not thoroughly cleaned using the proper cleaning methods.

5 Whatever the source, these foreign objects often end up embedded in the soft bearing material, and are easily recognised. Large particles will not embed in the bearing, and will score or gouge the bearing and journal. The best prevention for this cause of bearing failure is to clean all parts thoroughly, and keep everything spotlessly-clean during engine assembly. Frequent and regular engine oil and filter changes are also recommended.

6 Lack of lubrication (or lubrication breakdown) has a number of interrelated causes. Excessive heat (which thins the oil), overloading (which squeezes the oil from the bearing face) and oil leakage (from excessive bearing clearances, worn oil pump or high engine speeds) all contribute to lubrication

breakdown. Blocked oil passages, which usually are the result of misaligned oil holes in a bearing shell, will also oil-starve a bearing and destroy it. When lack of lubrication is the cause of bearing failure, the bearing material is wiped or extruded from the steel backing of the bearing. Temperatures may increase to the point where the steel backing turns blue from overheating.

7 Driving habits can have a definite effect on bearing life. Full-throttle, low-speed operation (labouring the engine) puts very high loads on bearings, which tends to squeeze out the oil film. These loads cause the bearings to flex, which produces fine cracks in the bearing face (fatigue failure). Eventually, the bearing material will loosen in pieces and tear away from the steel backing. Short-trip driving leads to corrosion of bearings, because insufficient engine heat is produced to drive off the condensed water and corrosive gases. These products collect in the engine oil, forming acid and sludge. As the oil is carried to the engine bearings, the acid attacks and corrodes the bearing material.

8 Incorrect bearing installation during engine assembly will lead to bearing failure as well. Tight-fitting bearings leave insufficient bearing oil clearance, and will result in oil starvation. Dirt or foreign particles trapped behind a bearing shell result in high spots on the bearing, which lead to failure.

9 Do not touch any shell's bearing surface with your fingers during reassembly; there is a risk of scratching the delicate surface, or of depositing particles of dirt on it.

10 As mentioned at the beginning of this Section, the bearing shells should be renewed as a matter of course during engine overhaul; to do otherwise is false economy.

16 Engine overhaul – reassembly sequence

1 Before reassembly begins, ensure that all new parts have been obtained and that all necessary tools are available. Read through the entire procedure to familiarise yourself with the work involved, and to ensure that all items necessary for reassembly of the engine are at hand. In addition to all normal tools and materials, flange sealant and thread-locking compound will be needed during engine reassembly. Do not use any kind of silicone-based sealant on any part of the fuel system or inlet manifold, and never use exhaust sealants upstream (on the engine side) of the catalytic converter.

2 In order to save time and avoid problems, engine reassembly can be carried out in the following order:
a) *Crankshaft and main bearings.*
b) *Pistons and connecting rods.*
c) *Cylinder head.*
d) *Timing sprockets and chain.*
e) *Timing chain cover (including oil pump).*

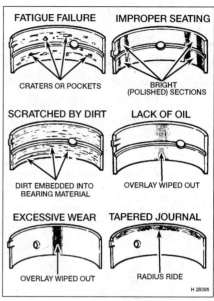

15.2 Typical bearing failures

f) *Sump.*
g) *Flywheel.*
h) *Engine external components (including inlet and exhaust manifolds).*

3 Ensure that everything is clean prior to reassembly. As mentioned previously, dirt and metal particles can quickly destroy bearings and result in major engine damage. Use clean engine oil to lubricate during reassembly.

17 Crankshaft – refitting

Selection of new bearing shells

1 Have the crankshaft inspected and measured by a franchised dealer or engine-reconditioning specialist. They will be able to carry out any regrinding/repairs, and supply suitable main and big-end bearing shells.

Refitting

2 It is assumed at this point that the cylinder block/crankcase and crankshaft have been cleaned and repaired or reconditioned as necessary. Position the engine upside-down.

3 Wipe clean the main bearing shell seats in the crankcase and bearing caps, and clean the backs of the bearing shells. Insert the respective upper shells (dry) into position in the crankcase. Note that the upper shells have grooves and oil holes in them (the lower shells are plain). The shell oil holes must align with the oil supply holes in the crankcase. Where the old main bearings are being refitted, ensure that they are located in their original positions. Make sure that the tab on each bearing shell fits into the notch in the block or cap **(see illustration)**.

17.3 The bearing shell tabs locates in the notch in the upper seat

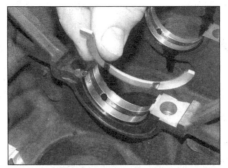

17.4a Apply a little grease to the backs of the thrustwashers before fitting...

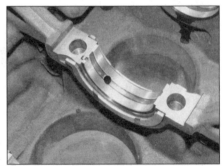

17.4b... and ensure they are fitted with the oil grooves facing outwards

17.5 Lubricate the bearing shells before fitting the crankshaft

17.6 Fit the main bearing caps with the arrow marks facing the timing chain end

9 Rotate the crankshaft a number of times by hand, to check for any obvious binding.
10 Check the crankshaft endfloat (refer to Section 11).
11 Fit new crankshaft oil seals as described in Chapter 2A Section 15 (as applicable).
12 Refit the pistons and connecting rods as described in Section 18.

18 Pistons/connecting rods – refitting

1 Clean the backs of the big-end bearing shells, and the recesses in the connecting rods and big-end caps. If new shells are being fitted, ensure that all traces of the protective grease are cleaned off using paraffin. Wipe the shells and connecting rods dry with a lint-free cloth.
2 Lubricate No 1 piston and piston rings, and check that the ring gaps are spaced as described in Section 13.
3 Fit the connecting rod bearing shells in place, making sure the shell's locating tab engages correctly **(see illustration)**.
4 Fit a ring compressor to No 1 piston, then insert the piston and connecting rod into No 1 cylinder. Make sure that the dot on the piston

4 Place the crankshaft thrust washers into position in the crankcase, either side of the No 3 bearing, so that their oil grooves are facing outwards (away from the central web) **(see illustrations)**. Hold them in position with a little grease. Clean the bearing surfaces of the shells in the block, and the crankshaft main bearing journals with a clean, lint-free cloth.
5 Clean the bearing surfaces of the shells in the block, then apply a thin layer of clean engine oil to each shell **(see illustration)**. Lubricate the thrust washer bearing surfaces as well.
6 Make sure the crankshaft journals are clean, and then lay the crankshaft back in place in the

block. Clean the bearing surfaces of the shells in the caps, and then lubricate them with oil. Install the caps in their respective positions, with the arrows pointing to the timing chain end of the engine **(see illustration)**.
7 Working in sequence (and ensuring that each cap is tightened down squarely and evenly onto the block), tighten the main bearing cap bolts to the Stage 1, specified torque **(see illustration)**.
8 With all the main bearing bolts tightened to the Stage 1 setting, go round again in the same sequence and tighten them further to the Stage 2 specified torque.

17.7 Tightening sequence for main bearing caps

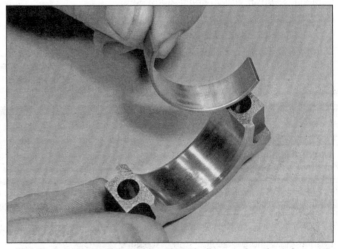

18.3 Fit the connecting rod bearing shell, ensuring the tab seats correctly

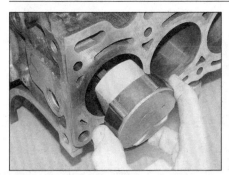

18.4a Fit a ring compressor, and offer in the piston...

18.4b... then tap the piston through the compressor using a hammer handle

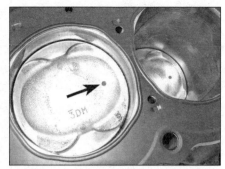

18.4c Dot on the piston crown should face the timing chain end

crown is facing the timing end of the engine. With No 1 crankpin at its lowest point, drive the piston carefully into the cylinder with the wooden handle of a hammer, at the same time guiding the connecting rod onto the crankpin **(see illustrations)**.

5 Press the big-end bearing shells into the connecting rod caps, aligning each shell with its locating groove.

6 Liberally lubricate the crankpin journals and big-end bearing shells. Refit the bearing caps, which have dowels to ensure correct positioning. Tighten the new bearing cap bolts to the specified torque in Section 0 and angles, and turn the crankshaft each time to make sure that it is free before moving on to the next assembly **(see illustrations)**.

19 Engine –
initial start-up after overhaul

1 With the engine refitted in the car, double-check the engine oil and coolant levels (see *Weekly checks*). Make a final check that everything has been reconnected, and that there are no tools or rags left in the engine compartment.

2 With the ignition and fuel injection systems

18.6a Oil and refit the connecting rod bearing caps...

18.6b... then fit the new bolts and tighten as specified

disabled by disconnecting the ignition coil wiring plugs (Chapter 5B Section 3) and removing the fuel pump fuse (Chapter 4A or Chapter 12 wiring diagrams), crank the engine on the starter motor until the oil pressure light goes out.

3 Reconnect the ignition coils, and refit the fuel pump fuse.

4 Start the engine, noting that this may take a little longer than usual.

5 While the engine is idling, check for fuel, water and oil leaks. Do not be alarmed if there are some odd smells and smoke from parts getting hot and burning off oil deposits.

6 Keep the engine idling until hot water is felt circulating through the top hose, then switch it off.

7 After a few minutes, recheck the oil and coolant levels, and top-up as necessary (see *Weekly checks*).

8 If new pistons, rings or crankshaft bearings have been fitted, the engine must be run-in for the first 500 miles. Do not operate the engine at full-throttle, nor allow it to labour in any gear during this period. It is recommended that the oil and filter be changed at the end of this period.

Notes

Chapter 3
Cooling, heating and air conditioning systems

Contents

Degrees of difficulty

| Easy, suitable for novice with little experience 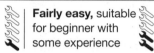 | Fairly easy, suitable for beginner with some experience | Fairly difficult, suitable for competent DIY mechanic | Difficult, suitable for experienced DIY mechanic | Very difficult, suitable for expert DIY or professional |

Specifications

General

Coolant capacity	See Chapter 1
Thermostat temperature:	
Start to open	80 to 84°C
Fully open	95°C
Radiator cap opening pressure	0.93 to 1.23 bar
Cooling fan starts to operate	93°C
Cooling fan motor amperage:	
With air conditioning	7.5 to 9.3 amps
Without air conditioning	2.5 to 4.5 amps
Coolant temperature sensor resistance:	
At 20°C	2320 to 2590 ohms
At 80°C	310 to 326 ohms

Air conditioning

Compressor:	
Make	Valeo-Zexel
Model	DKV-06R
Compressor oil:	
Type	ZXL 200PG
Quantity	80 cc
Refrigerant:	
Type	R134a
Quantity	450 g
Circuit pressure:	
Low-pressure side	1.5 to 2.5 bar
High-pressure side	13.7 to 15.7 bar

Torque wrench settings

	Nm	lbf ft
Air conditioning compressor mounting bolts	25	18
Air conditioning pipe retaining bolts	10	7
Coolant drain plug (on timing chain side of engine)	20	15
Coolant pump mounting bolts	28	21
Coolant temperature sensor	20	15
Thermostat cover nut/bolt	8	6

1 General information and precautions

1 The cooling system is of pressurised type, comprising a pump driven by the auxiliary drivebelt, an aluminium crossflow radiator, electric cooling fan, and a thermostat.
2 The system functions as follows. Cold coolant from the radiator passes through the hose to the water pump, where it is pumped around the cylinder block and head passages.
3 After cooling the cylinder bores, combustion surfaces and valve seats, the coolant reaches the underside of the thermostat, which is initially closed. The coolant passes through the heater, and is returned via the cylinder block to the water pump.
4 When the engine is cold, the thermostat is shut, and the coolant circulates only through the cylinder block, cylinder head and heater.
5 When the coolant reaches a predetermined temperature, the thermostat opens and the coolant passes through the top hose to the radiator.
6 As the coolant circulates through the radiator, it is cooled by the inrush of air when the car is in forward motion. Airflow is supplemented by the action of the electric cooling fan when necessary. Once the coolant has passed through the radiator, and has cooled, the cycle is repeated.
7 The coolant temperature is signaled to the engine ECU, and to the temperature display on the instrument panel, by a sensor fitted to the cylinder head at the transmission end of the cylinder head. This also controls the operation of the electric cooling fan, mounted on the rear of the radiator.
8 An expansion tank is fitted to allow for the expansion of the coolant. The expansion tank is part of the cooling fan shroud, and is connected to the top of the radiator by a hose.
9 Refer to Section 10 for information on the air conditioning system.

⚠ **Warning: Do not attempt to remove the expansion tank filler cap or disturb any part of the cooling system while the engine is hot, as there is a high risk of scalding.**

2.3a Release the spring clip with a pair of pliers...

If the expansion tank filler cap must be removed before the engine and radiator have fully cooled (even though this is not recommended) the pressure in the cooling system must first be relieved. Cover the cap with a thick layer of cloth, to avoid scalding, and slowly unscrew the filler cap until a hissing sound can be heard. When the hissing has stopped, indicating that the pressure has reduced, slowly unscrew the filler cap until it can be removed; if more hissing sounds are heard, wait until they have stopped before unscrewing the cap completely. At all times keep well away from the filler cap opening.

⚠ **Warning: Do not allow antifreeze to come into contact with skin or painted surfaces of the vehicle.** Rinse off spills immediately with plenty of water. Never leave antifreeze lying around in an open container or in a puddle in the driveway or on the garage floor. Children and pets are attracted by its sweet smell. Antifreeze can be fatal if ingested.

⚠ **Warning: If the engine is hot, the electric cooling fan may start rotating even if the engine is not running; be careful to keep hands, hair and loose clothing well clear when working in the engine compartment.**

⚠ **Warning: Refer to Section 10 for precautions to be observed when working on models equipped with air conditioning.**

2 Cooling system hoses – disconnection and renewal

Note: *Refer to the warnings given in Section 1 of this Chapter before proceeding. Do not attempt to disconnect any hose while the system is still hot.*
1 If the checks described in the relevant part of Chapter 1 reveal a faulty hose, it must be renewed as follows.
2 First drain the cooling system as described in Chapter 1 Section 23. If the coolant is not due for renewal, it may be re-used if it is collected in a clean container.

2.3b... and remove the pipe from the union

3 Before disconnecting a hose, first note its routing in the engine compartment, and whether it is secured by any retaining clips or ties. Use a pair of pliers to release the spring clamps (or a screwdriver to slacken screw-type clamps) then move them along the hose, clear of the relevant inlet/outlet union. Carefully work the hose free **(see illustrations)**.
4 Note that the coolant unions are fragile (some are made of plastic); do not use excessive force when attempting to remove the hoses. If a hose proves to be difficult to remove, try to release it by rotating the hose ends before attempting to free it – if this fails, try gently prising up the end of the hose with a small screwdriver to 'break' the seal.

> **HAYNES HiNT** *If all else fails, cut the coolant hose with a sharp knife, then slit it so that it can be peeled off in two pieces. Although this may prove expensive if the hose is otherwise undamaged, it is preferable to buying a new radiator.*

5 When fitting a hose, first slide the clamps onto the hose, and then work the hose into position. If spring-type clamps were originally fitted, it is a good idea to use screw-type clamps when refitting the hose (if only to make removal easier, next time). If the hose is stiff, use a little soapy water (washing-up liquid is ideal) as a lubricant, or soften the hose by soaking it in hot water.
6 Work the hose into position, checking that it is correctly routed and secured. Slide each clamp along the hose until it passes over the flared end of the relevant inlet/outlet union before tightening the clamps securely.
7 Refill the cooling system with reference to Chapter 1 Section 23.
8 Check thoroughly for leaks as soon as possible after disturbing any part of the cooling system.

3 Radiator – removal, inspection and refitting

Note: *If leakage is the reason for removing the radiator, bear in mind that minor leaks can often be cured using a radiator sealant with the radiator in position.*

Removal

1 Apply the handbrake, then jack up the front of the car and support securely on axle stands (see *Jacking and vehicle support*).
2 Drain the cooling system as described in Chapter 1 Section 23.
3 Remove the front bumper as described in Chapter 11 Section 6.
4 Undo the retaining bolts and remove the plastic 'honeycomb' panel from under the front crossmember **(see illustration)**.

5 Undo the retaining bolt and remove the horn from the front of the radiator. Release the retaining clips and remove the air deflectors from each side of the radiator **(see illustrations)**.

6 If not already removed to drain cooling system, release the securing clip and disconnect the bottom hose from the lower part of the radiator **(see illustration)**.

7 Disconnect the cooling fan wiring plug, and unclip the wiring harness as necessary **(see illustration)**.

8 Release the securing clip and disconnect the top hose from the filler neck of the radiator **(see illustrations)**. Unclip the hose from the retaining clip on the rear of the fan cowling.

9 On models with air conditioning, undo the two retaining bolts at the top of the condenser and then lift it up to disconnect it from the bottom of the radiator. Secure the condenser to the upper crossmember, making sure the air conditioning pipes do not get damaged **(see illustrations)**.

10 Undo the three bolts at each side of the front lower crossmember and remove it from the vehicle. As the crossmember is removed, carefully lower the radiator, complete with cooling fan, out from under the upper crossmember. Note the two lower mounting rubbers in the crossmember and the two mounting rubbers on the top of the radiator **(see illustrations)**.

11 If required, the cooling fan and shroud could be removed, after undoing the upper mounting bolt and releasing the upper securing clip. Then lift the cooling fan shroud upwards to disengage it from the bottom of the radiator **(see illustrations)**.

12 To remove the fan and motor from the shroud, see Section 5 of this Chapter.

3.4 Remove the plastic panel from the front lower crossmember

3.5b... and remove the air deflectors

3.5a Unbolt the horn...

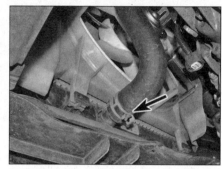

3.6 Release the bottom hose securing clip – arrowed

Inspection

13 If the radiator has been removed due to suspected blockage, reverse-flush it as described in Chapter 1 Section 23. Clean dirt

3.7 Disconnect the fan wiring connector

3.8a Release the top hose securing clip (arrowed)...

3.8b... and unclip it from the fan cowling

3.9a Undo the two retaining bolts...

3.9b... and lift the condenser from the lower mounting brackets...

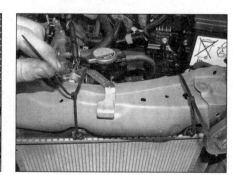

3.9c... and secure to the upper crossmember

3.10a Undo the lower mounting bolts (one side shown)...

3.10b... and remove the lower crossmember

3.10c Radiator upper mounting rubbers

and debris from the radiator fins, using an airline (in which case, wear eye protection) or a soft brush. Be careful, as the fins are easily damaged, and are sharp.

14 If necessary, a radiator specialist can perform a 'flow test' on the radiator, to establish whether an internal blockage exists.

15 A leaking radiator must be referred to a specialist for permanent repair. Do not attempt to weld or solder a leaking radiator, as damage may result.

Refitting

16 Refitting is a reversal of removal, bearing in mind the following points:

a) *Make sure the upper and lower mounting rubbers are fitted correctly **(see illustration)**.*

b) *Ensure that all hoses are correctly reconnected, and their retaining clips securely fitted (or tightened).*

c) *Reconnect the radiator fan wiring, and ensure the harness is routed clear of the fan blades or hot components.*

d) *On models with air conditioning, make sure there are no leaks from the pipes and it is working correctly.*

e) *On completion, refill the cooling system as described in Chapter 1 Section 23.*

4 Thermostat – removal, testing and refitting

1 As the thermostat ages, it will become slower to react to changes in water temperature ('lazy'). Ultimately, the unit may stick in the open or closed position, and this causes problems. A thermostat that is stuck open will result in a very slow warm-up; a thermostat which is stuck shut will lead to rapid overheating.

2 Before assuming the thermostat is to blame for a cooling system problem, check the coolant level. If the system is draining due to a leak, or has not been properly filled, there may be an airlock in the system (refer to the coolant renewal procedure in Chapter 1).

3 If the engine seems to be taking a long time to warm-up (based on heater output), the thermostat could be stuck open. Don't necessarily believe the temperature gauge reading – some gauges never seem to register very high in normal driving.

4 A lengthy warm-up period might suggest that the thermostat is missing – it may have been removed or inadvertently omitted by a previous owner or mechanic. Don't drive the car without a thermostat – the engine management system's ECU will then stay in warm-up mode for longer than necessary, causing emissions and fuel economy to suffer.

5 If the engine runs hot, use your hand to check the temperature of the radiator top hose. If the hose isn't hot, but the engine clearly is, the thermostat is probably stuck closed, preventing the coolant inside the engine from escaping to the radiator – renew the thermostat. Again, this problem may also be due to an airlock (refer to the coolant renewal procedure in Chapter 1).

6 If the radiator top hose is hot, it means that the coolant is flowing (at least as far as the radiator) and the thermostat is open. Consult the Fault finding section at the end of this manual to assist in tracing possible cooling system faults, but a lack of heater output would now definitely suggest an airlock or a blockage.

7 To gain a rough idea of whether the thermostat is working properly when the engine is warming up, without dismantling the system, proceed as follows.

8 With the engine completely cold, start the engine and let it idle, while checking the temperature of the radiator top hose. Periodically check the temperature indicated on the instrument panel – if overheating is indicated, switch the engine off immediately.

9 The top hose should feel cold for some time as the engine warms-up, and should then get warm quite quickly as the thermostat opens.

10 The above is not a precise or definitive test of thermostat operation, but if the system

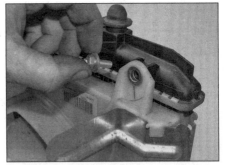

3.11a Remove the upper securing bolt...

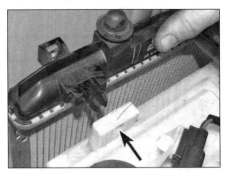

3.11b... release the securing clip...

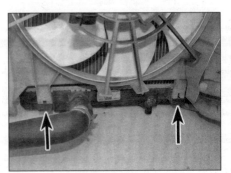

3.11c... and lift out of lower mounting points

3.16a Make sure the rubber mountings are fitted

4.12 Thermostat housing – arrowed

4.13 Disconnect the coolant hose

4.14a Undo the two retaining bolts...

4.14b... and remove the thermostat housing

4.21a The thermostat air bleed valve should be at the top

4.21b Use a new rubber seal when refitting the thermostat

does not perform as described, remove and test the thermostat as described below.

Removal

11 Allow the engine to cool completely, then drain the coolant as described in Chapter 1 Section 23.

12 The thermostat housing is located at the transmission end of the cylinder head **(see illustration)**.

13 Release the securing clip and disconnect the large-diameter radiator hose from the thermostat housing **(see illustration)**.

14 Undo the two retaining bolts and remove the thermostat cover and thermostat **(see illustrations)**. Pull out the thermostat and recover the O-ring seal – the seal should be renewed.

Testing

Note: *If there is any question about the operation of the thermostat, it's best to renew it – they are not expensive items. Testing involves heating in, or over, an open pan of boiling water, which carries with it the risk of scalding. A thermostat which has seen more than five years' service may well be past its best already.*

15 If the thermostat remains in the open position at room temperature, it is faulty, and must be renewed as a matter of course.

16 Check to see if there's an open temperature marking stamped on the thermostat.

17 Using a thermometer and container of water, heat the water until the temperature corresponds with the temperature marking stamped on the thermostat. If no marking is found, start the test with the water hot, and heat slowly until it boils.

18 Suspend the (closed) thermostat on a length of string in the water, and check that maximum opening occurs within two minutes, or before the water boils.

19 Remove the thermostat and allow it to cool down, and then check that it closes fully.

20 If the thermostat does not open and close as described, or if it sticks in either position, it must be renewed.

Refitting

21 Refitting is a reversal of removal, noting the following points:

a) *The thermostat has a 'jiggle pin' (air bleed valve) fitted, this should be at the top when refitting (see illustration).*

b) *Use a new O-ring seal (see illustration).*

c) *Tighten the cover bolts to the specified torque.*

d) *On completion, refill the cooling system as described in Chapter 1 Section 23.*

5.2 Disconnect the coolant hose from the radiator

5 Radiator cooling fan – removal and refitting

Note: *The cooling fan and shroud is removed in Section 3, complete with radiator. This Section shows how to remove the cooling fan and shroud without removing the radiator.*

Removal

1 Drain the cooling system as described in Chapter 1 Section 23.

2 If not already removed to drain cooling system, release the securing clip and disconnect the bottom hose from the lower part of the radiator **(see illustration)**.

3 Disconnect the cooling fan wiring plug at the top of the radiator **(see illustration)**.

4 Disconnect the hose from the radiator filler neck **(see illustration)**. This goes to the

5.3 Disconnect the fan wiring connector

5.4 Disconnect the overflow pipe

5.5a Remove the upper securing bolt...

5.5b... release the securing clip...

5.5c... and lift out of lower mounting points

5.7a Fan motor securing bolts

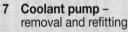

5.7b Unclip the wiring from the cowling

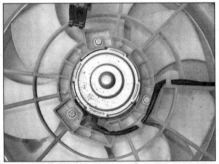

6.2 Coolant temperature sensor – arrowed

6.3 Disconnect the wiring connector

expansion tank, which is part of the cooling fan shroud.

5 Undo the upper mounting bolt and release the securing clip at the top of the radiator **(see illustrations)**.

6 Lift the cooling fan shroud upwards to disengage it from the bottom of the radiator and then withdraw the cooling fan and shroud out from under the vehicle.

7 To remove the fan and motor, undo the three motor retaining bolts and remove it from the cooling fan shroud. Unclip the wiring from the shroud as the fan/motor is removed **(see illustrations)**.

Refitting

8 Refitting is a reversal of removal. Reconnect the radiator fan wiring securely, and ensure the harness is routed clear of the fan blades or hot components.

6 Coolant temperature sensor – removal and refitting

⚠ *Warning: Do not attempt to remove any sensors while the cooling system is hot and/or pressurised, as there is a great risk of scalding.*

1 Allow the engine to cool, then slowly remove the cap from the coolant expansion tank to depressurise the cooling system. To avoid any chance of coolant spillage, the system can be drained as described in Chapter 1 Section 23, but this is not essential if a new sensor is being fitted, and can quickly be substituted for the old one. Otherwise, if the system is not drained and the sensor will be left out for some time, a plug of some kind should be inserted to reduce coolant loss.

2 The sensor is screwed into the cylinder head at the transmission end **(see illustration)**.

3 Disconnect the sensor wiring plug, then unscrew the sensor and remove it **(see illustration)**. Recover the sealing washer – a new one should be used when refitting.

4 The sensor can be checked by using an ohmmeter across the two terminals of the sensor. Check the resistance, as stated in the specifications at the beginning of this Chapter.

5 Refitting is a reversal of removal. Tightening the sensor to the specified torque.

6 Refill or top-up the cooling system as described in Chapter 1 or 'Weekly checks'.

7 Coolant pump – removal and refitting

Removal

1 Drain the cooling system as described in Chapter 1 Section 23 **(see illustration)**.

7.1 Cooling system engine drain plug – arrowed

2 Raise the front of the car, and support it on axle stands (see *Jacking and vehicle support*). Remove the driver's side plastic inner wing cover.

3 Remove the auxiliary drivebelt as described in Chapter 1 Section 21.

4 Unscrew the five bolts, and withdraw the coolant pump. Be prepared for coolant spillage as the pump is removed. Recover the gasket – a new one will be needed for reassembly **(see illustrations)**.

Inspection

5 If the pump has been removed for reasons other than to fit a new one, inspect it as follows.

6 Check around the drain hole on the pump body for signs of coolant leakage (typically, white- or antifreeze-coloured deposits). Even a slight leak is a sign of impending failure, and the pump should be renewed.

7 Spin the pump impeller, and listen for a noisy bearing. A rough scraping sound indicates that the pump is not worth refitting, and a new one should be obtained.

Refitting

8 Commence refitting by thoroughly cleaning the mating faces of the pump and the cylinder block.

9 Refit the pump, using a new gasket, and tighten the securing bolts to the specified torque **(see illustrations)**.

10 Further refitting is a reversal of removal, bearing in mind the following points:
a) Tighten all fixings to the specified torque (where given).
b) Refit the auxiliary drivebelt as described in Chapter 1 Section 21.
c) On completion, refill the cooling system as described in Chapter 1 Section 23.

8 Heating and ventilation system – general information

1 The heater/ventilation system consists of a four-speed blower motor (housed behind the facia), face-level vents at each end of the facia, and air ducts to the front footwells.

2 The control unit is located in the centre of the facia, and the controls operate flap valves to deflect and mix the air flowing through the various parts of the heater/ventilation system. The flap valves are contained in the air distribution housing which acts as a central distribution unit, passing air to the various ducts and vents.

3 Cold air enters the system through the grille at the rear of the engine compartment, and is filtered by a fine-mesh filter (pollen filter) mounted behind the glovebox to remove particles like dust and pollen before they enter the cabin.

4 The air (boosted by the four-speed blower fan if required) then flows through the various ducts, according to the settings of the controls. Stale air is expelled through ducts at the rear of the car. If warm air is required, the cold air is passed through the heater matrix, which is heated by the engine coolant.

5 A recirculation control enables the outside air supply to be closed off, while the air inside the car is recirculated. This can be useful to prevent unpleasant odours entering from outside the car, but should only be used briefly, as the recirculated air inside the car will soon deteriorate.

9 Heater/ventilation system components – removal and refitting

Heater/ventilation control panel

1 Carefully pull the heater control knob to release it from the bottom of the radio/CD trim panel, and undo the retaining screw **(see illustrations)**.

2 Using a plastic trim tool, carefully lever the radio/CD unit trim panel from the facia **(see illustration)**. Disconnect the wiring connectors from the switches and radio/CD on removal.

7.4a Undo the retaining bolts...

7.4b... and remove the coolant pump and sealing ring – arrowed

7.9a Fit new sealing ring to the cover...

7.9b... and fit the coolant pump

9.1a Remove the heater switch...

9.1b... and undo the retaining screw

9.2 Carefully lever the trim panel from the facia

9.3 Disconnect the wiring plug from the back of the heater control panel

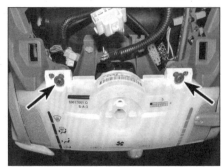

9.4a Undo the two retaining screws...

9.4b... and withdraw the control panel

9.6 Unclip the outer cable, then detach the inner cable from the lever

9.7 Note how the air distribution and temperature cables are routed

3 Disconnect the wiring connector from the rear of the heater control panel **(see illustration)**.

4 Undo the two retaining screws from the top of the heater control panel and withdraw it from the facia panel **(see illustrations)**. Note: The panel cannot be completely withdrawn at this moment, as the control cables are still connected.

5 For reference, the heater control cables to the back of the unit are colour-coded as follows:
a) *Recirculation control (centre) – white.*
b) *Air distribution control (left) – blue.*
c) *Temperature control (right) – black.*

6 Working inside the driver's side footwell, disconnect the heater temperature control cable (black), from the right-hand side of the heater unit **(see illustration)**. This will allow the heater control panel to be withdrawn from the facia at the right-hand side to access the other two cables.

7 With the control panel withdrawn, release the blue and white heater cables from the rear of the control panel **(see illustration)**, noting their fitted position (see paragraph 5).

8 The control panel can now be completely removed, complete with temperature control cable (black). Note the routing of the cables as the panel is withdrawn.

9 Refit the control panel to the facia, making sure the cables are routed in the correct way and the ends are securely attached to the rear of the control panel.

10 Further refitting is a reversal of removal. Check the operation of the heater controls before refitting the radio/CD.

Heater blower motor switch

11 Remove the heater control panel as described earlier in this Section.

12 Release the retaining clips and withdraw the heater blower motor switch from the rear of the control panel **(see illustrations)**.

13 Refitting is a reversal of removal.

Recirculation control cable

14 Remove the heater control panel as described earlier in this Section.

15 Remove the upper section of the facia panel as described in Chapter 11 Section 26.

16 Trace the cable (white) from the rear of the heater control panel across to the upper left-hand side of the heater unit, noting its routing. Release the cable from any clips or ties.

17 Unclip the outer cable at the control lever on the heater unit **(see illustration)**, then slide the end fitting off sideways.

18 Refitting is a reversal of removal. Ensure that the cable is routed as before, and then hook on the end fitting and clip in the outer cable exactly as before. Check its operation before refitting the upper panel.

Air distribution cable

19 Remove the heater control panel as described earlier in this Section.

20 Remove the upper section of the facia panel as described in Chapter 11 Section 26.

21 Trace the cable (blue) from the rear of the heater control panel across to the upper left-hand side of the heater unit, noting its routing. Release the cable from any clips or ties.

22 Unclip the outer cable at the control lever on the heater unit **(see illustration)**, then slide the end fitting off sideways.

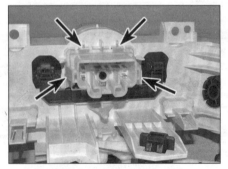

9.12a Release the retaining clips (arrowed)...

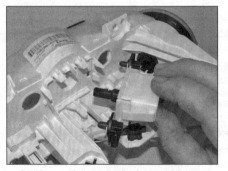

9.12b... and remove the heater blower switch

9.17 Unclip the outer cable from the retaining clip

9.22 Unclip the outer cable, then detach the inner cable from the lever

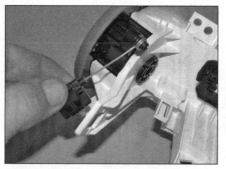

9.25a Unclip the outer cable retaining clip...

9.25b... and release the securing clip to remove the inner cable

23 Refitting is a reversal of removal. Ensure that the cable is routed as before, and then hook on the end fitting and clip in the outer cable exactly as before. Check its operation before refitting the upper panel.

Temperature control cable

24 Remove the heater control panel as described earlier in this Section.
25 Unclip the outer cable (black) at the control lever and then slide the end fitting off the temperature control switch **(see illustrations)**. Do not disturb the position of the control lever, if possible.
26 Refitting is a reversal of removal. Ensure that the cable is routed as before, and then hook on the end fitting and clip in the outer cable exactly as before. Check its operation before refitting the upper panel.

Heater blower motor

27 Remove the upper section of the facia panel as described in Chapter 11 Section 26.
28 With reference to Chapter 6, unbolt the clutch pedal from the bulkhead to allow the heater blower motor to be withdrawn from the right-hand rear of the heater unit housing.
29 Disconnect the wiring connector from the top of the heater blower motor **(see illustration)**.
30 Release the securing clip on the top of the heater motor, then turn it anti-clockwise and withdraw the motor from the heater unit **(see illustrations)**.
31 Refitting is a reversal of removal.

Heater blower motor resistor

32 Remove the upper section of the facia panel as described in Chapter 11 Section 26.
33 Disconnect the wiring connector **(see illustration)** from the upper left-hand side

of the heater unit housing at the rear of the heater blower motor.
34 Withdraw the resistor from the top of the heater unit **(see illustration)**.
35 Refitting is a reversal of removal.

Heater matrix

Models with air-conditioning

Note: *On models with air conditioning, the heater matrix can be removed without removing the complete heater unit, as follows.*
36 Drain the cooling system as described in Chapter 1 Section 23.
37 Remove the centre console and upper section of the facia panel as described in Chapter 11.
38 Unclip the passenger side kick-panel from the bottom of the A-pillar and remove the facia lower retaining bolt **(see illustrations)**.

9.29 Disconnect the blower motor wiring connector

9.30a Release the retaining clip...

9.30b... and twist the motor to remove from the housing

9.33 Disconnect the blower motor resistor wiring connector

9.34 Unclip the resistor from the top of the housing

9.38a Unclip the side trim panel...

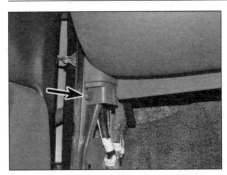

9.38b... and undo the retaining bolt –
arrowed

9.39 Undo the facia lower mounting bolt

9.40a Undo the two retaining bolts...

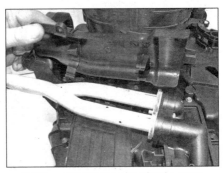

9.40b... and remove the plastic cover

9.41a Undo the retaining screw...

9.41b... and withdraw the pipes from the
heater matrix

39 Undo the facia panel lower retaining bolt **(see illustration)**, and then pull the bottom of the facia outwards to access the heater matrix coolant pipes.

40 Working inside the passenger footwell, undo the two retaining bolts and remove the plastic cover from the coolant pipes on the left-hand side of the heater unit housing **(see illustrations)**.

41 Undo the retaining screw and remove the coolant pipes from the heater matrix noting their fitted position **(see illustrations)**. Note the alignment marks on the pipes for refitting.

42 Remove the two retaining bolts, and then carefully slide the heater matrix out from the side of the heater unit **(see illustration)**. Pull the lower part of the facia outwards, taking care not to damage the heater matrix, as it is withdrawn.

43 Refitting is a reversal of removal, noting the following points:
a) *Check the condition of the rubber O-ring seals where the pipes join the heater matrix – if necessary, fit new ones.*
b) *Make sure the marks on the coolant pipes, noted on removal, are aligned.*
c) *Refit the centre console and upper facia panel with reference to Chapter 11.*
d) *On completion, fill and bleed the cooling system as described in Chapter 1 Section 23.*

Models without air-conditioning

Note: *To remove the heater matrix on models without air conditioning, the complete heater unit will need to be removed. This is because the coolant pipes that pass through the bulkhead are a complete part of the heater matrix.*

44 Remove the heater unit as described in paragraphs 47 to 55, later in this Section.

45 Remove the two retaining bolts, and then carefully slide the heater matrix out from the side of the heater unit.

46 Refitting is a reversal of removal, noting the following points:
a) *Refit the heater unit as described later in this Section.*
b) *On completion, fill and bleed the cooling system as described in Chapter 1 Section 23.*

Heater unit

⚠️ *Warning: On models with air conditioning, the system must be discharged before starting this procedure. The air conditioning pipes must be disconnected where they pass through the bulkhead (see Section 10 of this Chapter). Discharging the air conditioning system must be carried out by a specialist, or by a Peugeot dealer. Do not carry out this work unless the system has been discharged.*

47 Drain the cooling system as described in Chapter 1 Section 23.

48 Where fitted, have the air conditioning system professionally discharged.

49 At the rear of the engine compartment, release the spring-type hose clips and disconnect the two coolant hoses which pass through the bulkhead to the heater **(see illustration)**.

50 Remove the upper and lower sections of

9.42 Carefully slide the heater matrix out of
the heater unit

9.49 Release the spring clips and disconnect
the heater hoses from the bulkhead

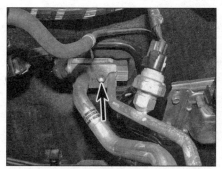

9.51 Air conditioning pipe retaining clamp bolt – arrowed

9.52a Disconnect the wiring connectors from the blower resistor...

9.52b... the evaporator sensor...

9.52c...and the heater blower motor

9.53 Disconnect the heater drain tube

9.54a Undo the three heater housing upper mounting nuts (arrowed)

the facia panel as described in Chapter 11 Section 26. Also remove the facia cross-member.

51 On models with air conditioning, there will be two additional pipes passing through the bulkhead, with a single bolt securing their retaining plate – once the bolt is removed, the plate can be released, and the pipes disconnected **(see illustration)**. New seals will be required on refitting. Do not disturb the refrigerant pipes unless the system has been discharged first (see Section 10) – for maximum personal safety, have these pipes disconnected by the engineer who discharges the system for you, and ensure the system is kept switched off afterwards.

52 Disconnect the three wiring connectors from the top of the heater unit **(see**

illustrations). Check around the heater unit housing and disconnect any wiring clips securing the wiring loom.

53 Disconnect the heater unit drain tube from the front right-hand side of the housing **(see illustration)**.

54 The heater unit is secured to the bulkhead by five securing nuts. Three nuts at the top of the unit, one nut on the passenger side, and one at the driver's side of the unit **(see illustrations)**.

55 Remove the nuts, and then with the aid of an assistant, ease the heater unit away from the bulkhead **(see illustration)**. Keep the unit tilted back slightly to avoid coolant spilling onto the carpet. Plug the heater matrix pipes as soon as possible.

56 Refitting is a reversal of removal, noting the following points:

a) Check the condition of the rubber

grommet(s) where the pipes pass through the bulkhead – if necessary, fit new ones.

b) Refit the facia and trim panels with reference to Chapter 11 Section 26.

c) On completion, fill and bleed the cooling system as described in Chapter 1 Section 23.

d) On models with air conditioning, have the refrigerant pipes reconnected (using new O-ring seals) and the system recharged by a specialist or a franchised dealer.

Facia vents

57 The facia air vents are part of the upper facia panel and do not appear to separate from the upper panel. If required, remove the upper facia panel, as described in Chapter 11 Section 26.

58 Each end vent has an outer ring trim,

9.54b Undo the heater housing left-hand lower mounting nut...

9.54c... and the right-hand lower mounting nut

9.55 Withdraw the heater unit away from the bulkhead

9.58a Unclip the heater vent outer ring trim...

9.58b... noting its locating peg for refitting

10.2 Air conditioning low- and high-pressure refrigerant pipes

which can be removed by carefully unclipping from the facia panel **(see illustrations)**.

59 Refitting is a reversal of removal. If removed, refit the upper facia panel as described in Chapter 11 Section 26.

10 Air conditioning system – general information and precautions

General information

1 Air conditioning is available on certain models. It enables the temperature of incoming air to be lowered, and also dehumidifies the air, which makes for rapid demisting and increased comfort.

2 The cooling side of the system works in the same way as a domestic refrigerator. Refrigerant gas is drawn into a belt-driven compressor, and passes into a condenser mounted in front of the radiator, where it loses heat and becomes liquid. The liquid passes through an expansion valve to an evaporator, where it changes from liquid under high pressure to gas under low pressure **(see illustration)**. This change is accompanied by a drop in temperature, which then cools the evaporator. The refrigerant returns to the compressor, and the cycle begins again.

3 Air blown through the evaporator passes to the heater assembly, where it is mixed with hot air blown through the heater matrix, to achieve the desired temperature in the passenger compartment.

4 The heating side of the system works

in the same way as on models without air conditioning (see Section 8).

5 The operation of the system is controlled electronically. Any problems with the system should be referred to a franchised dealer or an air conditioning specialist in the first instance.

Precautions

6 Warning: The air conditioning system is under high pressure. Do not loosen any fittings or remove any components until after the system has been discharged. Air conditioning refrigerant should be properly discharged at a dealer service department or an automotive air conditioning repair facility capable of handling R134a refrigerant. Always wear eye protection when disconnecting air conditioning system fittings.

7 When an air conditioning system is fitted, it is necessary to observe the following special precautions whenever dealing with any part of the system, its associated components, and any items which necessitate disconnection of the system:

a) *While the refrigerant used – R134a – is less damaging to the environment than the previously-used R12, it is still a very dangerous substance. It must not be allowed into contact with the skin or eyes, as there is a risk of frostbite. It must also not be discharged in an enclosed space – while it is not toxic, there is a risk of suffocation. The refrigerant is heavier than air, and so must never be discharged over a pit.*

b) *The refrigerant must not be allowed to come in contact with a naked flame, otherwise a poisonous gas will be created*

– *under certain circumstances, this can form an explosive mixture with air. For similar reasons, smoking in the presence of refrigerant is highly dangerous, particularly if the vapour is inhaled through a lighted cigarette.*

c) *Never discharge the system to the atmosphere – R134a is not an ozone-depleting ChloroFluoroCarbon (CFC) like R12, but is instead a hydro fluorocarbon, which causes environmental damage by contributing to the 'greenhouse effect' if released into the atmosphere.*

d) *R134a refrigerant must not be mixed with R12; the system uses different seals and has different fittings requiring different tools, so that there is no chance of the two types of refrigerant becoming mixed accidentally.*

e) *If for any reason the system must be disconnected, entrust this task to your franchised dealer or a refrigeration engineer.*

f) *It is essential that the system be professionally discharged prior to using any form of heat – welding, soldering, brazing, etc – in the vicinity of the system, before having the car oven-dried at a temperature exceeding 70°C after repainting, and before disconnecting any part of the system.*

11 Air conditioning system components – removal and refitting

⚠ **Warning: Read the precautions given in Section 10, and have the system discharged by a franchised dealer or an air conditioning specialist. Do not carry out the following work unless the system has been discharged.**

Pressure relief valve

Removal

1 The pressure relief valve can be removed by disconnecting the two pipes passing through the bulkhead at the rear of the engine compartment.

2 With the system discharged, undo the retaining bolt and disconnect the refrigerant lines from the pressure relief valve **(see illustrations)**. Plug the ends of the lines to

11.2a Undo the retaining bolt...

11.2b... and disconnect the refrigerant pipes

prevent dirt ingress. Discard the O-ring seals – new ones must be used when refitting. Do not disturb the refrigerant pipes unless the system has been discharged first (see Section 10) – for maximum personal safety, have these pipes disconnected by the engineer who discharges the system for you, and ensure the system is kept switched off afterwards.

3 Undo the two retaining bolts and remove the pressure relief valve from the heater unit **(see illustration)**. New seals will be required on refitting.

Refitting

4 Refitting is a reversal of removal, noting the following points:

a) *Use new O-rings* **(see illustration)**, *coated with refrigerant oil, when reconnecting the refrigerant lines.*

b) *Have the system professionally recharged and tested on completion.*

Pressure switch (Pressostat)

Removal

5 The pressure switch is located in the high-pressure refrigerant line at the rear of the engine compartment **(see illustration)**.

6 With the system discharged, disconnect the wiring connector and unscrew the pressure switch from the high-pressure refrigerant line. Discard the O-ring seals – new ones must be used when refitting. Do not disturb the system unless it has been discharged (see Section 10)

Refitting

7 Refitting is a reversal of removal, noting the following points:

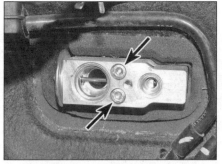

11.3 Pressure relief valve retaining bolts – arrowed

a) *Use new O-rings, coated with refrigerant oil, when reconnecting the refrigerant lines.*

b) *Have the system professionally recharged and tested on completion.*

Compressor

Note: *If the compressor is being removed as part of another procedure, it may not be necessary to have the system discharged. Usually, the compressor can be unbolted and tied to one side without the need to disturb the refrigerant lines* **(see illustration).**

Removal

8 Jack up the front of the car, and support it on axle stands (see *Jacking and vehicle support*). Remove the driver's side front wheel and inner wheel arch liner.

9 Remove the auxiliary drivebelt as described in Chapter 1 Section 21.

11.4 Fit new O-rings to the refrigerant pipes

10 Disconnect the compressor wiring plug **(see illustration)**, and release the wiring from the securing clip.

11 With the system discharged, disconnect the refrigerant lines from the compressor **(see illustration)**. Plug the ends of the lines and the compressor to prevent dirt ingress. Discard the O-ring seals – new ones must be used when refitting.

12 Support the compressor, then remove the three mounting bolts, and alternator adjusting bracket retaining bolt. Lower the compressor out from the engine compartment **(see illustrations)**.

Refitting

13 Refitting is a reversal of removal, noting the following points:

a) *Use new O-rings, coated with refrigerant oil, when reconnecting the refrigerant lines.*

11.5 Air conditioning pressure switch – arrowed

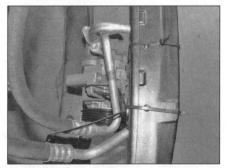

11.8 Secure the compressor to the vehicle crossmember if required

11.10 Disconnect the compressor wiring connector

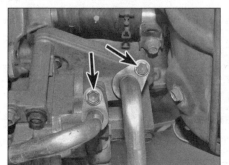

11.11 Undo the refrigerant pipe retaining bolts – arrowed

11.12a Undo the retaining bolts...

11.12b... and remove the compressor from the engine

11.15 Slide the heater matrix upwards out of the heater unit

11.16 Unclip the evaporator sensor wiring from the housing

11.17a Peel back the foam pad...

11.17b... undo the two retaining bolts...

11.17c... and slide the plastic housing from the relief valve

15 Remove the two retaining bolts, and then carefully slide the heater matrix out from the left-hand side of the heater unit housing **(see illustration)**.

16 Unclip the evaporator sensor wiring from the heater housing and move it to one side, noting its fitted position **(see illustration)**.

17 Peel back the foam sealing ring, undo the two retaining bolts and slide the plastic cover from around the pressure relief valve **(see illustrations)**.

18 Slacken and remove the retaining bolts that secure the air intake/pollen filter housing to the main heater unit housing, release the securing clip and twist the housing to remove it from the main heater housing **(see illustrations)**.

19 Undo the three retaining bolts and remove the plastic cover from the end of the evaporator **(see illustrations)**.

20 Unclip the evaporator sensor wiring and withdraw the evaporator from the heater unit housing **(see illustrations)**.

Refitting

21 Refitting is a reversal of removal, noting the following points:

a) Refit the heater unit as described in Section 9.

b) Refit the facia and trim panels with reference to Chapter 11 Section 26.

c) On completion, fill and bleed the cooling system as described in Chapter 1 Section 23.

d) Have the refrigerant pipes reconnected

b) Tighten the compressor mounting bolts to the specified torque.

c) Have the system professionally recharged and tested on completion.

Evaporator

Removal

14 Remove the heater unit as described in Section 9.

11.18a Remove the two securing bolts...

11.18c... and twist the housing to remove

11.18b... release the securing clip...

11.19a Undo the retaining bolts...

11.19b... and remove the plastic cover

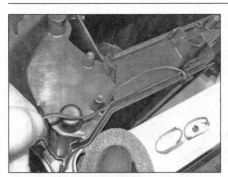
11.20a Unclip the sensor wiring from the housing...

11.20b... and slide the evaporator out from the heater unit

11.22 Carefully unclip the sensor from the fins in the evaporator

11.25a Unbolt the horn...

11.25b... and remove the air deflectors

11.26a Disconnect the refrigerant lines from the top...

(using new O-ring seals) and the system recharged by a specialist or a Peugeot dealer.

Evaporator sensor

22 The evaporator sensor is a press-fit in the side of the evaporator. Remove the evaporator as described in paragraphs 14 to 20, and then pull the sensor to remove it from the evaporator, taking care not to damage the evaporator **(see illustration)**.

Condenser

Removal

23 Apply the handbrake, then jack up the front of the car and support securely on axle stands (see *Jacking and vehicle support*).
24 Remove the front bumper as described in Chapter 11 Section 6.
25 Undo the retaining bolt and remove the horn from the front of the condenser. Release the retaining clips and remove the air deflectors from each side of the condenser **(see illustrations)**.
26 With the system discharged, disconnect the refrigerant lines from the condenser **(see illustrations)**. Discard the O-rings – new ones must be used when refitting.
27 Remove the two bolts from the top of the condenser, tilt the top of the condenser forwards and lift it upwards to disengage it from the bottom of the radiator **(see illustrations)**. The condenser can then be lowered out from the front of the vehicle.

Refitting

28 Refitting is a reversal of removal, noting the following points:
a) Use new O-rings **(see illustration)**, coated

with refrigerant oil, when reconnecting the refrigerant lines.
b) Have the system professionally recharged and tested on completion.

11.26b... and bottom of the condenser

11.27a Undo the two upper retaining bolts...

11.27b... unclip the lower part of the condenser from the radiator

11.28 Fit new O-rings to the refrigerant pipes

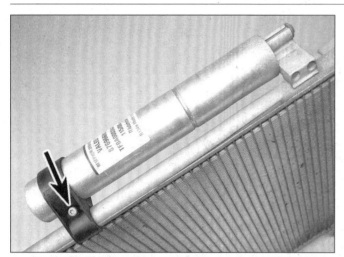

11.30 Undo the support bracket retaining screw – arrowed

11.31 Remove the cartridge lower retaining bolt – arrowed

Condenser filtering/ drying cartridge

Removal

29 Remove the condenser as described in paragraphs 23 to 27 of this Section.

30 Slacken and remove the retaining screw from the upper support bracket (see illustration).

31 Undo the retaining bolt and withdraw the filtering/drying cartridge from the condenser (see illustration). Discard the O-rings – new ones must be used when refitting.

Refitting

32 Refitting is a reversal of removal, noting the following points:

a) Use new O-rings, coated with refrigerant oil, when reconnecting the refrigerant lines.

b) Have the system professionally recharged and tested on completion.

Chapter 4 Part A
Fuel system

Contents

Degrees of difficulty

Easy, suitable for novice with little experience		Fairly easy, suitable for beginner with some experience		Fairly difficult, suitable for competent DIY mechanic		Difficult, suitable for experienced DIY mechanic		Very difficult, suitable for expert DIY or professional	

Specifications

General

System type	Bosch ME 7.9.5, EFI sequential multiport fuel injection
Fuel octane requirement.	Unleaded 95 RON or higher
Injection period when idling (ECU-controlled):	
Up to 12/08.	1.92 to 3.37 ms
From 12/08	1.30 to 3.10 ms
Fuel pressure	3.0 to 3.5 bars
Fuel injector assembly:	
Resistance	11.6 to 12.4 ohms @ 20°C
Injector volume (per 15 seconds)	47 to 58 cc
Difference between each injector	15 cc or less
Fuel pump assembly resistance.	0.2 to 3.0 ohms @ 20°C
Ignition timing advance (ECU-controlled).	8 to 12° BTDC
Idle speed (ECU-controlled)	840 ± 50 rpm

Sensor resistances

Camshaft or crankshaft position sensor (at 20°C)	1850 to 2450 ohms

Torque wrench settings

	Nm	lbf ft
Camshaft position sensor	8	6
Crankshaft position sensor	8	6
Fuel rail mounting bolts	27	20
Fuel tank mounting bolts	14	10
Inlet manifold nuts/bolts.	19	14
Manifold Absolute Pressure (MAP) sensor.	5	4
Throttle body mounting bolts.	10	7

1.5 Crankshaft sensor target ring, with flat (arrowed) for timing mark

1.6 Camshaft sensor target pegs (three) on the end of the inlet camshaft

1 General information and precautions

General information

1 The fuel system consists of a fuel tank (mounted under the floor, beneath the rear seats), fuel hoses, an electric fuel pump mounted in the fuel tank, and a sequential electronic fuel injection system controlled by an engine management electronic control unit (ECU).

2 The electric fuel pump supplies fuel under pressure to the fuel rail, which distributes fuel to the injectors. A pressure regulator fitted to the pump itself controls the system pressure at the pump end. With this system there is no fuel return line, reducing evaporative emissions caused by warmer fuel returning to the fuel tank. From the fuel rail, fuel is injected into the inlet ports, just above the inlet valves, by three fuel injectors. The fuel rail is mounted to the cylinder head, just above the plastic inlet manifold.

3 The amount of fuel supplied by the injectors is precisely controlled by the ECU. The ECU uses the signals from the crankshaft position sensor and the camshaft position sensor to trigger each injector separately in cylinder firing order (sequential injection), with benefits in terms of better fuel economy and leaner exhaust emissions.

4 The ECU is the heart of the entire engine management system, controlling the fuel injection, ignition and emissions control systems. The ECU receives information from various sensors, which is then computed and compared with preset values stored in its memory, to determine the required period of injection.

5 Information on crankshaft position and engine speed is generated by a crankshaft position sensor. The inductive head of the sensor runs just inboard of the crankshaft sprocket, and scans the teeth on a special sensor plate fitted behind the timing chain cover **(see illustration)**. As the crankshaft rotates, the sensor transmits a pulse to the ECU every time a tooth passes it. The teeth are 10° apart, and there are missing teeth

together on the sensor plate – the ECU recognises the absence of a pulse from the crankshaft position sensor at this point to establish a reference mark for crankshaft position. Similarly, the time interval between absent pulses is used to determine engine speed. This information is then fed to the ECU for further processing.

6 The camshaft position sensor is located at the transmission end of the cylinder head, and functions similarly to the crankshaft position sensor. In this case, however, there are three lugs – one for each cylinder – **(see illustration)** fitted to a plate on the end of the inlet camshaft. These provide a sensor signal which is used by the ECU to calculate the correct fuel and ignition timing, and is also used to control the variable valve timing system (VVT-i).

7 Engine temperature information is supplied by the coolant temperature sensor (see Chapter 3). The sensor is an NTC (Negative Temperature Coefficient) thermistor – that is, a semi-conductor whose electrical resistance decreases as its temperature increases. The sensor provides the ECU with a constantly varying (analogue) voltage signal, corresponding to the temperature of the engine coolant. This is used to refine the calculations made by the ECU when determining the correct amount of fuel required to achieve the ideal air/fuel mixture ratio.

8 Inlet air temperature and pressure for air/ fuel mixture ratio calculations is provided by a manifold absolute pressure (MAP) sensor fitted to the inlet manifold.

9 The throttle valve inside the throttle body is controlled by the driver, through the accelerator pedal. This is either done electronically or by cable depending on model. As the valve opens, the amount of air that can pass through the system increases. As the throttle valve opens further, the MAP sensor signal alters, and the ECU opens each injector for a longer duration, to increase the amount of fuel delivered to the inlet ports.

10 A throttle position sensor is mounted on the end of the throttle valve spindle to provide the ECU with a constantly varying (analogue) voltage signal corresponding to the throttle opening. This allows the ECU to register the

driver's input when determining the amount of fuel required by the engine. An idle speed control valve allows the ECU to adjust the idle speed as necessary, to aid driveability, and to provide an anti-stall function determined by engine temperature and the load caused by engine-driven accessories.

11 Roadspeed is monitored by the vehicle speed sensor. This component is a Hall-effect generator, mounted on top of the transmission, in place of the old speedometer drive. It supplies the ECU with a series of pulses corresponding to the car's roadspeed, enabling the ECU to control features such as the fuel shut-off on overrun.

12 An oxygen sensor in the exhaust system provides the ECU with constant feedback – 'closed-loop' control, which enables it to adjust the mixture to provide the best possible operating conditions for the catalytic converter. A further sensor is fitted downstream of the converter, to monitor the converter's operation, and this provides an even finer degree of emission control.

13 Both the idle speed and mixture are under the control of the ECU, and cannot be adjusted.

Precautions

⚠️ *Warning: Many of the procedures in this Chapter require the removal of fuel lines and connections, which may result in some fuel spillage. Before carrying out any operation on the fuel system, refer to the precautions given in Safety first! at the beginning of this manual, and follow them implicitly. Petrol is a highly dangerous and volatile liquid, and the precautions necessary when handling it cannot be overstressed.*

Note: *Residual pressure will remain in the fuel lines long after the car was last used. When disconnecting any fuel line, first depressurise the fuel system as described in Section 2.*

Note: *Before disconnecting any of the fuel injection system sensor wiring plugs, ensure at least that the ignition is switched off (ideally, disconnect the battery). If this is not done, it could result in a fault code being logged in the system memory, and may even cause damage to the component concerned.*

2 Fuel system – depressurisation

⚠️ *Warning: The following procedure will merely relieve the pressure in the fuel system – remember that fuel will still be present in the system components, and take precautions accordingly before disconnecting any of them.*

Note: *Refer to the warning note in Section 1 before proceeding.*

1 The fuel system referred to in this Chapter is defined as the fuel tank and tank-mounted fuel

4.3a Unclip the plastic cover...

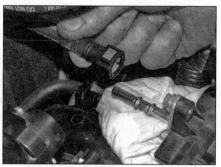

4.3b... disconnect the fuel pipe...

4.3c... and plug the ends to prevent dirt ingress

pump/fuel gauge sender unit, fuel pressure regulator, the fuel filter, the fuel injectors, and the metal pipes and flexible hoses of the fuel lines between these components. All these contain fuel which will be under pressure while the engine is running and/or while the ignition is switched on.

2 The pressure will remain for some time after the ignition has been switched off, and must be relieved before any of these components is disturbed for servicing work.

3 The simplest depressurisation method is to disconnect the fuel pump electrical supply by removing the fuel pump fuse. Make sure the ignition is switched off, and then remove the fuel system fuse, with reference to Chapter 12 Section 3.

4 Start the engine; allow the engine to idle until it stops through lack of fuel. Turn the engine over once or twice on the starter to ensure that all pressure is released, then switch off the ignition; do not forget to refit the fuse when work is complete.

5 Note that once the fuel system has been depressurised and drained (even partially), it will take significantly longer to restart the engine – perhaps several seconds of cranking – before the system is refilled and pressure restored.

3 Unleaded petrol – general information and usage

1 All petrol models are designed to run on fuel with a minimum octane rating of 95 (RON). All models have a catalytic converter, and so must be run on unleaded fuel only. Under no circumstances should leaded fuel (UK '4-star' or LRP) be used, as this will damage the converter.

2 Super unleaded petrol (98/99 octane) can also be used in all models if wished, though there is no advantage in doing so.

4 Fuel lines and fittings – general information

Note: Refer to the warning note in Section 1 before proceeding.

Quick-release couplings

1 Quick-release couplings are employed at many of the unions in the fuel feed and return lines.

2 Before disconnecting any fuel system component, relieve the residual pressure in the system (see Section 2), and equalise tank pressure by removing the fuel filler cap.

⚠️ Warning: This procedure will merely relieve the increased pressure necessary for the engine to run – remember that fuel will still be present in the system components, and take precautions accordingly before disconnecting any of them.

3 Unclip the plastic shield fitted around the connector, and then release the securing clips and pull off the fuel pipe (see illustrations). Use a rag to soak up any spilt fuel. Note which pipe is connected to which, and ensure that they are correctly reconnected on refitting. Plug the ends of the fuel lines to prevent dirt ingress.

4 To reconnect one of these couplings, line them up, press them firmly together, and twist the fitting clockwise to secure. Clip on the plastic collar to finish. Switch the ignition on and off five times to pressurise the system, and check for any sign of fuel leakage around the disturbed coupling before attempting to start the engine.

Checking fuel lines

5 Checking procedures for the fuel lines are included in Chapter 1.

Component renewal

6 If any damaged sections are to be renewed, use original-equipment hoses or pipes, constructed from the same material as the section being renewed. Do not install substitutes constructed from inferior or inappropriate material; this could cause a fuel leak or a fire.

7 Before detaching or disconnecting any part of the fuel system, note the routing of all hoses and pipes, and the orientation of all clamps and clips. New sections must be installed in exactly the same manner.

8 Before disconnecting any part of the fuel system, be sure to relieve the fuel system pressure (see Section 2), and equalise tank pressure by removing the fuel filler cap. Also disconnect the battery negative (earth) lead – see Disconnecting the battery in Reference. Cover the fitting being disconnected with a rag to absorb any fuel that may spray out.

5 Air cleaner assembly – removal and refitting

Removal

1 The lower part of the air cleaner assembly is part of the cylinder head cover.

2 Release the four spring clips on the side of the air cleaner cover (see illustration).

3 Slacken the two securing clips from the throttle housing and breather pipe (see illustration), and then lift the air cleaner cover from the top of the engine.

5.2 Release the four retaining clips...

5.3... and two hose clips...

5.4... and remove the air filter element

6.2 Unclip the cable retaining clip from the top of the pedal

6.4 Slacken the cable adjuster nuts

6.5 Unclip the inner cable from the throttle linkage

6.10 Adjust the nuts (arrowed) to take up the slack in the cable

4 Noting how it is fitted, withdraw the air filter element from the housing **(see illustration)**.

5 If required, remove the cylinder head cover (lower part of the air cleaner assembly), with reference Chapter 2A, Section 4.

Refitting

6 Refitting is a reversal of removal. If removed, refit the cylinder head cover as described in Chapter 2A Section 4, and refit the air filter element with reference to Chapter 1 Section 18.

---

6 Accelerator cable – removal, refitting and adjustment

Note: *On some models, there is no accelerator cable fitted, these have an electronic throttle body, which is controlled through wiring to the ECU and sensors on the throttle body.*

7.2 Throttle pedal retaining bolts (cable-operated)

Removal

1 To improve access, move the driver's seat fully to the rear.

2 Disconnect the inner cable from the top of the pedal by releasing the end fitting and sliding the cable out sideways **(see illustration)**.

3 Remove the air cleaner cover as described in Section 5, paragraphs 2 and 3.

4 At the throttle body, loosen the adjuster nuts and detach the outer cable from the adjuster/support bracket. If the same cable is being refitted, it may be worth measuring the amount of exposed thread on the cable adjuster, so it can be reset to its original setting **(see illustration)**.

5 Disconnect the inner cable from the quadrant on the throttle body **(see illustration)**.

6 Release the cable from the securing clips in the engine compartment, and withdraw it from the bulkhead.

7.3 Disconnect the wiring connector – arrowed

Refitting

7 Refitting is a reversal of removal, ensuring that the cable is routed as before, and secured by all the clips. Make sure the rubber grommet is fitted correctly in the bulkhead. When the cable is reconnected at each end, adjust the cable as follows.

Adjustment

8 Refit the outer cable to the support bracket, and tighten the nuts by hand.

9 Check that the throttle quadrant moves smoothly and easily from the fully closed to the fully open position and back again as the assistant depresses and releases the accelerator pedal.

10 If there is excess slack in the cable when the accelerator is released, use the adjuster nuts to take up the slack **(see illustration)**. The cable should not however be too tight; otherwise the cable will hold the throttle open when the pedal is released. Adjust as necessary, checking the action of the pedal each time, as described in paragraph 9. On completion, tighten the nuts securely.

11 Take the car for a short road test to confirm correct operation, especially at idle. Remember that a feature of some modern engine management systems is to hold the engine speed above idle, even with the accelerator fully released, until the car comes to a complete stop – this is not a symptom of cable over-adjustment.

---

7 Accelerator pedal – removal and refitting

Note: *On some models, there is no accelerator cable fitted, these have wiring connectors to the accelerator pedal and throttle body.*

Removal

Models with accelerator cable

1 Where fitted, detach the accelerator cable from the pedal (see Section 6).

2 Unscrew the two mounting bolts and remove the pedal assembly from the bulkhead **(see illustration)**.

Models without accelerator cable

3 On models with an electronic throttle body, disconnect the wiring connector from the top of the pedal **(see illustration)**.
4 Unscrew the two mounting nuts and remove the pedal assembly from the mounting bracket studs **(see illustration)**.

Refitting

5 Refit in the reverse order of removal. On completion, check the action of the pedal to ensure that the throttle has full unrestricted movement, and fully returns when released.
6 Where fitted, check and if necessary adjust the accelerator cable as described in Section 6.

8 Fuel pump/fuel pressure – checking

Note: *Refer to the warning note in Section 1 before proceeding.*

Fuel pump

1 Switch on the ignition, and listen for the fuel pump (the sound of an electric motor running, audible from beneath the rear seats). Assuming there is sufficient fuel in the tank, the pump should start and run for approximately one or two seconds, then stop, each time the ignition is switched on.
2 If the pump does not run at all, check the fuse, relay and wiring (refer to the wiring diagrams in Chapter 12).

Fuel pressure

3 A fuel pressure gauge will be required for this check, and should be connected in the fuel line at the fuel inlet connection at the rear of the engine compartment, in accordance with the gauge maker's instructions.
4 Start the engine and allow it to idle. Note the gauge reading as soon as the pressure stabilises, and compare it with the regulated fuel pressure as specified by the manufacturer (see your local dealer).
a) If the pressure is high, renew the fuel pressure regulator.
b) If the pressure is low, this also suggests a fuel pressure regulator problem. However, low voltage to the fuel pump, a faulty fuel

7.4 Throttle pedal retaining nuts (electronically-operated)

pump, or a blocked fuel pump filter (or other blockage in the fuel line) could be the cause.
5 Switch off the engine. Verify that a significant pressure remains for five minutes after the engine is turned off.
6 Carefully disconnect the fuel pressure gauge, depressurising the system first as described in Section 2. Be sure to cover the fitting with a rag before slackening it. Mop-up any spilt petrol.
7 Run the engine, and check that there are no fuel leaks.

9 Fuel tank – removal, inspection and refitting

Note: *Refer to the warning note in Section 1 before proceeding.*

9.5 Slacken the retaining clip – arrowed

Removal

1 Before removing the fuel tank, all the fuel must be drained from the tank. Since a fuel tank drain plug is not provided, it is therefore preferable to carry out the removal operation when the tank is nearly empty. Before proceeding, disconnect the battery negative terminal (refer to *Disconnecting the battery* in Reference), and siphon or hand-pump the remaining fuel from the tank.
2 Relieve the residual pressure in the fuel system (see Section 2), and equalise tank pressure by removing the fuel filler cap.
3 Referring to Section 10, working inside the vehicle, disconnect the wiring plug and pipes from the top of the fuel pump/gauge sender unit.
4 Chock the front wheels, then jack up the rear of the car and support it on axle stands (see *Jacking and vehicle support*). Remove the left-hand rear wheel, to access the fuel filler pipe.
5 Slacken the securing clip from the fuel filler pipe to the rubber hose on the fuel tank **(see illustration)**.
6 Undo the retaining bolt, and disconnect the fuel filler pipe from the fuel tank rubber hose and the rubber grommet in the left-hand rear body panel **(see illustrations)**. Remove the fuel filler pipe; be prepared for fuel spillage when the filler pipe is disconnected. Note the fuel tank breather tube runs up the inside of the filler pipe.
7 Remove the two fasteners securing the tank lower heat shield to remove the shield **(see illustration)**. This does not need to be

9.6a Undo the retaining bolt (arrowed)...

9.6b... withdraw the fuel filler pipe from the fuel tank...

9.6c... and disconnect it from the rear wing panel

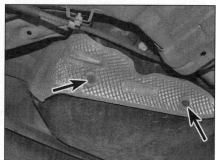
9.7 Heat shield retaining screws

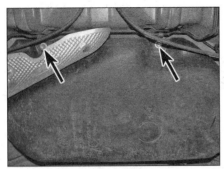

9.9a Undo the two front fuel tank mounting bolts...

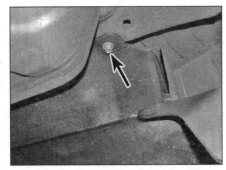

9.9b... right-hand rear mounting bolt...

9.9c... and left-hand rear mounting bolt

9.10a Unclip the outer retaining clip...

9.10b... inner retaining clip...

9.10c... and remove the filler neck rubber grommet

removed, unless you are fitting a new fuel tank.

8 Check round the tank as far as possible to ensure that no pipes or wires are still connected which would prevent it from being lowered.

9 Have either an assistant or a trolley jack with a block of wood support the tank, then work round the tank seam, loosening the four mounting bolts (see illustrations). When the tank is free, lower it to the ground (keeping it level, to reduce the chance of fuel spillage) and remove it from under the car.

10 If required, remove the two inner retaining clips and remove the filler neck rubber grommet from the rear body panel (see illustrations).

Inspection

11 Whilst removed, the fuel tank can be inspected for damage or deterioration. Removal of the fuel pump/fuel gauge sender unit (see Section 10) will allow a partial inspection of the interior. If the tank is contaminated with sediment or water, swill it out with clean fuel. Do not under any circumstances undertake any repairs on a leaking or damaged fuel tank; this work must be carried out by a professional who has experience in this critical and potentially-dangerous work.

12 Whilst the fuel tank is removed from the car, it should be placed in a safe area where sparks or open flames cannot ignite the fumes coming out of the tank. Be especially careful inside garages where a natural-gas type appliance is located, because the pilot light could cause an explosion.

13 Check the condition of the filler pipe and rubber connections, renew if necessary.

Refitting

14 Refitting is a reversal of the removal procedure, noting the following points:
a) Ensure that all pipe and wiring connections are securely fitted.
b) Tighten the tank retaining bolts to the specified torque.
c) If evidence of contamination was found, do not return any previously-drained fuel to the tank unless it is carefully filtered first.

10 Fuel pump/ fuel gauge sender unit – removal and refitting

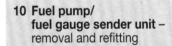
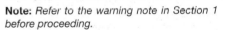

Note: Refer to the warning note in Section 1 before proceeding.

Removal

1 A combined fuel pump, fuel gauge sender unit, pressure regulator and charcoal canister is located in the top face of the fuel tank. An access cover is provided below the rear seat, meaning that the tank does not have to be removed.

2 Disconnect the battery negative (earth) lead (see Disconnecting the battery in the Reference chapter).

3 Remove the rear seat base, as described in Chapter 11 Section 22.

4 Prise up the access cover, which is stuck down with a bead of mastic (see illustration).

5 Disconnect the wiring plug from the top of the pump/sender unit, using a small screwdriver to release the clip (see illustration).

10.4 Cut the seal around the access cover under the rear seat

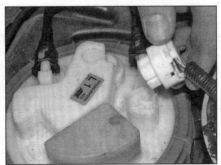

10.5 Disconnect the wiring connector from the pump/sender unit

10.6a Press the securing clips...

10.6b... and disconnect the fuel feed pipe

10.6c Press the securing clips...

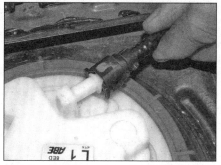

10.6d... and disconnect the fuel return pipe

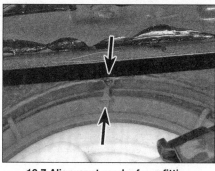

10.7 Alignment marks for refitting

10.8a Using a special tool to unscrew...

6 Squeeze the retaining clips to release the fuel pipes from the top of the unit **(see illustrations)**. Anticipate a small amount of fuel spillage as this is done. Plug the open unions on top of the unit, and also over the disconnected pipes, to prevent dirt getting in.

7 Check the alignment marks on the tank and locking ring for refitting **(see illustration)**.

8 Unscrew the locking ring and remove it from the tank. A special tool is available which fits over the collar and allows it to be released using a socket or spanner **(see illustrations)**. As the locking ring is rotated, take care not to damage the fuel pipe connections.

9 Carefully lift out the fuel pump/sender unit, noting its fitted position. Take care not to damage the pump filter, nor to bend the sender unit float arm (which can get caught up on the tank lip as the unit is removed) **(see illustration)**. Allow any remaining fuel to drain into the tank before finally lifting it clear.

Caution: After the pump/sender unit has been removed from the fuel tank, temporarily refit the locking ring onto the top of the fuel tank to prevent any distortion.

10 At the time of writing, the fuel pump was only available as a complete assembly – check with your local dealer if separate components are available (e.g. pump, sender unit, pressure regulator and charcoal canister).

Refitting

11 Refitting the pump/sender unit is a reversal of removal, noting the following points:

a) Check the condition of the fuel foam filter, and clean it if necessary **(see illustrations)**.

b) Fit a new rubber seal to the top of the fuel tank, before refitting the fuel pump **(see illustration)**.

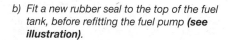

10.8b... and remove the pump/sender unit locking ring

10.9 Lift out the fuel pump/sender unit, and let the excess fuel drain

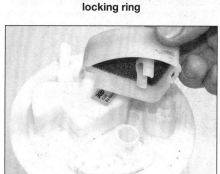

10.11a Unclip the plastic cover...

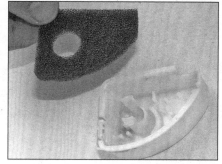

10.11b... and check the foam filter

10.11c Fit new O-ring seal when refitting

c) Tighten the locking ring, until the alignment marks are aligned (see illustration 10.7).
d) Once the unit has been refitted and the pipes connected, reconnect the battery and switch on the ignition. Check for correct pump operation, and for any sign of leaks from the supply pipe before refitting the access cover.

11 Fuel injection system – checking

Note: Refer to the warning note in Section 1 before proceeding.

1 If a fault appears in the fuel injection system, first ensure that all the system wiring connectors are securely connected and free of corrosion – also refer to paragraphs 6 to 9 below. Then ensure that the fault is not due to poor maintenance; ie, check that the air cleaner filter element is clean, the spark plugs are in good condition and correctly gapped, the cylinder compression pressures are correct, the ignition system wiring is in good condition and securely connected, and the engine breather hoses are clear and undamaged, referring to Chapter 1, Chapter 2A and Chapter 5B.

2 If these checks fail to reveal the cause of the problem, the car should be taken to a suitably-equipped franchised dealer for testing. A diagnostic connector is fitted below the steering column (see illustration) into which dedicated electronic test equipment can be plugged. The test equipment is capable

11.2 Diagnostic plug connector in the lower part of the facia

of 'interrogating' the engine management system ECU electronically and accessing its internal fault log (reading fault codes).

3 Fault codes can only be extracted from the ECU using a dedicated fault code reader. A franchised dealer will obviously have such a reader, but they are also available from other suppliers. It is unlikely to be cost-effective for the private owner to purchase a fault code reader, but a well-equipped local garage or auto-electrical specialist will have one.

4 Using this equipment, faults can be pinpointed quickly and simply, even if their occurrence is intermittent. Testing all the system components individually in an attempt to locate the fault by elimination is a time-consuming operation that is unlikely to be fruitful (particularly if the fault occurs dynamically), and carries a high risk of damage to the ECU's internal components.

5 Experienced home mechanics equipped with an accurate tachometer and a carefully-calibrated exhaust gas analyser may be able to check the exhaust gas CO content and the engine idle speed; if these are found to be out of specification, then the car must be taken to a suitably-equipped Peugeot dealer for assessment. Neither the air/fuel mixture (exhaust gas CO content) nor the engine idle speed are manually adjustable; incorrect test results indicate the need for maintenance (possibly, injector cleaning) or a fault within the fuel injection system.

Limited Operation Strategy

6 Certain faults, such as failure of one of the engine management system sensors,

will cause the system will revert to a backup (or 'limp-home') mode, often referred to as 'Limited Operation Strategy' (LOS). This is intended to be a 'get-you-home' facility only – the engine management warning light will come on when this mode is in operation.

7 In this mode, the signal from the defective sensor is substituted with a fixed value (it would normally vary), which may lead to loss of power, poor idling, and generally poor running, especially when the engine is cold.

8 However, the engine may in fact run quite well in this situation, and the only clue (other than the warning light) would be that the exhaust CO emissions (for example) would be higher than they should be.

9 Bear in mind that, even if the defective sensor is correctly identified and renewed, the engine will not return to normal running until the fault code is erased, taking the system out of LOS. This also applies even if the cause of the fault was a loose connection or damaged piece of wire – until the fault code is erased, the system will continue in LOS.

12 Fuel injection system components – removal and refitting

Note: Refer to the precautions in Section 1 before proceeding.

Throttle body (models with accelerator cable)

Note: At the time of writing, the throttle body could only be purchased as a complete unit, which includes the throttle position sensor (TPS) and idle speed control valve (ISCV) as part of the assembly.

Removal

1 Remove the air cleaner cover as described in Section 5, paragraphs 2 and 3.
2 Detach the accelerator cable from the throttle body as described in Section 6.
3 Disconnect the wiring plugs from the throttle position sensor and the idle speed control valve (see illustrations).
4 Remove the three mounting bolts, and lift off the throttle body from the inlet manifold (see illustration).

12.3a Disconnect the wiring connectors from the throttle position sensor...

12.3b... and the idle speed control valve

12.4 Throttle body mounting bolts

5 Recover the seal or O-ring from the top of the inlet manifold – a new one must be obtained for refitting **(see illustration)**. Any air leak from the base of the throttle body, caused by re-using the old seal, will cause all sorts of running problems.

Inspection

6 To check the throttle body assembly, first make sure the throttle housing is thoroughly clean.
7 Check the throttle valve flap opens and closes smoothly and the throttle valve shaft has no wear.
8 When the throttle closes, make sure there is no gap between the stop screw and the throttle lever **(see illustration)**. DO NOT adjust the throttle stop screw.
9 Using an ohmmeter, the throttle position sensor (TPS) can be checked by the following method **(see illustration)**:
a) *a) Measure the resistance between number 1 and 2 terminals on the throttle position sensor. The reading should be 2.5 to 5.0 k ohms at 25°C.*
b) *Measure the resistance between number 3 and 2 terminals on the throttle position sensor. With the throttle fully-closed, the reading should be 0.2 to 0.9 k ohms.*
c) *Measure the resistance between number 3 and 2 terminals on the throttle position sensor. With the throttle fully-open, the reading should be 1.85 to 4.22 k ohms.*
d) *If any of the above readings are not as specified, then the throttle body will need to be renewed.*
10 Using an ohmmeter, the idle speed control valve (ISCV) can be checked by the following method **(see illustration)**:
a) *Measure the resistance between number 1 and 3 terminals – the reading should be 39 to 65 ohms.*
b) *Measure the resistance between number 2 and 4 terminals – the reading should be 39 to 65 ohms.*
c) *Measure the resistance between number 1 and 2 terminals – the reading should be 10 k ohms or higher.*
d) *Measure the resistance between number 1 and 4 terminals – the reading should be 10 k ohms or higher.*
e) *Measure the resistance between number 2 and 3 terminals – the reading should be 10 k ohms or higher.*
f) *Measure the resistance between number 3 and 4 terminals – the reading should be 10 k ohms or higher.*
g) *If any of the above readings are not as specified, then the throttle body will need to be renewed.*

Refitting

11 Refitting is a reversal of removal, noting the following points:
a) *Use a new throttle body seal, and fit it to the inlet manifold.*
b) *Reconnect the wiring plugs securely.*
c) *Tighten the retaining bolts to the torque specified.*

12.5 Fit new O-ring seal when refitting

12.8 There should be no gap (arrowed) at the stop screw

12.9 Terminal numbers for checking the throttle position sensor (TPS)

12.10 Terminal numbers for checking the idle speed control valve (ISCV)

d) *Refit the accelerator cable and adjust as described in Section 6.*

Electronic throttle body (models without accelerator cable)

Note: *At the time of writing, the throttle body could only be purchased as a complete unit, which includes the throttle position sensor/control motor as part of the assembly.*

Removal

12 The throttle body receives a supply of coolant via two hoses at the rear – because of this; the cooling system should be drained as described in Chapter 1 before removing the throttle body. However, the amount of coolant lost will be quite small if the system is not drained, and it may be sufficient to disconnect the hoses (when engine is cold) and point their ends upwards to avoid much loss. If the hoses can be clamped prior to disconnection, this is better still **(see illustration)**.
13 Remove the air cleaner cover as described in Section 5, paragraphs 2 and 3.
14 Disconnect the wiring plug from the throttle position sensor/control motor **(see illustration)**. Release the wiring loom from the clip on top of the throttle housing and move it to one side.
15 Disconnect the two coolant hoses from the rear of the throttle body, noting the advice in paragraph 12.
16 Remove the four mounting bolts, and lift off the throttle body from the inlet manifold **(see illustration)**.

12.12 Disconnect the coolant hose retaining clips

12.14 Disconnect the throttle housing wiring plug

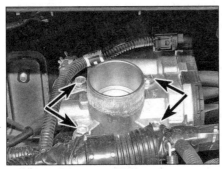

12.16 Undo the throttle body mounting bolts

12.24a Unclip the plastic cover...

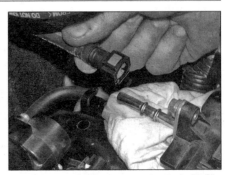

12.24b... and disconnect the fuel pipe

17 Recover the seal or O-ring from the top of the inlet manifold – a new one must be obtained for refitting. Any air leak from the base of the throttle body, caused by re-using the old seal, will cause all sorts of running problems.

Inspection

18 The electronic throttle body can only be checked using special diagnostic equipment. This will need to be carried out while the throttle body is fitted to the vehicle. If a problem with the throttle body is suspected, have your findings confirmed by a franchised dealer or other specialist, as a complete new throttle body may have to be fitted.

Refitting

19 Refitting is a reversal of removal, noting the following points:
a) Use a new throttle body seal and fit it to the inlet manifold.

b) Tighten the retaining bolts to the torque specified.
c) Reconnect the wiring plugs and hoses correctly and securely.
d) On completion, check and if necessary top-up the cooling system as described in 'Weekly checks'.

Fuel rail and injectors

Removal

20 Relieve the residual pressure in the fuel system (see Section 2), and equalise tank pressure by removing the fuel filler cap.

⚠️ *Warning: This procedure will merely relieve the increased pressure necessary for the engine to run – remember that fuel will still be present in the system components, and take precautions accordingly before disconnecting any of them.*

21 Disconnect the battery negative (earth) lead (see *Disconnecting the battery*).
22 Remove the air cleaner cover as described in Section 5, paragraphs 2 and 3.
23 Place some rags underneath the transmission end of the fuel rail, as there will be some spillage of fuel as the fuel pipe is removed.
24 Unclip the plastic collar fitted around the connector, and then release the securing clips, and pull off the fuel pipe to the fuel rail (see illustrations). Move the pipe to one side, clear of the fuel rail, and either plug the ends or wrap a plastic bag around the open joint face to prevent dirt getting in.
Caution: DO NOT fold or bend the fuel pipe or damage may occur.
25 Disconnect the wiring plug connectors from the three ignition coils (see illustration).
26 Disconnect the wiring plug connectors from the three fuel injectors (see illustration) – though it should not be possible to mix them up when refitting, it may pay to label them as they are disconnected. Unclip the wiring loom from the retaining bracket and move the wiring loom to one side.
27 Undo the retaining bolt and remove the wiring loom retaining bracket from the top of the inlet manifold (see illustration).
28 Slacken and remove the two fuel rail securing bolts from the top of the cylinder head (see illustration).
29 Carefully pull the fuel rail upwards complete with the injectors – there will be some resistance from the injector O-ring seals/vibration dampers fitted in the cylinder head (see illustration).

12.25 Disconnect the three ignition coil wiring plugs

12.26 Disconnect the three fuel injector wiring plugs

12.27 Undo the wiring loom mounting bracket bolt

12.28 Undo the fuel rail mounting bolts...

12.29... and withdraw the fuel rail from the cylinder head

12.30 Recover the seals/dampers from the cylinder head

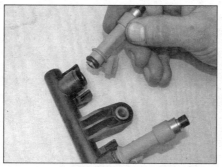

12.31a Twist the injectors from the fuel rail...

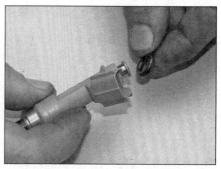

12.31b... and renew the upper injector seal

30 Recover the injector lower seals/dampers – new ones must be used when refitting **(see illustration)**.

31 Carefully pull the injectors from the fuel rail, using a twisting motion to free them. Recover the small O-ring from the top of each injector – these should also be renewed when they are disturbed **(see illustrations)**. Note: The injectors are fragile, take care not to drop them, or subject them to any other kind of impact.

Refitting

32 Refitting is the reverse of the removal procedure, noting the following points:

a) Fit new injector O-rings and seals/dampers to the cylinder head **(see illustration)**, lubricate them with a small amount of grease to aid refitting. Turn the injectors so that the wiring plug sockets will face forwards when the fuel rail is refitted.

b) Fit the fuel rail into place **(see illustration)**, and push the injectors into the seals/vibration dampers inside the cylinder head. Refit the bolts to the specified torque; check that the injectors are seated correctly.

c) Ensure that the hoses and wiring are routed correctly, and secured on reconnection by any clips or ties provided. Refit the wiring loom retaining bracket back to the top of the inlet manifold.

d) On completion, switch the ignition on to activate the fuel pump and pressurise the system, without cranking the engine.

Check for signs of fuel leaks around all disturbed unions and joints before attempting to start the engine.

Fuel pulsation damper

Removal

33 The pulsation damper is located in the end of the fuel rail, at the transmission end **(see illustration)**.

34 If required, remove the canister discharge electro-valve from the rear of the cylinder head cover to make access easier (see paragraph 65).

35 Relieve the residual pressure in the fuel system (see Section 2), and equalise tank pressure by removing the fuel filler cap.

36 Remove the retaining clip from the end of the fuel rail and withdraw the pulsation damper from the end of the fuel rail **(see illustrations)**. There will be some resistance

from the O-ring seal fitted on the damper, discard the seal as this will need to be renewed on refitting.

Refitting

37 Refitting is the reverse of the removal procedure, noting the following points:

a) Fit new O-ring seal to the pulsation damper **(see illustration)**, lubricate with a small amount of grease to aid refitting.

b) On completion, switch the ignition on to activate the fuel pump and pressurise the system, without cranking the engine. Check for signs of fuel leaks around all disturbed unions and joints before attempting to start the engine.

Fuel pressure regulator

38 The pressure regulator is combined with the fuel pump, which is fitted to the fuel tank. Refer to Section 10.

12.32a Fit new seals/dampers to the cylinder head...

12.32b... and refit the injectors and fuel rail

12.33 Fuel pulsation damper (arrowed) in the end of the fuel rail

12.36a Withdraw the securing clip...

12.36b... and pull out the pulsation damper

12.37 Fit new seal to the damper

12.45 Engine management ECU is located behind the fuse/relay box – arrowed

12.47 Slide out the locking clips and disconnect the wiring connectors

Idle speed control valve (ISCV)

39 The control valve is located on the throttle body. According to the manufacturer, the valve is not available separately from the throttle body, and is not intended to be removed. See the throttle body removal and refitting procedure, at the start of this Section for further information.

40 The idle speed control valve can be checked using an ohmmeter, as described in paragraph 10 of this section.

41 If a problem with the valve is suspected, have your findings confirmed by a franchised dealer or other specialist, as a complete new throttle body may have to be fitted.

Throttle position sensor (TPS)

42 The sensor is located on the throttle body. According to the manufacturer, the sensor is not available separately from the throttle body, and is not intended to be removed. See the throttle body removal and refitting procedure, at the start of this Section for further information.

43 The throttle position sensor can be checked using an ohmmeter, as described in paragraph 9 of this section.

44 If a problem with the valve is suspected, have your findings confirmed by a franchised dealer or other specialist, as a complete new throttle body may have to be fitted.

Engine management ECU

Note: *The ECU is fragile. Take care not to drop it, or subject it to any other kind of impact. Do not subject it to extremes of temperature, or allow it to get wet.*

45 The engine management ECU is located on a bracket bolted to the bulkhead at the rear of the engine compartment, behind the battery and fuse/relay box **(see illustration)**.

46 Disconnect the battery negative lead, and place the lead away from the terminal (see *Disconnecting the battery*). It is essential that the battery is disconnected before separating the ECU wiring plug, or the ECU itself could be damaged.

47 Release the locking clips and disconnect the two wiring plugs from the top of the ECU **(see illustration)**.

48 Remove the four ECU mounting bolts (two at each side), then pull the unit out, and remove it from the mounting bracket **(see illustration)**.

Crankshaft position sensor

Removal

49 The sensor is located at the base of the timing chain cover, next to the crankshaft pulley **(see illustration)**.

50 With the ignition switched off, disconnect the sensor wiring plug, then unscrew the mounting bolt and withdraw the sensor **(see illustrations)**. Discard the O-ring seal as this will need to be renewed on refitting.

51 The sensor resistance is quoted in the Specifications at the start of this Chapter – check by connecting a multimeter, set to the resistance function, across the sensor's plug terminals. A zero or infinity reading suggests the sensor is faulty.

Refitting

52 Refitting is a reversal of removal. Ensure that the sensor is clean and a new seal is fitted, and then tighten the bolt to the specified torque.

12.48 ECU mounting bolts

12.49 Location of crankshaft sensor

12.50a Disconnect the wiring connector...

12.50b... undo the retaining bolt and remove the sensor

12.53 Location of camshaft sensor

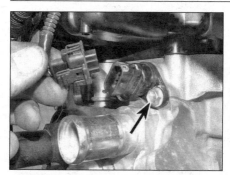

12.54 Disconnect the wiring connector and undo the retaining bolt – arrowed

12.57 Location of manifold absolute pressure (MAP) sensor

12.59a Disconnect the wiring connector...

Camshaft position sensor

Removal

53 The sensor is located at the transmission end of the cylinder head **(see illustration)**, under the left-hand rear end of the cylinder head cover. Access to the sensor may be hampered by coolant hoses nearby – for this reason, remove the sensor when the engine is cold.

54 With the ignition switched off, disconnect the sensor wiring plug, then unscrew the mounting bolt and withdraw the sensor from the cylinder head **(see illustration)**. Discard the O-ring seal, as this will need to be renewed on refitting.

55 The sensor resistance is quoted in the Specifications at the start of this Chapter – check by connecting a multimeter, set to the resistance function, across the sensor's plug terminals. A zero or infinity reading suggests the sensor is faulty.

Refitting

56 Refitting is a reversal of removal. Ensure that the sensor is clean and a new seal is fitted, and then tighten the bolt to the specified torque.

Manifold absolute pressure (MAP) sensor

Removal

57 The MAP sensor detects the vacuum pressure in the inlet manifold and also the inlet air temperature. This information is then sent to the engine management ECU. The sensor is located in the top of the inlet manifold, behind the throttle body **(see illustration)**.

58 Remove the air cleaner cover as described in Section 5, paragraphs 2 and 3.

59 With the ignition switched off, disconnect the sensor wiring plug, and then unscrew the two retaining bolts and withdraw the sensor **(see illustrations)**. Discard the O-ring seal, as this will need to be renewed on refitting.

60 Using an ohmmeter, the manifold absolute pressure (MAP) sensor, can be checked by the following method **(see illustration)**:

a) *Measure the resistance between number 2 and 4 terminals on the pressure sensor.*
b) *At -20°C the reading should be 14.6 to 17.8 k ohms.*

12.59b... undo the retaining bolts and remove the sensor

c) *At 20°C the reading should be 2.21 to 2.69 k ohms.*
d) *At 80°C the reading should be 0.29 to 0.35 k ohms.*
e) *If any of the above readings are not as specified, then the manifold absolute pressure sensor will need to be renewed.*

Refitting

61 Refitting is a reversal of removal. Ensure that the sensor is clean and a new seal is fitted, and then tighten the bolt to the specified torque.

Coolant temperature sensor

62 The sensor is located at the transmission end of the cylinder head, behind the thermostat housing. See Chapter 3, Section 4, for the removal and refitting procedure.

Oxygen sensor

63 There are two sensors fitted, one is located in the top of the exhaust manifold (before the catalytic converter), and the other one is in the exhaust front pipe (after the catalytic converter). Refer to Chapter 4B for further information.

Knock sensor

64 The sensor is located at the rear of the cylinder block, under the inlet manifold. Refer to Chapter 5B Section 4, for further information.

Canister discharge electrovalve (fuel venting valve)

65 The fuel venting valve is located at the

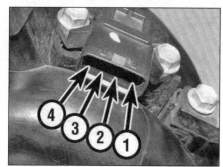

12.60 Terminal numbers for checking the MAP sensor

rear left-hand end of the cylinder head/air cleaner cover. Refer to Chapter 4B for further information.

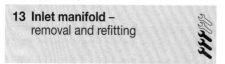

13 Inlet manifold –
removal and refitting

Note: *Refer to the warning note in Section 1 before proceeding. Note that the inlet manifold is made of plastic – do not strike it, nor use any great force when removing it.*

Removal

1 To give better access at the rear of the engine compartment, remove the windscreen motor/wiper linkage and rear scuttle panel, as described in Chapter 12 Section 14 **(see illustration)**.

13.1 Remove the rear scuttle panel

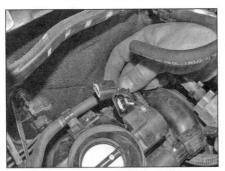

13.3 Disconnect the wiring connector from the MAP sensor

13.4 Undo the wiring loom mounting bracket bolt

13.5 Disconnect the breather hose from the cylinder head cover

13.6a Disconnect the brake vacuum hose...

13.6b.. and unclip it from the rear of the inlet manifold

13.7 Disconnect the fuel venting hose from the manifold

2 Remove the throttle body as described in Section 12.

3 Disconnect the manifold pressure sensor wiring connector at the rear of the inlet manifold **(see illustration)**.

4 Unclip the wiring from across the top of the fuel rail and move it to one side, then undo the retaining bolt and remove the wiring loom bracket **(see illustration)**.

5 Disconnect the breather hose from the left-hand rear of the cylinder head cover **(see illustration)**.

6 Working at the transmission end of the inlet manifold, release the securing clips and disconnect the brake servo vacuum hose from the inlet manifold, unclip the hose from along the rear of the manifold and move it to one side **(see illustrations)**.

7 Also at the transmission end of the manifold, release the securing clips and disconnect the fuel venting valve hose from the inlet manifold, and move it to one side **(see illustration)**.

8 Slacken and remove the mounting bolt from the support bracket under the right-hand rear of the inlet manifold **(see illustration)**.

9 Undo the four mounting bolts and remove the inlet manifold from the rear of the engine **(see illustrations)**.

10 Recover the one-piece gasket – a new one should be used when refitting **(see illustration)**.

13.8 Undo the inlet manifold lower securing bracket bolt

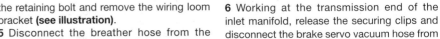

13.9a Undo the right-hand side mounting bolts...

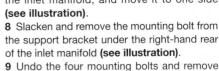

13.9b... left-hand side mounting bolts...

13.10 Fit new one-piece rubber type inlet manifold gasket

Refitting

11 Refitting is a reversal of removal, noting the following points:

a) Ensure that the mating faces are clean, and use a new manifold gasket.

b) Tighten the inlet manifold bolts to the specified torque.

c) Refit the throttle body (see Section 12).

d) If removed, refit the wiper motor/linkage and scuttle, with reference to Chapter 12 Section 14.

Chapter 4 Part B
Emission control and exhaust systems

Contents

Degrees of difficulty

Easy, suitable for novice with little experience	**Fairly easy,** suitable for beginner with some experience	**Fairly difficult,** suitable for competent DIY mechanic	**Difficult,** suitable for experienced DIY mechanic	**Very difficult,** suitable for expert DIY or professional

Specifications

Canister discharge electrovalve (fuel venting valve)
Resistance . . . . 30 to 34 ohms at 20°C

Exhaust front pipe assembly
Minimum length of spring. . . . . 40.5 mm

Torque wrench settings	Nm	lbf ft
Exhaust centre section-to-rear silencer clamp bolt	32	24
Exhaust manifold nuts/bolts.	24	18
Exhaust manifold support bracket:		
Mounting bolt	24	18
Mounting nut	19	14
Exhaust manifold/catalytic converter-to-front pipe bolts.	45	33
Oxygen (lambda) sensors.	44	32

1 General Information

Emission control systems

1 All models are designed to use unleaded petrol, and are controlled by engine management systems that are programmed to give the best compromise between driveability, fuel consumption and exhaust emissions. A crankcase emission control system is fitted, which reduces the release of pollutants from the engine's lubrication system, and a catalytic converter is fitted which reduces exhaust gas pollutant. An evaporative loss emission control system is fitted which reduces the release of gaseous hydrocarbons from the fuel tank.

Crankcase emission control

2 To reduce the emission of unburned hydrocarbons from the crankcase into the atmosphere, the engine is sealed and the blow-by gases and oil vapour are drawn from inside the crankcase into the inlet tract to be burned by the engine during normal combustion. There is an oil separator fitted to the front of the cylinder block, this separates the oil from the blow-by gases in order to reduce degradation and consumption of the engine oil.
3 Under conditions of high manifold pressure, the gases will be sucked positively out of the crankcase. Under conditions of low manifold depression, the gases are forced out of the crankcase by the (relatively) higher crankcase pressure. If the engine is worn, the raised crankcase pressure (due to increased blow-by) will cause some of the flow to return under all manifold conditions.

Exhaust emission control

4 To minimise the amount of pollutants which escape into the atmosphere, all models are fitted with a three-way catalytic converter in the exhaust system. The fuelling system is of the closed-loop type, in which the oxygen (lambda) sensors in the exhaust system provide the engine management system ECU with constant feedback, enabling the ECU to adjust the air/fuel mixture to optimise combustion.
5 All models have two oxygen sensors – one before the catalytic converter and one after.

This enables more efficient monitoring of the exhaust gas, allowing a faster response time. The overall efficiency of the converters can also be checked.
6 The oxygen sensors have a built-in heating element, controlled by the ECU through the oxygen sensor relay, to quickly bring the sensor's tip to its optimum operating temperature. The sensor's tip is sensitive to oxygen, and sends a voltage signal to the ECU that varies according on the amount of oxygen in the exhaust gas. If the inlet air/fuel mixture is too rich, the exhaust gases are low in oxygen so the sensor sends a low-voltage signal, the voltage rising as the mixture weakens and the amount of oxygen rises in the exhaust gases. Peak conversion efficiency of all major pollutants occurs if the inlet air/fuel mixture is maintained at the chemically correct ratio for the complete combustion of petrol of 14.7 parts (by weight) of air to 1 part of fuel (the stoichiometric ratio). The sensor output voltage alters in a large step at this point, the ECU using the signal change as a reference point and correcting the inlet air/fuel mixture accordingly by altering the fuel injector pulse width.

2.2 Fuel venting valve on rear of cylinder head cover

Evaporative emission control

7 To minimise the escape of unburned hydrocarbons into the atmosphere, an evaporative loss emission control system is fitted to all models. The fuel tank filler cap is sealed, and a charcoal canister is mounted inside the top of the fuel pump/sender unit, inside the fuel tank. This collects the petrol vapours released from the fuel contained inside the fuel tank. It stores them until they can be drawn from the canister (under the control of the engine management ECU) via the canister discharge electrovalve (fuel venting valve), where the engine then burns them during normal combustion.

8 To ensure the engine runs correctly when it is cold and/or idling, and to protect the catalytic converter from the effects of an over-rich mixture, the fuel venting valve is not opened by the ECU until the engine has warmed up, and the engine is under load; the venting valve is

3.2 Oil separator plate on the front of the cylinder block

4.1 Disconnect the wiring connector...

then modulated on and off to allow the stored vapour to pass into the inlet manifold.

Exhaust systems

9 The exhaust system comprises of the three parts:
a) Exhaust manifold, which includes catalytic converter and first oxygen sensor.
b) Centre section, which includes front pipe and second oxygen sensor.
c) Rear silencer, which is positioned across the rear of the vehicle.

10 The exhaust system is supported by various metal brackets, which are attached to the underside of the vehicle, with rubber vibration dampers fitted to suppress noise.

2 Evaporative loss emission control system – information and component renewal

1 The evaporative loss emission control system consists of the canister discharge electrovalve (fuel venting valve), the charcoal canister, and a series of connecting hoses. The resistance of the fuel venting valve is given in the specifications at the beginning of this Chapter.

Canister discharge electrovalve (fuel venting valve)

2 The fuel venting valve is bolted to the left-hand rear of the cylinder head cover/air cleaner cover **(see illustration)**.
3 With the ignition switched off, disconnect the valve wiring plug, then unscrew the

2.3a Disconnect the wiring connector...

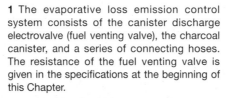

4.2... unbolt the wiring bracket...

2.3b... and undo the retaining bolt

mounting bolt and withdraw the valve from the cylinder head cover **(see illustrations)**.
4 Release the retaining clips to disconnect the two venting hoses from the valve.
5 Refitting is a reversal of removal.

Charcoal canister

6 The charcoal canister is mounted inside the top of the fuel pump/sender unit, inside the fuel tank.
7 This can only be purchased as a complete unit, see Chapter 4A, Section 10, for the removal and refitting procedure of the fuel pump/sender unit.

3 Crankcase emission system – general information

1 The crankcase emission control system consists of a series of hoses that connect the crankcase vent to the cylinder head cover vent and the inlet manifold.
2 There is also an oil separator fitted to the front of the cylinder block **(see illustration)**, this separates the oil from the blow-by gases in order to reduce degradation and consumption of the engine oil.
3 The system requires no attention other than to check at regular intervals that the hose(s) are free of blockages and undamaged.

4 Oxygen sensors – removal and refitting

Note: The oxygen sensors are delicate and will not work if dropped or knocked, if their power supply is disrupted, or if any cleaning materials are used on them.

Removal

Sensor 1

1 Open the bonnet and trace the wiring back from the upper oxygen sensor to the connector at the front of the cylinder head cover, disconnect the wiring connector **(see illustration)**.
2 Undo the retaining bolt and remove the wiring bracket from the front of the cylinder head cover **(see illustration)**.

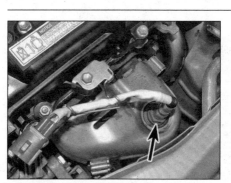

4.3... and remove the upper oxygen sensor

4.5 Disconnect the wiring connector...

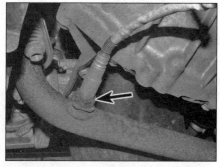

4.6... and remove the lower oxygen sensor

3 Unscrew and remove the sensor from its location in the top of the exhaust manifold – an open-ended spanner will be needed, as the sensor wiring means a normal socket cannot be fitted (see illustration).

Sensor 2

4 Jack up the front of the car, and support it on axle stands (see *Jacking and vehicle support*).

5 Trace the wiring back from the oxygen sensor to the connector on the front of the transmission housing, disconnect the wiring connector and unclip the wire from the bracket (see illustration).

6 Unscrew and remove the sensor from its location in the front of the exhaust pipe – an open-ended spanner will be needed, as the sensor wiring means a normal socket cannot be fitted (see illustration).

Refitting

7 Refitting is a reversal of removal, noting the following points:

a) *Clean the threads of the sensor and the threads in the exhaust manifold.*

b) *Ideally, the sensor should be tightened to the specified torque. However, unless a slotted socket is available, this will not be possible – use the figure quoted as a guide to hand-tightening using a spanner.*

c) *Reconnect the wiring; making sure that it is in no danger of contacting the exhaust or other moving parts.*

5 Exhaust manifold/ catalytic converter – removal and refitting

⚠️ *Warning: Allow ample time for the exhaust system to cool before starting work. In particular, note that the catalytic converter runs at very high temperatures. If there is any chance that the system may still be hot, wear suitable gloves. When removing the exhaust front section, take care not to damage the oxygen sensors if they are not removed from their locations.*

Removal

1 Jack up the front of the car, and support it on axle stands (see *Jacking and vehicle support*).

2 Remove the front bumper as described in Chapter 11 Section 6.

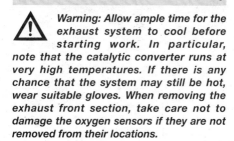

5.3a Remove the exhaust front pipe securing bolts...

3 Remove the two bolts securing the exhaust front pipe to the bottom of the manifold/catalytic converter, and recover the springs. Lower the front part of the exhaust down (unhook the rubber mountings as necessary), and support the exhaust on an axle stand. Make sure the wiring to the oxygen sensor is not damaged, disconnect if required. Recover the metal O-ring gasket from the joint – a new one should be used when refitting (see illustrations).

4 Undo the lower mounting bolt and nut, then remove the support bracket from the side of the catalytic converter (see illustration).

5 Working on top of the engine, trace the oxygen sensor wiring to the connector plug, and disconnect it (see illustration).

6 Undo the retaining bolt and remove the wiring bracket from the front of the cylinder head cover (see illustration).

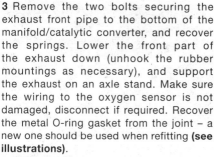

5.3b... and disconnect the oxygen sensor wiring plug

5.4 Remove the nut and bolt from the manifold support bracket

5.5 Disconnect the upper oxygen sensor wiring connector...

5.6... and unbolt the sensor wiring bracket

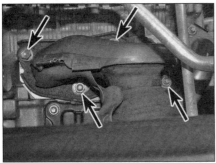

5.7 The exhaust manifold is secured by two upper bolts, and two lower nuts

5.8 Removing the exhaust manifold/catalytic converter

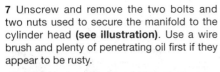

5.10a Fit a new manifold-to-front pipe sealing ring...

5.10b... and a new manifold-to-head gasket

7 Unscrew and remove the two bolts and two nuts used to secure the manifold to the cylinder head **(see illustration)**. Use a wire brush and plenty of penetrating oil first if they appear to be rusty.

8 Carefully withdraw the manifold from the cylinder head studs **(see illustration)**.

9 Recover the manifold gasket – a new one must be used when refitting. Examine the condition of the manifold mounting studs/nuts

and bolts, and obtain new ones for refitting if necessary.

Refitting

10 Refitting is a reversal of the removal procedure, noting the following points:
a) *Always fit new gasket sealing ring to the manifold/catalytic converter-to-front pipe* **(see illustration)**.
b) *Always fit new gasket to the manifold-to-head joint* **(see illustration)**.
c) *Clean the threads thoroughly to remove all traces of rust.*
d) *Tighten all fittings to the specified torque*

---

6 Exhaust system – component renewal

> ⚠ *Warning: Allow ample time for the exhaust system to cool before starting work. When removing the exhaust front section, take care not to damage the oxygen sensors if they are not removed from their locations.*

Removal

1 The original system fitted in the factory is in two sections. The centre section includes the front pipe, and can be removed complete. The rear silencer can be removed and renewed separately.

2 To remove part of the system, first jack up the front or rear of the car and support it on axle stands (see *Jacking and vehicle support*). Alternatively, position the car over an inspection pit or on car ramps.

Centre section

3 Trace the wiring back from the oxygen sensor at the front of the exhaust, and disconnect the wiring connector **(see illustration)**. Unclip the wiring from any clips or brackets, noting how it is routed for refitting.

4 If a new exhaust section is being fitted, unscrew the oxygen sensor from the old pipe, and fit it to the new section, using the information in Section 4.

5 Remove the two bolts at the front securing the manifold/catalytic converter to the front pipe, and recover the springs **(see illustration)**. Lower the front part of the exhaust down, and support the exhaust on an axle stand. Recover the metal O-ring gasket from the joint – a new one should be used when refitting. If the springs are worn, they will need to be renewed, check the length with the specifications at the beginning of this Chapter.

6 At the rear of the centre section, in front of the rear axle, slacken and remove the securing clamp, noting the fitted position of the two parts of exhaust **(see illustrations)**. Tap the flange if necessary, to separate it.

7 The centre section is now supported by the rubber mounting(s) on the back of the

6.3 Disconnect the lower oxygen sensor wiring connector

6.5 Remove the exhaust front pipe securing bolts...

6.6a Undo the retaining bolt...

6.6b... and remove the clamp...

6.6c... and then split the centre exhaust from the rear

6.7 Release the exhaust rubber mountings

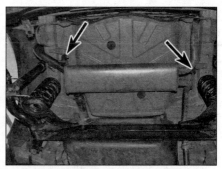

6.9 Rear silencer rubber exhaust mountings – arrowed

subframe **(see illustration)**. Carefully unhook the rubber(s), and lower the section to the floor.

Rear silencer

8 Disconnect the centre section of the exhaust sytem from the rear silencer as described in paragraph 6.

9 Unhook the rear silencer from the rubber mountings at the left and right, and remove it from under the car **(see illustration)**.

Refitting

10 Each section is refitted by a reversal of the removal sequence, noting the following points:

a) *Ensure that all traces of corrosion have been removed from the flanges or pipe ends, and renew all necessary gaskets (see illustration 5.10a).*

b) *Align the markings when joining the centre section to the rear silencer (see illustration).*

c) *If the flange bolts and springs are in poor condition, obtain new ones for refitting. Exhaust fitting kits are now widely available from car accessory shops, which contain all the necessary parts (often including new gaskets).*

d) *Inspect the rubber mountings for signs of damage or deterioration, and renew as necessary.*

e) *If using exhaust assembly paste, make sure this is only applied to joints downstream (after) of the catalyst.*

f) *Ensure that all rubber mountings are correctly located, and that there is adequate clearance between the exhaust system and vehicle underbody. Providing good-quality parts are fitted, the bolted flange joints should mean the exhaust alignment is preserved.*

---

7 Catalytic converter –
general information
and precautions

General information

1 The catalytic converter reduces harmful exhaust emissions by chemically converting the more poisonous gases to ones that

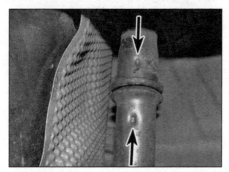

6.10 Align the markings (arrowed) on the exhaust when refitting

(in theory at least) are less harmful. The chemical reaction is known as an 'oxidising' reaction, or one where oxygen is 'added' **(see illustration)**.

2 Inside the converter is a honeycomb structure made of ceramic material and coated with the precious metals palladium, platinum and rhodium (the 'catalyst' which promotes the chemical reaction). The chemical reaction generates heat, which itself promotes the reaction – therefore, once the car has been driven several miles, the body of the converter will be very hot.

3 The ceramic structure contained within the converter is understandably fragile, and will not withstand rough treatment. Since the converter runs at a high temperature, driving through deep standing water (in flood conditions, for example) is to be avoided, since the thermal stresses imposed when plunging the hot converter into cold water may well cause the ceramic internals to fracture, resulting in a 'blocked' converter – a common cause of failure. A converter that has been damaged in this way can be checked by shaking it (do not strike it) – if a rattling noise is heard, this indicates probable failure.

Precautions

4 The catalytic converter is a reliable and simple device which needs no maintenance in itself, but there are some facts of which an owner should be aware if the converter is to function properly for its full service life:

a) *DO NOT use leaded petrol (or lead-*

7.1 Catalytic converter (arrowed) is part of the exhaust manifold

   replacement petrol, LRP) in a car equipped with a catalytic converter – the lead (or other additives) will coat the precious metals, reducing their converting efficiency and will eventually destroy the converter.

b) *Always keep the ignition and fuel systems well-maintained in accordance with the manufacturer's schedule (see Chapter 1).*

c) *If the engine develops a misfire, do not drive the car at all (or at least as little as possible) until the fault is cured.*

d) *DO NOT push- or tow-start the car – this will soak the catalytic converter in unburned fuel, causing it to overheat when the engine does start.*

e) *DO NOT switch off the ignition at high engine speeds – ie, do not 'blip' the throttle immediately before switching off the engine.*

f) *DO NOT use fuel or engine oil additives – these may contain substances harmful to the catalytic converter.*

g) *DO NOT continue to use the car if the engine burns oil to the extent of leaving a visible trail of blue smoke.*

h) *Remember that the catalytic converter operates at very high temperatures. DO NOT, therefore, park the car in dry undergrowth, over long grass or piles of dead leaves after a long run.*

i) *As mentioned above, driving through deep water should be avoided if possible. The sudden cooling effect may fracture the ceramic honeycomb, damaging it beyond repair.*

j) Remember that the catalytic converter is FRAGILE – do not strike it with tools during servicing work, and take care handling it when removing it from the car for any reason.

k) In some cases, a sulphurous smell (like that of rotten eggs) may be noticed from the exhaust. This is common to many catalytic converter-equipped cars, and has more to do with the sulphur content of the brand of fuel being used than the converter itself.

l) If a substantial loss of power is experienced, remember that this could be due to the converter being blocked. This can occur simply as a result of high mileage, but may be due to the ceramic element having fractured and collapsed internally (see paragraph 3). A new converter is the only cure in this instance

m) The catalytic converter, used on a well-maintained and well-driven car, should last at least 100 000 miles – if the converter is no longer effective, it must be renewed.

Chapter 5 Part A
Starting and charging systems

Contents

Degrees of difficulty

Easy, suitable for novice with little experience	**Fairly easy,** suitable for beginner with some experience	**Fairly difficult,** suitable for competent DIY mechanic	**Difficult,** suitable for experienced DIY mechanic	**Very difficult,** suitable for expert DIY or professional

Specifications

System type . . . . 12 volt, negative earth

Battery
Type . . . . Lead acid 'maintenance-free'
Charge condition:
  Poor . . . . 11.5 volts
  Normal . . . . 12.0 volts
  Good . . . . 12.5 volts

Alternator
Type A1151
Supplier . . . . DMIT
Output (typical) . . . . 70 or 80 amps
Regulated voltage . . . . 12.9 to 14.9 volts
Brush exposed length:
  Standard . . . . 12.5 mm
  Minimum . . . . 6.5 mm

Starter motor
Valeo
  Type D7E
  Output power . . . . 1.0 kW
Bosch
  Type R70M
  Output power . . . . 1.1 kW
Maximum output (at 11.5 V) . . . . 90 amps
Brush length:
  Standard . . . . 10.7 mm
  Minimum . . . . 4.4 mm

Torque wrench settings	Nm	lbf ft
Alternator lower adjuster bracket bolt	34	25
Alternator upper pivot bolt	54	40
Starter motor mounting bolts	37	27

1 General information, precautions and battery disconnection

General information

1 The engine electrical system consists mainly of the charging and starting systems. Because of their engine-related functions, these components are covered separately from the body electrical devices such as the lights, instruments, etc (which are covered in Chapter 12). Information on the ignition system is covered in Part B of this Chapter.

2 The electrical system is of 12 volt negative earth type.

3 The battery is of the 'maintenance-free' (sealed for life) type and is charged by the alternator, which is belt-driven from the crankshaft pulley.

4 The starter motor is of the pre-engaged type incorporating an integral solenoid. On starting, the solenoid moves the drive pinion into engagement with the flywheel ring gear before the starter motor is energised. Once the engine has started, a one-way clutch prevents the motor armature being driven by the engine until the pinion disengages from the flywheel.

Precautions

5 It is necessary to take extra care when working on the electrical system to avoid damage to semi-conductor devices (diodes and transistors), and to avoid the risk of personal injury. In addition to the precautions given in *Safety first!* at the beginning of this manual, observe the following when working on the system:

• *Always remove rings, watches, etc, before working on the electrical system*. Even with the battery disconnected, capacitive discharge could occur if a component's live terminal is earthed through a metal object. This could cause a shock or nasty burn.

• *Do not reverse the battery connections*. Components such as the alternator, electronic control units, or any other components having semi-conductor circuitry could be irreparably damaged.

• *If the engine is being started using jump leads and a slave battery, connect the batteries positive-to-positive and negative-to-negative (see Jump starting). This also applies when connecting a battery charger*.

• *Never disconnect the battery terminals, the alternator, any electrical wiring or any test instruments when the engine is running*.

• *Do not allow the engine to turn the alternator, when the alternator is not connected*.

• *Never 'test' for alternator output by 'flashing' the output lead to earth*.

• *Never use an ohmmeter of the type incorporating a hand-cranked generator for circuit or continuity testing*.

• *Always ensure that the battery negative lead is disconnected when working on the electrical system*.

• *Before using electric-arc welding equipment on the car, disconnect the battery, alternator and components such as the fuel injection/ignition electronic control unit to protect them from the risk of damage*.

Battery disconnection

Refer to the precautions listed in '*Disconnecting the battery*' in the Reference chapter of this manual.

2 Electrical fault finding – general information

1 Refer to Chapter 12 Section 2.

3 Battery – testing and charging

Testing

1 Maintenance-free batteries are fitted to these models, which are 'sealed for life'. Topping-up and testing of the electrolyte in each cell is not possible. The condition of the battery can therefore only be tested using a battery condition indicator or a voltmeter.

2 If testing the battery using a voltmeter, connect the voltmeter across the battery and compare the result with those given in the Specifications under 'charge condition'. The test is only accurate if the battery has not been subjected to any kind of charge for the previous six hours. If this is not the case, switch on the headlights for 30 seconds, then wait four to five minutes before testing the battery after switching off the headlights. All other electrical circuits must be switched off, so check that the doors and tailgate are fully shut when making the test.

3 If the voltage reading is less than 12.0 volts, then the battery is discharged.

4 If the battery is to be charged, remove it from the car (Section 4) and charge it as described later in this Section.

Charging

Note: *The following is intended as a guide only. Always refer to the manufacturers recommendations (often printed on a label attached to the battery), and always disconnect both terminals before charging a battery.*

5 A maintenance-free type of battery takes considerably longer to fully recharge than the standard type, the time taken being dependent on the extent of discharge, but it can take anything up to three days.

6 A constant voltage type charger is required, to be set, when connected, to 13.9 to 14.9 volts with a charger current below 25 amps. Using this method, the battery should be usable within three hours, giving a voltage reading of 12.5 volts, but this is for a partially-discharged battery and, as mentioned, full charging can take considerably longer.

7 If the battery is to be charged from a fully-discharged state (condition reading less than 12.2 volts), have it recharged by your franchised dealer or local automotive electrician, as the charge rate is higher and constant supervision during charging is necessary.

4 Battery and tray – removal and refitting

Note: *Refer to the warnings given in 'Safety first!' and in Section 1 of this Chapter before starting work.*

Battery

Removal

1 The battery is located on the left-hand side of the engine compartment, on a battery tray above the transmission.

2 Loosen the clamp nut, and then detach the earth lead from the battery negative (earth) terminal post **(see illustrations)**. This is the terminal to disconnect before working on, or disconnecting, any electrical component

4.2a Loosen the clamp nut...

4.2b... and disconnect the negative lead

4.3a Unclip the red plastic cover...

4.3b... loosen the clamp nut and disconnect the positive lead

4.4 Undo the bolt and remove the battery clamp from the front of the battery

4.5 Lift out the battery from the engine compartment

4.8a Undo the fuse/relay box upper securing bolt...

4.8b... and lower securing bolt

on the car. Position the lead away from the battery.

3 Unclip the red plastic cover from the positive terminal, then loosen the positive lead clamp nut. Detach the positive lead from the terminal, and position it away from the battery **(see illustrations)**.

4 Undo the bolt from the battery clamping plate and remove it from the front of the battery tray **(see illustration)**.

5 Lift out the battery, keeping it as level as possible. Take care, as the battery is heavy **(see illustration)**.

Refitting

6 Refitting is a reversal of removal. Reconnect the battery negative lead last. Make sure the battery terminals and clamps are clean before refitting, and that the clamp nuts are tightened securely.

Battery tray

Removal

7 A metal tray/mounting plate is fitted under the battery; this will need to be removed if working on the transmission. Remove the battery as described earlier in this Section.

8 Undo the two retaining bolts and unclip the fuse/relay box from the rear of the battery tray **(see illustrations)**.

9 As the fuse/relay box is disconnected from the battery tray, unclip the wiring loom retaining clips from the tray **(see illustrations)**.

10 Undo the three retaining bolts from the battery tray (one is down inside a hole in the

front of the tray), and then remove the battery tray. Unclip the wiring loom from under the front of the tray as it is being removed **(see illustrations)**.

Refitting

11 Refitting is a reversal of removal. Refit the battery as described earlier in this Section.

4.9a Release the wiring loom securing clips...

4.9b... and move the fuse/relay box to one side

4.10a Undo the three securing bolts...

4.10b... and withdraw the battery tray from the engine compartment

7.4 Unclip the plastic cover cap...

7.5... then unscrew the cable securing nuts

7.6 Release the wiring loom securing clip from the bracket

5 Charging system – testing

Note: *Refer to the warnings given in 'Safety first!' and in Section 1 of this Chapter before starting work.*

1 If the charge warning light fails to illuminate when the ignition is switched on, first check the alternator wiring connections for security. If the light still fails to illuminate, check the continuity of the warning light feed wire from the alternator to the instrument panel. If all is satisfactory, the alternator is at fault and should be renewed or taken to an auto-electrician for testing and repair.

2 If the ignition warning light illuminates when the engine is running, stop the engine and check that the drivebelt is intact and correctly tensioned (see Chapter 1 Section 7), and that the alternator connections are secure. If all is so far satisfactory, have the alternator checked by an auto-electrician for testing and repair.

3 If the alternator output is suspect even though the warning light functions correctly, the regulated voltage may be checked as follows.

4 Connect a voltmeter across the battery terminals and start the engine.

5 Increase the engine speed until the voltmeter reading remains steady; the reading should be approximately 12 to 13 volts, and no more than 14 volts.

6 Switch on as many electrical accessories (eg, the headlights, heated rear window and heater blower) as possible, and check that the

alternator maintains the regulated voltage at around 13 to 14 volts.

7 If the regulated voltage is not as stated, the fault may be due to worn brushes, weak brush springs, a faulty voltage regulator, a faulty diode, a severed phase winding or worn or damaged slip-rings. The alternator should be renewed or taken to an auto-electrician for testing and repair.

6 Alternator drivebelt – removal, refitting and tensioning

1 Refer to the procedure given for the auxiliary drivebelt in Chapter 1 Section 21.

7 Alternator – removal and refitting

Note: *Refer to the warnings given in 'Safety first!' and in Section 1 of this Chapter before starting work.*

Removal

1 Slacken the clamp nut, then detach the earth lead from the battery negative (earth) terminal post. Position the lead well away from the battery.

2 Apply the handbrake, then jack up the front of the car and support on axle stands (see *Jacking and vehicle support*).

3 Remove the auxiliary drivebelt as described in Chapter 1 Section 21.

4 Unclip the plastic cover from the terminals on the rear of the alternator **(see illustration)**.

5 Undo the two nuts and disconnect the wiring connectors from the alternator **(see illustration)**.

6 Unclip the wiring loom from the retaining clip at the top of the alternator and move it to one side **(see illustration)**. On models with air conditioning, it may be necessary to disconnect the wiring connector from the compressor to allow the wiring loom to be moved to one side.

7 Support the alternator, then remove the lower adjuster lockbolt and upper pivot bolt, and remove the alternator from its mounting lugs on the engine **(see illustrations)**. Lift the alternator upwards and out from the engine compartment.

Refitting

8 Refitting is a reversal of removal, noting the following points:
a) Only fit the pivot and lockbolts hand-tight to begin with.
b) Ensure that the wiring is reconnected correctly, and that the retaining nuts are tight.
c) Refit and tension the auxiliary drivebelt, as described in Chapter 1 Section 21.

8 Alternator – testing and overhaul

1 If the alternator is thought to be suspect, it should be removed from the car and taken

7.7a Remove the lower adjuster bolt...

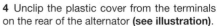

7.7b... and upper pivot bolt...

7.7c... and then withdraw the alternator from the engine

10.3 Undo the two cable securing nuts and the wiring bracket bolt

10.4a Remove the starter motor upper bolt...

10.4b... and the lower bolt

to an auto-electrician for testing. Most auto-electricians will be able to supply and fit brushes at a reasonable cost. However, check on the cost of repairs before proceeding, as it may prove more economical to obtain a new or exchange alternator.

9 Starting system – testing

Note: *Refer to the precautions given in 'Safety first!' and in Section 1 of this Chapter before starting work.*

1 If the starter motor fails to operate when the ignition key is turned to the appropriate position, the following possible causes may be to blame:
a) *The battery is faulty.*
b) *The electrical connections between the switch, solenoid, battery and starter motor are somewhere failing to pass the necessary current from the battery through the starter to earth.*
c) *The solenoid is faulty.*
d) *The starter motor is mechanically or electrically defective.*

2 To check the battery, switch on the headlights. If they dim after a few seconds, this indicates that the battery is discharged – recharge (see Section 3) or renew the battery. If the headlights glow brightly, operate the ignition switch and observe the lights. If they dim, then this indicates that current is reaching the starter motor; therefore the fault must lie in the starter motor. If the lights continue to glow brightly (and no clicking sound can be heard from the starter motor solenoid), this indicates that there is a fault in the circuit or solenoid – see following paragraphs. If the starter motor turns slowly when operated, but the battery is in good condition, then this indicates that either the starter motor is faulty, or there is considerable resistance somewhere in the circuit.

3 If a fault in the circuit is suspected, disconnect the battery leads (including the earth connection to the body), the starter/solenoid wiring and the engine/transmission earth strap. Thoroughly clean the connections, and reconnect the leads

and wiring, then use a voltmeter or test light to check that full battery voltage is available at the battery positive lead connection to the solenoid, and that the earth is sound. Smear petroleum jelly around the battery terminals to prevent corrosion – corroded connections are amongst the most frequent causes of electrical system faults.

4 If the battery and all connections are in good condition, check the circuit by disconnecting the wire from the solenoid terminal. Connect a voltmeter or test light between the wire end and a good earth (such as the battery negative terminal), and check that the wire is live when the ignition switch is turned to the 'start' position. If it is, then the circuit is sound – if not, the circuit wiring can be checked as described in Chapter 12 Section 2.

5 The solenoid contacts can be checked, by connecting a voltmeter or test light between the battery positive feed connection on the starter side of the solenoid and earth. When the ignition switch is turned to the start position, there should be a reading or lighted bulb, as applicable. If there is no reading or lighted bulb, the solenoid is faulty and should be renewed.

6 If the circuit and solenoid are proved sound, the fault must lie in the starter motor. In this event, it may be possible to have the starter motor overhauled by a specialist, but check on the cost of spares before proceeding, as it may prove more economical to obtain a new or exchange motor.

10 Starter motor – removal and refitting

Note: *Refer to the warnings given in 'Safety first!' and in Section 1 of this Chapter before starting work.*

Removal

1 Slacken the clamp nut, then detach the earth lead from the battery negative (earth) terminal post. Position the lead well away from the battery.

2 Apply the handbrake, then jack up the front of the car and support on axle stands (see *Jacking and vehicle support*).

3 Working beneath the rear of the engine, remove the rubber covers and undo the retaining nuts to disconnect the wiring connectors from the starter motor. Undo the bolt for the wiring loom retaining bracket and move the wiring to one side **(see illustration)**.

4 Support the starter motor, then unscrew and remove the two starter mounting bolts from the transmission bellhousing **(see illustrations)**.

5 Withdraw the starter motor from the rear of the bell housing, and then remove the plastic spacer from the cylinder block **(see illustrations)**.

Refitting

6 Refitting is a reversal of removal, noting the following points:

10.5a Remove the starter motor...

10.5b... and the plastic spacer from the bellhousing

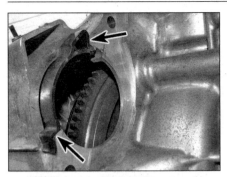

10.6 Make sure the plastic spacer is located in the bellhousing when refitting

a) Make sure the plastic spacer is fitted correctly **(see illustration)** before refitting the starter motor.
b) Ensure that the wiring is reconnected correctly, and that the retaining nuts are tight.
c) Tighten the mounting bolts to the specified torque.

11 Starter motor – testing and overhaul

1 If the starter motor is thought to be suspect, it should be removed from the car and taken to an auto-electrician for testing. Most auto-electricians will be able to supply and fit brushes at a reasonable cost. However, check on the cost of repairs before proceeding, as it may prove more economical to obtain a new or exchange motor.

Chapter 5 Part B
Ignition system

Contents

Degrees of difficulty

Easy, suitable for novice with little experience	Fairly easy, suitable for beginner with some experience	Fairly difficult, suitable for competent DIY mechanic	Difficult, suitable for experienced DIY mechanic	Very difficult, suitable for expert DIY or professional

Specifications

General

System type	Direct ignition system (DIS) with one ignition coil per cylinder, controlled by the engine ECU
Firing order.	1-2-3
Location of No 1 cylinder.	Timing chain end
Ignition timing (ECU-controlled)	Not adjustable

Ignition system data

Ignition timing advance (ECU-controlled).	8 to 12° BTDC
Ignition coil resistances (typical):	
Primary windings	0.4 to 0.6 ohms
Secondary windings.	10 500 to 16 500 ohms

Torque wrench settings

	Nm	lbf ft
Ignition coil mounting bolts	8	6
Knock sensor	20	15
Spark plugs	25	18

1 General information and precautions

General information

1 The ignition system is integrated with the fuel injection system to form a combined engine management system under the control of the engine management ECU (see Chapter 4A Section 1 for further information). The main ignition system components include the ignition switch, the battery, the crankshaft speed/position sensor, the camshaft position sensor, the knock sensor, the three ignition coils, and the spark plugs.
2 A Direct Ignition System (DIS) is fitted, where the main functions of a conventional distributor are performed by a computerised module within the engine ECU. Based on the inputs from the crankshaft and camshaft position sensors (besides all the input on engine load, temperature, etc, from the fuel

system sensors), the engine ECU is able to calculate precisely the best ignition timing for any given situation. The ECU sends out the trigger to each coil in the firing order, and the coils, which are fitted directly to their individual spark plugs, ignite the fuel/air mixture in the cylinders. Having one coil per cylinder gives an even greater control refinement, as the timing can be altered rapidly to suit changing conditions. Unlike the distributorless ignition systems seen on many modern cars, there is no 'wasted spark' with the coil-on-plug direct system, which theoretically means extended spark plug life. Greater potential reliability is also derived from having no ignition HT leads.
3 The information contained in this Chapter concentrates on the ignition-related components of the engine management system. Information covering the fuel, exhaust and emission control components can be found in the applicable Parts of Chapter 4.

Precautions

4 The following precautions must be

observed, to prevent damage to the ignition system components and to reduce risk of personal injury:
a) *Do not keep the ignition on for more than 10 seconds if the engine will not start.*
b) *Ensure that the ignition is switched off before disconnecting any of the ignition wiring.*
c) *Ensure that the ignition is switched off before connecting or disconnecting any ignition test equipment.*
d) *Do not earth the coil primary or secondary circuits.*

⚠ ***Warning: Voltages produced by an electronic ignition system are considerably higher than those produced by conventional ignition systems. Extreme care must be taken when working on the system with the ignition switched on. Persons with surgically implanted cardiac pacemaker devices should keep well clear of the ignition circuits, components and test equipment.***

3.2 Unclip the air cleaner cover retaining clips

3.3a Release the hose clips from the throttle housing...

3.3b... and the breather pipe

2 Ignition system – testing

Note: *Don't overlook the possibility of a problem with the immobiliser system on a non-starting engine (see Chapter 12). Genuine keys will contain the necessary transponder chip, but ones supplied from other sources may not.*

1 If the engine either will not turn over at all, or only turns very slowly, check the battery and starter motor as described in Chapter 5A.

2 Check each coil's primary and secondary winding resistance as described in Section 3; renew the coil if faulty, but be careful to carefully check the wiring connections themselves before doing so, to ensure that the fault is not due to dirty or poorly-fastened connectors.

3 If the engine runs but has an irregular misfire, check the wiring plugs on the ignition coils, ensuring that all connections are clean and securely fastened. Also ensure that there is no damage to the wiring harness leading to each coil. It's not unknown for a coil to break down under load, especially in hot conditions. Check the spark plugs (by substitution, if necessary).

4 The most likely cause of total failure would be a problem with the crankshaft sensor (the camshaft sensor would perhaps be a close second). Check the condition of the wiring, and that the wiring plugs are clean and

secure, as a first step. These components are both relatively easy to renew, but first weigh up their cost compared with having the car checked by a franchised dealer or other specialist – the fault may lie elsewhere.

5 If simple checks fail to reveal the cause of the problem, the car should be taken to a franchised dealer or suitably-equipped garage for diagnostic testing. A wiring connector is incorporated in the engine management circuit (under the steering column) into which a special electronic diagnostic tester can be plugged. The tester will locate the fault quickly and simply, alleviating the need to test all the system components individually, which is a time-consuming operation that carries a high risk of damaging the ECU. If necessary, the system wiring and wiring connectors can be checked as described in Chapter 12.

3 Ignition coils – removal, testing and refitting

Removal

1 Make sure the ignition is switched off (take out the key) and open the bonnet.

2 Release the four spring clips on the side of the air cleaner cover **(see illustration)**.

3 Slacken the two securing clips from the throttle housing and breather pipe **(see illustrations)**, and then lift the air cleaner cover from the top of the engine.

4 Disconnect the wiring plug from the first coil to be removed **(see illustration)**. Though it seems unlikely that the wiring plugs could be mixed up, it might be safest to disconnect and remove one coil at a time. If all the coils are to be removed, mark them and their respective wiring plugs with labels or tape to indicate their fitted positions (No 1 at the timing chain end).

5 Remove the coil mounting bolt, then pull upwards to remove the coil from its spark plug **(see illustrations)**.

Testing

6 Using an ohmmeter, measure the resistances of the ignition coil's primary and secondary windings, and compare with the information given in the Specifications – measure between the two wiring plug terminals, then between each terminal and the connection for the spark plug. Confirm your findings with a Peugeot dealer before renewing the coil – a variation in the resistances found is not likely to be significant, but a zero or infinity reading would suggest a problem with the coil.

7 Check for battery voltage at the positive terminal of the coil wiring plug, with the ignition temporarily switched on.

Refitting

8 Refitting is a reversal of removal. Repeat the procedure for the remaining coils as necessary.

3.4 Disconnect the wiring connector

3.5a Undo the retaining bolt...

3.5b... and withdraw the ignition coil

4 Ignition system sensors – removal and refitting

Note: *Several of the more fuel-related sensors described in Chapter 4A, Section 12, may also have a bearing on the ignition system. Those listed below are the most likely to give rise to an ignition system fault.*
a) *Crankshaft position sensor.*
b) *Camshaft position sensor.*
c) *Manifold absolute pressure (MAP) sensor.*

Knock sensor

Removal

1 The sensor is used to detect the onset of pinking (pre-ignition or detonation, usually noticed in hot conditions, or when running on sub-standard or low-octane fuel). It is screwed into the engine block at the rear of the engine, and works by detecting the specific vibrations produced by pinking. When signaled by the knock sensor, the ECU retards the ignition timing until the pinking stops, and then advances it slowly until it just recurs, thus maintaining maximum engine efficiency while avoiding the risk of engine damage.
2 Chock the rear wheels, then jack up the front of the car and support it on axle stands (see *Jacking and vehicle support*).
3 Working from under the vehicle, at the rear of the cylinder block, disconnect the wiring plug from the sensor **(see illustration)**.
4 Unscrew the retaining bolt and remove the sensor from the rear of the engine **(see illustration)**. Note the position of the sensor before removal, as it needs to be refitted in the same position.

Refitting

5 Refitting is a reversal of removal. Make sure the contact face between the sensor and cylinder block are clean. It is essential that the

4.3 Disconnect the wiring connector

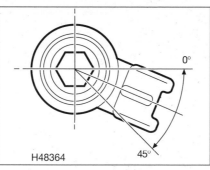

H48364   0°   45°

4.5 The sensor should be angled between 0° to 45°

sensor be tightened to the specified torque, and at the right angle **(see illustration)**, as failure to do so may prevent it from working properly.

5 Ignition timing – checking and adjustment

1 Due to the nature of the ignition system, the ignition timing is constantly being monitored and adjusted by the engine management ECU

4.4 Knock sensor securing bolt

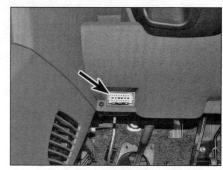

5.2 Diagnostic plug connector in lower part of facia

(refer to Chapter 4A Section 1), and nominal values cannot be given. Therefore, it is not possible for the home mechanic to check the ignition timing.
2 The only way, in which the ignition timing can be checked is using special electronic test equipment, connected to the engine management system diagnostic connector **(see illustration)**. No adjustment of the ignition timing is possible. Should the ignition timing be incorrect, a fault must be present in the engine management system.

Notes

Chapter 6
Clutch

Contents

Degrees of difficulty

Easy, suitable for novice with little experience	**Fairly easy,** suitable for beginner with some experience	**Fairly difficult,** suitable for competent DIY mechanic	**Difficult,** suitable for experienced DIY mechanic	**Very difficult,** suitable for expert DIY or professional

Specifications

General

Clutch type	Single dry plate with diaphragm spring
Manual transmission	Cable-operated release mechanism
Multi-Mode Transmission (MMT)	Electrically-operated release mechanism
Make:	
Manual Transmission	LUK
Multi-Mode Transmission	ASIN or Valeo
Disc diameter:	
Manual Transmission	181.0 mm
Multi-Mode Transmission	190.0 mm
Friction material thickness (new)	3.5 mm (approximate)
Disc run-out (maximum)	0.8 mm

Clutch pedal

Pedal height from floor:	
Right-hand drive	166.0 ± 5.0 mm
Left-hand drive	140.0 ± 5.0 mm
Pedal free play	18.0 to 28.0 mm
'Bite' point	25.0 mm (minimum) from floor

Torque wrench setting	**Nm**	**lbf ft**
Pressure plate-to-flywheel bolts	19	14

2.2 Release the clutch return spring

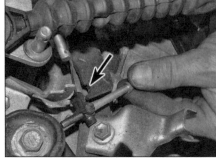

2.3a Unhook the adjuster from the lever...

2.3b... and pull the outer cable from the bracket

1 General Information

1 The clutch consists of a friction disc, a pressure plate assembly, and a release bearing sandwiched between the engine and the transmission.

2 The clutch friction disc is fitted between the engine flywheel and the clutch pressure plate, and is allowed to slide on the transmission input shaft splines.

3 The pressure plate assembly is bolted to the engine flywheel. When the engine is running, drive is transmitted from the crankshaft, via the flywheel, to the friction disc (these components being clamped securely together by the pressure plate assembly) and from the friction disc to the transmission input shaft.

4 On manual transmissions, the release mechanism is mechanical and is operated by a cable. To interrupt the drive, the spring pressure must be relaxed by the clutch release mechanism. Depressing the clutch pedal operates the cable, which in turn operates the clutch lever and presses the release bearing against the pressure plate spring fingers. This causes the springs to deform and releases the clamping force on the pressure plate.

5 On Multi-Mode Transmissions (MMT), the release mechanism is electrical and an actuator on top of the transmission operates the clutch lever. When a gear is selected, and the brake pedal is released, the MMT electronic control unit (ECU) partially engages

the clutch via the actuator. When the driver depresses the accelerator pedal, the clutch is then fully engaged and the vehicle can be driven. As the vehicle speed decreases and the brakes are applied, the MMT ECU then sends a signal to the actuator to disengage the clutch. The actuator operates the clutch lever and presses the release bearing against the pressure plate spring fingers. This causes the springs to deform and releases the clamping force on the pressure plate.

6 When the pedal is released, the diaphragm spring forces the pressure plate into contact with the friction linings on the friction disc. The disc is now firmly sandwiched between the pressure plate and the flywheel, thus transmitting engine power to the transmission.

7 On manual transmissions, it is recommended that adjustment of the clutch cable be carried out every 18 000 miles.

8 On Multi-Mode Transmissions, the pressure plate has a self-adjusting mechanism, which automatically compensates for wear of the friction material on the clutch disc.

2 Clutch cable – removal and refitting

Removal

1 Open the bonnet and remove the battery and battery tray as described in Chapter 5A Section 4.

2 Release the return spring from the end of

the operating lever (see illustration), and remove it from the engine compartment.

3 Unhook the adjuster nut from the end of the operating lever and then pull the outer cable back, to release it from the mounting bracket (see illustrations). If required, slacken the adjustment on the cable, but note its position for refitting.

4 Working inside the driver's side footwell, move the driver's seat fully to the rear. Remove the facia lower trim panels as described in Chapter 11 Section 26 to access the clutch pedal. If required, remove the upper facia panel to make access easier.

5 Reach up to the top of the clutch pedal assembly, and then unhook the cable from the recess in the top of the pedal (see illustration).

6 Working under the bonnet, release the clutch cable from the retaining clips along the rear of the engine compartment and withdraw the cable from the rubber grommet in the bulkhead (see illustrations).

Refitting

7 Refit the cable through the rubber grommet in the bulkhead and secure the outer cable in the retaining clips.

8 Working inside the driver's side footwell, reconnect the inner cable to the recess in the top of the clutch pedal, making sure it has located correctly. Apply a small amount of grease to the inner cable.

9 Working inside the engine compartment, reconnect the other end of the outer cable to the mounting bracket on the transmission,

2.5 Unhook the cable from the recess (arrowed) in the top of the pedal

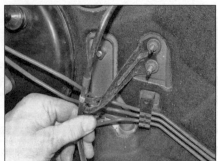

2.6a Unclip the cable from the retaining clip...

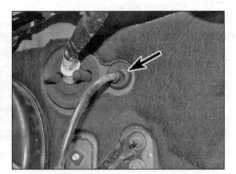

2.6b... and pull the rubber grommet from the bulkhead

3.4 Clutch pedal pivot bolt

3.9a Clutch pedal height adjuster bolt

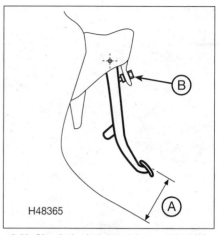

H48365

3.9b Check the height of the pedal at (A) and adjust stop (B)

and the inner cable to the operating lever. Refit to the position noted on removal.

10 To check the free play in the pedal and adjust the clutch pedal height, see Section 3.

11 Refit the facia trim panels as described in Chapter 11 Section 26.

12 Refit the battery and tray as described in Chapter 5A Section 4.

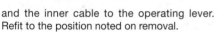

3 Clutch pedal – removal, refitting and adjustment

Removal

1 Working inside the driver's side footwell, move the driver's seat fully to the rear. Remove the facia lower trim panels as described in Chapter 11 Section 26, to access the clutch pedal. If required, remove the upper facia panel to make access easier.

2 It will be necessary to release the return spring and slacken the adjustment on the cable at the transmission end before removal. See Section 2.

3 Reach up to the top of the clutch pedal assembly, and then unhook the cable from the recess in the top of the pedal.

4 Unscrew and remove the pedal pivot bolt/ nut, and remove the pedal **(see illustration)**.

Refitting

5 Refitting is a reversal of removal. Tighten the pedal pivot bolt/nut securely, and check the operation of the clutch thoroughly before taking the car out on the road. Adjust the pedal if necessary, as described below.

Adjustment

6 With the pedal released, measure the distance from the floor (directly below the pedal) to the top of the rubber pad (pedal height). Do not lift the pedal when making the measurement.

7 Check the pedal free play by depressing the pedal until resistance is felt, and measure the distance from the fully-released position to this point. It may be easier, therefore, to press the pedal by hand for this check.

8 If the first two measurements are correct, the final check is that the clutch pedal 'bite' point (the point where the clutch begins

to engage) should be at least the distance specified from the pedal to the floor.

9 If the pedal height or bite point require adjustment, this is achieved by loosening the locknut and turning the adjuster bolt at the top of the pedal as necessary **(see illustrations)**. Some trial-and-error will be required until the height falls into the range specified. Tighten the locknut on completion.

10 If the pedal free play is excessive, turn the plastic nut on the outer cable at the transmission end of the cable, and turn the nut until the free play dimension is as specified **(see illustration)**.

4 Clutch assembly – removal, inspection and refitting

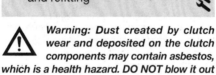

> **Warning: Dust created by clutch wear and deposited on the clutch components may contain asbestos, which is a health hazard. DO NOT blow it out with compressed air, or inhale any of it. DO NOT use petrol or petroleum-based solvents to clean off the dust. Brake system cleaner or methylated spirit should be used to flush the dust into a suitable receptacle. After the clutch components are wiped clean with rags, dispose of the contaminated rags and cleaner in a sealed, marked container.**
> **Note:** Although some friction materials may no longer contain asbestos, it is safest to assume that they do, and to take precautions accordingly.

3.10 Clutch cable adjuster nut

Removal

1 Unless the complete engine/transmission unit has to be removed from the car (see Chapter 2B Section 4), the clutch can be reached by removing the transmission as described in Chapter 7A or Chapter 7B.

2 Unless a new clutch is being fitted, use chalk or a marker pen to mark the relationship of the pressure plate assembly to the flywheel **(see illustration)**.

3 Hold the flywheel stationary using a suitable tool engaged with the starter ring gear teeth – a piece of metal can be tightened to one of the bolt holes, or alternatively an assistant can use a wide-bladed screwdriver engaged with the teeth **(see illustration)**.

4.2 Mark the position of the pressure plate to the flywheel

4.3 Locking the flywheel in position with a homemade tool

4.5 Remove the pressure plate and friction disc

4.13a Special tool presses down on diaphragm spring to adjust pressure plate

4.13b Turn the adjusting ring anti-clockwise, then release pressure on the diaphragm spring

4 Working in a diagonal sequence, slacken the pressure plate bolts by half a turn at a time, until spring pressure is released and the bolts can be unscrewed by hand. Discard the bolts – new ones should be used when refitting.

5 Prise the pressure plate assembly off its locating dowels, and collect the friction disc, noting which way round the disc is fitted **(see illustration)**.

Inspection

Note: *Due to the amount of work necessary to remove and refit clutch components, it is usually considered good practice to renew the clutch friction disc, pressure plate assembly and release bearing as a matched set, even if only one of these is actually worn enough to require renewal. It is also worth considering the renewal of the clutch components on a preventive basis if the engine and/or transmission have been removed for some other reason.*

Caution: On Multi-Mode Transmissions (MMT), the clutch friction disc and pressure plate are a paired item and cannot be renewed separately

6 When cleaning clutch components, read first the warning at the beginning of this Section; remove the dust using a clean, dry cloth, and working in a well-ventilated atmosphere.

7 Check the friction disc linings for signs of wear, damage or oil contamination. If the friction material is cracked, burnt, scored or damaged, or if it is contaminated with oil or grease (shown by shiny black patches),

the clutch friction disc must be renewed. Check the depth of the rivets below the friction material surface. If any are at or near the surface of the friction material, then the friction disc must be renewed.

8 If the friction material is still serviceable, check that the centre boss splines are unworn, that the torsion springs are in good condition and securely fastened, and that all the rivets are tight. If any wear or damage is found, the friction disc must be renewed.

9 If the friction material is fouled with oil, this must be due to an oil leak from the crankshaft oil seal, or from the transmission input shaft.

10 Check the pressure plate assembly for obvious signs of wear or damage; shake it to check for loose rivets or worn or damaged fulcrum rings, and check that the drive straps securing the pressure plate to the cover do not show signs of overheating (such as a deep yellow or blue discoloration). If the diaphragm spring is worn or damaged, or if its pressure is in any way suspect, the pressure plate assembly should be renewed.

11 Examine the machined bearing surfaces of the pressure plate and of the flywheel; they should be clean, completely flat, and free from scratches or scoring. If either is discoloured from excessive heat, or shows signs of cracks, it should be renewed – although minor damage of this nature can sometimes be polished away using emery paper.

12 Check that the release bearing contact surface rotates smoothly and easily, with no sign of noise or roughness. Also check that the surface itself is smooth and unworn, with no signs of cracks, pitting or scoring. If there

is any doubt about its condition, the bearing must be renewed.

Refitting

13 On Multi-Mode Transmissions (MMT), if you are re-using the pressure plate, the adjustment ring will need to be reset. Position the pressure plate in a hydraulic press; technicians use a special tool **(see illustration)**, with a block of wood placed under the central portion of the pressure plate, directly below the diaphragm spring fingers (not on the friction face). Apply pressure to the diaphragm spring fingers until the adjusting ring is loose. While still applying pressure, use a screwdriver to rotate the adjusting ring anti-clockwise **(see illustration)**. Hold the adjustment ring in place, and then release the pressure on the diaphragm spring fingers. New pressure plates are pre-set ready for fitting.

14 On reassembly, ensure that the disc contact surfaces of the flywheel and pressure plate are completely clean, smooth, and free from oil or grease. Use solvent to remove any protective grease from new components.

15 Apply a smear of molybdenum disulphide grease to the splines of the friction disc hub, then offer the disc to the flywheel, with the greater projecting side of the hub facing away from the flywheel (most friction discs will have an Engine side marking which should face the flywheel). Hold the friction disc against the flywheel while the pressure plate assembly is offered into position, or alternatively use the centralising tool described in paragraph 17 to hold the disc on the flywheel.

16 Fit the clutch pressure plate assembly, where applicable aligning the marks with those on the flywheel. Ensure that the pressure plate assembly locates over the dowels on the flywheel. Insert the securing bolts and washers, and tighten them finger-tight, so that the friction disc is gripped, but can still be moved.

17 The friction disc must now be centralised, to ensure correct alignment of the transmission input shaft with the spigot bearing in the crankshaft/flywheel **(see illustrations)**. To do this, a proprietary tool may be used, or alternatively, use a wooden mandrel made to fit inside the friction disc hub and spigot bearing. Insert the tool through the

4.17a Centralise the clutch plate...

4.17b... and fit the assembly onto the flywheel

friction disc into the spigot bearing, and make sure that it is central.

18 Tighten the clutch pressure plate bolts progressively and in diagonal sequence, until the specified torque setting is achieved, and then remove the centralising tool.

19 Check the release bearing in the front of the transmission for smooth operation, and if necessary renew it with reference to Section 5.

20 Apply a thin smear of molybdenum disulphide grease to the splines of the friction disc and the transmission input shaft **(see illustration)**.

Caution: Do not apply too much grease, as there is a risk that it will contaminate the friction disc material.

21 Refit the transmission as described in Chapter 7A or Chapter 7B.

5 Clutch release bearing – removal, inspection and refitting

Removal

1 For access to the clutch release bearing, the transmission must be removed as described in Chapter 7A or Chapter 7B.

2 Release the retaining clip and release the bearing from the release arm, withdraw the bearing along the guide and remove it from the input shaft **(see illustrations)**.

Inspection

3 It is often considered worthwhile to renew the release bearing as a matter of course regardless of its condition, considering the amount of work necessary to access it. Check that the contact surface rotates smoothly and

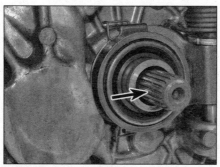
4.20 Apply a small amount of grease to the splines

5.2b... and withdraw the thrust bearing

easily, with no sign of noise or roughness, and that the surface itself is smooth and unworn, with no signs of cracks, pitting or scoring. If there is any doubt about its condition, the bearing must be renewed.

Refitting

4 Apply a little molybdenum disulphide

5.2a Release the retaining clips...

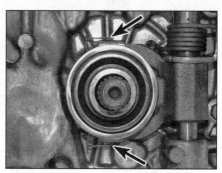
5.5 Make sure the retaining clips (arrowed) are located correctly

grease to the release bearing contact points on the release arm.

5 Slide the bearing onto the guide and secure to the lever with the retaining clip **(see illustration)**.

6 Refit the transmission with reference to Chapter 7A or Chapter 7B.

Notes

Chapter 7 Part A
Manual transmission

Contents

Degrees of difficulty

Easy, suitable for novice with little experience	Fairly easy, suitable for beginner with some experience	Fairly difficult, suitable for competent DIY mechanic	Difficult, suitable for experienced DIY mechanic	Very difficult, suitable for expert DIY or professional

Specifications

General

Transmission type.	Five forward speeds, one reverse. Synchromesh on all forward gears. Gearchange linkage operated by twin cables
Transmission code	C551
Transmission oil	Refer to *Lubricants and fluids* on page 0•16
Transmission weight.	28.2 kg

Gear ratios

1st	3.545: 1
2nd	1.913: 1
3rd	1.310: 1
4th	1.027: 1
5th	0.850: 1
Reverse	3.214: 1
Final drive.	3.550: 1

Torque wrench settings

	Nm	lbf ft
Drain plug.	29	21
Engine/transmission mountings:		
Left-hand mounting bolts.	52	38
Rear mounting through-bolt.	120	89
Filler/level plug	39	29
Gear lever assembly mounting bolts	12	9
Gear neutral switch (engaged sensor)	40	30
Gear select and shift actuator mounting bolts.	18	13
Reversing light switch	40	30
Roadwheel bolts.	100	74
Starter motor mounting bolts.	37	27
Transmission revolution sensor	8	6
Transmission-to-engine bolts.	64	47
Transmission-to-engine lower plate bolts	40	30

2.4 Transmission oil filler/level plug

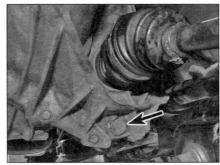

2.5 Transmission oil drain plug

2.6 Remove the drain plug and allow the oil to drain

1 General Information

1 This Part of Chapter 7 contains information on the manual transmission. In Chapter 7B, service procedures for the Multi-Mode Transmission (MMT) system will be found – this is also known as a '2-Tronic' transmission in Peugeot handbooks and 'SensoDrive' in Citroen handbooks.

2 The transmission is contained in a cast-aluminium alloy casing bolted to the engine's left-hand end, and consists of the gearbox and final drive differential – often called a transaxle.

3 The 5-speed transmission has a cable-actuated gearchange linkage, with gear selection via a floor-mounted lever and two cables.

4 Drive is transmitted from the crankshaft via the clutch to the input shaft, which has a splined extension to accept the clutch friction disc. From the input shaft, drive is transmitted to the output shaft, from where the drive is transmitted to the differential crownwheel, which rotates with the differential and planetary gears, thus driving the sun gears and driveshafts. The rotation of the planetary gears on their shaft allows the inner roadwheel to rotate at a slower speed than the outer roadwheel when the car is cornering.

5 The transmission selector mechanism causes the appropriate selector fork to move its respective synchro-sleeve along the

output shaft, to lock the gear pinion to the synchro-hub. Since the synchro-hubs are splined to the output shaft, this locks the pinion to the shaft, so that drive can be transmitted. To ensure that gearchanging can be made quickly and quietly, a synchromesh system is fitted to all forward gears, consisting of baulk rings and spring-loaded fingers, as well as the gear pinions and synchro-hubs. The synchromesh cones are formed on the mating faces of the baulk rings and gear pinions.

Transmission overhaul

6 Because of the complexity of the assembly, possible unavailability of parts and special tools necessary, internal repair procedures for the transmission are not recommended for the home mechanic. The bulk of the information in this Chapter is devoted to removal and refitting procedures.

2 Transmission oil renewal

1 This operation is much quicker and more efficient if the car is first taken on a journey of sufficient length to warm the engine/transmission up to normal operating temperature. However, take care to avoid burning yourself on any hot components when working underneath the car.

2 Park the car on a level surface, switch off the ignition and apply the handbrake firmly. For improved access to the filler/level plug, apply the handbrake, then jack up the front

of the vehicle and support it on axle stands (see *Jacking and vehicle support*), Note that the car can be raised at the front only for oil draining, but the vehicle will need to be level when refilling the transmission, to ensure an accurate level check.

3 Where fitted, remove the engine lower cover panels from under the car.

4 Remove all traces of dirt, and then unscrew the filler/level plug from the front face of the transmission **(see illustration)**. This will probably be tight – use a good-quality spanner or socket to unscrew it, and take care to avoid personal injury. Where applicable, a new washer should be fitted to the filler/level plug when refitting.

5 Wipe clean the area around the drain plug, which is situated on the base of the transmission, just below the left-hand driveshaft inner CV joint **(see illustration)**. Position a suitable container under the drain plug, and unscrew the plug – this will also probably be tight, and will need a new washer when refitting.

6 Allow the oil to drain completely into the container **(see illustration)**. If the oil is hot, take precautions against scalding. Clean the drain plug, being especially careful to wipe any metallic particles off the magnetic insert. Discard the sealing washer; it should be renewed whenever it is disturbed.

7 When the oil has finished draining, clean the drain plug threads and those of the transmission casing, fit a new sealing washer and refit the drain plug **(see illustration)**, tightening it to the specified torque wrench setting.

8 Refilling the transmission is an awkward operation. Above all, allow plenty of time for the oil level to settle properly before checking it. Note that the car must be parked on flat level ground (or if it is raised, it must be level) when checking the oil level.

9 Fill the transmission with the specified grade of oil (see *Lubricants and fluids*) until the oil just starts to run out **(see illustration)**. Allow any excess oil to flow out until the level stabilises.

10 When the level is correct, clean and refit the filler/level plug (with a new washer, where fitted), then tighten it to the specified torque **(see illustration)**.

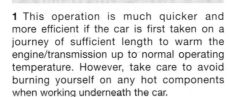

2.7 Fit new sealing washer when refitting

2.9 Fill the transmission until the oil starts to run out

2.10 Refit the filler/level plug

3.2a On the left-hand cable, pull out the spring clip...

3.2b... then unhook the end fitting from the operating lever

11 Where applicable, refit the lower cover panels, and lower the car to the ground.
12 Although not strictly necessary, to ensure maximum accuracy take the car on a short journey so that the new oil is distributed fully around the transmission components, then check the level again on your return.

3.2c On the right-hand cable, spread the spring clip (arrowed) to release the ball fitting

3.3 Both cables are detached at the front by prising upwards

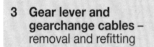

3 Gear lever and gearchange cables – removal and refitting

Removal

Cables

1 Remove the centre console as described in Chapter 11 Section 25.
2 Noting their positions for refitting, remove the spring clips and disconnect the two cables from their respective operating levers on the gearchange unit (see illustrations).
3 Prise up the gearchange outer cables to detach their collars from the front of the gearchange unit (see illustration).
4 Jack up the front of the car, and support it on axle stands (see *Jacking and vehicle support*).
5 Under the car, remove the two nuts securing the cables' floor plate/grommet, and also release the cable bracket attached to the underside of the car (see illustrations).
6 With the cables free to move, draw them through from the inside of the car, and let them hang down. Take care not to kink or bend the cables during removal. Check for any further mounting brackets, clips, or ties, and

disconnect them as necessary. If preferred, the car can now be lowered to the ground.
7 To make access to the cables better, it may be necessary to remove the battery and battery tray, as described in Chapter 5A Section 4.

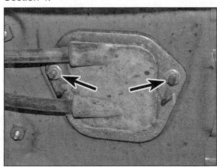

3.5a Undo the two securing nuts from the cable floor plate...

3.5b... and release the cables from the securing bracket

8 On top of the transmission, slide out the metal clips used to hold the cables to the support bracket on the transmission, noting their positions (see illustrations). Alternatively (and depending on the nature of the work being carried out), the support bracket itself

3.8a Slide out the metal retaining clips...

3.8b... and unhook the cables from the support bracket...

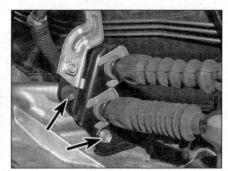

3.8c... or undo the bracket retaining bolts

3.9a Pull out the spring clips...

3.9b... then lift off the cable end fittings

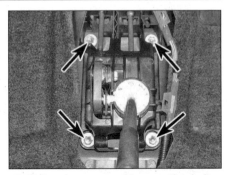

3.13 Gear lever assembly mounting bolts

may be unbolted from the transmission housing, with the cables still attached.

9 Again noting their positions for refitting, pull out the spring clips and recover the washers, then unhook the cable end fittings from the transmission shift/select mechanism **(see illustrations)**. The cables can now be removed completely, taking care not to kink or bend the cables as they are removed.

Gear lever (gearchange unit)

10 Remove the centre console as described in Chapter 11 Section 25.

11 Noting their positions for refitting, remove the spring clips and disconnect the two cables from their respective operating levers on the gearchange unit, as described previously in paragraph 2 of this Section.

12 Lift the cables to detach the retaining plates from the front of the gearchange unit,

as described previously in paragraph 3 of this Section. Move the cables to one side.

13 Remove the four bolts securing the unit to the floor, then lift it out and remove it from the car **(see illustration)**.

Refitting

14 Refitting is a reversal of removal. Check that all gears can be selected before taking the car out on the road.

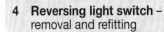

4 Reversing light switch – removal and refitting

Removal

1 The switch is located on the top of the transmission, at the far left-hand side. With

the transmission fitted to the vehicle, the switch is covered by the battery tray and transmission mounting **(see illustration)**.

2 Trace the wiring from the switch, and disconnect it at the in-line connector, which is on the front of the unit **(see illustration)**.

3 Remove the battery and battery tray, as described in Chapter 5A Section 4.

4 Support the transmission using a trolley jack, then undo the retaining bolts and remove the transmission mounting **(see illustration)**, with reference to Chapter 2A Section 17.

5 Unscrew and remove the switch from the top of the transmission, release the wiring from any retaining clips.

Refitting

6 Refitting is a reversal of removal. Tighten the switch securely.

5 Oil seals – renewal

1 Oil leaks frequently occur due to wear or deterioration of the driveshaft oil seals, or even the vehicle speed sensor O-ring. Renewal of these seals is relatively easy, since the repairs can be performed without removing the transmission from the car.

Driveshaft oil seals

2 The driveshaft oil seals are located at the sides of the transmission, where the driveshafts enter the transmission. If leakage at the seal is suspected, raise the car and support it securely on axle stands. If the seal is leaking, oil will be found on the side of the transmission below the driveshaft.

3 Refer to Chapter 8 Section 2 and remove the appropriate driveshaft.

4 Check the fitted depth of the seal in the housing, so that the new seal can be fitted the same **(see illustration)**.

5 Using a large screwdriver or lever, carefully prise the oil seal out of the transmission casing, taking care not to damage the transmission casing **(see illustration)**.

6 Wipe clean the oil seal seating in the transmission casing **(see illustration)**.

7 Press it a little way into the casing by hand,

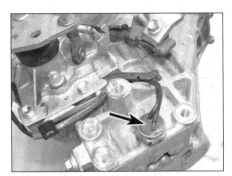

4.1 Reversing light switch in the top of the transmission

4.2 Disconnect the reversing light switch wiring plug on the front of the transmission

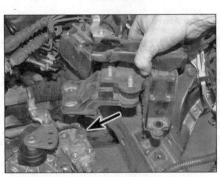

4.4 The reversing light switch is located under the engine/transmission mounting

5.4 Using a vernier gauge to check the depth of the seal in the casing

making sure that it is square to its seating **(see illustration)**.

8 Using suitable tubing or a large socket **(see illustration)**, carefully drive the oil seal into the casing, until it is fitted to the depth noted on removal. Do not tap it all the way into the casing, as this may cause it not to seal against the driveshaft when it is fitted.

9 Refit the driveshaft with reference to Chapter 8 Section 2.

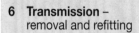

6 Transmission – removal and refitting

Note: *Read through this procedure before starting work to see what is involved, particularly in terms of lifting equipment. Depending on the facilities available, the home mechanic may prefer to remove the engine and transmission together, and then separate them on the bench, as described in Chapter 2B. The help of an assistant is highly recommended if the transmission is to be removed (and later refitted) on its own.*

Removal

1 Remove the air cleaner as described in Chapter 4A Section 5.

2 Remove the battery and battery tray, as described in Chapter 5A Section 4. Also working from the information in Chapter 5A Section 10, remove the starter motor.

3 Pull out the spring clips and then unhook the gearchange cable end fittings from the transmission shift/select mechanism, noting

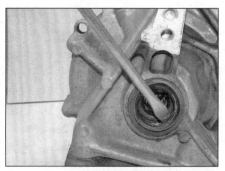

5.5 Carefully prise the seal from the casing

5.7 Position the seal in the casing...

their fitted positions **(see illustrations)**.

4 Unbolt the mounting bracket and move the cables clear of the transmission, taking care not to kink or bend them **(see illustrations)**.

5 Disconnect the clutch cable from the clutch operating lever on the top of the transmission,

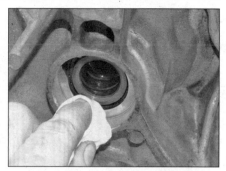

5.6 Clean out the recess in the casing

5.8... and tap the seal into the position noted on removal

refer to Chapter 6 Section 2 for further information.

6 Disconnect the wiring from the reversing light switch and disconnect it. Unclip the wiring from the bracket on the transmission **(see illustrations)**.

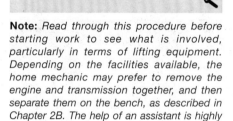

6.3a Pull out the spring clips...

6.3b... then lift off the cable end fittings

6.4a Undo the retaining bolts...

6.4b... and move the cable bracket to one side

6.6a Disconnect the reversing light wiring connector...

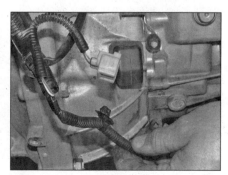

6.6b... and unclip the wiring loom retaining clip

6.8 Unbolt the earth cable from the front of the transmission

6.9 Disconnect the lower oxygen sensor wiring connector

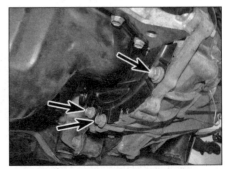

6.10 Undo the lower shield retaining bolts

6.13a Slacken the two front transmission bolts...

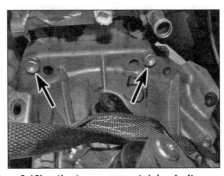

6.13b... the two upper retaining bolts...

6.13c... and the lower rear transmission bolt

7 Jack up the front of the car, and support it on axle stands (see *Jacking and vehicle support*). The car must be raised sufficiently that the transmission can be lowered out and removed underneath. Consideration should also be given to the need to support the engine, once the rear and left-hand mountings are disconnected.

8 Unbolt and remove the earth cable from the front of the transmission housing **(see illustration)**. Unclip the wiring from the bracket on the transmission.

9 Disconnect the wiring plug from the oxygen (lambda) sensor on front of the transmission **(see illustration)**. Unclip the wiring from the bracket on the transmission.

10 Undo the three retaining bolts and remove the lower shield from the bottom of the transmission **(see illustration)**.

11 Drain the oil from the transmission, as described in Section 2.

12 Remove both driveshafts as described in Chapter 8 Section 2.

13 Slacken, but do not remove the five transmission-to-engine mounting bolts. There are two at the front of the transmission, two upper transmission bolts and one at the rear of the engine **(see illustrations)**. Leave them in place for now – this avoids using any substantial force to remove the bolts when the transmission is only supported on a jack.

14 Using a substantial hydraulic ('trolley') jack with a block of wood, raise the transmission slightly, to take the weight off its mountings. Supporting the transmission securely in this way can be difficult to achieve – due to its shape, there is a danger the transmission will roll off once disconnected. For this reason, it pays to have an assistant on hand, to steady the unit as it is lowered out.

15 Before the engine rear mounting

and left-hand transmission mounting are disconnected, the engine must be supported, preferably from above, using either an engine crane or support bar. If the engine is supported from below, using another jack (and block of wood, to protect the sump), this seriously reduces the working room for removing the transmission.

16 With the engine securely supported, first remove the through-bolts from the engine rear mounting, and then remove the mounting from the mounting bracket **(see illustrations)**.

17 Remove the three mounting-to-body bolts and four mounting-to-transmission bolts and remove the complete mounting from the engine compartment **(see illustration)**.

18 Make a final check all around the transmission, to check that there is nothing left attached to the transmission, nor anything

6.16a Undo the mounting bolts...

6.16b... and remove the rear engine mounting

6.17 Left-hand engine/transmission mounting bolts – arrowed

in the way which would prevent the unit from being lowered out.

19 Check that the transmission is securely supported (preferably with the help of an assistant), and then remove the five bolts from around the transmission bellhousing. These are the bolts that where slackened in paragraph 13.

20 Carefully lower the transmission, checking all the time that nothing is getting caught or stretched. Also take care that the engine right-hand mounting is not being too distorted, or placed under excess strain. To help support the transmission, fasten a strap around the transmission to help support it on the trolley jack **(see illustration)**.

21 As the transmission is withdrawn from the engine, make sure its weight is supported at all times – the transmission input shaft (or the clutch) may otherwise be damaged as it is withdrawn through the clutch assembly bolted to the engine flywheel. As this is done, be prepared for the unit to start separating – have your assistant support it. If the transmission does not separate, prise it gently apart – it is located on dowels, and they may stick.

22 Once the transmission is clear of the engine, keep the transmission steady on the jack head, and carefully lower it down. With the help of your assistant, remove it from under the car.

23 The clutch components can now be inspected with reference to Chapter 6, and renewed if necessary. Unless they are virtually new, it is worth renewing the clutch components as a matter of course, even if the transmission has been removed for some other reason.

Refitting

24 If removed, refit the clutch components (see Chapter 6).

25 With the transmission secured to the trolley jack as on removal, raise it into position, and then carefully slide it onto the engine, at the same time engaging the input shaft with the clutch friction disc splines.

26 Do not use excessive force to refit the transmission – if the input shaft does not slide into place easily, re-adjust the angle of the transmission so that it is level, and/or turn the input shaft so that the splines engage properly with the disc. If problems are still experienced, check that the clutch friction disc is correctly centralised (Chapter 6 Section 4).

27 Once the transmission is successfully mated to the engine, insert as many of the transmission-to-engine bolts as possible, and tighten them progressively, to draw the transmission fully onto the locating dowels.

28 Raise the transmission into position, then refit the engine left-hand and rear mountings. Tighten the bolts hand-tight only at this stage, but sufficiently to support the transmission so that the support bar, engine hoist or supporting jack can be removed.

29 Refit the lower bell housing plate, and then tighten its three bolts, and the five transmission-to-engine bolts, to the specified torque.

30 Tighten the engine mounting bolts to the specified torque.

31 Further refitting is a reversal of removal, noting the following points:

a) *Refit the gearchange cables, as described in Section 3.*

b) *Refit the clutch cable and adjust, as described in Chapter 6 Section 2.*

c) *Refit the starter motor and battery, as described in Chapter 5A Section 4.*

d) *Refit the driveshafts as described in Chapter 8 Section 2.*

e) *Refill the transmission with oil as described in Section 2.*

7   Transmission overhaul – general information

1 The overhaul of a manual transmission is a complex (and often expensive) engineering task for the DIY home mechanic to undertake, which requires access to specialist equipment. It involves dismantling and reassembly of many small components, measuring clearances precisely and if

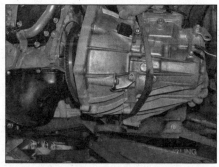

6.20 Withdraw the transmission from the engine, keeping it supported with a strap

necessary, adjusting them by the selection of shims and spacers. Internal transmission components are also often difficult to obtain and in many instances, extremely expensive. Because of this, if the transmission develops a fault or becomes noisy, the best course of action is to have the unit overhauled by a specialist repairer or to obtain an exchange reconditioned unit.

2 Nevertheless, it is not impossible for the more experienced mechanic to overhaul the transmission, if the special tools are available and the job is carried out in a deliberate step-by-step manner, to ensure that nothing is overlooked.

3 The tools necessary for an overhaul include internal and external circlip pliers, bearing pullers, a slide hammer, a set of pin punches, a dial test indicator, and possibly, a hydraulic press. In addition, a large, sturdy workbench and a vice will be required.

4 During dismantling of the transmission, make careful notes of how each component is fitted to make reassembly easier and accurate.

5 Before dismantling the transmission, it will help if you have some idea of where the problem lies. Certain problems can be closely related to specific areas in the transmission, which can make component examination and renewal easier. Refer to *Fault finding* at the end of this manual for more information.

Notes

Chapter 7 Part B
Multi-Mode transmission

Contents

Degrees of difficulty

Easy, suitable for novice with little experience 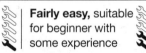	**Fairly easy,** suitable for beginner with some experience	**Fairly difficult,** suitable for competent DIY mechanic	**Difficult,** suitable for experienced DIY mechanic	**Very difficult,** suitable for expert DIY or professional

Specifications

General

Transmission type.	Five forward speeds, one reverse. Synchromesh on all forward gears. Gearchange operated electrically by an ECU, actuators and sensors
Transmission code	C551A
Transmission oil	Refer to *Lubricants and fluids* on page 0•16
Transmission weight.	32.8 kg

Gear ratios

1st	3.545: 1
2nd	1.913: 1
3rd	1.310: 1
4th	1.027: 1
5th	0.850: 1
Reverse	3.214: 1
Final drive.	3.550: 1

Torque wrench settings

	Nm	lbf ft
Clutch actuator mounting bolts	17	13
Drain plug.	29	21
Engine/transmission mountings:		
Left-hand mounting bolts.	52	38
Rear mounting through-bolt	120	89
Filler/level plug	39	29
Gear select and shift actuator mounting bolts.	18	13
Gear lever assembly mounting bolts	12	9
Gear neutral switch (engaged sensor)	40	30
Reversing light switch	40	30
Roadwheel bolts.	100	74
Starter motor mounting bolts.	37	27
Transmission revolution sensor	8	6
Transmission-to-engine bolts.	64	47
Transmission-to-engine lower plate bolts	40	30

2.4 Transmission oil filler/level plug

2.5 Transmission oil drain plug

1 General Information

1 This Part of Chapter 7 contains information on the Multi-Mode Transmission (MMT), also known as '2-Tronic' in the Peugeot handbook and 'SensoDrive' in the Citroen handbook. Service procedures for the manual transmission system are contained in Part A.

2 The Multi-Mode Transmission system consists of a manual transmission (as seen in Chapter 7A), a self-adjusting clutch pressure plate (see Chapter 6), a transmission ECU, actuators, sensors and switches. This allows the manual transmission to be electro-mechanically controlled. The transmission has a reverse and neutral position and also has two types of shift modes:

a) The E-mode that shifts automatically to suit the driving conditions, this is selected by the Multi-Mode Transmission ECU, which chooses an optimal gear position that will suit the driving conditions. This will give good fuel efficiency and ease of driving.

b) The M-mode that allows the driver to manually operate the shift lever to select the gears without having to apply the clutch. When the shift lever is operated in the '+' or '-' direction, the Multi-Mode Transmission ECU controls the gearshift selection. This allows a more sporty drive.

3 The transmission is contained in a cast-aluminium alloy casing bolted to the engine's left-hand end, and consists of the gearbox and final drive differential – often called a transaxle.

4 Drive is transmitted from the crankshaft via the clutch to the input shaft, which has a splined extension to accept the clutch friction disc. From the input shaft, drive is transmitted to the output shaft, from where the drive is transmitted to the differential crownwheel, which rotates with the differential and planetary gears, thus driving the sun gears and driveshafts. The rotation of the planetary gears on their shaft allows the inner roadwheel to rotate at a slower speed than the outer roadwheel when the car is cornering.

5 The transmission selector mechanism causes the appropriate selector fork to move its respective synchro-sleeve along the output shaft, to lock the gear pinion to the synchro-hub. Since the synchro-hubs are splined to the output shaft, this locks the pinion to the shaft, so that drive can be transmitted. To ensure that gearchanging can be made quickly and quietly, a synchromesh system is fitted to all forward gears, consisting of baulk rings and spring-loaded fingers, as well as the gear pinions and synchro-hubs. The synchromesh cones are formed on the mating faces of the baulk rings and gear pinions.

Transmission overhaul

6 Because of the complexity of the assembly, possible unavailability of parts and special tools necessary, internal repair procedures for the transmission are not recommended for the home mechanic. The bulk of the information in this Chapter is devoted to removal and refitting procedures.

2 Transmission oil renewal

1 This operation is much quicker and more efficient if the car is first taken on a journey of sufficient length to warm the engine/transmission up to normal operating temperature. However, take care to avoid burning yourself on any hot components when working underneath the car.

2 Park the car on a level surface, switch off the ignition and apply the handbrake firmly. For improved access to the filler/level plug, apply the handbrake, then jack up the front of the vehicle and support it on axle stands (see *Jacking and vehicle support*), Note that the car can be raised at the front only for oil draining, but the vehicle will need to be level when refilling the transmission, to ensure an accurate level check.

3 Where fitted, remove the engine lower cover panels from under the car.

4 Remove all traces of dirt, and then unscrew the filler/level plug from the front face of the transmission **(see illustration)**. This will probably be tight – use a good-quality spanner or socket to unscrew it, and take care to avoid personal injury. Where applicable, a new washer should be fitted to the filler/level plug when refitting.

5 Wipe clean the area around the drain plug, which is situated on the base of the transmission, just below the left-hand driveshaft inner CV joint **(see illustration)**. Position a suitable container under the drain plug, and unscrew the plug – this will also probably be tight, and will need a new washer when refitting.

6 Allow the oil to drain completely into the container **(see illustration)**. If the oil is hot, take precautions against scalding. Clean the drain plug, being especially careful to wipe any metallic particles off the magnetic insert. Discard the sealing washer; it should be renewed whenever it is disturbed.

7 When the oil has finished draining, clean the drain plug threads and those of the transmission casing, fit a new sealing washer and refit the drain plug **(see illustration)**, tightening it to the specified torque wrench setting.

8 Refilling the transmission is an awkward operation. Above all, allow plenty of time for the oil level to settle properly before checking it. Note that the car must be parked on flat level ground (or if it is raised, it must be level) when checking the oil level.

9 Fill the transmission with the specified grade of oil (see *Lubricants and fluids*) until the oil just starts to run out **(see illustration)**. Allow any excess oil to flow out until the level stabilises.

2.6 Remove the drain plug and allow the oil to drain

2.7 Fit new sealing washer when refitting

10 When the level is correct, clean and refit the filler/level plug (with a new washer, where fitted), then tighten it to the specified torque **(see illustration)**.

11 Where applicable, refit the lower cover panels, and lower the car to the ground.

12 Although not strictly necessary, to ensure maximum accuracy take the car on a short journey so that the new oil is distributed fully around the transmission components, then check the level again on your return.

3 Multi-Mode electrical components – removal and refitting

Note: *The following removal and refitting procedures are to be carried out after the system has been set using diagnostic equipment.*

Caution: Before removing any of the following Multi-Mode electrical components, diagnostic equipment will be required to set the system to the required dismantling/fitting position. Also after the work has been completed, the system will need to be reprogrammed with diagnostic equipment.

Clutch actuator

Removal

1 Set the transmission to the neutral (N) position, and switch of the ignition.

2 Open the bonnet and remove the battery and battery tray, as described in Chapter 5A Section 4.

3.3a Remove the blanking plug...

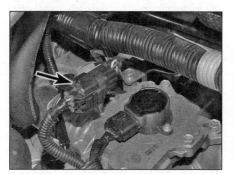

3.4 Disconnect the wiring loom block connector

2.9 Fill the transmission until the oil starts to run out

3 To check the transmission is in neutral, remove the blanking plug from the top of the transmission and check the position of the slot in the shaft **(see illustrations)**.

4 Disconnect the wiring connector, then undo the wiring bracket mounting bolt and move the wiring loom to one side **(see illustration)**.

5 Disconnect the wiring connectors from the clutch sensor and clutch motor **(see illustration)**.

6 Mark the fitted position of the clutch actuator unit (the mounting bolt holes are elongated, for adjustment), then slacken and remove the three mounting bolts **(see illustration)**.

7 Withdraw the clutch actuator from the top of the transmission, disengaging the pushrod from the clutch operating lever. DO NOT attempt to move the clutch actuator by pulling on the pushrod, as this will result in damage.

3.3b... and check the position of the slot (arrowed) inside the transmission

3.5 Disconnect the wiring connectors from the clutch sensor and motor

2.10 Refit the filler/level plug

Inspection

8 Check the pushrod gaiter is in good condition and making good seal to prevent ingress of dirt.

9 Using an ohmmeter, check the resistance between the two terminals of the clutch motor terminal. The reading should be between 0.1 and 100 ohms, if not renew the clutch actuator.

10 Before refitting, make sure the lower

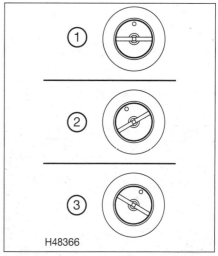

3.3c Slot positions (illustration 3.3b is in the Neutral position)

1 Neutral
2 1st, 3rd and 5th
3 2nd, 4th and Reverse

3.6 Clutch actuator mounting bolt holes, which are elongated for adjustment

3.14 Undo the wiring bracket retaining bolt

3.16 Disconnect the wiring connectors from the shift and select motors

3.17 Disconnect the wiring connectors from the shift and select sensors

surface of the clutch actuator and the top of the transmission is clean and dry. Making sure the clutch actuator sits squarely on the transmission.

Refitting

11 Refitting is a reversal of removal, noting the following points:

a) *Make sure the transmission is still in the neutral position.*

b) *Grease the end of the clutch operating arm, to locate the pushrod.*

c) *As the clutch actuator is fitted, make sure the pushrod engages with the operating arm correctly.*

d) *As the clutch actuator mounting bolts are tightened to their specified torque, make sure there is no clearance between the pushrod and the operating arm.*

e) *On completion, the system will need to be programmed, with diagnostic equipment.*

Gear select and shift actuator

Removal

12 Set the transmission to the neutral (N) position, and switch of the ignition.

13 Open the bonnet and remove the battery and battery tray, as described in Chapter 5A Section 4.

14 Undo the retaining bolt and disconnect the wiring bracket from the top of the transmission **(see illustration)**.

15 Remove the clutch actuator, as described in paragraphs 3 to 7.

16 Disconnect the wiring connectors from the shift and select motors at the rear of the transmission **(see illustration)**.

17 Disconnect the wiring connectors from the shift and select sensors at the front of the transmission **(see illustration)**.

18 Slacken and remove the six mounting bolts

and withdraw the gear select and shift actuator from the top of the transmission. Clean the sealant of the mating face of the transmission and actuator unit, ready for refitting.

Refitting

19 Refitting is a reversal of removal, noting the following points:

a) *Apply sealant to the mating face of the transmission before refitting the actuator unit.*

b) *Make sure the transmission is still in the neutral position.*

c) *Refit the clutch actuator as described previously in this Section.*

d) *Check all wiring connections are made securely.*

e) *On completion, the system will need to be programmed with diagnostic equipment.*

Clutch stroke sensor

20 The clutch stroke sensor is located on top of the clutch actuator **(see illustration)**, disconnect the wiring connector, and undo the two retaining screws to remove the sensor. Renew the O-ring seal on refitting.

Shift stroke sensor

21 The shift stroke sensor is located on top of the gear select and shift actuator **(see illustration)**, disconnect the wiring connector, and undo the two retaining screws to remove the sensor. Renew the O-ring seal on refitting.

Select stroke sensor

22 The select stroke sensor is located on top of the gear select and shift actuator **(see illustration)**, disconnect the wiring connector, and undo the two retaining screws to remove the sensor. Renew the O-ring seal on refitting.

Neutral start switch

23 The neutral switch is located on the front of the transmission. Disconnect the wiring connector from the neutral switch, and unscrew the switch to remove **(see illustration)**. Renew the sealing washer on refitting (where fitted).

Transmission revolution sensor

24 The revolution sensor is located on the bottom of the transmission. Undo the retaining bolt and remove the shield, then undo the retaining bolt from the sensor and

3.20 Disconnect the wiring connector from the clutch stroke sensor

3.21 Disconnect the wiring connector from the shift stroke sensor

3.22 Disconnect the wiring connector from the select stroke sensor

3.23 Disconnect the wiring connector from the neutral start switch

3.24a Undo the sensor shield retaining bolt

3.24b Undo the revolution sensor retaining bolt

3.26 Disconnect the wiring connectors from the gear lever unit

remove from the casing (see illustrations). Trace the wiring to the top of the transmission and disconnect the wiring connector. Renew the O-ring seal on refitting.

Gear lever (gearchange unit)

Removal

25 Remove the centre console as described in Chapter 11 Section 25.

26 Noting their positions for refitting, disconnect the wiring connectors from the right-hand side of the gear change unit (see illustration).

27 Remove the four bolts securing the unit to the floor, then lift it out and remove it from the car (see illustration).

Refitting

28 Refitting is a reversal of removal. Check that all gear positions can be selected before taking the car out on the road.

Shift position sensor

29 The shift position sensor is located on the right-hand side of the gear change unit. Remove the gearchange unit as described in paragraphs 25 to 27. Remove the two retaining screws, from the shift position sensor and remove it from the gearchange unit (see illustration).

Electronic control unit (ECU)

30 The ECU is located inside the vehicle on the A-pillar under the upper part of the facia. Remove the upper part of the facia as described in Chapter 11 Section 26. Disconnect the wiring connector and unbolt the ECU from the A-pillar.

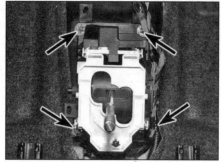

3.27 Gear lever assembly mounting bolts

4 Reversing light switch – removal and refitting

Removal

1 The switch is located on the top of the transmission, at the far left-hand side. With the transmission fitted to the vehicle, the switch is covered by the battery tray and transmission mounting (see illustration).

2 Trace the wiring from the switch, and disconnect it at the in-line connector, which is on the front of the transmission housing (see illustration).

3 Remove the battery and battery tray, as described in Chapter 5A Section 4.

4 Support the transmission using a trolley jack, then undo the retaining bolts and remove

3.29 Gear shift position sensor retaining screws

the transmission mounting (see illustration), with reference to Chapter 2A Section 17.

5 Unscrew and remove the switch from the top of the transmission, release the wiring from any retaining clips.

Refitting

6 Refitting is a reversal of removal. Tighten the switch securely.

5 Oil seals – renewal

1 Oil leaks frequently occur due to wear or deterioration of the driveshaft oil seals, or even the vehicle speed sensor O-ring. Renewal of these seals is relatively easy, since the repairs can be performed without removing the transmission from the car.

4.1 Reversing light switch in the top of the transmission

4.2 Disconnect the reversing light switch wiring plug on the front of the transmission

4.4 The reversing light switch is located under the engine/transmission mounting

5.4 Using a vernier gauge to check the depth of the seal in the casing

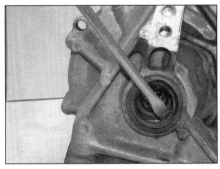

5.5 Carefully prise the seal from the casing

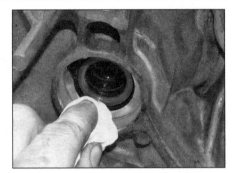

5.6 Clean out the recess in the casing

5.7 Position the seal in the casing...

5.8... and tap the seal into the position noted on removal

4 Check the fitted depth of the seal in the housing, so that the new seal can be fitted the same **(see illustration)**.
5 Using a large screwdriver or lever, carefully prise the oil seal out of the transmission casing, taking care not to damage the transmission casing **(see illustration)**.
6 Wipe clean the oil seal seating in the transmission casing **(see illustration)**.
7 Press it a little way into the casing by hand, making sure that it is square to its seating **(see illustration)**.
8 Using suitable tubing or a large socket **(see illustration)**, carefully drive the oil seal into the casing, until it is fitted to the depth noted on removal.
9 Refit the driveshaft with reference to Chapter 8.

Driveshaft oil seals

2 The driveshaft oil seals are located at the sides of the transmission, where the driveshafts enter the transmission. If leakage at the seal is suspected, raise the car and support it securely on axle stands. If the seal is leaking, oil will be found on the side of the transmission below the driveshaft.
3 Refer to Chapter 8 Section 2 and remove the appropriate driveshaft.

<table>
<tr><td>6</td><td>Transmission –
removal and refitting</td><td></td></tr>
</table>

Note: *Read through this procedure before starting work to see what is involved, particularly in terms of lifting equipment. Depending on the facilities available, the home mechanic may prefer to remove the engine and transmission together, and then separate them on the bench, as described in Chapter 2B. The help of an assistant is highly recommended if the transmission is to be removed (and later refitted) on its own.*

Removal

1 Remove the air cleaner cover as described in Chapter 4A Section 5.
2 Remove the battery and battery tray, as described in Chapter 5A Section 4.
3 Disconnect the two wiring connectors from the shift and select actuator motors at the rear of the transmission **(see illustration)**.
4 Disconnect the wiring connector from the clutch actuator motor on top of the transmission **(see illustration)**.
5 Disconnect the wiring block connector on top of the transmission **(see illustration)**.
6 Disconnect the wiring block connector for the reversing light switch; unclip the wiring from the bracket on the transmission **(see illustration)**.

6.3 Disconnect the wiring connectors from the shift and select motors

6.4 Disconnect the wiring connectors from the clutch motor

6.5 Disconnect the wiring loom block connector

6.6 Disconnect the reversing light wiring connector

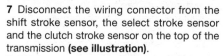

6.7 Disconnect the wiring connectors from the clutch, shift and select sensors

6.8 Disconnect the wiring connector from the neutral start switch

6.13 Unbolt the earth cable from the front of the transmission

7 Disconnect the wiring connector from the shift stroke sensor, the select stroke sensor and the clutch stroke sensor on the top of the transmission **(see illustration)**.

8 Disconnect the wiring connector from the neutral switch on the front of the transmission housing **(see illustration)**.

9 If not already done, jack up the front of the car, and support it on axle stands (see *Jacking and vehicle support*). The car must be raised sufficiently that the transmission can be lowered out and removed underneath. Consideration should also be given to the need to support the engine, once the rear and left-hand mountings are disconnected.

10 Remove the front bumper as described in Chapter 11 Section 6.

11 Secure the radiator and air conditioning condenser (where fitted) to the upper crossmember, then undo the bolts from each end of the lower crossmember and remove it from the front of the vehicle. Take care not to damage the radiator or the condenser as the transmission is removed.

12 Working from the information in Chapter 5A Section 10, remove the starter motor.

13 Unbolt and remove the earth cable from the front of the transmission housing **(see illustration)**. Unclip the wiring from the bracket on the transmission.

14 Disconnect the wiring plug from the oxygen (lambda) sensor on front of the transmission **(see illustration)**. Unclip the wiring from the bracket on the transmission.

15 Undo the three retaining bolts and remove

the lower plate/shield from the bottom of the transmission **(see illustration)**.

16 Drain the oil from the transmission, as described in Section 2.

17 Remove both driveshafts as described in Chapter 8 Section 2.

18 Slacken, but do not remove the five transmission-to-engine mounting bolts. There are two at the front of the transmission, two upper transmission bolts and one at the rear of the engine **(see illustrations)**. Leave them in place for now – this avoids using any substantial force to remove the bolts when the transmission is only supported on a jack.

19 Using a substantial hydraulic ('trolley') jack with a block of wood, raise the transmission slightly, to take the weight off its mountings. Supporting the transmission securely in this way can be difficult to achieve – due to its

shape, there is a danger the transmission will roll off once disconnected. For this reason, it pays to have an assistant on hand, to steady the unit as it is lowered out.

20 Before the engine rear mounting and left-hand transmission mounting are disconnected, the engine must be supported, preferably from above, using either an engine crane or support bar. If the engine is supported from below, using another jack (and block of wood, to protect the sump), this seriously reduces the working room for removing the transmission.

21 With the engine securely supported, first remove the through-bolts from the engine rear mounting, and then remove the mounting from the mounting bracket **(see illustrations)**.

22 Remove the three mounting-to-body bolts and four mounting-to-transmission bolts

6.14 Disconnect the lower oxygen sensor wiring connector

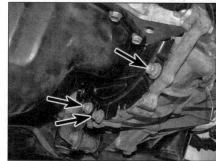

6.15 Undo the lower shield retaining bolts

6.18a Slacken the two front transmission bolts...

6.18b... the two upper retaining bolts...

6.18c... and the lower rear transmission bolt

6.21a Undo the mounting bolts...

6.21b... and remove the rear engine mounting

and remove the complete mounting from the engine compartment **(see illustration)**.
23 Make a final check all around the transmission, to check that there is nothing left attached to the transmission, nor anything in the way which would prevent the unit from being lowered out.
24 Check that the transmission is securely supported (preferably with the help of an assistant), and then remove the five bolts from around the transmission bellhousing. These are the bolts that where slackened in paragraph 18.
25 Carefully lower the transmission, checking all the time that nothing is getting caught or stretched. Also take care that the engine right-hand mounting is not being too distorted, or placed under excess strain. To help support the transmission, fasten a strap around the transmission to help support it on the trolley jack.
26 As the transmission is withdrawn from the engine, make sure its weight is supported at all times – the transmission input shaft (or the clutch) may otherwise be damaged as it is withdrawn through the clutch assembly bolted to the engine flywheel. As this is done, be prepared for the unit to start separating – have your assistant support it. If the transmission does not separate, prise it gently apart – it is located on dowels, and they may stick.
27 Once the transmission is clear of the engine, keep the transmission steady on the jack head, and carefully lower it down. With the help of your assistant, remove it

from under the car. As the transmission is lowered, take care not to damage the transmission revolution sensor on the lower part of the transmission housing **(see illustration)**.
28 The clutch components can now be inspected with reference to Chapter 6, and renewed if necessary. Unless they are virtually new, it is worth renewing the clutch components as a matter of course, even if the transmission has been removed for some other reason.

Refitting

29 If removed, refit the clutch components (see Chapter 6).
30 With the transmission secured to the trolley jack as on removal, raise it into position, and then carefully slide it onto the engine, at the same time engaging the input shaft with the clutch friction disc splines.
31 Do not use excessive force to refit the transmission – if the input shaft does not slide into place easily, re-adjust the angle of the transmission so that it is level, and/or turn the input shaft so that the splines engage properly with the disc. If problems are still experienced, check that the clutch friction disc is correctly centralised (Chapter 6 Section 4).
32 Once the transmission is successfully mated to the engine, insert as many of the transmission-to-engine bolts as possible, and tighten them progressively, to draw the transmission fully onto the locating dowels.
33 Raise the transmission into position, then refit the engine left-hand and rear mountings.

Tighten the bolts hand-tight only at this stage, but sufficiently to support the transmission so that the support bar, engine hoist or supporting jack can be removed.
34 Refit the lower bellhousing plate, and then tighten its three bolts, and the five transmission-to-engine bolts, to the specified torque.
35 Tighten the engine mounting bolts to the specified torque.
36 Further refitting is a reversal of removal, noting the following points:
a) Refit all the wiring connectors securely and to their correct location.
b) Refit the starter motor and battery, as described in Chapter 5A.
c) Refit the driveshafts as described in Chapter 8 Section 2.
d) Refit the front bumper, with reference to Chapter 11 Section 6.
e) Refill the transmission with oil as described in Section 2.

7 Transmission overhaul – general information

1 The overhaul of a multi-mode transmission is a complex (and often expensive) engineering task for the DIY home mechanic to undertake, which requires access to specialist equipment. It involves dismantling and reassembly of many small components, measuring clearances precisely and if necessary, adjusting them by the selection of shims and spacers. Internal transmission components are also often difficult to obtain and in many instances, extremely expensive. Because of this, if the transmission develops a fault or becomes noisy, the best course of action is to have the unit overhauled by a specialist repairer or to obtain an exchange reconditioned unit.
2 Nevertheless, it is not impossible for the more experienced mechanic to overhaul the transmission, if the special tools are available and the job is carried out in a deliberate step-by-step manner, to ensure that nothing is overlooked.
3 The tools necessary for an overhaul include internal and external circlip pliers, bearing pullers, a slide hammer, a set of pin punches, a dial test indicator, and possibly, a hydraulic press. In addition, a large, sturdy workbench and a vice will be required.
4 During dismantling of the transmission, make careful notes of how each component is fitted to make reassembly easier and accurate.
5 Before dismantling the transmission, it will help if you have some idea of where the problem lies. Certain problems can be closely related to specific areas in the transmission, which can make component examination and renewal easier. Refer to *Fault finding* at the end of this manual for more information.

6.22 Left-hand engine/transmission mounting bolts – arrowed

6.27 As the transmission is lowered, take care not to damage the revolution sensor

Chapter 8
Driveshafts

Contents

Degrees of difficulty

Easy, suitable for novice with little experience	**Fairly easy,** suitable for beginner with some experience	**Fairly difficult,** suitable for competent DIY mechanic	**Difficult,** suitable for experienced DIY mechanic	**Very difficult,** suitable for expert DIY or professional

Specifications

General

Driveshaft type.	Solid steel shafts with inner and outer constant velocity (CV) joints. Outer joints of the ball-and-cage (Rzeppa) type, inner joints of the spider-and-yoke (tripod) type
Shaft length (complete):	
Left	411 mm
Right	601 mm
Shaft diameter.	20.7 mm
Driveshaft gaiter type:	
Transmission end	Neoprene (Neo)
Roadwheel end.	Thermoplastic (TP)
Lubricant:	
Type/specification.	Special grease supplied in sachets with gaiter kits – inner and outer joints use different grease types
Quantity (per joint):	
Inner joint	85 to 105 g
Outer joint.	80 to 100 g

Torque wrench settings	Nm	lbf ft
Driveshaft (hub) nut*.	216	159
Lower arm balljoint nut.	98	72
Roadwheel nuts	100	74
Swivel hub-to-suspension strut pinch-bolt/nut	48	35
Track rod end nut.	33	24

* Use new nut

---

1 General Information

1 Drive is transmitted from the differential to the front wheels by means of two, unequal-length driveshafts. The driveshaft on the left-hand side (near-side) is shorter than the one on the right-hand side (off-side).

2 Each driveshaft is fitted with an inner and outer constant velocity (CV) joint. The inner constant velocity joint is of the spider- and-yoke (tripod) type and the outer joint is of the ball-and-cage (Rzeppa) type. Each outer joint is splined to engage with the wheel hub, and is threaded so that it can be fastened to the hub by a large nut. The inner joint is also splined to engage with the differential sunwheel gears.

2.2 Tap up the deformed portion of the nut so it can be unscrewed

2 Driveshafts – removal and refitting

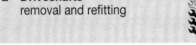

Removal

1 Remove the relevant wheel trim, or the wheel centre cover (alloy wheels) for access to the driveshaft nut. On some models with alloy wheels, access to the driveshaft nut is not possible, this will need to be slackened once the wheel has been removed.

2 Using a hammer and punch, relieve the staking on the driveshaft nut **(see illustration)**. Make sure the staking has been released completely, as this can damage the threads on the driveshaft as the nut is removed.

3 Ensure that the handbrake is applied (ideally, have an assistant apply the

2.5 Using a homemade holding tool to prevent the front hub from turning

footbrake), and then slacken the driveshaft nut using a socket and extension bar. Loosen the driveshaft nut almost to the end of its threads, but do not remove it at this stage.

> ⚠ **Warning: The driveshaft nut is done up extremely tight, and considerable effort will be required to loosen it. Do not use poor-quality, badly-fitting tools for this task, due to the risk of personal injury.**

4 Slacken the relevant front wheel nuts, then jack up the front of the car, and support securely on axle-stands (see *Jacking and vehicle support*). Remove the roadwheel.

5 If the driveshaft retaining nut was not able to be slackened as described in paragraphs 1 and 2, then a tool will be required to hold the hub stationary while the nut is slackened to the end of the threads **(see illustration)**.

6 Drain the transmission oil as described in Chapter 7A or 7B. If this is not done, be prepared for considerable loss of oil or fluid when the driveshafts are removed from the transmission.

7 Extract the split pin from the track rod end balljoint nut, then unscrew the nut and use a balljoint splitter to separate the track rod from the swivel hub **(see illustrations)**. Take care not to damage the balljoint rubber during the separation procedure. A new split pin should be used when refitting.

8 Remove the spring clip, then slacken the lower arm balljoint nut, and unscrew it as far as the ends of the threads. Push the end of the lower arm down to free the balljoint from the swivel hub. If the balljoint is very tight, it may be necessary to lever down using a long lever bar, or similar tool, but take care not to damage the balljoint rubber seal **(see illustrations)**.

9 The splined end of the driveshaft now has to be released from its location in the hub. It's likely that the splines will be tight (corrosion may even be a factor, if the driveshaft has not been disturbed for some time), and considerable force may be needed to push the driveshaft out. Carefully tap the shaft out with a plastic or hide mallet. If an ordinary hammer is used, place a small piece of wood over the end of the driveshaft – in addition to the loosened driveshaft nut; this will protect the threads from damage.

10 Once the splines have been released, remove the driveshaft nut and discard it – the nut is only intended to be used once.

2.7a Remove the split pin...

2.7b... and the retaining nut...

2.7c... and separate the track rod end with a balljoint splitter

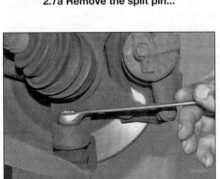

2.8a Remove the split pin and retaining nut...

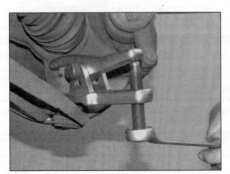

2.8b... then separate the balljoint with a balljoint splitter

2.8c If necessary, use a bar and chain to lever the balljoint out of position

2.11 Separate the driveshaft from the inside of the hub

2.12a Use the slotted shoulders (arrowed) on the inner joint...

2.12b... to tap against when using a drift to remove driveshaft

11 Pull the hub outwards, and pull the driveshaft inwards, to separate the splined end from the hub **(see illustration)**. It is helpful to have an assistant on hand, to pull either the hub or the shaft. Do not bend the driveshaft excessively at any stage, or the joints may be damaged – the inner and outer joints should not be bent through more than 18° and 45° respectively. Do not let the driveshaft hang down under its own weight – tie it up level if necessary.

12 The driveshafts are held into the transmission by a spring circlip, which can take some effort to release. Using a suitable drift on the slotted shoulder of the driveshaft inner joint, tap the joint out of the transmission **(see illustrations)**. Take care not to damage the driveshaft boot or the securing clips. Be prepared for a small amount of oil loss when the driveshaft releases (or a large amount, if the transmission was not drained).

13 Manoeuvre the driveshaft out of position **(see illustration)**, ensuring that the constant velocity joints are not placed under excessive strain, and remove the driveshaft from underneath the car.

14 Whilst the driveshaft is removed, plug the differential aperture with a clean, lint-free cloth to prevent dirt getting in.

15 Extract the circlip from the groove on the inner end of the driveshaft, and obtain a new one **(see illustration)**.

16 Check the condition of the differential oil seals, and if necessary renew them as described in Chapter 7A or 7B.

Caution: If the car is lowered back onto its wheels while the driveshafts are removed, this could cause damage to the wheel bearings, especially if the car is moved. The manufacturers special tool for this eventuality is a very large bolt (identical in diameter to the driveshaft), which fits through the hub and supports the bearing – if a large enough bolt could be obtained, a homemade substitute could be made.

Refitting

17 Locate the new circlip in the groove on the inner end of the driveshaft, and turn the clip so its open side is facing downwards

(see illustration). Use a small amount of grease to keep the circlip central in the groove.

18 Lubricate the driveshaft inner splines with transmission oil. Carefully refit the driveshaft into the transmission, taking care not to damage the oil seal. Turn the driveshaft until it engages the splines on the differential gears.

19 Push the driveshaft fully home, so that the circlip engages. Try pulling the shaft out, to make sure the circlip is fully engaged.

20 Apply a little molybdenum disulphide grease to the driveshaft outer splines. Pull the hub outwards, and insert the outer end of the driveshaft. Turn the driveshaft to engage the splines in the hub, and fully push on the hub.

21 Screw on the new driveshaft nut **(see illustration)**, and use it to draw the driveshaft

fully through the hub. Delay fully-tightening the nut until the wheel is back on, and the car has been lowered to the ground. If the nut cannot be accessed when the wheel is fitted, then tighten the driveshaft nut using the holding tool as described on removal, see paragraph 5.

22 Locate the hub onto the lower balljoint, and secure with the nut and retaining clip. Tighten the nut to the specified torque. If the split pin hole is not lined up, the nut may be tightened up to a further 60°.

23 Locate the track rod end balljoint into the swivel hub. Tighten the nut to the specified torque, then secure with a new split pin. If the split pin hole is not lined up, the nut may be tightened up to a further 60°.

24 Fill the transmission, and check the level as described in Chapter 7A or 7B.

25 Fully tighten the driveshaft nut to the

2.13 Withdraw the driveshaft from the splines in the transmission

2.15 Prising out the old driveshaft circlip

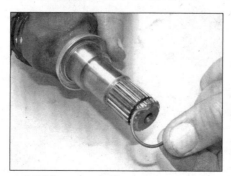

2.17 Fit a new circlip to the end of the driveshaft

2.21 Fit a new hub/driveshaft retaining nut

2.25 Use a punch to stake the nut in position on completion

specified torque, and then stake the nut into the driveshaft groove **(see illustration)**.

26 Refit the wheel, and lower the car to the ground. Tighten the wheel nuts to the specified torque.

3 Driveshaft inner joint gaiter – renewal

1 The inner joint gaiter is best renewed with the driveshaft removed from the car, as described in Section 2. Note that if both the inner and outer gaiters are being renewed at the same time, the outer gaiter can only be removed from the inner end of the driveshaft, once the inner joint and gaiter have been removed.

2 If required, mount the driveshaft in a vice.

3 Note the fitted location of both of the inner joint gaiter retaining clips, then release the clips from the gaiter, and slide the gaiter back along the driveshaft a little way **(see illustrations)**.

4 Mark the driveshaft in relation to the joint housing, to ensure correct refitting **(see illustration)**.

5 Remove the inner joint housing from the tripod **(see illustration)**.

6 Extract the circlip retaining the tripod on the driveshaft **(see illustration)**.

7 Check that the inner end of the driveshaft is marked in relation to the splined tripod hub. If not, use dabs of paint on the driveshaft and one end of the tripod **(see illustration)**.

8 Using a soft-metal drift on the tripod centre hub (not on the outer rollers), tap off the tripod from the end of the driveshaft **(see illustrations)**.

9 Finally, slide off the inner gaiter **(see illustration)**.

10 If the outer gaiter is also to be renewed, remove it with reference to Section 4.

11 Clean the driveshaft, and obtain a new joint retaining circlip. The gaiter retaining clips must also be renewed.

3.3a Using a screwdriver, release the securing clips...

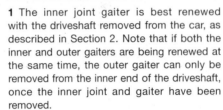

3.3b... and remove them from the gaiter

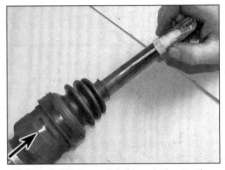

3.4 Mark the inner joint in relation to the shaft

3.5 Separate the inner joint from the tripod

3.6 Extract the circlip from the end of the driveshaft

3.7 Mark the tripod in relation to the shaft

3.8a Tap the inner casting of the tripod...

3.8b... to remove it from the shaft

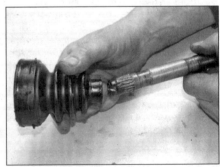

3.9 Slide off the inner joint gaiter

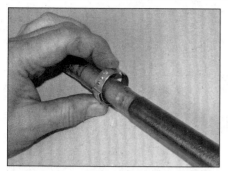

3.12a Slide the new small retaining clip onto the shaft...

3.12b... followed by the new gaiter

3.13a Line up the paint marks and refit the tripod...

12 Slide the new gaiter on the driveshaft, together with new clips **(see illustrations)**.
13 Refit the tripod on the driveshaft splines, if necessary using a soft-faced mallet and a suitable socket to drive it fully onto the splines. It must be fitted with the previously-made marks aligned **(see illustrations)**. Secure it in position using a new circlip. Ensure that the circlip is fully engaged in its groove.
14 Scoop out all of the old grease from the joint housing, then pack the joint and gaiter with new grease (see Specifications at the beginning of this Chapter) **(see illustration)**. Guide the joint housing onto the tripod joint, making sure that the previously-made marks are aligned.
15 Slide the gaiter along the driveshaft, and locate it on the tripod joint housing. The small-diameter end of the gaiter must be located in the groove on the driveshaft, while the larger end of the gaiter should also locate in a groove on the housing.
16 Ensure that the gaiter is not twisted or distorted, then insert a small screwdriver under the lip of the gaiter at the housing end. This will allow trapped air to escape.
17 Remove the screwdriver, then fit the retaining clips and tighten them **(see illustrations)**.

4 Driveshaft outer joint gaiter – renewal

1 The outer CV joint gaiter can only be

3.13b... using a new circlip

renewed by removing the inner gaiter first as described in Section 3.
2 If required, mount the driveshaft in a vice.
3 Note the fitted location of both of the outer joint gaiter retaining clips, then release the

3.17a Fit new gaiter retaining clips and secure them using pliers...

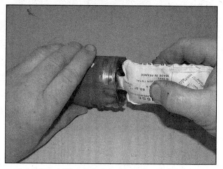

3.14 Pack the joint and gaiter with new grease

clips from the gaiter, and slide the gaiter back along the driveshaft, and off the inner end **(see illustrations)**.
4 Slide the new gaiter (together with new clips) onto the driveshaft.

3.17b... or special securing clip pliers

4.3a Using a screwdriver, release the outer joint gaiter's smaller...

4.3b... and larger-diameter clips...

4.3c... then slide the gaiter off the CV joint, and off the inner end of the shaft

4.6a Locate the gaiter onto the CV joint

4.6b... and secure in place with new retaining clips

4.8 Use special pliers (as seen), long-nose pliers or side-cutters depending on type of clip fitted

5 Scoop out all of the old grease, then pack the joint and gaiter with new grease (see Specifications). Take care that the fresh grease does not become contaminated with dirt or grit as it is being applied.

6 Move the gaiter along the driveshaft, and locate it over the joint and onto the outer CV joint housing (see illustrations). The small-diameter end of the gaiter must be located in the groove on the driveshaft.

7 Ensure that the gaiter is not twisted or distorted, then insert a small screwdriver under the lip of the gaiter at the housing end, to allow any trapped air to escape.

8 Remove the screwdriver, fit the retaining clips in their previously-noted positions, and tighten them (see illustration).

5 Driveshafts – inspection and joint renewal

1 If any of the checks described in the relevant part of Chapter 1 Section 14 reveal apparent excessive wear or play in any driveshaft joint, first remove the wheel, and check the condition of the driveshaft nut. As it should have been staked in place when it was fitted, it is unlikely to be loose. If this is a concern, however, relieve the staking with a hammer and punch, and check that it is tightened to the specified torque. Repeat this check on the other side of the car.

2 Road test the car, and listen for a metallic clicking from the front as the car is driven slowly in a circle on full lock. If a clicking noise is heard, this indicates wear in the outer constant velocity joint, which means that the joint must be renewed; reconditioning is not possible.

3 The outer CV joint is part of the driveshaft, and is not available separately.

4 If vibration, consistent with roadspeed, is felt through the car when accelerating, there is a possibility of wear in the inner tripod joints.

5 To renew an inner tripod joint, remove the driveshaft as described in Section 2, then separate the joint from the driveshaft with reference to Section 3.

Chapter 9
Braking system

Contents

Degrees of difficulty

Easy, suitable for novice with little experience | **Fairly easy,** suitable for beginner with some experience | **Fairly difficult,** suitable for competent DIY mechanic | **Difficult,** suitable for experienced DIY mechanic | **Very difficult,** suitable for expert DIY or professional

Specifications

Brake pedal
Pedal height (with engine running):
  Right-hand drive vehicles . . . . 121.6 to 131.6 mm
  Left-hand drive vehicles . . . . 135.8 to 145.8 mm
Pedal free play . . . . 1.0 to 6.0 mm
Brake light switch clearance . . . . 1.5 to 2.5 mm

Front brakes
Type . . . . Ventilated disc, with single sliding-piston caliper
Caliper make . . . . Bosch
Brake pad make . . . . JURID 682
Brake pad thickness:
  New . . . . 11.0 mm
  Minimum . . . . 1.0 mm
Disc diameter . . . . 247.0 mm
Disc thickness:
  New . . . . 20.0 mm
  Minimum . . . . 18.0 mm
Maximum disc thickness variation . . . . 0.025 mm
Maximum disc/hub run-out . . . . 0.050 mm
Caliper piston diameter . . . . 48.0 mm
Brake pad thickness (minimum) . . . . 1.0 mm

Rear drum brakes
Type . . . . Leading and trailing shoes, with automatic adjusters
Brake shoe make . . . . Ferodo 3627 F
Brake shoe thickness:
  New . . . . 4.5 mm
  Minimum . . . . 1.0 mm
Drum internal diameter:
  New . . . . 200.0 mm
  Maximum . . . . 201.0 mm
  Width . . . . 30.0 mm
Wheel cylinder diameter . . . . 17.5 mm

Master cylinder

Type	Valve type
Diameter	20.64 mm
Travel (primary/secondary)	18.0 mm
Reservoir:	
Capacity	0.22 litres
Make	Bosch
Fluid type	See *Lubricants and fluids* on page 0•16

Brake servo

Diameter	228.6mm (9 inches)
Make	Bosch
Type	Single action

ABS hydraulic valve block

Type	ABS REF 8.0
Make	Bosch

Torque wrench settings

	Nm	lbf ft
ABS hydraulic unit to body	19	14
ABS wheel sensor securing bolts	8	6
Brake pipe unions	15	11
Caliper guide pin bolts	30	22
Caliper hose union	30	22
Caliper mounting bracket (carrier) bolts	89	66
Handbrake lever mounting bolts	22	16
Master cylinder-to-servo mounting nuts	20	15
Rear hub bolts	55	39
Rear wheel cylinder mounting bolt	8	6
Roadwheel nuts	100	74
Servo pushrod locknut	22	16
Servo-to-body mounting nuts	20	15

1 General Information

1 The braking system is of diagonally split, dual-circuit design, with ventilated discs at the front, and drum brakes at the rear. All models have an anti-lock braking system (ABS) as standard. The front calipers are of single sliding-piston design, using asbestos-free pads. The rear drum brakes are of the leading and trailing shoe type, and are self-adjusting.

2 The vacuum servo unit uses inlet manifold depression (generated only when the engine is running) to boost the effort applied by the driver at the brake pedal and transmits this increased effort to the master cylinder pistons.

3 Models are also equipped with Electronic Brake force Distribution (EBD). This is an electronically-managed version of the rear brake regulator valve (fitted to non-ABS vehicles). To prevent rear wheel lock-up, the ABS unit software limits the brake fluid pressure supplied to the rear wheels.

4 The handbrake is cable-operated, and acts on the rear brakes. The cables operate on the rear trailing brake shoe operating levers.

5 All models have a conventional brake system, together with an ABS hydraulic unit fitted between the master cylinder and the four brake units at each wheel. For more information on the system, refer to Section 15.

Precautions

6 The car's braking system is one of its most important safety features. When working on the brakes, there are a number of points to be aware of, to ensure that your health (or even your life) is not being put at risk.

• When servicing any part of the system, work carefully and methodically – do not take short-cuts; also observe scrupulous cleanliness when overhauling any part of the hydraulic system.

• Always renew components in axle sets, where applicable – this means renewing brake pads, shoes, etc, on BOTH sides, even if only one set of pads is worn, or one wheel cylinder is leaking (for example). In the instance of uneven brake wear, the cause should be investigated and fixed (on front brakes, sticking caliper pistons is a likely problem).

• Use only genuine parts, or at least those of known good quality.

• Although brake pads and shoes are asbestos-free, the dust created by wear of the brakes can be a health hazard. Never blow them out with compressed air, and don't inhale any of the dust.

• DO NOT use petroleum-based solvents to clean brake parts; use brake cleaner or methylated spirit only.

• DO NOT allow any brake fluid, oil or grease to contact the brake pads or disc.

⚠ *Warning: Brake fluid is poisonous. Take care to keep it off bare skin, and in particular not to get splashes in your eyes. The fluid also attacks paintwork and plastics – wash off spillages immediately with cold water. Finally, brake fluid is highly inflammable, and should be handled with the same care as petrol.*

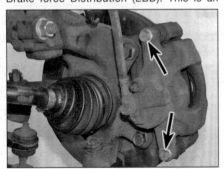
2.2 Unscrew and remove the guide pin bolts

2 Front brake pads – renewal

Note: *Refer to the precautions in Section 1 before proceeding.*

1 Apply the handbrake. Loosen the front wheel nuts, and then jack up the front of the car and support it on axle stands (see *Jacking and vehicle support*). Remove the front wheels. Work on one brake assembly at a time, using the assembled brake for reference if necessary.

2 Slacken and remove the caliper guide pin bolts **(see illustration)**.

3 With the guide pin bolts removed, withdraw the caliper from the brake pads **(see illustration)**. If required, the upper guide pin bolt can be left in place, and the caliper swiveled upwards from the brake pads.

4 Make a note of how the pads are fitted, and remove the outer and inner brake pads from the brake mounting bracket **(see illustrations)**.

5 With the two brake pads removed, check the anti-rattle shims are still located in the mounting bracket **(see illustration)**.

6 First measure the thickness of each brake pad's friction material (not including the backing plate). If either pad is worn at any point to the specified minimum thickness or less, all four pads must be renewed. Also, the pads should be renewed if any are fouled with oil or grease; there is no satisfactory way of degreasing friction material, once contaminated. If any of the brake pads are worn unevenly, or are fouled with oil or grease, trace and rectify the cause before reassembly.

7 If the brake pads are still serviceable, carefully clean them using a clean, fine wire brush or similar, paying particular attention to the sides and back of the metal backing. If the pads are 'glazed' (have a shiny appearance) it may be helpful to roughen the surface of the friction material in order to restore the pads' braking effectiveness. Clean out the grooves in the friction material (where applicable), and pick out any large embedded particles of dirt or debris. Carefully clean the pad locations in the caliper body/mounting bracket.

8 Prior to fitting the pads, check that the guides are free to slide easily in the caliper mounting bracket, and the rubber boots are not damaged. Brush the dust and dirt from the caliper and piston, but do not inhale it, as it may contain asbestos, which is a health hazard. Inspect the dust seal around the piston for damage, and the piston for evidence of fluid leaks, corrosion or damage. If attention to any of these components is necessary, refer to Section 3.

9 The caliper piston must be pushed back into the caliper to make room for the new pads – this may require considerable effort. Either use a G-clamp, sliding-jaw (water pump) pliers, or suitable pieces of wood as levers **(see illustration)**.

2.3 Remove the caliper to access the pads

2.4b... and inner brake pads

2.4a Remove the outer...

2.5 If required, withdraw the anti-rattle shims from the mounting bracket

Caution: Pushing back the piston causes a reverse-flow of brake fluid, which has been known to 'flip' the master cylinder rubber seals, resulting in a total loss of braking. To avoid this, clamp the caliper flexible hose and open the bleed screw – as the piston is pushed back, the fluid can be directed into a suitable container using a hose attached to the bleed screw. Close the screw just before the piston is pushed fully back, to ensure no air enters the system.

10 If the recommended method of opening a bleed screw before pushing back the piston is not used, the fluid level in the reservoir will rise, and possibly overflow. Make sure that there is sufficient space in the brake fluid reservoir to accept the displaced fluid and, if necessary, siphon some off first. Any brake fluid spilt on paintwork should be washed off

with clean water without delay – brake fluid is also a highly effective paint-stripper.

11 Where applicable, refit the pad upper and lower anti-rattle shims to the mounting bracket **(see illustration)**.

12 Although not essential, it is useful to apply a little copper brake grease to the edges of the pads in the areas which will slide in the mounting bracket (such as the end lugs, or 'ears') **(see illustration)**. Though anti-squeal shims are fitted, there is no harm in applying a little brake grease to the backs of the pads, where they will contact the caliper pistons. Ensure that no grease ends up on the pad friction material, or on the disc.

13 Install the pads, ensuring that the friction material of each pad is against the brake disc. On genuine manufacturers parts, the inner pad may have a wear indicator plate – if so, this should be facing upwards.

2.9 Using a DIY clamping tool to squeeze back the caliper pistons

2.11 Make sure the anti-rattle springs are fitted correctly

2.12 Apply a little copper grease to the pad-to-bracket surfaces

14 Refit the brake caliper or pivot the caliper down into position. Install the guide pin bolt(s), tightening them to the specified torque **(see illustration)**.

15 On completion, firmly depress the brake pedal a few times, to bring the pads to their normal working position. Check the level of the brake fluid in the reservoir, and top-up if necessary.

16 Give the car a short road test, to make sure that the brakes are functioning correctly, and to bed-in the new linings to the contours of the disc. New linings will not provide maximum braking efficiency until they have bedded-in; avoid heavy braking as far as possible for the first hundred miles or so.

3 Front brake caliper – removal, overhaul and refitting

Note: *Refer to the precautions in Section 1 before proceeding.*

Removal

1 Apply the handbrake. Loosen the front wheel nuts, and then jack up the front of the car and support it on axle stands (see *Jacking and vehicle support*). Remove the appropriate front wheel.

2 If the caliper is to be completely removed (as opposed to simply being unbolted and moved to one side for other servicing work to be carried out) fit a brake hose clamp to the flexible hose leading to the caliper. This will minimise brake fluid loss during subsequent

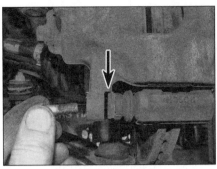
2.14 Make sure the guide fits in the flat of the caliper to prevent it from turning

operations. Loosen the union on the caliper end of the flexible hose **(see illustration)**. Once loosened, do not try to unscrew the hose at this stage.

3 Unscrew and remove the upper and lower guide pin bolts **(see illustration)**.

4 The caliper can now be removed from the mounting bracket. If it is simply to be unbolted and moved aside, support it from a convenient point under the wheel arch, using a piece of wire, string, or a cable-tie. Do not allow the caliper to hang unsupported on its flexible hose.

5 To remove the caliper completely, support it in one hand, and prevent the hydraulic hose from turning with the other hand. Unscrew the caliper from the hose, making sure that the hose is not twisted unduly or strained. Once the caliper is detached, plug the open hydraulic unions in the caliper and hose, to keep out dust and dirt.

6 If required (for instance, when renewing the discs), the caliper carrier bracket can be unbolted from the hub carrier **(see illustration)**.

Overhaul

Note: *Before starting work, check on the availability of parts (caliper overhaul kit/seals).*

7 With the caliper on the bench, brush away all traces of dust and dirt, but take care not to inhale any dust, as it may be harmful to your health.

8 Pull the dust cover rubber seal from the end of the piston.

9 Apply air pressure to the fluid inlet union to eject the piston. Only low air pressure is required for this, such as is produced by a foot-operated tyre pump.

Caution: The piston may be ejected with some force. Position a thin piece of wood between the piston and the caliper body to prevent damage to the end face of the piston in the event of it being ejected suddenly.

10 Using a suitable blunt instrument, prise the piston seal from the groove in the cylinder bore. Take care not to scratch the surface of the bore.

11 Clean the piston and caliper body with methylated spirit, and allow to dry. Examine the surfaces of the piston and cylinder bore for wear, damage and corrosion. If the piston alone is unserviceable, a new piston must be obtained, along with seals. If the cylinder bore is unserviceable, the complete caliper must be renewed. The seals must be renewed, regardless of the condition of the other components.

12 Coat the piston and seals with clean brake fluid, and then manipulate the piston seal into the groove in the cylinder bore.

13 Push the piston squarely into its bore, taking care not to damage the seal.

14 Fit the dust cover rubber seal onto the piston and caliper, and then depress the piston fully.

15 Prior to fitting the caliper, check that the guides are free to slide easily in the caliper mounting bracket, and the rubber boots are not damaged. Remove the guides and lubricate them with grease, to make sure they are free to slide **(see illustrations)**.

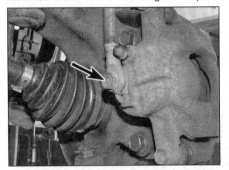
3.2 Slacken the brake pipe union on the caliper

3.3 Unscrew and remove the guide pin bolts

3.6 Caliper mounting bracket retaining bolts

3.15a Withdraw the guide...

3.15b... and rubber boot/gaiter

Refitting

16 Refit the caliper by reversing the removal operations. Make sure that the flexible brake hose is not twisted. Tighten the mounting bolts and wheel nuts to the specified torque.

17 Bleed the brake circuit according to the procedure given in Section 11, remembering to remove the brake hose clamp from the flexible hose. Make sure there are no leaks from the hose connections. Test the brakes carefully before returning the car to normal service.

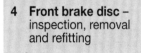

4 Front brake disc – inspection, removal and refitting

Note: *Refer to the precautions in Section 1 before proceeding.*

Inspection

1 Apply the handbrake. Loosen the relevant wheel nuts, jack up the front of the car and support it on axle stands. Remove the appropriate front wheel.

2 Slacken and remove the two caliper mounting bracket securing bolts **(see illustrations)**, and then withdraw the caliper, complete with mounting bracket from the front brake disc. Do not disconnect the flexible hose. Support the caliper on an axle stand, or suspend it out of the way with a piece of wire, taking care to avoid straining the flexible hose.

3 Temporarily refit two of the wheel nuts to diagonally opposite studs, with the flat sides of the nuts against the disc. Tighten the nuts progressively, to hold the disc firmly.

4 Scrape any corrosion from the disc. Rotate the disc, and examine it for deep scoring, grooving or cracks. Using a micrometer, measure the thickness of the disc in several places. The minimum thickness is stamped on the disc hub. Light wear and scoring is normal, but if excessive, the disc should be removed, and either reground by a specialist, or renewed. If regrinding is undertaken, the minimum thickness must be maintained. Obviously, if the disc is cracked, it must be renewed.

5 Using a dial gauge or a flat metal block and feeler gauges, check that the disc run-out 10

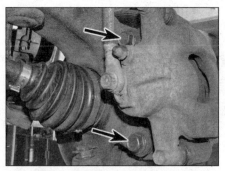

4.2a Undo the caliper mounting bracket retaining bolts...

mm from the outer edge does not exceed the limit given in the Specifications. To do this, fix the measuring equipment, and rotate the disc, noting the variation in measurement as the disc is rotated. The difference between the minimum and maximum measurements recorded is the disc run-out.

6 If the run-out is greater than the specified amount, check for variations of the disc thickness as follows. Mark the disc at eight positions 45° apart then, using a micrometer, measure the disc thickness at the eight positions, 15 mm in from the outer edge. If the variation between the minimum and maximum readings is greater than the specified amount, the disc should be renewed.

7 The hub face run-out can also be checked in a similar way. First remove the disc as described later in this Section, fix the measuring equipment, then slowly rotate the hub, and check that the run-out does not exceed the amount given in the Specifications. If the hub face run-out is excessive, this should be corrected (by renewing the hub bearings – see Chapter 10 Section 3) before rechecking the disc run-out.

Removal

8 With the wheel and caliper removed, remove the wheel nuts, which were temporarily refitted in paragraph 3.

9 Mark the disc in relation to the hub, if it is to be refitted.

10 Remove the Torx retaining screw, and withdraw the disc from the front hub **(see illustrations)**.

4.2b... and withdraw the caliper and mounting bracket

11 If the disc is a tight fit, two bolt holes are provided in the disc, which can be used to draw it off. Screw two bolts into these holes, and tighten them evenly to pull the disc off **(see illustration)**.

Refitting

12 Make sure that the disc and hub mating surfaces are clean, then locate the disc on the front hub. Align the previously-made marks if the original disc is being refitted.

13 Refit the Torx retaining screw.

14 Refit the brake caliper and mounting bracket.

15 Refit the wheel, and lower the car to the ground. Tighten wheel nuts to their specified torque.

16 Test the brakes carefully before returning the car to normal service.

5 Rear brake drum – removal, inspection and refitting

Note: *Refer to the precautions in Section 1 before proceeding.*

Removal

1 Chock the front wheels, release the handbrake and engage 1st gear. Loosen the relevant wheel nuts, jack up the rear of the car and support it on axle stands (see *Jacking and vehicle support*). Remove the appropriate rear wheel.

2 Undo the Torx retaining screw from the rear

4.10a Remove the securing screw...

4.10b... and remove the brake disc

4.11 Fit two suitable bolts into the holes provided, and tighten them evenly

5.2 Remove the drum securing screw

5.3a Fit two suitable bolts into the holes provided, and tighten them evenly

5.3b... to draw the drum off without damaging the shoes

5.4 Rear brake shoe adjuster wheel

brake drum **(see illustration)**. It should be possible to pull the drum off by hand – if not, first check that the handbrake is fully released. Removal often means turning the drum, and trying to pull a little at either side. Another

option is to try loosening the handbrake adjuster nut inside the car (refer to Section 19). Do not use too much force in removing the drum, or the shoe components could be damaged.

6.2 Note how the components are fitted before dismantling

6.4a Use pliers to depress and twist the cups...

6.4b... which releases the cups and hold-down springs...

6.4c... and allows the pins to be withdrawn from the rear

3 Two bolt holes are provided in the drum, which can be used to draw the drum off. Screw two bolts into these holes, and tighten them evenly to pull the drum off **(see illustrations)**.
4 The last option is to insert a slim, flat-bladed screwdriver through the wheel bolt hole, and try to turn the toothed wheel which operates the shoe adjuster **(see illustration)**.
5 With the brake drum removed, clean the dust from the drum, brake shoes, wheel cylinder and backplate, using brake cleaner or methylated spirit. Take care not to inhale the dust, as it may be harmful.

Inspection

6 Clean the inside surfaces of the brake drum, and then examine the internal friction surface for signs of scoring or cracks. If the drum was difficult to remove, this may have been due to a wear lip on the outer edge. If it is cracked, deeply scored, or has worn to a diameter greater than the maximum given in the Specifications, then it should be renewed, together with the drum on the other side.
7 Regrinding of the brake drum is not recommended.
8 Check the wheel cylinder for signs of fluid leakage. A clue to a cylinder that may have just started leaking is a build-up of black brake dust around the cylinder rubber boots. Carefully lift their rubber boots with a small screwdriver, and look for dampness. Renew if necessary, as described in Section 7.

Refitting

9 Refitting is a reversal of removal, noting the following points:
a) Secure the drum with the Torx retaining screw.
b) With the wheel refitted and the car lowered to the ground, apply the footbrake and handbrake fully several times, to centre up the shoes and to set the automatic adjuster.
c) Test the brakes carefully before returning the car to normal service.

6 Rear brake shoes – renewal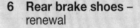

Note: Refer to the precautions in Section 1 before proceeding.
1 Remove the rear brake drums as described in Section 5.
2 Before going any further, note the fitted position of the springs and the brake shoes (if possible, take a digital picture) **(see illustration)**.
3 Clean the components with brake cleaner, and allow to dry. Position a tray beneath the backplate to catch the fluid and residue.
4 Remove the two shoe hold-down springs, use a pair of pliers to depress and twist the cups so that they can be withdrawn off the pins. Remove the hold-down pins from the backplate **(see illustrations)**.

6.5a Unhook the brake shoe from the lower pivot...

5 Noting how it is fitted, unhook and remove the shoe from the lower mounting, and then using a pair of thin-nosed pliers unclip the lower spring **(see illustrations)**.

6 Noting how the upper spring is fitted, unhook and remove the front shoe from the adjusting rod **(see illustrations)**.

7 Remove the upper spring from the rear shoe **(see illustration)**.

8 Pull out the rear shoe, complete with adjusting mechanism, and unhook the handbrake cable end fitting from the operating lever **(see illustrations)**.

9 To prevent the wheel cylinder pistons from being accidentally ejected, fit a suitable elastic band or wire lengthways over the cylinder/pistons **(see illustration)**. DO NOT press the brake pedal while the shoes are removed.

10 Working on a clean bench, pull the leading shoe from the strut and brake shoe adjuster, noting how it is attached, then unhook the upper return spring from the shoes. Pull the adjustment strut to release it from the trailing brake shoe, and remove the strut rear return spring **(see illustration)**.

11 If the wheel cylinder shows signs of fluid leakage, or if there is any reason to suspect it of being defective, inspect it now, as described in the next Section.

12 Clean the backplate, and apply small amounts of high melting-point brake grease to the brake shoe contact points **(see illustration)**. Be careful not to get grease on any friction surfaces.

13 Lubricate the sliding components of the brake shoe adjuster with a little high

6.9 Wrap an elastic band around the wheel cylinder while the shoes are removed

6.5b... and unhook and remove the shoe lower spring

6.6b... and remove the brake shoe, complete with adjuster wheel and thread

melting-point brake grease, but leave the serrations on the eccentric cam clean.

14 Fit the new brake shoes using a reversal of the removal procedure, but set the adjuster to its minimum length before assembling it to the trailing shoe.

6.8a Withdraw the rear brake shoe with adjuster bar...

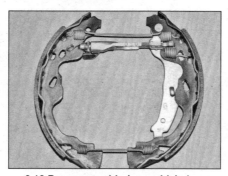

6.10 Passenger side (near side) shoe assembly – front view

6.6a Release the upper spring from the brake shoe...

6.7 Unhook and remove the shoe upper spring

15 Carry out the renewal procedures on the remaining rear brake.

16 Before refitting the drum, check its condition as described in Section 5.

17 With the drum in position, refit the wheel.

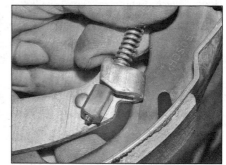

6.8b... and disconnect the handbrake cable from the brake lever

6.12 Clean the backplate and apply brake grease to the positions shown

7.3 Using a brake hose clamp

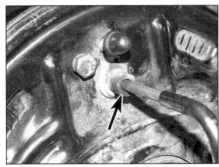

7.5 Slacken the wheel cylinder union nut

18 Lower the car to the ground, and tighten the wheel nuts to the specified torque.

19 Depress the brake pedal several times, in order to operate the self-adjusting mechanism and set the shoes at their normal operating position.

20 Make several forward and reverse stops, and operate the handbrake fully two or three times (adjust the handbrake as required – see Section 19). Give the car a road test, to make sure that the brakes are functioning correctly, and to bed-in the new shoes to the contours of the drum. Remember that the new shoes will not give full braking efficiency until they have bedded-in.

7 Rear wheel cylinder – removal, overhaul and refitting

Note: *Refer to the precautions in Section 1 before proceeding. Also bear in mind that if the brake shoes have been contaminated by fluid leaking from the wheel cylinder, they must be renewed. The shoes on BOTH sides of the car must be renewed, even if they are only contaminated on one side.*

Removal

1 Remove the brake drum as described in Section 5. If the wheel cylinders have been leaking, there will probably be a significant build-up of brake dust on the failed seals (the dust sticks to the leaking fluid). A leak can be confirmed by carefully prising up the outer

lip of the seal – any wetness means a new cylinder will be needed.

2 In recent years, the availability of wheel cylinder repair kits has greatly decreased, but it may still be worth asking. Wheel cylinders do not have to be fitted in pairs (providing they are the same size), but if one is leaking, it's reasonable to assume the other one soon will be too. If the leak has been going on for some time, it may be serious enough to have contaminated the brake shoes, in which case new shoes should be fitted on BOTH sides.

3 Minimise fluid loss either by removing the master cylinder reservoir cap, and then tightening it down onto a piece of polythene to obtain an airtight seal, or by using a brake hose clamp or similar tool, to clamp the flexible hose at the nearest convenient point to the wheel cylinder **(see illustration)**.

4 Pull the brake shoes apart at their top ends, so that they are just clear of the wheel cylinder. The automatic adjuster will hold the shoes in this position so that the cylinder can be withdrawn.

5 Wipe away all traces of dirt around the hydraulic union at the rear of the wheel cylinder, then undo the union nut **(see illustration)**. This nut may well be very tight – it pays to apply penetrating oil (or WD-40) in advance, and to use a proper brake spanner when loosening it.

6 Unscrew the bolt securing the wheel cylinder to the backplate.

7 Withdraw the wheel cylinder from the

backplate so that it is clear of the brake shoes. Plug the open hydraulic unions to prevent entry of dirt, and to minimise further fluid loss whilst the cylinder is detached.

Overhaul

8 No overhaul procedures or parts were available at the time of writing – check availability of spares before dismantling. Renewing a wheel cylinder as a unit is recommended.

Refitting

9 Wipe clean the backplate and remove the plug from the end of the hydraulic pipe. Fit the cylinder onto the backplate and screw in the hydraulic union nut by hand, being careful not to cross-thread it.

10 Tighten the mounting bolt, and then fully tighten the hydraulic union nut.

11 Retract the automatic brake adjuster mechanism, so that the brake shoes engage with the pistons of the wheel cylinder. To do this, prise the shoes apart slightly, turn the automatic adjuster to its minimum position, and release the shoes.

12 Remove the clamp from the flexible brake hose, or the polythene from the master cylinder (as applicable).

13 Refit the brake drum with reference to Section 5.

14 Bleed the hydraulic system as described in Section 11. Providing suitable precautions were taken to minimise loss of fluid, it should only be necessary to bleed the relevant rear brake.

15 Test the brakes carefully before returning the car to normal service.

8 Master cylinder – removal and refitting

Note: *Refer to the precautions in Section 1 before proceeding.*

Removal

1 Disconnect the wiring plug for the fluid level warning sensor from the top of the reservoir **(see illustration)**.

2 Draw off the hydraulic fluid from the reservoir, using an old battery hydrometer or similar. Alternatively, raise the car, remove the wheels, then slacken the front bleed nipples and drain the fluid from the reservoir.

3 Identify the locations of the brake pipes on the master cylinder, then unscrew the union nuts and disconnect the pipes **(see illustration)**. Use a proper brake pipe spanner when loosening them. Plug the open hydraulic unions in the master cylinder and pipes to keep out dust and dirt.

4 Undo the master cylinder securing nuts, and then withdraw the master cylinder from the studs on the servo unit **(see illustration)**. Recover the O-ring – a new one will be needed when refitting.

8.1 Disconnect the brake fluid level sensor wiring connector

8.3 Unscrew the pipe unions on the side of the master cylinder

5 If required, the reservoir can be removed from the cylinder by releasing the plastic legs on the bottom of the reservoir from the mounting pins on the master cylinder **(see illustration)**. Recover the reservoir seals, and fit new ones when reassembling.

6 If the master cylinder is faulty, it must be renewed. At the time of writing, no overhaul kits were available.

Refitting

7 Refitting is a reversal of the removal procedure, noting the following points:
a) *Clean the contact surfaces of the master cylinder and servo, and locate a new O-ring on the back of the master cylinder*
b) *Refit and tighten the nuts to the specified torque.*
c) *Carefully insert the brake pipes in the apertures in the master cylinder, and then tighten the union nuts. Make sure that the nuts enter their threads correctly.*
d) *Fill the reservoir with fresh brake fluid.*
e) *Bleed the brake hydraulic system as described in Section 11.*
f) *Test the brakes carefully before returning the car to normal service.*

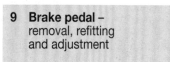

9 Brake pedal –
removal, refitting and adjustment

Note: *Refer to the precautions in Section 1 before proceeding.*

Removal

1 Working inside the car, move the driver's seat fully to the rear, to allow maximum working area.

2 Reach up under the facia panel and pull out the spring clip used to secure the servo pushrod clevis pin **(see illustration)**.

3 Pull out the clevis pin and detach the pushrod from the pedal **(see illustration)**.

4 Unscrew the pedal pivot bolt nut, then slide out the bolt and remove the pedal from the car **(see illustration)**. Recover the pedal pivot sleeve/bush – if it appears worn, obtain a new one for reassembly.

5 If required, the pedal mounting bracket can be removed – it is secured to the bulkhead by the four servo unit mounting

9.4 Brake pedal pivot bolt nut

8.4 Unscrew the master cylinder mounting nuts

9.2 Remove the spring clip...

nuts and by a further lower mounting bolt **(see illustration)**.

Refitting

6 Prior to refitting the pedal, apply a little grease to the pivot shaft, pedal sleeve/bush and actuator rod.

7 Refitting is the reversal of the removal procedure, but make sure that the pedal sleeve/bush and servo operating rod are correctly located.

8 Check and adjust the pedal height if necessary as described below.

Adjustment

Note: *For maximum accuracy, the brakes should be bled as described in Section 11 before carrying out any adjustments.*

9 With the pedal released, measure the distance from the floor (directly below the pedal), and compare with the specified dimension.

9.5 Brake pedal mounting bracket retaining nuts and bolt

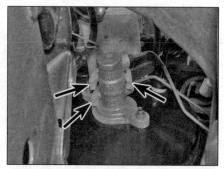

8.5 Release the securing clips (arrowed) to release the reservoir

9.3... and withdraw the clevis pin from the pushrod

10 If adjustment is necessary, first disconnect the wiring plug from the brake light switch. Twist the switch and remove it from the pedal bracket.

11 Loosen the locknut on the brake servo pushrod, and turn the adjuster as required until the pedal height falls within the specified range **(see illustration)**. Tighten the locknut to the specified torque on completion.

12 Refit the brake light switch, reconnect its wiring plug and adjust the switch as described in Section 17.

13 Now press the pedal repeatedly using

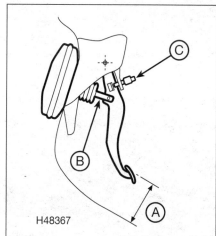

9.11 Adjust the pushrod (B) to get the right height at (A)

C Brake light switch

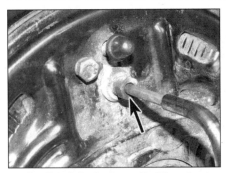

10.2 Check for leaks around the wheel cylinder union nut

your foot, until the vacuum in the servo is dissipated and the pedal has a firm feel.

14 Check the pedal free play by depressing the pedal with your hand until resistance is felt – this should be no more than a very few millimeters. If the free play is incorrect, recheck the servo pushrod adjustment. Incorrect free play suggests a problem elsewhere in the braking system.

15 On completion, test the brakes care- fully before returning the car to normal service.

10 Hydraulic pipes and hoses – inspection, removal and refitting

Note: *Refer to the precautions in Section 1 before proceeding.*

Inspection

1 Jack up the front and rear of the car, and

10.9a Slacken the union nut...

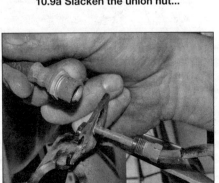

10.9c... and disconnect the brake hose

10.8 Using a brake hose clamp

support on axle stands. Make sure the car is safely supported on a level surface.

2 Check for signs of leakage at the pipe unions **(see illustration)**, then examine the flexible hoses for signs of cracking, chafing and fraying.

3 The brake pipes should be examined carefully for signs of dents, corrosion or other damage. Corrosion should be scraped off, and if the depth of pitting is significant, the pipes renewed. This is particularly likely in those areas underneath the car body where the pipes are exposed and unprotected.

4 Renew any defective brake pipes and/or hoses.

Removal

5 If a section of pipe or hose is to be removed, loss of brake fluid can be reduced by unscrewing the filler cap, and completely sealing the top of the reservoir with cling film

10.9b... slide out the securing clip...

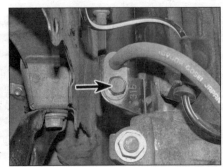

10.11a Make sure the hose is secured with bolt...

or adhesive tape. Alternatively, the reservoir can be emptied (see Section 11).

6 To remove a section of pipe, hold the adjoining hose union nut with a spanner to prevent it from turning, then unscrew the union nut at the end of the pipe, and release it. Repeat the procedure at the other end of the pipe, and then release the pipe by pulling out the clips attaching it to the body.

7 Where the union nuts are exposed to the weather, they can sometimes be quite tight. If an open-ended spanner is used, burring of the flats on the nuts is not uncommon, and for this reason it is preferable to use a split ring (brake) spanner, which will engage all the flats. If such a spanner is not available, self-locking grips may be used as a last resort; these may well damage the nuts, but if the pipe is to be renewed, this does not matter.

8 To further minimise the loss of fluid when disconnecting a flexible brake line from a rigid pipe, clamp the hose as near as possible to the pipe to be detached, using a brake hose clamp or similar **(see illustration)**.

9 To remove a flexible hose, first clean the ends of the hose and the surrounding area, and then unscrew the union nuts from the hose ends. Remove the spring clip, and withdraw the hose from the support bracket **(see illustrations)**. Where applicable, unscrew the hose from the caliper.

10 Brake pipes supplied with flared ends and union nuts can be obtained individually or in sets from a franchised dealer or accessory shops. The pipe is then bent to shape, using the old pipe as a guide, and is ready for fitting. Be careful not to kink or crimp the pipe when bending it; ideally, a proper pipe-bending tool should be used.

Refitting

11 Refitting of the pipes and hoses is a reversal of removal. Make sure that all brake pipes are securely supported in their clips, and ensure that the hoses are not kinked **(see illustrations)**.

12 Check also that the hoses are clear of all suspension components and underbody fittings **(see illustration)**, and will remain clear during movement of the suspension and steering.

10.11b... and all retaining clips are secure

13 On completion, remove any hose clamps that have been used and bleed the hydraulic system as described in Section 11.

11 Hydraulic system – bleeding

Note: *Refer to the precautions in Section 1 before proceeding.*

1 If the master cylinder has been disconnected and reconnected, then the complete system (all circuits) must be bled of air. If a component of one circuit has been disturbed, then only that particular circuit need be bled.

2 Bleeding should start with the furthest bleed nipple from the master cylinder, followed by the next one until the bleed nipple nearest the master cylinder is bled last.

3 There are many do-it-yourself 'one-man' brake bleeding kits available from motor accessory shops, and it is recommended that one of these kits be used wherever possible, as they greatly simplify the brake bleeding operation.

4 During the bleeding operation, do not allow the brake fluid level in the reservoir to drop below the minimum level mark. If the level is allowed to fall so far that air is drawn in, the whole procedure will have to be started again from the beginning. **Note:** *The ignition must be switched off (remove the key from the ignition).* Only use new fluid for topping-up, preferably from a freshly-opened container. Never use fluid bled from the system.

5 Before starting, check that all rigid pipes and flexible hoses are in good condition, and that all hydraulic unions are tight. Take great care not to allow hydraulic fluid to come into contact with the car paintwork; otherwise the finish will be seriously damaged. Wash off any spilt fluid immediately with cold water.

Bleeding

Basic (two-man) method

6 Collect together a clear container of reasonable size, a suitable length of plastic or rubber tubing, which is a tight fit over the bleed screw, and a ring spanner to fit the screw. The help of an assistant will also be required.

7 Remove the dust cap from the first bleed screw in the sequence (see illustration). Fit the spanner and tube to the screw, place the other end of the tube in the container, and pour in sufficient fluid to cover the end of the tube.

8 Ensure that the master cylinder reservoir fluid level is maintained at least above the MIN level line throughout the procedure (see illustration).

9 Have the assistant fully depress the brake pedal several times to build-up pressure, and then maintain it on the final downstroke.

10 While pedal pressure is maintained, unscrew the bleed screw (approximately one

10.12a Check the front brake hoses...

turn) and allow the compressed fluid and air to flow into the container. The assistant should maintain pedal pressure, following it down to the floor if necessary, and should not release it until instructed to do so. When the flow stops, tighten the bleed screw again, have the assistant release the pedal slowly, and recheck the reservoir fluid level.

11 Repeat the steps given in paragraphs 9 and 10 until the fluid emerging from the bleed screw is free from air bubbles. If the master cylinder has been drained and refilled, and air is being bled from the first screw in the sequence, allow approximately five seconds between cycles for the master cylinder passages to refill.

12 When no more air bubbles appear, tighten the bleed screw securely, remove the tube and spanner, and refit the dust cap. Do not overtighten the bleed screw.

13 Repeat the procedure on the remaining

11.7 Remove the dust cap from the rear wheel cylinder bleed screw

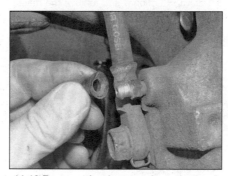
11.13 Remove the dust cap from the front caliper bleed screw

10.12b... and rear brake hoses

bleed screws (see illustration), until all air is removed from the system and the brake pedal feels firm again.

Using a one-way valve kit

14 As their name implies, these kits consist of a length of tubing with a one-way valve fitted, to prevent expelled air and fluid being drawn back into the system; some kits include a translucent container, which can be positioned so that the air bubbles can be more easily seen flowing from the end of the tube.

15 The kit is connected to the bleed screw, which is then opened (see illustration). The user returns to the driver's seat, depresses the brake pedal with a smooth, steady stroke, and slowly releases it; this is repeated until the expelled fluid is clear of air bubbles.

16 Note that these kits simplify work so much that it is easy to forget the master

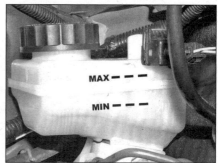
11.8 Keep the fluid level above the minimum level at all times

11.15 Using a one-man brake bleeding kit

12.4 Remove the scuttle panel from the rear of the engine compartment

12.5 Brake vacuum hose one-way valve

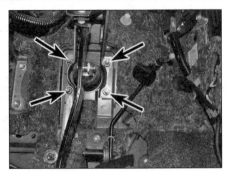

12.10 Four brake servo mounting nuts

cylinder reservoir fluid level; ensure that this is maintained at least above the MIN level line at all times.

Using a pressure-bleeding kit

17 These kits are usually operated by the reservoir of pressurised air contained in the spare tyre. However, note that it will probably be necessary to reduce the pressure to a lower level than normal; refer to the instructions supplied with the kit.

18 By connecting a pressurised, fluid-filled container to the master cylinder reservoir, bleeding can be carried out simply by opening each screw in turn (in the sequence given in paragraph 2), and allowing the fluid to flow out until no more air bubbles can be seen in the expelled fluid.

19 This method has the advantage that the large reservoir of fluid provides an additional safeguard against air being drawn into the system during bleeding.

20 Pressure-bleeding is particularly effective when bleeding 'difficult' systems, or when bleeding the complete system at the time of routine fluid renewal.

All methods

21 When bleeding is complete, and firm pedal feel is restored, wash off any spilt fluid, tighten the bleed screws securely, and refit their dust caps.

22 Check the hydraulic fluid level in the master cylinder reservoir, and top up if necessary (see 'Weekly checks').

23 Discard any hydraulic fluid that has been bled from the system; it will not be fit for re-use.

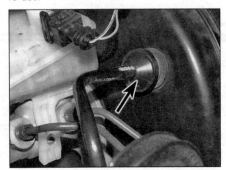

13.2 Disconnect the vacuum hose/valve from the servo

24 Check the feel of the brake pedal. If it feels at all spongy, air must still be present in the system, and further bleeding is required. Failure to bleed satisfactorily after a reasonable repetition of the bleeding procedure may be due to worn master cylinder seals.

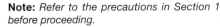

12 Vacuum servo unit – testing, removal and refitting

Note: *Refer to the precautions in Section 1 before proceeding.*

Testing

1 To test the operation of the servo unit, depress the footbrake four or five times to dissipate the vacuum, then start the engine while keeping the footbrake depressed. As the engine starts, there should be a noticeable give in the brake pedal as vacuum builds-up. Allow the engine to run for at least two minutes, and then switch it off. If the brake pedal is now depressed again, it should be possible to hear a hiss from the servo when the pedal is depressed. After four or five applications, no further hissing should be heard, and the pedal should feel harder.

2 Before assuming that a problem exists in the servo unit itself, inspect the non-return valve as described in the next Section.

Removal

3 Refer to Section 8 and remove the master cylinder.

4 To give better access, remove the wiper motor/linkage and scuttle panel from the rear of the engine compartment **(see illustration)**, as described in Chapter 12 Section 14.

5 Pull the vacuum hose/valve from the rubber grommet on the front of the servo unit **(see illustration)**.

6 On left-hand-drive models, remove the battery and battery tray as described in Chapter 5A Section 4.

7 Working inside the car, move the driver's seat fully to the rear, to allow maximum working room.

8 Reach up under the facia panel and pull

out the spring clip used to secure the servo pushrod clevis pin **(see illustration 9.2)**.

9 Pull out the clevis pin and detach the pushrod from the pedal **(see illustration 9.3)**.

10 Have an assistant support the servo unit under the bonnet, then unscrew and remove the four nuts from the brake pedal mounting bracket **(see illustration)**.

11 Have your assistant carefully withdraw the servo unit into the engine compartment – this will also loosen the pedal mounting bracket inside the car, but it should remain in place due to the lower mounting bolt to the bulkhead.

12 Recover the servo mounting gasket – a new one should be used when refitting.

Refitting

13 Refitting is a reversal of the removal procedure, noting the following points:
a) *Make sure the new gasket is correctly positioned on the servo.*
b) *Refit the master cylinder, as described in Section 8.*
c) *Refit the scuttle panel and wiper motor/ linkage, as described in Chapter 12 Section 14.*
d) *Test the brakes carefully before returning the car to normal service.*

13 Vacuum servo unit vacuum hose and non-return valve – removal, testing and refitting

Note: *Refer to the precautions in Section 1 before proceeding.*

Removal

1 With the engine switched off, depress the brake pedal four or five times, to dissipate any remaining vacuum from the servo unit.

2 Remove the vacuum hose/non-return valve by pulling it free from the rubber grommet in the servo unit **(see illustration)**. If it is reluctant to move, carefully prise it free, taking care not to damage the rubber grommet.

3 Release the securing clips and detach the other end of the vacuum hose from the inlet manifold connection **(see illustrations)**.

4 Unclip the vacuum hose from across the rear of the inlet manifold, noting its fitted

13.3a Disconnect the servo vacuum hose...

13.3b... release the securing clips...

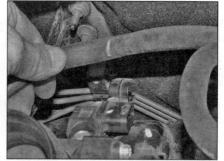

13.4... and unclip it from the rear of the inlet manifold

position **(see illustration)**. The hose has yellow markings to aid refitting.

5 If the hose or the fixings are damaged or in poor condition, they must be renewed. The vacuum hose and non-return valve is a complete unit and can only be renewed as one part.

Testing

6 Examine the non-return valve for damage and signs of deterioration, and renew it if necessary. The valve may be tested by blowing through its connecting hoses in both directions. It should only be possible to blow from the servo end towards the inlet manifold.

Refitting

7 Refitting is a reversal of the removal procedure.

14 Anti-lock braking system (ABS) – general information

1 ABS is fitted to all models as standard. The system comprises a hydraulic regulator unit and the four roadwheel sensors. The regulator unit contains the electronic control unit (ECU), the hydraulic solenoid valves and the electrically-driven return pump. The purpose of the system is to prevent the wheel(s) locking during heavy braking. This is achieved by automatic release of the brake on the relevant wheel, followed by re-application of the brake.

2 The solenoid valves are controlled by the ECU, which itself receives signals from the four wheel sensors fitted to the wheel hubs which monitor the speed of rotation of each wheel. By comparing these signals, the ECU can determine the speed at which the vehicle is travelling – this information is used instead of a vehicle speed sensor signal on some models. It can use this speed to determine when a wheel is decelerating at an abnormal rate, compared to the speed of the car, and therefore predicts when a wheel is about to lock. During normal operation, the system functions in the same way as a non-ABS braking system.

3 If the ECU senses that a wheel is about to lock, it closes the relevant outlet solenoid valves in the hydraulic unit, which then isolates the relevant brake(s) on the wheel(s) which is/

are about to lock from the master cylinder, effectively sealing-in the hydraulic pressure.

4 If the speed of rotation of the wheel continues to decrease at an abnormal rate, the ECU opens the inlet solenoid valves on the relevant brake(s), and operates the electrically-driven return pump which pumps the hydraulic fluid back into the master cylinder, releasing the brake. Once the speed of rotation of the wheel returns to an acceptable rate, the pump stops; the solenoid valves switch again, allowing the hydraulic master cylinder pressure to return to the caliper, which then re-applies the brake. This cycle can be carried out many times a second.

5 The action of the solenoid valves and return pump creates pulses in the hydraulic circuit. When the ABS system is functioning, these pulses can be felt through the brake pedal.

6 The operation of the ABS system is entirely dependent on electrical signals. To prevent the system responding to any inaccurate signals, a built-in safety circuit monitors all signals received by the ECU. If an inaccurate signal or low battery voltage is detected, the ABS system is automatically shut-down, and the warning light on the instrument panel is illuminated to inform the driver that the ABS system is not operational. Normal braking should still be available, however.

7 It is also equipped with an additional safety feature called EBD (Electronic Brake force Distribution), which automatically apportions braking effort between the front and rear wheels. The EBD function is built into the system's software, and the intention is to limit braking effort (fluid pressure) to the rear

15.3 Disconnect the wiring plug from the ABS unit

wheels, to further prevent them locking up under heavy braking.

8 If a fault does develop in the any of these systems, the vehicle must be taken to a franchised dealer or suitably-equipped specialist for fault diagnosis and repair.

15 ABS hydraulic unit – removal and refitting

Note: *Refer to the precautions in Section 1 before proceeding.*

Removal

1 The ABS unit is somewhat inaccessible, at the rear left-hand corner of the engine compartment.

2 Remove the battery, fuse/relay box and battery tray as described in Chapter 5A Section 4.

3 Release the locking clip and disconnect the wiring multi-plug from the ABS unit **(see illustration)**.

4 Taking precautions against the spillage of brake fluid, and noting their positions for refitting, unscrew the six brake pipe unions on the top and side of the unit, and disconnect the pipes **(see illustration)**. Use a proper brake spanner on the unions, to avoid rounding them off if they are tight. Plug the ends of the brake pipes and the connections in the ABS unit, to prevent dirt ingress and to prevent further loss of fluid from the ABS unit.

5 Working under the ABS unit, unbolt the mounting bracket from the inner wing, and

15.4 Disconnect the six brake pipes from the top of the unit

15.5 Unbolt the ABS unit mounting bracket from the inner wing

remove the hydraulic unit from the engine compartment, together with its mounting bracket **(see illustration)**. If refitting the old ABS unit, keep it in the upright position, with the fluid still inside and the connections plugged.

6 If required, the hydraulic unit can be separated from its mounting bracket, after removing the two nuts.

Refitting

7 Refitting is a reversal of removal, noting the following points:

a) *Ensure that the six brake pipes are fitted in the correct locations in the ABS unit, as noted on removal.*

b) *Make sure the multiplug is securely connected.*

c) *Tighten the brake pipe unions to their specified torque.*

d) *On completion, bleed the hydraulic system as described in Section 11.*

16 ABS wheel sensors – testing, removal and refitting

Note: *Refer to the precautions in Section 1 before proceeding.*

Testing

1 Checking of the sensors is done before removal by connecting a voltmeter to the disconnected sensor multiplug. Using an analogue (moving coil) meter is not practical, since the meter does not respond quickly enough. A digital meter having an ac facility should be used to check that the sensor is operating correctly.

2 To do this, raise the relevant wheel then disconnect the wiring to the ABS sensor and connect the meter to it.

3 Spin the wheel and check that the output voltage is between 1.5 and 2.0 volts, depending on how fast the wheel is spun.

4 Alternatively, an oscilloscope may be used to check the output of the sensor – an alternating current will be traced on the screen, of magnitude depending on the speed of the rotating wheel.

5 If the sensor output is low or zero, renew the sensor.

Removal

Front wheel sensor

6 Apply the handbrake and loosen the relevant front wheel nuts. Jack up the front of

the car and support it on axle stands. Remove the wheel.

7 Undo the retaining bolt and remove the shield from the wheel sensor in the top of the hub **(see illustration)**.

8 Unscrew the sensor mounting bolt from the hub and withdraw the sensor **(see illustrations)**. The sensors can prove difficult to remove, due to corrosion – try soaking the sensor in penetrating oil (or WD-40). Do not use any great force to remove a sensor, or it will be damaged. If the sensor does not have to be removed, trace the wire and unclip it from its retaining clips and disconnect its wiring connector instead.

9 Working along the length of the sensor wiring, unclip it from any retaining clips **(see illustration)**.

10 If necessary remove the inner wheel arch liner, and then trace the wiring up the inner wing and disconnect the wiring connector **(see illustration)**. Withdraw the sensor and wiring from the vehicle.

Rear wheel sensor

11 Apply the handbrake and loosen the relevant rear wheel nuts. Chock the front wheels, and then jack up the rear of the car and support it on axle stands. Remove the wheel.

12 Unscrew the sensor mounting bolt from the rear of the hub and withdraw the sensor **(see illustrations)**. Do not use any great force to remove a sensor, or it will be damaged.

13 Working along the length of the sensor

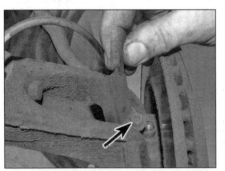

16.7 Unbolt the shield from the top of the hub assembly

16.8a Undo the retaining bolt...

16.8b... and remove the wheel sensor

16.9 Unclip the sensor wiring from its securing brackets

16.10 Disconnect the wiring connector from under the wing panel

16.12a Undo the retaining bolt...

wiring, unclip it from any retaining clips **(see illustration)**.

14 Trace the wiring up to the floor panel and through the rubber grommet into the luggage compartment and under the rear seat cushion. Disconnect the wiring connector and withdraw the sensor and wiring from the vehicle **(see illustrations)**.

Refitting

15 Refitting is a reversal of the removal procedure.

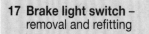

17 Brake light switch – removal and refitting

Note: *Refer to the precautions in Section 1 before proceeding.*

Removal

1 Working inside the car, move the driver's seat fully to the rear, to allow maximum working space.

2 Disconnect the wiring plug from the brake light switch at the top of the brake pedal bracket **(see illustration)**.

3 Twist the switch and withdraw it from the plastic spacer/nut in the pedal bracket **(see illustrations)**.

4 If required, unclip the plastic spacer/nut from the pedal bracket **(see illustration)**.

Refitting

5 If removed insert the plastic spacer/nut back into the pedal bracket.

17.2 Disconnect the brake light switch wiring plug

17.3b... and withdraw it from the pedal bracket

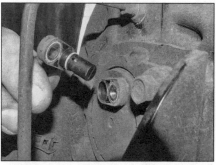

16.12b... and remove the wheel sensor

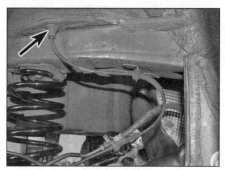

16.14a Unclip the rubber grommet in the floor panel...

6 Refit the brake light switch back into the top of the pedal bracket, push it all the way in until the switch housing (white part), touches the top of the pedal, then twist it to lock it in position. As the switch is twisted in the plastic spacer/

17.3a Twist the brake light switch...

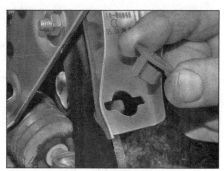

17.4 Unclip the plastic nut from the bracket

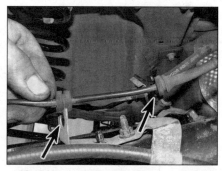

16.13 Unclip the sensor wiring from its securing brackets

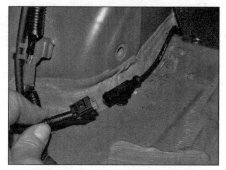

16.14b... and disconnect the wiring connector from under the rear seat

nut, it will release slightly to allow a small gap (1.5 to 2.5 mm) between the pedal and the switch housing. Just the plunger (black part) will remain against the pedal **(see illustration)**.

7 Reconnect the wiring connector to the switch and check the operation of the brake lights.

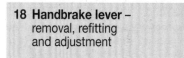

18 Handbrake lever – removal, refitting and adjustment

Note: *Refer to the precautions in Section 1 before proceeding.*

Removal

1 Chock the front wheels, and engage 1st gear.

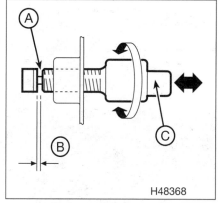

17.6 Check the gap at (B)

A plunger   C Switch

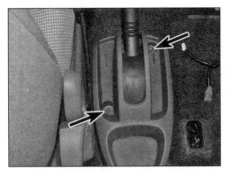

18.2a Undo the two retaining bolts...

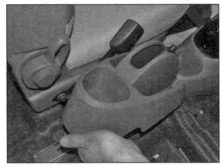

18.2b... and remove the handbrake cover

18.3a Slacken the locknut/adjuster nut...

18.3b... and unhook the cables from the equaliser bar

18.4 Unplug the handbrake warning light switch

18.5 Remove the two mounting bolts and remove the lever assembly

2 Undo the two retaining bolts and remove the console from around the handbrake lever (see illustrations).
3 Slacken the adjuster nut completely, to the end of the threads, and unhook the equaliser bar from the cable end fittings at the rear (see illustrations).
4 Disconnect the electrical connector from the handbrake warning light switch (see illustration).
5 Remove the two bolts securing the lever assembly to the floor, and remove it from the car (see illustration).

Refitting

6 Refitting is a reversal of removal.
7 When refitting the lever, it will be necessary to reset and adjust the mechanism, as described below.

Adjustment

8 Refer to the adjustment procedure in Chapter 1 Section 8. If new cables have been fitted, recheck the adjustment after about, one month or 1000 miles.

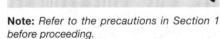
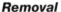

19 Handbrake cables – removal and refitting

Note: *Refer to the precautions in Section 1 before proceeding.*
Caution: *Since the cables are routed close to the exhaust system in several places, this procedure should only be attempted when the engine and exhaust system are completely cool. The engine should have been switched off for at least a few*

hours (preferably, after it has been left overnight).

Removal

1 Chock the front wheels, and engage 1st gear. Loosen the wheel nuts on the relevant rear wheel, and then jack up the rear of the car and support it on axle stands (see *Jacking and vehicle support*). Fully release the handbrake lever.
2 Remove the brake shoes as described in Section 6.
3 Using a small ring spanner to release the retaining clips, free the cable from the brake backplate (see illustrations).
4 Unclip the ABS sensor wiring from the support clip, then unscrew the first cable support bracket nut, on the rear suspension arm (see illustrations).

19.3a Using a ring spanner to release the cable securing clips...

19.3b... and then remove the cable from the backplate

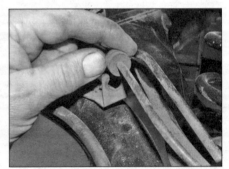

19.4a Unclip the wheel speed sensor wiring...

19.4b... and remove the cable support bracket

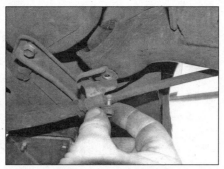

19.5a Unbolt the cable support bracket from the rear arm...

19.5b... and the rear floor panel

5 Trace the cable forwards, unbolting the support brackets to free it from the underside of the car **(see illustrations)**. Note how it is routed for refitting.

6 At the front, unscrew the bolt which secures the cable to the floor where it enters the car **(see illustrations)**.

7 Undo the two retaining bolts and remove the console from around the handbrake lever (see illustrations 18.2a and 28.2b).

8 Slacken the adjuster nut completely, to the end of the threads, and unhook the equaliser bar from the cable end fittings at the rear (see illustrations 18.3a and 18.3b).

9 Feed the cable downwards and out from under the car. If one cable is being renewed due to wear or other problems, consider renewing them both as a pair to ensure even operation.

Refitting

10 Refitting is a reversal of the removal procedure, noting the following points:

a) *Make sure that the cable end fittings are correctly located, and that the cables are routed as before, without any kinks or sharp bends.*

b) *Adjust the handbrake as described in Chapter 1 Section 8.*

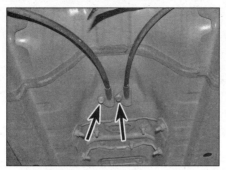

19.6a Unbolt the cable support brackets from the floor...

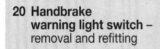

20 Handbrake warning light switch – removal and refitting

Note: *Refer to the precautions in Section 1 before proceeding.*

Removal

1 Undo the two retaining bolts and remove the console from around the handbrake lever **(see illustrations 18.2a and 18.2b).**

19.6b... and withdraw the handbrake cables

2 The switch is located on the front of the handbrake lever mounting bracket **(see illustration)**.

3 Disconnect the wiring plug from the front of the switch.

4 Slide the passenger seat as far back as possible and remove the switch securing screw, and then withdraw the switch from the mounting bracket **(see illustrations)**.

Refitting

5 Refitting is a reversal of removal.

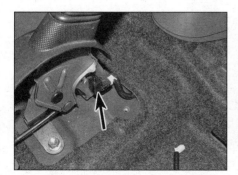

20.2 Handbrake warning light switch

20.4a Undo the retaining screw (arrowed)...

20.4b... and remove the switch from the handbrake lever bracket

Notes

Chapter 10
Suspension and steering

Contents

Degrees of difficulty

Easy, suitable for novice with little experience	**Fairly easy,** suitable for beginner with some experience	**Fairly difficult,** suitable for competent DIY mechanic	**Difficult,** suitable for experienced DIY mechanic	**Very difficult,** suitable for expert DIY or professional

Specifications

Wheel alignment and steering angles

Steering axis inclination (non-adjustable)	9° 33'
Maximum side-to-side variation	30'
Front wheel:	
Toe-setting/tracking (adjustable)	0° 07' ± 0° 12'
Camber (non-adjustable)	-0° 47' ± 0° 45'
Maximum side-to-side variation	30'
Castor (non-adjustable)	2° 47' ± 0° 45'
Maximum side-to-side variation	30'
Rear wheel:	
Toe-setting/tracking (non-adjustable)	0° 21' ± 0° 13'
Camber (non-adjustable)	-0° 56' ± 0° 30'
Maximum side-to-side variation	30'

Torque wrench settings

	Nm	lbf ft
Front suspension		
Anti-roll bar:		
Bracket bolts	18	13
Drop link nuts	18	13
Driveshaft (hub) nut*	216	159
Lower arm:		
Balljoint nut	98	72
Front pivot bolt	100	74
Rear mounting bolt	100	74
Subframe mounting bolts:		
Front bolts (side-chassis leg)	70	52
Rear bolts (floor panel)	48	35
Rear bolts (lower arm rear mounting)	100	74
Suspension strut:		
Piston rod nut*	55	41
Top mounting nut	55	41
Swivel hub-to-suspension strut pinch-bolt/nut	48	35
Rear suspension		
Rear axle beam-to-body mounting bolts	123	91
Rear hub mounting bolts	60	44
Shock absorber:		
Lower mounting bolt	48	35
Upper mounting nuts	25	18

Torque wrench settings (continued)

	Nm	lbf ft
Steering		
Steering column:		
Lower knuckle joint pinch-bolts	35	26
Mounting bolts	25	18
Protector plate bolt	25	18
Steering rack securing bolts	89	66
Steering wheel securing nut	50	37
Track rod end:		
Balljoint nut	33	24
Locknuts	47	35
Roadwheels		
Roadwheel nuts	100	74

* Use new nut/bolt.

---

1 General Information

1 The front suspension is of independent type, with a subframe, MacPherson struts, lower arms, and an anti-roll bar. The struts, which incorporate coil springs and integral shock absorbers, are attached at their upper ends to the reinforced strut mountings on the body shell. The lower end of each strut is bolted to the top of a cast swivel hub, which carries the hub, and the brake disc and caliper. The hubs run within non-adjustable bearings in the swivel hubs. The lower end of each swivel hub is attached, via a balljoint, to a pressed-steel lower arm assembly. The balljoints are integral with the lower arms. Each lower arm is attached at its inboard end to the subframe, via flexible rubber bushes, and controls both lateral and fore-and-aft movement of the front wheels. An anti-roll bar is fitted to all models. The anti-roll bar is mounted on the subframe, and is connected to the suspension struts via vertical drop links.

2 The rear suspension is semi-independent, with a U-section beam welded between pressed-steel trailing arms. This U-section beam allows a limited torsional flexibility, giving each rear wheel a certain degree of independent movement, whilst maintaining optimum track and wheel camber control. This type of arrangement is called a 'twist beam' rear axle. The axle is attached to the body via rubber bushes, which are designed to allow a certain amount of 'rear steering' (toe correction) during fast cornering. The rear suspension commonly used on small cars is separate springs and shock absorbers. The compact springs are mounted under the car; so only the shock absorber housings encroach on the boot area, resulting in more boot space. The shock absorbers are bolted to the trailing arm section of the rear axle at the base, and to the body housings at the top. The rear hubs are integral with the stub axles, which are bolted to the rear of the trailing arms, and the brake drums are separate.

3 The steering is of conventional rack-and-pinion type, incorporating a collapsible safety column. The column is joined to the steering rack via a flexible coupling. The steering rack is mounted on the front suspension subframe. The steering rack track rods are attached via the track rod ends to the steering arms on the swivel hubs. All models have an electric power steering system, with a motor incorporated into the steering column to provide the steering assistance.

2 Front swivel hub – removal and refitting

Removal

1 Remove the relevant wheel trim, or the wheel centre cover (alloy wheels) for access to the driveshaft nut.

2 Using a hammer and punch, relieve the staking on the driveshaft nut **(see illustration)**. Make sure the staking has been released completely, as this can damage the threads on the driveshaft as the nut is removed (see Chapter 8 Section 2).

> **HAYNES HiNT** *A tool to hold the front hub stationary whilst the driveshaft retaining nut is slackened can be fabricated from two lengths of steel strip (one long, one short) and a nut and bolt; the nut and bolt forming the pivot of a forked tool.*

3 Ensure that the handbrake is applied (ideally, have an assistant apply the footbrake), and then slacken the driveshaft nut using a suitable socket (30 mm on our car) and extension bar. Slacken the driveshaft nut almost to the end of its threads, but do not remove it at this stage.

> ⚠ *Warning: The driveshaft nut is done up extremely tight, and considerable effort will be required to loosen it. Do not use poor-quality, badly-fitting tools for this task, due to the risk of personal injury.*

4 Apply the handbrake, slacken the relevant front wheel nuts, then jack up the front of the car and support securely on axle stands (see *Jacking and vehicle support*). Remove the roadwheel and the engine lower cover.

5 If the driveshaft retaining nut was not able to be slackened as described in paragraphs 1 and 2, then a tool will be required to hold the hub stationary while the nut is slackened **(see illustration)**.

6 Unscrew the bolts securing the brake caliper mounting bracket to the swivel hub, then slide the caliper/bracket assembly from the swivel hub and brake disc (there is no need to remove the brake pads **(see illustrations)**. Undo the brake hose retaining bolt and suspend the caliper/bracket assembly from the strut coil spring using wire or string – do not allow the caliper to hang on the brake hose.

7 Mark the brake disc in relation to the hub (assuming it is to be refitted), then remove any

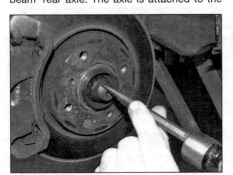

2.2 Tap up the deformed portion of the nut so it can be unscrewed

2.5 Using a home-made holding tool to prevent the front hub from turning

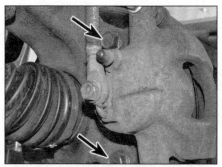

2.6a Caliper mounting bracket retaining bolts – arrowed

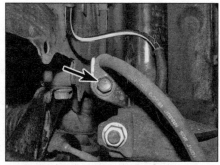

2.6b Undo the brake hose bracket retaining bolt

2.10 Separate the track rod end balljoint

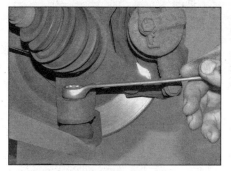

2.11a Remove the split pin and retaining nut...

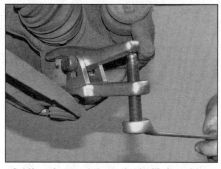

2.11b... then separate the balljoint with a balljoint splitter

2.11c If necessary, use a bar and chain to lever the balljoint out of position

retaining clips or washers holding it in place, and withdraw it from the hub (see Chapter 9 Section 4).

8 Unscrew the (ABS) wheel sensor retaining bolt, then withdraw the wheel sensor from the top of the hub. **Note:** *The sensors can prove difficult to remove, due to corrosion – see Chapter 9, Section 16.*

9 Remove the split pin, then slacken the track rod end balljoint nut, and unscrew it as far as the ends of the threads.

10 Disconnect the track rod end balljoint from the swivel hub using a balljoint separator tool (leave the nut fitted to protect the threads), taking care not to damage the balljoint rubber seal **(see illustration)**. Once the balljoint has been released, remove the balljoint nut. See Section 18 for further information on the track rod end.

11 Remove the spring clip, then slacken the

lower arm balljoint nut, and unscrew it as far as the ends of the threads. Push the end of the lower arm down to free the balljoint from the swivel hub. If the balljoint is very tight, it may be necessary to lever down using a long lever bar, or similar tool, but take care not to damage the balljoint rubber seal **(see illustrations)**.

12 Remove the nut from the bolt used to secure the swivel hub to the base of the suspension strut. Note which way the bolt is fitted (this should be from the rear), then support the hub and tap the bolt out **(see illustrations)**.

13 The splined end of the driveshaft now has to be released from its location in the hub. It's likely that the splines will be very tight (corrosion may even be a factor, if the driveshaft has not been disturbed for some time), and considerable force may be needed to push the driveshaft out. It is recommend

that a plastic or hide mallet is used for tapping the shaft out. If an ordinary hammer is used, place a small piece of wood over the end of the driveshaft – in addition to the loosened driveshaft nut; this will protect the threads from damage.

14 Once the splines have been released, remove the driveshaft nut and discard it – the nut is only intended to be used once.

15 Pull the hub outwards, and pull the driveshaft inwards, to separate the splined end from the hub. It is helpful to have an assistant on hand, to pull either the hub or the shaft. Do not bend the driveshaft excessively at any stage, or the joints may be damaged – the inner and outer joints should not be bent through more than 18° and 45° respectively. Do not let the driveshaft hang down under its own weight – tie it up level if necessary. Pull off the hub, and remove it **(see illustrations)**.

2.12a Remove the strut-to-hub nut...

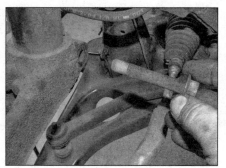

2.12b... and withdraw the retaining bolt

2.15a Pull the driveshaft out from the inside of the hub...

2.15b... and separate the hub from the base of the strut...

Refitting

16 Refitting is a reversal of removal, bearing in mind the following points:

a) *Fit the swivel hub-to-strut bolt in from the rear, and oil the nut threads before fitting.*

b) *Use a new split pin/spring clip on the track rod end and lower arm balljoint nuts, and a new driveshaft nut.*

c) *The track rod end and lower arm balljoint nuts can both be tightened up to 60° past their torque value, if necessary, to fit the split pin/spring clip.*

d) *Do not fully tighten the driveshaft nut until the car is resting on its wheels.*

e) *Tighten all fixings to the specified torque.*

f) *Have the front wheel alignment checked on completion.*

3.4a Using a metal tube and socket...

3.5b... or removing the bearing inner race with a puller

2.15c... using an Allen key to open up the fitting

3 Front hub bearings – renewal

Note: *A press, a suitable puller, or similar improvised tools will be required for this operation. Obtain a bearing overhaul kit before proceeding.*
Caution: The front swivel hub has an ABS wheel sensor fitted to the top of the hub; this picks up a signal from a target ring built into the front wheel bearing. Do not use a hammer to remove or refit the bearing, as damage to the target ring will occur. Make sure the bearing is fitted correctly for the sensor to pick up the signal. If the sensor is left in the hub, take care not to damage it as the bearing is being fitted.

1 With the swivel hub removed as described in Section 2, proceed as follows.

3.6 Extract the bearing circlip

2 The bearing removal process involves three stages – removing the hub flange (where the wheel mounts), tapping off the inner race from the hub flange, and then driving out the bearing itself from the hub.
3 The hub flange must first be removed from the bearing/swivel hub assembly. It is preferable to use a press to do this, but it is possible to drive out the hub using a metal tube of suitable diameter. Alternatively, a suitable puller can be used.
4 Have an assistant hold the hub assembly over a work surface then, using a metal bar, tube, or socket of suitable diameter, drive the hub flange through the bearing and remove it **(see illustrations)**. This process will destroy the bearing, as the inner race will separate with the flange.
5 The bearing inner race left on the hub flange must now be removed, which is most easily done using a puller. Otherwise, grip the edge of the flange in a vice, and tap the race off with a chisel, taking care not to damage the flange's bearing surface **(see illustrations)**. Tap the race at the top and both sides (even turn the flange over in the vice) to stop it jamming as it comes off.
6 Now the bearing itself must be removed. First, remove the large bearing retaining circlip, using a pair of circlip pliers **(see illustration)**.
7 After applying a generous amount of spray lubricant, we were able to draw the bearing out, using a spacer, large tube and threaded bar **(see illustrations)**. Once the bearing has moved most of the way, it

3.5a Use a chisel between the hub flange and the inner race...

3.7a Using a threaded bar and spacers...

3.7b... to remove the bearing (arrowed) from the hub

3.9a Make sure the bearing is fitted the correct way around...

3.9b... as the wheel sensor (arrowed) picks up a signal from a target ring in the bearing

3.10 Using a threaded rod and spacers to press in the new bearing

3.11 Fit the new retaining clip to the hub

3.12 Press the flange into the new bearing using a threaded rod and spacers

is possible to hit the end of the nut on the threaded bar to knock it the rest of the way out.

8 Using emery paper, clean off any burrs or raised edges from the hub flange and hub carrier which might stop the components going back together.

9 Apply a light coat of lubricant to the inside of the hub carrier, and to the outside of the new bearing. Start fitting the bearing by offering it squarely into the carrier, and then press it into the hub to locate it – keep the bearing square as this is done, or it will jam **(see illustrations)**. The bearing has got a target ring built into it for the wheel sensor; make sure the bearing is fitted the correct way around.

10 Fitting the bearing by tapping it in all the way with a hammer will likely damage the ABS target ring. We used a length of threaded bar

(available from motor factors, DIY stores, etc.), with a nut, some large washers and a spacer plate on the outside of the hub carrier. With the old bearing, a length of flat bar, spacer/washer, and a nut on the inside, the whole assembly was mounted in a vice, and the nuts tightened to press the new bearing in place **(see illustration)**.

11 When the bearing has been pressed in until fully home, refit the new bearing retaining circlip **(see illustration)**. Making sure that it has seated securely in the groove in the hub.

12 The hub flange can be pressed into the new bearing using a very similar method to the one just used for the bearing **(see illustration)**.

13 On completion, refit the swivel hub as described in Section 2.

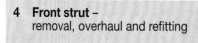

4 Front strut –
removal, overhaul and refitting

Note: *If renewing shock absorbers or springs, it is recommended that they be renewed in pairs.*

Removal

1 Apply the handbrake, slacken the relevant front wheel nuts, then jack up the front of the car and support securely on axle stands (see *Jacking and vehicle support*). Remove the roadwheel and the engine lower cover.

2 Unclip the ABS wiring from the bracket on the lower part of the strut **(see illustration)**.

3 Remove the retaining bolt securing the brake flexible hose support bracket to the suspension strut. Release the hose from the strut **(see illustrations)**.

4.2 Unclip the wheel sensor wiring from the strut

4.3a Remove the bolt on the inside of the strut...

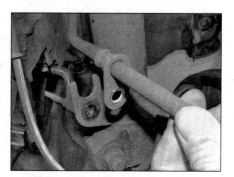

4.3b... which secures the brake hose

4.4 Use an Allen key (or similar) to open up the slot in the hub fitting

4.5 Remove the scuttle panel from the rear of the engine compartment

4.7a Remove the upper retaining nut...

4.7b... and withdraw the strut assembly from under the wheel arch...

4.7c... recover the large dished washer from the inner wing panel

4.8 Remove the rubber upper mounting

4 Remove the nut from the bolt used to secure the swivel hub to the base of the suspension strut. Note which way the bolt is fitted (this should be from the rear). Tap the bolt out, and then separate the strut base from the hub **(see illustration)**.

5 Remove the windscreen wiper motor/linkage as described in Chapter 12 Section 14, and then undo the mounting bolts and remove the scuttle panel from across the back of the engine compartment **(see illustration)**.

6 All that's holding the strut in place now is the upper mounting nut and large washer on top of the inner wing.

7 Support the strut from under the wheel arch then, working in the engine compartment, unscrew the suspension strut top mounting nut. Lower the strut out, and remove it under the wheel arch. Recover the strut top mounting plate **(see illustrations)**.

Overhaul

Note: *A spring compressor tool will be required for this operation. Always follow the instructions with the compressor to prevent any personal injury.*

8 Remove the upper rubber mounting from the top of the suspension strut **(see illustration)**.

9 With the suspension strut resting on a bench, or clamped in a vice, fit a spring compressor tool, and compress the coil spring to relieve the pressure on the spring seats **(see illustration)**. Ensure that the compressor tool is securely located on the spring, in accordance with the tool manufacturer's instructions.

10 The strut piston rod centre must now be prevented from turning while the retaining nut is loosened. Using an Allen key and spanner, loosen and remove the centre nut **(see illustrations)**. Discard the nut, and obtain a new one for refitting.

11 Remove the upper ball thrust bearing from the top of the strut, followed by the spring upper seat plate **(see illustrations)**.

12 Withdraw the rubber dust boot/gaiter

4.9 Fit spring compressor, making sure they are secure

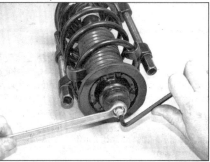

4.10a Hold the piston rod with an Allen key...

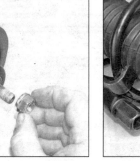

4.10b... slacken and remove the retaining nut

4.11a Remove the upper bearing...

4.11b... and spring upper seat plate

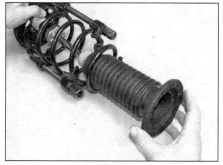

4.12a Remove the dust cover/gaiter...

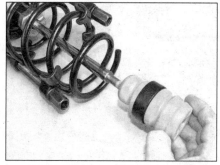

4.12b... and the rubber bump stop

and rubber bump stop from the centre of the coil spring **(see illustrations)**. Note the fitted position of the rubber dust boot/gaiter as it is removed; the top of the gaiter is also a rubber washer between the spring and the upper plate.

13 With the spring compressor tool still fitted, withdraw the spring from the suspension strut **(see illustration)**, noting its fitted position in the lower plate. Make sure the spring is stored in a safe place, to prevent the compressor tool from coming off the spring.

14 With the strut assembly now completely dismantled, examine all the components for wear, damage or deformation, and check the thrust bearing for smoothness of operation. Renew any of the components as necessary.

15 Examine the strut for signs of fluid leakage. Check the strut piston for signs of pitting along its entire length, and check the strut body for signs of damage. While holding it in an upright position, test the operation of the strut by moving the piston through a full stroke, and then through short strokes of 50 to 100 mm. In both cases, the resistance felt should be smooth and continuous. If the resistance is jerky or uneven or if there is any visible sign of wear or damage to the strut, renewal is necessary.

16 If any doubt exists as to the condition of the coil spring, carefully remove the spring compressors and check the spring for distortion and signs of cracking. Renew the spring if it is damaged or distorted, or if there is any doubt as to its condition.

17 Inspect all other components for damage or deterioration, and renew any that are suspect.

18 If the spring compressor tool has been removed from the spring, refit it and compress the spring sufficiently to enable it to be refitted to the strut.

19 Slide the spring over the strut, and position it so that the lower end of the spring is resting against the stop on the lower seat, as noted on removal.

20 Fit the rubber bump stop onto the strut piston and slide the dust boot/gaiter into position. Make sure the top of the rubber dust boot/gaiter is seated on top of the spring, as noted on removal.

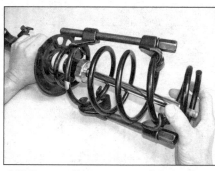

4.13 Remove the compressed spring from the strut

21 Refit the upper spring seat, and rotate it as necessary to position it against the rubber washer and upper end of the spring.

22 Fit the upper ball thrust bearing to the top of the strut, and then fit a new piston rod nut, and then tighten the nut to the specified torque. Prevent the strut piston rod centre from turning by using an Allen key and spanner as used on removal.

23 Slowly slacken the spring compressor tool to relieve the tension in the spring. Check that the ends of the spring locate correctly against the stops on the upper and lower spring seats. If necessary, turn the spring and the upper seat so that the components locate correctly before the compressor tool is removed. Remove the compressor tool when the spring is fully seated.

24 Refit the upper rubber mounting to the top of the suspension strut.

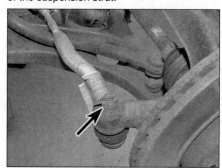

5.2 Separate the track rod end balljoint

4.25 Hold the piston rod with an Allen key and tighten the retaining nut

Refitting

25 Refitting is a reversal of removal, bearing in mind the following points:
a) Refit the suspension strut to the inner wing, and tighten the upper mounting nut to the specified torque **(see illustration)**.
b) Fit the swivel hub-to-strut bolt in from the rear, and oil the nut threads before fitting.
c) Tighten all fixings to the specified torque.
d) Have the front wheel alignment checked on completion.

5 Front anti-roll bar and links – removal and refitting

Note: To remove the anti-roll bar completely from the vehicle, you will need to first remove the steering rack, as described in Section 17 of this Chapter.

Removal

1 Apply the handbrake, loosen the front wheel nuts, then jack up the front of the car and support it on axle stands (see *Jacking and vehicle support*). Remove both front wheels and the engine lower covers (where fitted).

2 Remove the split pin either side, then unscrew and remove the track rod balljoint nuts. Using a balljoint separator tool if necessary, detach the track rods from the swivel hubs **(see illustration)**.

3 If the anti-roll bar is to be completely removed, then first remove the steering rack

5.3 Anti-roll bar-to-subframe mounting bracket securing bolts

5.4 Anti-roll bar-to-lower arm drop link

5.5 Anti-roll bar-to-subframe mounting brackets viewed from the top

5.7 Collar on anti-roll bar to align for refitting

as described in Section 17. If you just need access to the anti-roll bar bushes, take care not to damage the steering rack gaiters as you remove the mounting bracket bolts **(see illustration)**.

4 Holding the drop link against rotation using a spanner on the flats, remove the upper and lower nuts, and disconnect both links from the lower arms **(see illustration)**. Recover the washers and rubbers, noting the fitted order

6.2a Remove the spring clip and securing nut...

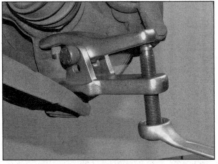

6.2b... and separate the lower arm balljoint

6.2c If necessary, use a bar and chain to lever the balljoint out of position

6.3 Prevent the drop link from turning by using a spanner on the flats – arrowed

and orientation of all components as they are removed.

5 Remove the two bolts securing each clamp to the subframe **(see illustration)**, and then lift the clamp from the anti-roll bar. The rubber bushes are split, and can be removed once the clamps are taken off, note the fitted position of the bushes, with the split facing forwards.

6 If required, with the steering rack removed, withdraw the anti-roll bar out between the subframe, and the underside of the car.

Refitting

7 Refitting is a reversal of removal, bearing in mind the following points:
a) *Make sure the split in the rubber bushes are facing forward, when refitting.*
b) *Make sure the rubber bushes are seated against the collar on the anti-roll bar **(see illustration)**.*
c) *Tighten all fixings to the specified torque.*
d) *Use a new split pin on the track rod end balljoint nuts.*
e) *The track rod end balljoint nuts can be tightened up to 60° past their torque value, if necessary, to fit the split pin.*
f) *If removed, refit the steering rack with reference to Section 17.*
g) *Have the front wheel alignment checked on completion.*

6 Front lower arm – removal and refitting

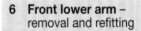

Removal

1 Slacken the front wheel nuts on the side concerned, then apply the handbrake, jack up the front of the car, and support securely on axle stands (see *Jacking and vehicle support*). Remove the roadwheel and the engine lower cover.

2 Remove the spring clip, and then unscrew the lower arm balljoint nut. Push the end of the lower arm down to free the balljoint from the swivel hub. If the balljoint is very tight, it may be necessary to lever down using a large screwdriver, or similar tool, but take care not to damage the balljoint rubber seal **(see illustrations)**.

3 Holding the drop link against rotation using a spanner on the flats, remove the upper and lower nuts, and disconnect both links from the lower arms **(see illustration)**. Recover the washers and rubbers, noting the fitted order and orientation of all components as they are removed.

4 Remove the lower arm front pivot bolt, then unscrew the rear mounting bolt and remove the lower arm from under the car **(see illustrations)**.

Overhaul

5 Examine the rubber bushes and the suspension lower balljoint for wear and

damage. At the time of writing, the balljoint and rubber bushes could not be renewed on the lower arm. Renew the complete lower arm if there is any wear or damage.

Refitting

6 Refitting is a reversal of removal, bearing in mind the following points:
a) *Tighten all fixings to the specified torque*
b) *The lower arm front pivot bolt and rear mounting bolt should be tightened firmly by hand initially. When the wheels are refitted and the car is lowered so the weight is fully on the suspension, tighten both bolts to their specified torques.*
c) *Use a new spring clip on the lower arm balljoint nut.*
d) *The lower arm balljoint nut can be tightened up to 60° past its torque value, if necessary, to fit the spring clip.*
e) *Have the front wheel alignment checked on completion.*

7 Front lower arm balljoint – renewal

1 If the lower arm balljoint is worn, or the rubber seal is damaged, the complete lower arm must be renewed as described in Section 6. At the time of writing, the balljoint could not be renewed separately from the lower arm, as it is riveted in place during manufacture. Check the latest parts availability situation with the franchised dealer, and with reputable motor factors.

8 Front subframe – removal and refitting

Removal

1 Make sure the front wheels (and steering wheel) are in the straight-ahead position. If possible, lock the steering in this position using the steering column lock.
2 Working in the driver's footwell, behind the pedals, unclip the plastic cover from the lower end of the steering column **(see illustration)**. Paint or scribe match-marks between the universal joint and the steering gear pinion. Loosen the joint upper bolt, then remove the lower one, and the steering gear pinion will be free to separate from the column when the subframe is lowered.
3 Slacken the front wheel nuts. Apply the handbrake, then jack up the front of the car, and support securely on axle stands (see *Jacking and vehicle support*). For obvious reasons, do not support the car under the subframe, nor in such a way as to hinder lowering the subframe out. Remove the roadwheels and the engine lower covers.
4 Remove the split pin each side, then slacken the track rod end balljoint nut, and unscrew it as far as the ends of the threads.

6.4a Lower arm front pivot bolt...

Disconnect the track rod end balljoints from the swivel hubs using a balljoint separator tool as described in Section 18.
5 Remove the spring clip each side, then slacken the lower arm balljoint nut, and unscrew it as far as the ends of the threads. Push the ends of the lower arms down to free the balljoints from the swivel hubs. If a balljoint is very tight, it may be necessary to lever down using a large lever, or similar tool, but take care not to damage the ball-joint rubber seal **(see illustrations 6.2a, 6.2b and 6.2c).**
6 Referring to Chapter 4B Section 6 if necessary, unbolt and remove the exhaust system front/centre pipe.
7 Remove the two mounting bolts, and then withdraw the engine rear mounting link bar from the subframe **(see illustration)**. The engine/transmission will be less stable once the mounting has been undone, but will still be

8.2 Unclip the lower steering column joint plastic cover

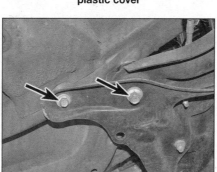
8.9a Subframe rear mounting bolts (one side shown)

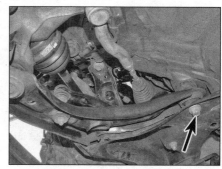
6.4b... and rear mounting bolt

safely supported on the left- and right-hand mountings.
8 Support the subframe from below, using at least two substantial jacks (one either side).
9 With the subframe securely supported, progressively loosen the six mounting bolts. There are two at the rear, into the car floor, two also at the rear which secure the rear mounting in the lower arm and one each side at the front, on a curved spur up to the base of the chassis leg **(see illustrations)**.
10 When all the bolts have been removed, check once more that nothing is still attached to the subframe, and that nothing is still fitted which would hinder it from being lowered. Note the steering rack and anti-roll bar are bolted to the top of the subframe and will be removed with the subframe.
11 With the help of an assistant, lower the subframe and remove it from under the car. In

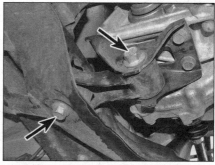
8.7 Undo the rear engine mounting bolts

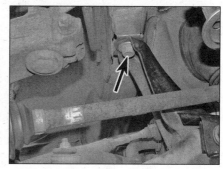
8.9b Subframe side mounting bolt (one side shown)

doing so, the steering gear pinion will be being disengaged from the column splines. Unclip the gaiter from the bulkhead and disengage from the steering column **(see illustration)**.

Refitting

12 With the help of an assistant, position the subframe on the jacks, then raise the jack to lift the subframe into position under the car. Line up the mounting holes and fit the rear mounting studs through as the subframe is raised into position. Also engage the steering gear pinion splines with those of the column inside the car.
13 The remainder of refitting is a reversal of removal, noting the following points:
a) Tighten all fixings to the specified torque.
b) Make sure the gaiter is secured in the bulkhead for the steering rack.
c) Have the front wheel alignment checked on completion.

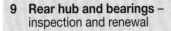

9 Rear hub and bearings – inspection and renewal

Note: The rear hub and bearing is a sealed unit. If the rear bearings are worn, a new hub must be fitted. The rear wheel sensor is fitted to the rear of the hub.

Inspection

1 The rear hub bearings are non-adjustable.
2 To check the bearings for excessive wear, chock the front wheels, then jack up the rear of the vehicle and support it on axle stands. Fully release the handbrake.

9.6 Remove the ABS wheel sensor

10.1 Prise out the trim clips and remove the carpet trim inside the luggage compartment

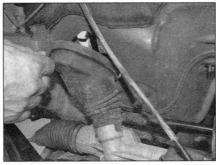

8.11 Unclip the lower steering column joint rubber cover

3 Grip the rear wheel at the top and bottom, and attempt to rock it. If excessive movement is noted, or if there is any roughness or vibration felt when the wheel is spun, it is indicative that the hub bearings are worn.

Removal

4 Loosen the rear wheel nuts, then chock the front wheels (or engage a gear). Jack up the rear of the car, and support it on axle stands (see Jacking and vehicle support). Remove the rear wheel.
5 Remove the brake drum as described in Chapter 9 Section 5. While the drum is removed, it would make sense to inspect the rear brake components for wear, and the wheel cylinder for signs of fluid leakage.
6 Undo the retaining bolt and remove the ABS rear wheel sensor from the back of the hub **(see illustration)**. Refer to Chapter 9, Section 16, for further information.

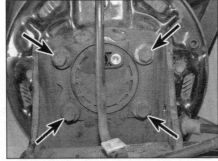

9.7a Remove the four hub mounting bolts...

10.2a Pull off the shock absorber rubber cover...

7 Loosen the four bolts securing the hub (and brake backplate) to the trailing arm. Support the hub and backplate, and remove the four bolts. Withdraw the hub through the rear shoe assembly **(see illustrations)**.
8 Temporarily refit the four bolts to hang the backplate onto, and cable-tie the backplate to the trailing arm to prevent straining the brake pipe and handbrake cable.

Refitting

9 Refitting is a reversal of removal, noting the following points:
a) When refitting the hub, clean away any corrosion on its mating surfaces with the backplate, and apply a little copper grease to make future removal easier.
b) Tighten all fixings to the specified torque
c) Refit the brake drum and wheel sensor, as described in Chapter 9 Section 5.

10 Rear shock absorber – removal and refitting

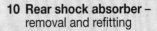

Note: When renewing shock absorbers, it is recommended that they be renewed in pairs.

Removal

1 Working in the boot, release the retaining clips and remove the inner carpet trim from the side of the luggage compartment **(see illustration)**.
2 Unclip the cover from the top of the shock absorber and, using a spanner to hold the lower nut, loosen the top nut and remove it **(see illustrations)**. If required, use a small

9.7b... and withdraw the hub through the brake shoes

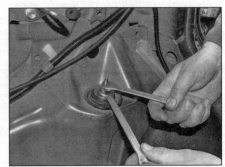

10.2b... and, using two spanners, slacken and remove the retaining nuts

spanner to hold the piston rod flats at the top, and loosen the shock absorber lower nut. Leave the lower nut fitted by a full nut of thread, until the lower mounting has been removed and the shock absorber is ready to be lowered out.

3 Chock the front wheels, select 1st gear, then jack up the rear of the car, and support securely on axle stands (see *Jacking and vehicle support*).

4 Support the 'trailing arm' section of the beam axle using a trolley jack, and then unscrew the shock absorber lower mounting bolt **(see illustration)**.

5 Support the shock absorber, then remove the upper mounting nut, and remove the unit from under the wheel arch. Recover the shock absorber top washer and rubber bush from the mounting inside the boot, noting their fitted position.

Refitting

6 Ensure that the shock absorber is fully reassembled before offering it into position – check that the upper rubber mounting(s) have been refitted (or transferred to the new unit, where applicable).

7 Refit the shock absorber under the rear wheel arch and locate it in the upper mounting hole, fit the upper rubber mounting, washer and securing nut and tighten it by hand at this stage.

8 If required lower or raise the trailing arm using the trolley jack, and fit the lower part of the shock absorber to the rear axle and insert the lower bolt **(see illustration)**. Tighten it by hand at this stage.

9 Lower the car to the ground, and bounce the rear of the car a couple of times to settle the rear suspension.

10 Working inside the luggage compartment, tighten the retaining nut on the top of the shock absorber to the specified torque. Fit the second nut to the first, then hold the first nut in position, and tighten the second to the specified torque. Note: There should be three to five threads showing at the top of the piston rod, once the two retaining nuts are in place.

11 Refit the rubber cover to the top of the shock absorber and refit the inner carpet to the side of the luggage compartment.

12 Tighten the shock absorber lower mounting bolt to the specified torque.

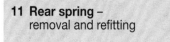

11 Rear spring –
removal and refitting

Note: *When renewing springs, it is recommended that they be renewed in pairs.*

Removal

1 Chock the front wheels, select 1st gear, then jack up the rear of the car, and support securely on axle stands (see *Jacking and vehicle support*).

10.4 Remove the lower mounting bolt

2 Support the 'trailing arm' section of the beam axle using a trolley jack, and then unscrew the shock absorber lower mounting bolt and disengage it from the axle.

3 Slowly lower the trailing arms on the jack, until the spring tension is released, and the springs can be pulled out of their location, noting its fitted position. We found it was best to remove the jack, and then press down the trailing arm to remove the spring – make sure, however, that no excess strain is placed on the brake hose **(see illustrations)**.

4 Recover the spring upper and lower mounting rubbers, noting how they are fitted **(see illustrations)**. If they are in poor condition, fit new ones.

Refitting

5 Refitting is a reversal of removal, noting the following points:

11.3a Note the fitted position of the spring and any paint markings

11.4a Check the spring upper mounting rubber...

10.8 Make sure the bolt locates correctly in the axle

a) Make sure the spring is properly engaged in the upper and lower mounts.
b) Delay tightening the shock absorber lower mounting bolt to its specified torque until the car is resting on its wheels.

12 Rear axle assembly –
removal and refitting

Removal

1 Slacken the rear wheel nuts. Chock the front wheels, select 1st gear, then jack up the rear of the car, and support securely on axle stands (see *Jacking and vehicle support*). Remove the rear roadwheels.

2 Remove the rear wheel sensor from the rear of the hub, as described in Chapter 9

11.3b Lower the jack until the spring tension is released, and remove the spring

11.4b... and lower mounting rubber

12.2 Unclip the ABS wheel sensor wiring from the bracket

12.3a Withdraw the handbrake cables from the passenger compartment...

12.3b... and unbolt them from the floor panel

Section 16, then unclip the wiring from the retaining brackets on the axle **(see illustration)**.

3 Disconnect the handbrake cables from the handbrake lever inside the vehicle, as described in Chapter 9; then undo the retaining bolts and remove the retaining brackets from the floor panel **(see illustrations)**.

4 Disconnect the rear brake flexible hoses from the rigid pipes leading to the backplates.

Anticipate some fluid spillage – if possible, clamp the hoses before disconnecting them. Slide out the metal clip used to secure the hose each side, and move the hoses clear of the axle **(see illustrations)**.

5 Remove the rear springs as described in Section 11.

6 Support the rear axle using two substantial jacks, one at each end. Having an assistant will also be useful – the axle is a heavy and awkward assembly to remove without help.

7 Make a final check that nothing is still attached to the axle that would hamper its removal. Move the cables, hoses and wiring clear as far as possible, so that they do not get caught up when the axle is lowered.

8 With the axle securely supported, unscrew and remove the pivot bolt each side **(see illustrations)**.

9 Lower the axle on the jacks, making sure that nothing gets caught, until it can be withdrawn from under the car **(see illustration)**.

12.4a Use brake hose clamps on both rear hoses

12.4b Slacken the brake pipe union...

Refitting

10 Refitting of the axle assembly is a reversal of removal, bearing in mind the following points:

a) *Do not fully-tighten the axle mounting bolts, or the shock absorber lower mounting nuts, until the weight of the car is resting on its wheels.*

b) *Tighten all fixings to the specified torque.*

c) *Refit the rear springs as described in Section 11.*

d) *Refit the handbrake cables and ABS wheel sensors, as described in Chapter 9.*

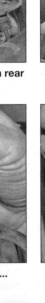

12.4c... slide out the retaining clip...

12.4d... and disconnect the brake hose

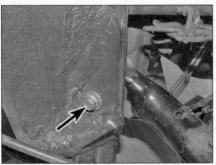

12.8a Slacken the rear axle pivot bolts...

12.8b... and remove them, once the axle is supported

12.9 Use the two trolley jacks to withdraw the axle from under the car

13.2 Alignment marks for refitting

13.3a Drill out the rubber...

13.3b... and remove the centre of the bush

13.4a Carefully cut through the outer sleeve of the bush...

13.4b... noting the outer part is raised

13.5 Use a drift to remove the outer sleeve

13 Rear axle pivot bushes – renewal

1 Remove the rear axle as described in Section 12.
2 Make alignment marks between the bush housing and the end of the bush **(see illustration)**. Note the triangle/arrow mark on the side of the rubber bush.
3 The bush is a very tight fit inside the axle; service technicians use a special tool to press the bush out from the axle. We found that the best way to remove the bush was to drill out the rubber part of the bush, working around until the centre could be removed **(see illustrations)**.
4 Using a hacksaw, cut through the outer sleeve of the bush **(see illustrations)**, taking care not to go through and damage the axle housing. The bush tapers down to the inside, so is only a tight fit on the outer half of the bush sleeve.
5 Use a drift to knock the outer sleeve from the axle housing **(see illustration)**, taking care not to damage the axle housing.
6 Once removed, thoroughly clean the bush housing in the axle.
7 Slightly lubricate the bush housing, and the new bush outer sleeve to aid fitting.
8 Locate the new bush in position against the housing, align the line made on the side of the housing with the alignment mark on the bush **(see illustration)**.
9 Using a metal tube, washers, bolt and nuts, draw the bush into the housing until it is fully engaged **(see illustration)**.

13.8 Align mark on bush with mark on axle made on removal

10 Repeat the procedure for the remaining bush.
11 On completion, refit the rear axle as described in Section 12.

14 Steering wheel – removal and refitting
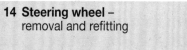

Removal

1 Disconnect the battery negative lead, and position the lead away from the battery (also see *Disconnecting the battery*). Wait at least one minute before proceeding. If this waiting period is not observed, there is a danger of accidentally activating the airbag(s).
2 Remove the airbag unit from the steering wheel as described in Chapter 12 Section 22.
3 Ensure that the front wheels are pointing in

13.9 Using a threaded rod and spacers to press the bearing into the axle

the straight-ahead position, and if possible, engage the steering lock in this position.
4 Prevent the steering wheel turning by grasping the rim firmly, then unscrew the steering wheel securing nut, until it is at the end of the threads **(see illustration)**. Do not

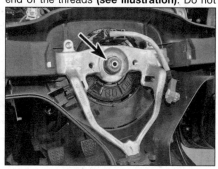
14.4 Steering wheel securing nut

14.5 Make alignment marks for refitting

14.6 Grip the wheel either side, and pull it off the splines

14.7 Two threaded holes are provided, either side of the nut for use with a puller

rely on the steering column lock to prevent the wheel turning, as this may damage the lock.

5 Before removing the steering wheel from the steering column shaft, make alignment mark for refitting **(see illustration)**.

6 Grip the steering wheel on each side (or top and bottom), then pull and withdraw it from the splines on the end of the column. Once the wheel has released, remove the securing nut completely, and withdraw the wheel **(see illustration)**.

7 The wheel may prove difficult to remove from its splines. There are two M8 threaded holes provided in the wheel hub, for use with a puller **(see illustration)**. To protect the end of the column, refit the steering wheel nut before the puller, leaving the nut just proud of the column.

8 If a puller is not available, a home-made alternative can be made out of a piece of bar and a couple of bolts. When tightening the two bolts into the holes in the wheel hub,

make sure they do not go to far through and damage the airbag clockspring behind.

Refitting

9 Make sure that the front wheels are pointing in the straight-ahead position, and then fit the steering wheel to the column.

10 Refit the steering wheel securing nut, and tighten to the specified torque – again, do not rely on the steering column lock to hold the wheel as the nut is tightened.

11 The remainder of the refitting procedure is a reversal of removal. Refit the airbag unit as described in Chapter 12 Section 22.

15 Steering column and motor – removal and refitting

Note: *The steering column and motor can*

15.4a Undo the two retaining screws...

15.4b... and remove the upper instrument panel shroud

only be renewed as a complete unit. The lower shaft and knuckle joints can be renewed separately.

Removal

1 Disconnect the battery negative lead, and position the lead away from the battery (also see *Disconnecting the battery*). Wait at least one minute before proceeding. If this waiting period is not observed, there is a danger of accidentally activating the airbag(s).

2 Remove the steering wheel as described in Section 14.

3 Move the driver's seat fully to the rear, to allow maximum working area.

4 Undo the two retaining screws and unclip the upper shroud from around the instrument panel **(see illustrations)**.

5 Undo the retaining screw and unclip the lower shroud from the steering column **(see illustration)**.

6 Remove the airbag clockspring and steering column switches, as described in Chapter 12.

7 Remove the instrument panel and rev counter (where fitted), as described in Chapter 12 Section 10, 11.

8 Remove the facia panel as described in Chapter 11 Section 26.

9 Disconnect the two wiring connectors from the ignition switch unclip the wiring securing clip, noting their fitted positions **(see illustrations)**.

10 Undo the retaining bolt and remove the steering column protector from the power steering motor assembly **(see illustration)**.

11 Working in the driver's footwell, behind

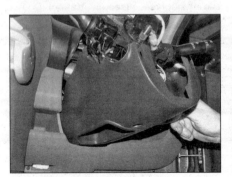

15.5 Remove the lower shroud

15.9a Disconnect the immobiliser transceiver wire...

15.9b... and the ignition switch wiring connector

15.10 Remove the steering column motor protector

15.11 Unclip the plastic cover from the lower steering joint

15.12 Remove the lower joint bolt (arrowed) and slacken the upper one

the pedals, unclip and remove the trim panel from the floor for access to the lower end of the steering column (see illustration).

12 Paint or scribe match-marks between the universal joint and the steering gear pinion. Loosen the joint upper bolt, then remove the lower one so the steering column can be separated from the steering gear pinion (see illustration).

13 Remove the column lower mounting bolt (just below the motor, inserted from the side) and the two upper bolts (see illustrations).

14 Check around the steering column and unclip any wiring connections that are still attached, and then move them to one side, noting their fitted position.

15 Unclip the column from its upper mounting, and carefully withdraw the column from the car (see illustrations). Free the lower joint from the steering rack pinion as it is removed.

16 If required, undo the retaining bolt to remove the lower shaft and knuckle joints from the steering column (see illustration). Mark the position of the lower shaft on the steering column for refitting.

Refitting

17 Refitting is a reversal of removal, bearing in mind the following points:
a) Tighten all fixings to the specified torque.
b) Refit the facia as described in Chapter 11 Section 26.

c) Refit the driver's airbag, airbag clockspring, instrument panel and rev counter (where fitted) with reference to Chapter 12 Section 22

16 Steering rack rubber gaiters – renewal

1 Remove the relevant track rod end as described in Section 18.

2 Remove the inboard and outboard securing clips, and then slide the gaiter off the end of the track rod (see illustration).

3 Thoroughly clean the track rod, and then slide the new gaiter into position.

15.13a Remove the column lower mounting bolt...

15.13b... and upper mounting bolts

15.15a Remove the steering column...

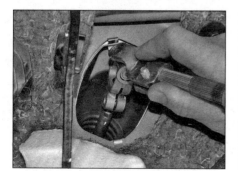

15.15b... and disconnect the lower joint from the steering rack pinion

15.16 Remove the retaining bolt to remove the joint from the column

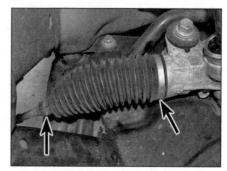

16.2 Steering rack gaiter retaining clips

16.4 Make sure the gaiter is not twisted when fitted

4 Fit the gaiter securing clips, using new clips if necessary, making sure that the gaiter is not twisted **(see illustration)**.
5 Refit the track rod end (see Section 18).

17 Steering rack – removal and refitting

Note: Access to the steering rack is best achieved by removing the front subframe as described in Section 8. However, if the subframe is lowered, it is possible to slide the steering rack out to the side (see text).

Removal

1 Slacken the front wheel nuts. Apply the handbrake, then jack up the front of the car, and support securely on axle stands (see *Jacking and vehicle support*). Remove the front roadwheels.

17.5 Unclip the pinion rubber cover from the bulkhead

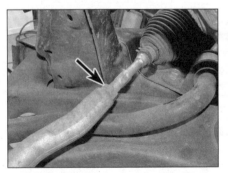

18.2 Slacken the track rod end locknut

17.3a Unclip the plastic cover from the lower steering joint...

2 Disconnect the track rod end as described in Section 18.
3 Working in the driver's footwell, behind the pedals, unclip the plastic cover from the lower end of the steering column **(see illustrations)**. Paint or scribe match-marks between the universal joint and the steering gear pinion. Loosen the joint upper bolt, then remove the lower one, and the steering gear pinion will be free to separate from the column when the subframe is lowered.
4 Remove the front subframe as described in Section 8, or lower it by approximately 30 mm, by slackening the subframe mounting bolts to allow the steering rack to slide out to the side. Refer to Section 8, to make sure that there is no damage done to any components when the subframe is lowered.
5 When the subframe is lowered, unclip the rubber gaiter from the bulkhead for the steering rack pinion **(see illustration)**.

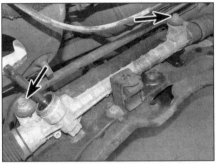

17.6 Steering rack mounting bolts

18.3a Remove the track rod end nut split pin...

17.3b... and remove the lower joint bolt (arrowed) and slacken the upper one

6 Remove the two steering rack mounting bolts, and recover the nuts from below the subframe **(see illustration)**. Withdraw the steering rack out through the side of the subframe.

Refitting

7 Refitting is a reversal of removal, noting the following points:
a) Tighten all fixings to the specified torque.
b) Refit the subframe as described in Section 8.
c) Fit the universal joint on the steering gear pinion, in the position noted on removal.

18 Track rod end – removal and refitting

Note: A balljoint separator tool will be required for this operation. Where applicable, Nyloc-type self-locking nuts must be renewed on refitting.

Removal

1 Slacken the relevant front wheel nuts. Apply the handbrake, then jack up the front of the car, and support securely on axle stands (see *Jacking and vehicle support*). Remove the roadwheel.
2 If the same track rod is to be refitted, mark its position relative to the steering rack. Slacken the track rod end locknut, noting its fitted position on the threads **(see illustration)**.
3 Pull out the split pin, then slacken the track rod end balljoint nut and remove from the threads **(see illustrations)**.

18.3b... and remove the securing nut...

18.4a Use a balljoint splitter...

18.4b... to separate the track rod end

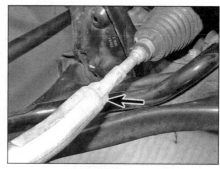

19.11 Track rod end locknut used for adjustment

4 Disconnect the track rod end balljoint from the swivel hub using a balljoint separator tool (depending on type of tool used, it may be necessary to leave the nut fitted to protect the threads), taking care not to damage the balljoint rubber seal **(see illustrations)**. Once the balljoint has been released, remove the balljoint nut.

5 Unscrew the track rod end from the track rod, counting the number of turns necessary to remove it.

Refitting

6 Screw the track rod end onto the track rod the number of turns noted during removal (or until the marks line up, where applicable), then tighten the locknut while holding the balljoint in position.

7 Engage the track rod end balljoint pin with the swivel hub, then the nut. Tighten the nut to the specified torque, and then fit a new split pin. The nut may be tightened by up to an extra 60° if necessary until the hole in the castle nut lines up for the split pin.

8 Refit the roadwheel, then lower the car to the ground, and tighten the wheel nuts.

9 Have the front wheel alignment checked at the earliest opportunity, to prevent any tyre wear.

19 Wheel alignment and steering angles – general information

Front wheel alignment

1 Accurate front wheel alignment is essential to precise steering and for even tyre wear. Before considering the steering angles, check that the tyres are correctly inflated, that the front wheels are not buckled, the hub bearings are not worn, and that the steering linkage and front suspension are in good order, without slackness or wear at the joints.

2 Wheel alignment consists of four factors:

Camber

3 • The angle at which the roadwheels are set from the vertical when viewed from the front or rear of the car. Positive camber is the angle (in degrees) that the wheels are tilted outwards at the top from the vertical. The camber angle is given for reference only, and cannot be adjusted.

Castor

4 • The angle between the steering axis and a vertical line when viewed from each side of the car. Positive castor is indicated when the steering axis is inclined towards the rear of the car at its upper end. This angle is not adjustable.

Steering axis inclination (kingpin inclination)

5 • The angle, when viewed from the front or rear of the car, between the vertical and an imaginary line drawn between the upper and lower front suspension strut mountings. This angle is not adjustable.

Toe

6 • The amount by which the distance between the front inside edges of the roadwheel rim differs from that between the rear inside edges. If the distance between the front edges is less than that at the rear, the wheels are said to toe-in. If the distance between the front inside edges is greater than that at the rear, the wheels toe-out.

7 Owing to the need for precision gauges to measure the small angles of the steering and suspension settings, it is preferable that checking of castor and camber is left to a service station having the necessary equipment. Camber and castor is set during production of the car, and any deviation from the specified angle will be due to accident damage or gross wear in the suspension mountings.

8 To check the front wheel alignment, first make sure that the lengths of both track rods are equal when the steering is in the straight-ahead position. The track rod lengths can be adjusted if necessary by releasing the locknuts from the track rod ends and rotating the track rods. If necessary, self-locking grips can be used to rotate the track rods.

9 Obtain a tracking gauge. These are available in various forms from accessory stores, or one can be fabricated from a length of steel tubing suitably cranked to clear the sump and transmission, and having a setscrew and locknut at one end.

10 With the gauge, measure the distances between the two wheel inner rims (at hub height) at the rear of the wheel. Push the car forward to rotate the wheel through 180° (half a turn) and measure the distance between the wheel inner rims, again at hub height, at the front of the wheel. This last measurement should differ from the first by the appropriate toe-in that is given in the Specifications. The car must be on level ground.

11 If the toe-in is found to be incorrect, release the track rod end locknuts and turn both track rods equally **(see illustration)**. Only turn them a quarter-of-a-turn at a time before rechecking the alignment. If necessary use self-locking grips to turn the track rods – do not grip the threaded part of the track rod during adjustment. It is important not to allow the track rods to become unequal in length during adjustment, otherwise the alignment of the steering wheel will become incorrect and tyre scrubbing will occur on turns.

12 On completion tighten the locknuts without disturbing the setting. Check that the track rod end balljoint is at the centre of its arc of travel (ie, not twisted to the front or rear).

Rear wheel alignment

13 Figures are provided in the Specifications for rear wheel camber and toe-setting but for reference only. No adjustment is possible, so any significant deviation from the quoted figures is likely to be due to accident damage, or possibly to poor reassembly.

Notes

Chapter 11
Bodywork and fittings

Contents

Degrees of difficulty

Easy, suitable for novice with little experience	Fairly easy, suitable for beginner with some experience	Fairly difficult, suitable for competent DIY mechanic	Difficult, suitable for experienced DIY mechanic	Very difficult, suitable for expert DIY or professional

Specifications

Torque wrench settings	Nm	lbf ft
Door check strap-to-A-pillar bolt	27	20
Door check strap-to-door bolts	10	7
Door exterior handle nuts.	5	4
Door lock bolts.	5	4
Seat belt bolts	42	31
Seat mounting bolts.	22	16
Window regulator mounting nuts	7	5

1 General Information

1 The bodyshell is of three- and five-door Hatchback configurations, and is made of pressed-steel sections. Most components are welded together, but some use is made of structural adhesives.

2 The bonnet, doors and some other vulnerable panels are made of zinc-coated metal, and are further protected by being coated with an anti-chip primer prior to being sprayed.

3 Extensive use is made of plastic materials, mainly in the interior, but also in exterior components. The front and rear bumpers are injection-moulded from a synthetic material, which is very strong, and yet light. Plastic components such as wheel arch liners are fitted to the underside of the car, to improve the body's resistance to corrosion.

2 Maintenance – bodywork and underframe

1 The general condition of a car's bodywork is the one thing that significantly affects its value. Maintenance is easy, but needs to be regular. Neglect, particularly after minor damage, can lead quickly to further deterioration and costly repair bills. It is important also to keep watch on those parts of the car not immediately visible, for instance the underside, inside all the wheel arches, and the lower part of the engine compartment.

2 The basic maintenance routine for the bodywork is washing – preferably with a lot of water, from a hose. This will remove all the loose solids that may have stuck to the car. It is important to flush these off in such a way as to prevent grit from scratching the finish. The wheel arches and underframe need washing in the same way, to remove any accumulated mud, which will retain moisture and tend to encourage rust. Paradoxically enough, the best time to clean the underframe and wheel arches is in wet weather, when the mud is thoroughly wet and soft. In very wet weather, the underframe is usually cleaned of large accumulations automatically, and this is a good time for inspection.

3 Periodically, except on models with a wax-based underbody protective coating, it is a good idea to have the whole of the underframe of the car steam-cleaned, engine compartment included, so that a thorough inspection can be carried out to see what minor repairs and renovations are necessary. Steam cleaning is available at many garages, and is necessary for the removal of the accumulation of oily grime, which sometimes is allowed to become thick in certain areas. If steam-cleaning facilities are not available, there are one or two excellent grease solvents available, which can be brush-applied; the dirt can then be simply hosed off. Note that these methods should not be used on cars with wax-based underbody protective coating, or the coating will be removed. Such cars should be inspected annually, preferably just prior to winter, when the underbody should be washed down, and any damage to the wax coating repaired. Ideally, a completely fresh coat should be applied. It would also be worth considering the use of such wax-based protection for injection into door panels, sills, box sections, etc, as an additional safeguard against rust damage, where such protection is not provided by the manufacturer.

4 After washing paintwork, wipe off with a chamois leather to give an unspotted clear finish. A coat of clear protective wax polish will give added protection against chemical pollutants in the air. If the paintwork sheen has dulled or oxidised, use a cleaner/polisher combination to restore the brilliance of the shine. This requires a little effort, but such dulling is usually caused because regular washing has been neglected. Care needs to be taken with metallic paintwork, as special non-abrasive cleaner/polisher is required to avoid damage to the finish. Always check that the door and ventilator opening drain holes and pipes are completely clear, so that water can be drained out. Brightwork should be treated in the same way as paintwork. Windscreens and windows can be kept clear of the smeary film that often appears, by the use of proprietary glass cleaner. Never use any form of wax, or other body or chromium polish, on glass.

3 Maintenance – upholstery and carpets

1 Mats and carpets should be brushed or vacuum-cleaned regularly, to keep them free of grit. If they are badly stained, remove them from the car for scrubbing or sponging, and make quite sure they are dry before refitting. Seats and interior trim panels can be kept clean by wiping with a damp cloth. If they do become stained (which can be more apparent on light-coloured upholstery), use a little liquid detergent and a soft nail brush to scour the grime out of the grain of the material. Do not forget to keep the headlining clean in the same way as the upholstery. When using liquid cleaners inside the car, do not over-wet the surfaces being cleaned. Excessive damp could get into the seams and padded interior, causing stains, offensive odours or even rot. If the inside of the car gets wet accidentally, it is worthwhile taking some trouble to dry it out properly, particularly where carpets are involved. Do not leave oil or electric heaters inside the car for this purpose.

4 Minor body damage – repair

Repairs of minor scratches

1 If the scratch is very superficial, and does not penetrate to the metal of the bodywork, repair is very simple. Lightly rub the area of the scratch with a paintwork renovator, or a very fine cutting paste, to remove loose paint from the scratch, and to clear the surrounding bodywork of wax polish. Rinse the area with clean water.

2 In the case of metallic paint (and some solid colours), the most commonly found scratches are not in the basecoat paint, but in the lacquer topcoat, and appear white. If care is taken, these can sometimes be rendered less obvious by very careful use of paintwork renovator (which would otherwise not be used on metallic paintwork); otherwise, repair of these scratches can be achieved by applying lacquer with a fine brush.

3 Apply touch-up paint to the scratch using a fine paintbrush; continue to apply fine layers of paint until the surface of the paint in the scratch is level with the surrounding paintwork. Allow the new paint at least two weeks to harden, and then blend it into the surrounding paintwork by rubbing the scratch area with a paintwork renovator or a very fine cutting paste. Finally, apply wax polish.

4 Where the scratch has penetrated right through to the metal of the bodywork, causing the metal to rust, a different repair technique is required. Remove any loose rust from the bottom of the scratch with a penknife, and then apply rust-inhibiting paint, to prevent the formation of rust in the future. Using a rubber or nylon applicator, fill the scratch with bodystopper paste. If required, this paste can be mixed with cellulose thinners, to provide a very thin paste, which is ideal for filling narrow scratches. Before the stopper-paste in the scratch hardens, wrap a piece of smooth cotton rag around the top of a finger. Dip the finger in cellulose thinners, and quickly sweep it across the surface of the stopper-paste in the scratch; this will ensure that the surface of the stopper-paste is slightly hollowed. The scratch can now be painted over as described earlier in this Section.

Repairs of dents

5 When deep denting of the bodywork has taken place, the first task is to pull the dent out, until the affected bodywork almost attains its original shape. There is little point in trying to restore the original shape completely, as the metal in the damaged area will have stretched on impact, and cannot be reshaped fully to its original contour. It is better to bring the level of the dent up to a point that is about 3 mm below the level of the surrounding bodywork. In cases where the dent is very shallow anyway, it is not worth trying to pull

it out at all. If the underside of the dent is accessible, it can be hammered out gently from behind, using a mallet with a wooden or plastic head. Whilst doing this, hold a suitable block of wood firmly against the outside of the panel, to absorb the impact from the hammer blows and thus prevent a large area of the bodywork from being 'belled-out'.

6 Should the dent be in a section of the bodywork that has a double skin, or some other factor making it inaccessible from behind, a different technique is called for. Drill several small holes through the metal inside the area – particularly in the deeper section. Then screw long self-tapping screws into the holes, just sufficiently for them to gain a good purchase in the metal. Now pulling on the protruding heads of the screws with a pair of pliers can pull out the dent.

7 The next stage of the repair is the removal of the paint from the damaged area, and from an inch or so of the surrounding 'sound' bodywork. This is accomplished most easily by using a wire brush or abrasive pad on a power drill, although it can be done just as effectively by hand, using sheets of abrasive paper. To complete the preparation for filling, score the surface of the bare metal with a screwdriver or the tang of a file, or alternatively, drill small holes in the affected area. This will provide a really good 'key' for the filler paste.

8 To complete the repair, see the Section on filling and re-spraying.

Repairs of rust holes or gashes

9 Remove all paint from the affected area, and from an inch or so of the surrounding 'sound' bodywork, using an abrasive pad or a wire brush on a power drill. If these are not available, a few sheets of abrasive paper will do the job most effectively. With the paint removed, you will be able to judge the severity of the corrosion, and therefore decide whether to renew the whole panel (if this is possible) or to repair the affected area. New body panels are not as expensive as most people think, and it is often quicker and more satisfactory to fit a new panel than to attempt to repair large areas of corrosion.

10 Remove all fittings from the affected area, except those that will act as a guide to the original shape of the damaged bodywork (e.g. body side mouldings etc). Then, using tin snips or a hacksaw blade, remove all loose metal and any other metal badly affected by corrosion. Hammer the edges of the hole inwards, in order to create a slight depression for the filler paste.

11 Wire-brush the affected area to remove the powdery rust from the surface of the remaining metal. Paint the affected area with rust-inhibiting paint; if the back of the rusted area is accessible, treat this also.

12 Before filling can take place, it will be necessary to block the hole in some way. This can be achieved by the use of aluminium or plastic mesh, or aluminium tape.

13 Aluminium or plastic mesh, or glass-fibre matting, is probably the best material to use for a large hole. Cut a piece to the approximate size and shape of the hole to be filled, then position it in the hole so that its edges are below the level of the surrounding bodywork. It can be retained in position by several blobs of filler paste around its periphery.

14 Aluminium tape should be used for small or very narrow holes. Pull a piece off the roll, trim it to the approximate size and shape required, then pull off the backing paper (if used) and stick the tape over the hole; it can be overlapped if the thickness of one piece is insufficient. Rub down the edges of the tape, using the handle of a screwdriver or similar, this will ensure that the tape is securely attached to the metal underneath.

Filling and respraying

15 Before using this Section, see the Sections on dent, deep scratch, rust holes and gash repairs.

16 Many types of bodyfiller are available, but generally speaking, those proprietary kits, which contain a tin of filler paste and a tube of resin hardener, are best for this type of repair. A wide, flexible plastic or nylon applicator will be found invaluable for imparting a smooth and well-contoured finish to the surface of the filler.

17 Mix up a little filler on a clean piece of card or board – measure the hardener carefully (follow the maker's instructions on the pack), otherwise the filler will set too rapidly or too slowly. Using the applicator, apply the filler paste to the prepared area; draw the applicator across the surface of the filler to achieve the correct contour and to level the surface. As soon as a contour that approximates to the correct one is achieved, stop working the paste – if you carry on too long, the paste will become sticky and begin to 'pick-up' on the applicator. Continue to add thin layers of filler paste at 20-minute intervals, until the level of the filler is just proud of the surrounding bodywork.

18 Once the filler has hardened, the excess can be removed using a metal plane or file. From then on, progressively finer grades of abrasive paper should be used, starting with a 40-grade production paper, and finishing with a 400-grade wet-and-dry paper. Always wrap the abrasive paper around a flat rubber, cork, or wooden block – otherwise the surface of the filler will not be completely flat. During the smoothing of the filler surface, the wet-and-dry paper should be periodically rinsed in water. This will ensure that a very smooth finish is imparted to the filler at the final stage.

19 At this stage, the 'dent' should be surrounded by a ring of bare metal, which in turn should be encircled by the finely 'feathered' edge of the good paintwork. Rinse the repair area with clean water, until all of the dust produced by the rubbing-down operation has gone.

20 Spray the whole area with a light coat of – this will show up any imperfections in the surface of the filler. Repair these imperfections with fresh filler paste or bodystopper, and once more smooth the surface with abrasive paper. If bodystopper is used, it can be mixed with cellulose thinners, to form a really thin paste that is ideal for filling small holes. Repeat this spray-and-repair procedure until you are satisfied that the surface of the filler, and the feathered edge of the paintwork, are perfect. Clean the repair area with clean water, and allow to dry fully.

21 The repair area is now ready for final spraying. Paint spraying must be carried out in a warm, dry, windless and dust-free atmosphere. This condition can be created artificially if you have access to a large indoor working area, but if you are forced to work in the open, you will have to pick your day very carefully. If you are working indoors, dousing the floor in the work area with water will help to settle the dust that would otherwise be in the atmosphere. If the repair area is confined to one body panel, mask off the surrounding panels; this will help to minimise the effects of a slight mis-match in paint colours. Bodywork fittings (e.g. chrome strips, door handles etc) will also need to be masked off. Use genuine masking tape, and several thicknesses of newspaper, for the masking operations.

22 Before commencing to spray, agitate the aerosol can thoroughly, and then spray a test area (an old tin, or similar) until the technique is mastered. Cover the repair area with a thick coat of primer; the thickness should be built up using several thin layers of paint, rather than one thick one. Using 400-grade wet-and-dry paper, rub down the surface of the primer until it is really smooth. While doing this, the work area should be thoroughly doused with water, and the wet-and-dry paper periodically rinsed in water. Allow to dry before spraying on more paint.

23 Spray on the topcoat, again building up the thickness by using several thin layers of paint. Start spraying at the top of the repair area, and then, using a side-to-side motion, work downwards until the whole repair area and about two inches of the surrounding original paintwork is covered. Remove all masking material 10 to 15 minutes after spraying on the final coat of paint.

24 Allow the new paint at least two weeks to harden, then, using a paintwork renovator or a very fine cutting paste, blend the edges of the paint into the existing paintwork. Finally, apply wax polish.

Plastic components

25 With the use of more and more plastic body components by the car manufacturers (e.g. bumpers, spoilers, and in some cases, major body panels), rectification of more serious damage to such items has become a matter of either entrusting repair work to a specialist in this field, or renewing complete components. Repair of such damage by the

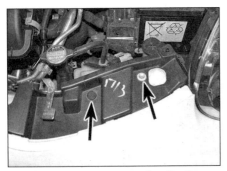

6.1 Prise up and remove the clip, then undo the upper bolt – arrowed

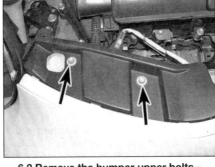

6.2 Remove the bumper upper bolts – arrowed

6.4a Remove the bumper lower bolts (one side shown)...

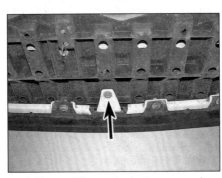

6.4b... and the centre bolt – arrowed

DIY owner is not really feasible, owing to the cost of the equipment and materials required for effecting such repairs. The basic technique involves making a groove along the line of the crack in the plastic, using a rotary burr in a power drill. The damaged part is then welded back together, using a hot air gun to heat up and fuse a plastic filler rod into the groove. Any excess plastic is then removed, and the area rubbed down to a smooth finish. It is important that a filler rod of the correct plastic is used, as body components can be made of a variety of different types (e.g. polycarbonate, ABS, polypropylene).

26 Damage of a less serious nature (abrasions, minor cracks etc), can be repaired by the DIY owner using a two-part epoxy filler repair. Once mixed in equal, this is used in similar fashion to the bodywork filler used on metal panels. The filler is usually cured in

twenty to thirty minutes, ready for sanding and painting.

27 If the owner is renewing a complete component himself, or if he has repaired it with epoxy filler, he will be left with the problem of finding a suitable paint for finishing which is compatible with the type of plastic used. At one time, the use of a universal paint was not possible, owing to the complex range of plastics encountered in body component applications. Standard paints, generally speaking, will not bond to plastic or rubber satisfactorily, but suitable paints to match any plastic or rubber finish, can be obtained from dealers. However, it is now possible to obtain a plastic body parts finishing kit that consists of a pre-primer treatment, a primer and coloured topcoat. Full instructions are normally supplied with a kit, but basically, the method of use is to

first apply the pre-primer to the component concerned, and allow it to dry for up to 30 minutes. Then the primer is applied, and left to dry for about an hour before finally applying the special-coloured topcoat. The result is a correctly coloured component, where the paint will flex with the plastic or rubber, a property that standard paint does not normally posses.

5 Major body damage – repair

1 Where serious damage has occurred, or large areas need renewal due to neglect, it means that complete new panels will need welding-in, and this is best left to professionals. If the damage is due to impact, it will also be necessary to check completely the alignment of the bodyshell, and a franchised dealer or body specialist, using special jigs, will only be able to carry this out accurately. If the body is left misaligned, it is primarily dangerous, as the car will not handle properly, and secondly, uneven stresses will be imposed on the steering, suspension and possibly transmission, causing abnormal wear, or complete failure, particularly to such items as the tyres.

6 Bumpers – removal and refitting

Front bumper

Removal

1 Open the bonnet, and prise out the single clip and undo the retaining bolt from the left-hand, top edge of the bumper **(see illustration)**.

2 Undo the two retaining bolts from the right-hand, top edge of the bumper **(see illustration)**.

3 Chock the rear wheels and jack up the front of the car, and support it on axle stands (see *Jacking and vehicle support*).

4 Working under the front edge of the bumper, remove the five retaining bolts (two at each side and one in the centre) securing the lower edge of the bumper **(see illustrations)**.

5 Under the edge of the front wheel arch each side, undo the retaining screw and remove the retaining clip from the bumper **(see illustration)**. Note: Undo the centre screw of the clip and then remove the complete clip.

6 Prise out and remove the plastic trim clips used to secure the front part of the wheel arch liner, and pull it away from the bumper.

7 On later models with daytime running lights fitted, reach up behind the bumper and disconnect the wiring plugs at each side **(see illustration)**.

6.5 Undo wheel arch retaining screw – arrowed

6.7 Disconnect the wiring connector

6.8 Disconnect the wiring connector

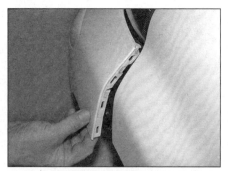

6.9 Pull the bumper end outwards to release the end clips

6.10a Unclip the top of the bumper...

6.10b...and remove bumper

6.13a Remove the securing clip (one side shown) – on C1 & 107 models...

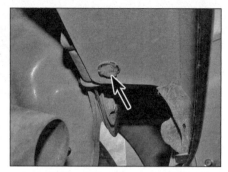

6.13b... and on Aygo models

8 On models with front foglights fitted, also reach up behind the light unit and disconnect the wiring plugs from the rear of the light units **(see illustration)**.

9 Carefully pull the ends of the bumper outwards to release them from the securing clips **(see illustration)**.

10 Once the ends are released, unclip the top of the bumper and then it can be pulled forwards and removed from the car **(see illustrations)**.

Refitting

11 Refitting is a reversal of removal. Have an assistant available to help align the bumper, and tighten the mountings securely.

Rear bumper

Removal

12 Chock the front wheels, jack up the rear of the car, and support it on axle stands (see *Jacking and vehicle support*).

13 Working under the rear edge of the bumper, remove the two securing clips (one at each side) securing the lower edge of the bumper **(see illustrations)**. **Note:** *Withdraw the centre part of the clips and then remove the complete clip*.

14 On C1 and 107 models, open the fuel filler flap on the left-hand rear of the vehicle and remove the bumper upper securing bolt **(see illustration)**.

15 Under the rear wheel arch each side, undo the retaining screw and remove the retaining clip from the front edge of the rear

bumper **(see illustration)**. Note: Undo the centre screw of the clip and then remove the complete clip.

16 Open the tailgate and undo the two

retaining screws (Torx 30), from the left and right-hand, top edges of the bumper **(see illustrations)**.

17 Pull the ends of the bumper outwards

6.14 Undo the retaining bolt (arrowed) – C1 & 107 models

6.15 Unscrew the centre and prise the clip from the wheel arch liner

6.16a Undo the Torx screw from the top of the bumper – C1 & 107 models...

6.16b... and on Aygo models

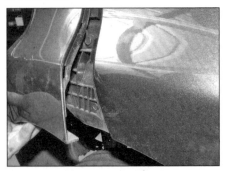

6.17a Pull the bumper end outwards to release the end clips – C1 & 107 models...

6.17b... and on Aygo models

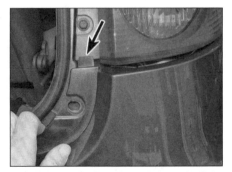

6.18 Release the locating tab from the light unit – C1 & 107 models

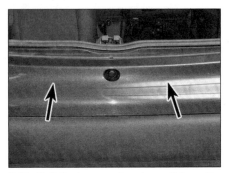

6.19a Pull the bumper to release it from the retaining clips...

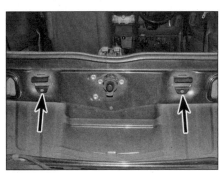

6.19b... retaining clips shown with bumper removed

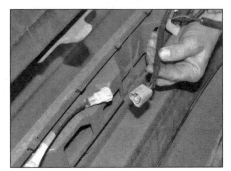

6.20 Disconnect the wiring connector as the bumper is removed

to release them from the securing clips **(see illustrations)**.

18 On C1 and 107 models, carefully pull the bumper downwards slightly, to release the locating tab from the bottom of the rear light units **(see illustration)**.

19 Once the ends are released, the bumper can be pulled rearwards and removed from the car. The bumper will need to be released from the two mounting clips at the rear centre of the bumper to remove **(see illustrations)**.

20 As the bumper is removed, reach behind the bumper and disconnect the wiring plug connector(s) **(see illustration)**.

Refitting

21 Refitting is a reversal of removal. Have an assistant available to help align the bumper, and tighten the mountings securely.

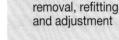

7 Bonnet –
removal, refitting and adjustment

Removal

1 Open the bonnet, and support it on its stay.
2 Using a marker pen or paint, mark around the hinge positions on the bonnet.
3 With the aid of an assistant, support the bonnet, and unscrew the four bolts (two each side) securing the bonnet to the hinges **(see illustration)**.
4 Lift off the bonnet and store in a safe place to prevent any damage.

Refitting

5 Align the marks made on the bonnet before

removal with the hinges, then refit and tighten the bonnet securing bolts.
6 Check the bonnet adjustment as follows.

Adjustment

7 Close the bonnet, and check that there is an equal gap at each side, between the bonnet and the wing panels. Check also that the bonnet sits flush in relation to the surrounding body panels.
8 The bonnet should close smoothly and positively without excessive pressure. If this is not the case, adjustment will be required.
9 To adjust the bonnet alignment, slacken the bonnet securing bolts, and move the bonnet on the bolts as required (the bolt holes in the hinges are elongated). To adjust the bonnet closure, adjustable bump stops are fitted to the bonnet **(see illustration)**. These may be screwed in or out to raise or lower the bonnet. If desired, the bonnet lock can be adjusted as described in, Section 9.

8 Bonnet release cable –
removal and refitting

Note: *If the cable has broken, use the information in this Section to establish which end of the cable has failed – if the break is inside the car, it may be possible to remove the release lever as described below, and operate the remains of the cable to get the bonnet open. It is also possible to gain access to the bonnet release cable under the left-hand front*

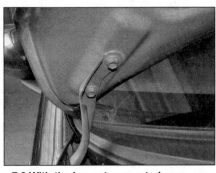

7.3 With the bonnet supported, unscrew the four hinge bolts (two each side)

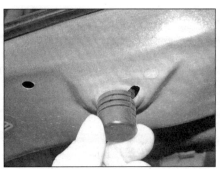
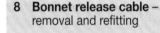

7.9 Adjust bump stop for bonnet closure height

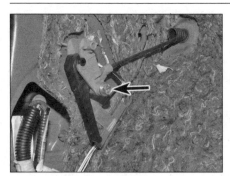

8.2a Undo the retaining bolt...

8.2b... and remove the release lever from the inner panel

8.3 Unclip the cable from the retaining clips – arrowed

wheel arch, under the liner. If the break is under the bonnet, the bonnet may be opened by reaching up the right-hand side of the radiator from underneath the vehicle. From underneath, with the car jacked up and supported on axle stands, access to the bonnet lock operating lever may be a little better.

Removal

1 The bonnet release lever is located on the lower part of the left-hand front A-pillar, under the edge of the facia.
2 From inside the passenger footwell, undo the retaining bolt and remove the release lever from the A-pillar **(see illustrations)**.
3 Open the bonnet and release the outer cable from the clips and brackets in the engine compartment, noting its routing **(see illustration)**.
4 Release the retaining clip and disconnect the inner cable from the lock operating lever **(see illustration)**.
5 Working under the left-hand front wheel arch, remove the retaining clips from the wheel arch liner and pull it away from the inner wing panel. Pull the cable through from the engine compartment, and then remove the rubber grommet and pull the release lever and cable out through the passenger compartment **(see illustration)**.

Refitting

6 Refitting is a reversal of removal. Ensure that the cable is routed as noted before removal, and make sure that the bulkhead grommet is correctly seated.

8.4 Unclip the inner cable from the bonnet lock

9 Bonnet lock – removal and refitting

Removal

1 Open the bonnet, and then unscrew the two securing bolts, and remove the lock assembly **(see illustration)**.
2 Release the securing clip and disconnect the inner cable from the lock operating lever **(see illustration 8.4)**.

Refitting

3 Refitting is a reversal of removal. If necessary, the position of the lock can be altered to adjust the lock operation by moving the lock within the elongated holes.

8.5 Push the cable and grommet out through into the passenger compartment

10 Door – removal and refitting

Note: *Before removing any electrical connections, it is advisable to disconnect the battery negative lead, and position the lead away from the battery (also see 'Disconnecting the battery').*

Removal

1 Open the door, and working inside the passenger compartment, remove the inner lower trim panel from the A-pillar (for front door) or B-pillar (for rear door), and then disconnect the wiring plug connectors **(see illustration)**.
2 Unbolt the door check strap from the door pillar **(see illustration)**.

9.1 Bonnet lock securing bolts on front panel

10.1 Disconnect the door wiring block connectors

10.2 Door check strap bolt on the door pillar

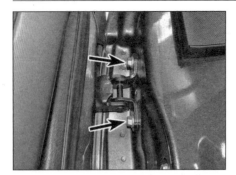

10.4a Upper door hinge retaining bolts...

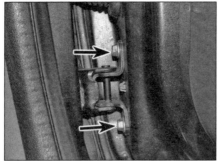

10.4b... and lower door hinge retaining bolts

10.5 Unclip the wiring rubber grommet from the door pillar

3 Ensure that the door is adequately supported with the aid of an assistant, or using wooden blocks or similar under the bottom edge of the door (take care not to damage the paintwork).

4 Mark the position of the hinges on the door, and with the door supported, unscrew the mounting bolts **(see illustrations)**.
5 As the door is removed from the car, release the wiring rubber grommet from the

door pillar and withdraw the wiring loom **(see illustration)**.

Refitting

6 Refitting is a reversal of removal.

11 Door inner trim panel – removal and refitting

Note: *Before removing any electrical connections, it is advisable to disconnect the battery negative lead, and position the lead away from the battery (also see 'Disconnecting the battery').*

Front door

Removal

1 With the door fully open, carefully unclip the trim from the inner door grab handle **(see illustration)**. Unclip it at the front edge and then release it at the rear to remove.
2 Remove the three retaining screws in the top of the door trim panel **(see illustration)**.
3 On models with manual front windows, carefully remove the winder handle by inserting a lever between the winder handle and door trim. Pull the winder handle, while turning the handle to release it from the spindle.
4 On models with electric windows, carefully prise up the window switch panel, and then disconnect the wiring plug underneath **(see illustrations)**.
5 The door trim panel is now secured by a number of plastic clips, all round the sides and base. Start at one of the bottom corners, and prise the panel with a wide-bladed tool to release the first few clips. Work along the base of the panel, then up the sides, releasing the clips as you go **(see illustration)**.
6 On models with speakers fitted, disconnect the wiring connector as the trim is removed.
7 To access the door inner components, it will usually be necessary to remove the membrane from the door. Use a sharp knife to slice along the bead of mastic, and carefully peel back the membrane without tearing it **(see illustrations)**.

11.1 Carefully unclip the trim panel from the inner door handle

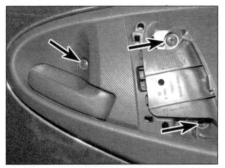

11.2 Remove the three screws from the door trim panel

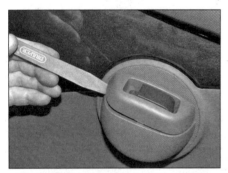

11.4a Unclip the electric window switch...

11.4b... and disconnect the wiring connector

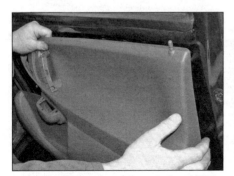

11.5 Unclip the door trim panel and lift it over the door lock button

11.7a Cut along the bead of mastic securing the membrane

11.7b There are two separate membranes fitted to the door panel

11.9a Carefully unclip the trim panel...

11.9b... from the inner door handle

Refitting

8 Refitting is a reversal of removal. Before starting, check to see whether any trim clips have been damaged on removal, renew as necessary.

Rear door

Removal

9 With the door fully open, carefully unclip the trim from the inner door grab handle **(see illustrations)**. Unclip it at the front edge and then release it at the rear to remove.
10 Remove the three retaining screw in the top of the door trim panel **(see illustration)**.
11 The door trim panel is now secured by a number of plastic clips, all round the sides and base. Start at one of the bottom corners, and prise the panel with a wide-bladed tool to release the first few clips. Work along the base of the panel, then up the sides, releasing the clips as you go **(see illustration)**.
12 On models with speakers fitted, disconnect the wiring connector as the trim is removed **(see illustration)**.
13 To access the door inner components, it will usually be necessary to remove the membrane from the door. Use a sharp knife to slice along the bead of mastic, and carefully peel back the membrane without tearing it **(see illustration)**.

Refitting

14 Refitting is a reversal of removal. Before starting, check to see whether any trim clips have been damaged on removal, renew as necessary.

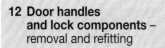

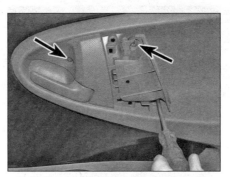

11.10 Remove the three screws from the door trim panel

11.11 Unclip the inner trim panel from the door

11.12 Disconnect the speaker wiring – where fitted

11.13 Cut along the bead of mastic securing the membrane

2 Unclip the door lock handle from the door, first releasing its locating peg at the rear edge **(see illustration)**.
3 Unhook the cable end from the handle,

and the handle can be removed **(see illustration)**.
4 To remove the cable, the membrane will also have to be peeled off, as described in

12 Door handles and lock components – removal and refitting

Note: *Before removing any electrical connections, it is advisable to disconnect the battery negative lead, and position the lead away from the battery (also see 'Disconnecting the battery').*

Interior handle

Removal

1 Remove the door inner trim panel as described in Section 11.

12.2 Unclip the door lock handle from the door panel

12.3 Release the outer cable from the housing and unclip the inner cable

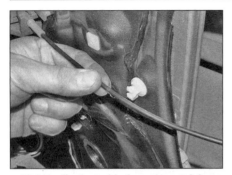

12.4 Unclip the cable from the retaining clip

12.7a Pull out the window guide seal...

12.7b... undo the retaining bolt...

12.7c... and remove the lower window guide

Section 11. Unclip the cable from the retaining clip in the door panel **(see illustration)**, and then unhook the end fitting from the lock assembly.

Refitting

5 Refitting is a reversal of removal. Refit the door trim panel with reference to Section 11.

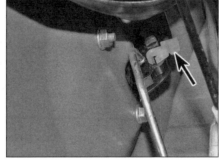

12.8 Release the link rod retaining clip – arrowed

Exterior handle

Removal

6 Remove the door trim panel as described in Section 11, and remove the membrane.
7 On front doors, with the window in the closed

position, undo the retaining bolt at the bottom of the rear window guide, and then remove it from inside the door aperture **(see illustrations)**.
8 Reach up inside the door, and prise off the clip from the link rod on the exterior handle **(see illustration)**. Disconnect the link rod from the handle. Move it to one side, noting how it is fitted.
9 Remove the two retaining nuts at the rear of the exterior handle, and then withdraw the handle from the outside of the door **(see illustrations)**. The two retaining nuts can be accessed through holes in the door panel.

Refitting

10 Refitting is a reversal of removal, noting the following points:
a) *Check the operation of the handle before refitting the trim panel.*
b) *Make sure the window guide rail locates correctly at the top, before refitting the lower mounting bolt.*
c) *Refit the panel as described in Section 11*

Front lock barrel

Removal

11 Remove the door trim panel as described in Section 11, and remove the membrane.
12 With the window in the closed position, undo the retaining bolt at the bottom of the rear window guide, and then remove it from inside the door aperture **(see illustrations 12.7a, 12.7b and 12.7c)**.
13 Reach up inside the door, and prise off the clip from the link rod on the lock barrel. Disconnect the link rod from the lock barrel **(see illustrations)**. Move it to one side, noting how it is fitted.

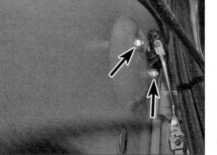

12.9a Exterior handle retaining nuts...

12.9b... can be accessed through the door panel...

12.9c... to remove the exterior handle

12.13a Release the retaining clip...

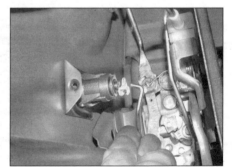

12.13b... and disconnect the link rod

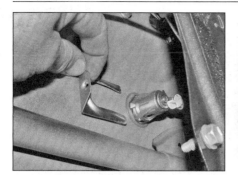

12.14a Slide out the retaining clip...

12.14b... and withdraw the lock barrel from the door

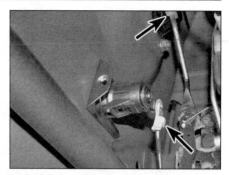

12.18 Release the two link rod retaining clips – arrowed

14 Pull the retaining clip to remove it from the rear of the lock barrel, and then withdraw the lock barrel from the outside of the door **(see illustrations)**.

Refitting

15 Refitting is a reversal of removal, noting the following points:
a) *Check the operation of the lock barrel before refitting the trim panel.*
b) *Make sure the window guide rail locates correctly at the top, before refitting the lower mounting bolt.*
c) *Refit the panel as described in Section 11*

Front lock assembly

Removal

16 Remove the door trim panel as described in Section 11, and remove the membrane.
17 With the window in the closed position, undo the retaining bolt at the bottom of the rear window guide, and then remove it from inside the door aperture **(see illustrations 12.7a, 12.7b and 12.7c)**.
18 Reach up inside the door, and prise off the clips from the link rods on the exterior handle and lock barrel. Disconnect the link rods from the exterior handle and lock barrel **(see illustration)**. Move them to one side, noting how they where fitted.
19 Remove the interior door handle and disconnect the door lock operating cable as described in paragraphs 1 to 4 in this Section.
20 On models with central locking, undo the retaining bolt on the locking motor bracket **(see illustration)**.

21 Undo the three screws securing the lock assembly to the rear edge of the door, and withdraw the lock assembly downwards and out from inside the door aperture **(see illustrations)**.
22 On models with central locking, disconnect the wiring connector from the central locking motor as it is removed **(see illustration)**.

Refitting

23 Refitting is a reversal of removal, bearing in mind the following points:
a) *Lubricate the moving parts of the lock assembly with multipurpose grease before refitting.*
b) *The three lock securing screws on the back edge of the door should have their threads cleaned and coated with thread-locking fluid before refitting them.*

12.20 Undo the lock motor bracket retaining bolt

12.21b... and remove the lock assembly from inside the door

12.22 Disconnect the central locking wiring plug

c) *Make sure the window guide rail locates correctly at the top before refitting the lower mounting bolt.*
d) *Check the operation of the lock mechanism before refitting the door inner trim panel.*
e) *Refit the door trim panel with reference to Section 11.*

Rear lock assembly

Removal

24 Remove the door trim panel as described in Section 11, and remove the membrane.
25 Unclip the door lock interior handle from the door, first releasing its locating peg at the rear edge **(see illustrations)**.
26 Release the door lock operating rod from the securing clip, and then release the securing clip and disconnect the

12.21a Remove the three Torx screws at the rear...

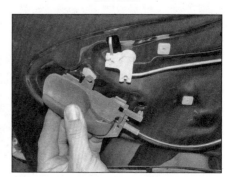

12.25a Unclip the door lock handle from the door panel...

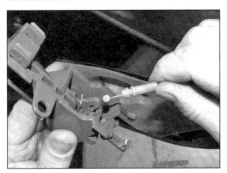

12.25b... and release the operating cable from the inner door handle

12.26a Unclip the linkage rod from the retaining clip in the door...

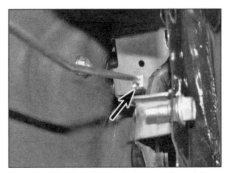

12.26b... and release the link rod retaining clip on the lock assembly

operating rod from the lock assembly (see illustrations).

27 On models with central locking, undo the retaining bolt on the locking motor bracket (see illustration).

28 Undo the three screws securing the lock assembly to the rear edge of the door, and withdraw the lock assembly downwards and out from inside the door aperture (see illustrations).

29 On models with central locking, disconnect the wiring connector from the central locking motor as it is removed (see illustration).

Refitting

30 Refitting is a reversal of removal, bearing in mind the following points:

a) Lubricate the moving parts of the lock assembly with multipurpose grease before refitting.

b) The three lock securing screws on the back edge of the door should have their threads cleaned and coated with thread-locking fluid before refitting them.

c) Check the operation of the lock mechanism before refitting the door inner trim panel.

d) Refit the door trim panel with reference to Section 11.

13 Door window glass and regulator – removal and refitting

Note: *Before removing any electrical connections, it is advisable to disconnect the battery negative lead, and position the lead away from the battery (also see 'Disconnecting the battery').*

Front door window glass

Removal

1 Remove the door trim panel as described in Section 11, and remove the membrane.

2 Reconnect the electric window switch (or window winder handle), and lower the glass until the door glass retaining bolts are visible in the access holes in the inner panel (see illustrations).

3 Unscrew the glass retaining bolts, then lift the glass slightly to remove the securing clips from the bottom of the window, note their fitted position (see illustration).

4 Tilt the window glass forwards to release it from the guide rails and then withdraw it upwards and out from the door (see illustration).

Refitting

5 Refitting is a reversal of removal, noting the following points:

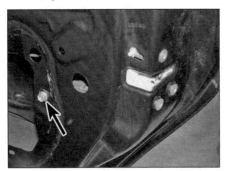

12.27 Undo the lock motor bracket retaining bolt

12.28a Remove the three Torx screws at the rear...

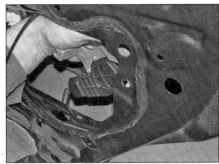

12.28b... and remove the lock assembly from inside the door

12.29 Disconnect the central locking wiring plug

13.2a Unclip the blanking plug from the door panel...

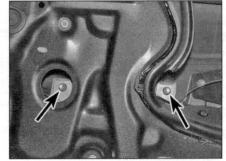

13.2b... to access the door glass retaining bolts

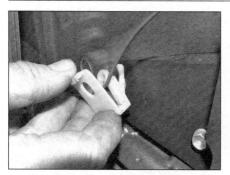

13.3 Release the securing clips from the bottom of the door glass...

a) *Refit the plastic securing clips to the bottom of the glass correctly.*
b) *Tighten the glass retaining bolts securely.*
c) *Refit the door trim panel as described in Section 11.*

Front regulator

Removal

6 Remove the door window glass as described previously in this Section.
7 On models with electric windows, disconnect the wiring plug from the motor **(see illustration)**.
8 Remove the retaining nuts from the window regulator (three nuts on electric windows and four nuts on manual windows), and then withdraw the regulator from the door **(see illustrations)**.

Refitting

9 Refitting is a reversal of removal, noting the following points:
a) *Lubricate the moving parts of the regulator with multipurpose grease before refitting.*
b) *Check the operation of the window regulator mechanism, before refitting the door trim panel.*
c) *Refit the door trim panel as described in Section 11.*

Rear window

Removal

10 Open the door and, with the window supported by an assistant, undo the two retaining screws from the rear window catch **(see illustration)**.
11 Working at the front edge of the door undo the two retaining nuts, and remove the rear window glass from the door **(see illustration)**.

Refitting

12 Refitting is a reversal of removal.

14 Tailgate and support struts
– removal, refitting and adjustment

Tailgate

Removal

1 Open the tailgate and remove the upper trim panel to disconnect wiring connectors

13.4... then lift the glass out of the door frame

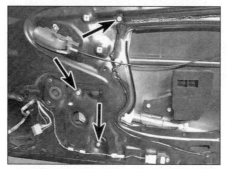

13.8a Undo the electric window regulator securing bolts...

13.10 Undo the catch retaining screws

from the wiper motor and heated rear window **(see illustration)**.
2 If required, remove the rear wipe motor as described in Chapter 12, Section 15.
3 With the aid of an assistant to support

14.1 Disconnect the wiring connector

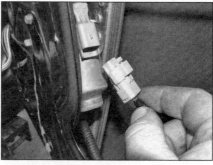

13.7 Disconnect the electric window wiring plug

13.8b... and remove the regulator assembly

13.11 Window front retaining nuts – arrowed

the tailgate, release the retaining clip and disconnect the support strut from the tailgate **(see illustration)**.
4 Ensure that the tailgate is supported, then unscrew the nuts securing the hinges to the

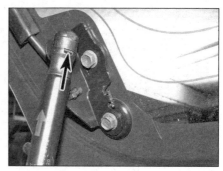

14.3 Release the strut upper retaining clip

14.4a Left-hand tailgate hinge securing nut...

14.4b... and right-hand hinge securing nut – arrowed

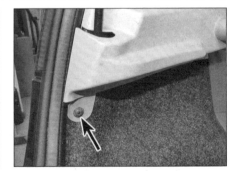

14.7a Undo the retaining screw...

14.7b... and pull the lower edge of the trim away

14.8 Release the strut lower retaining clip

vehicle body **(see illustrations)**, and lift the tailgate from the car.

Refitting

5 Refitting is a reversal of removal, bearing in mind the following points:

a) *Make sure that the hinges are aligned correctly before tightening.*
b) *If removed, refit the rear wiper motor as described in Chapter 12, Section 15.*
c) *On completion, check the alignment of the*

tailgate with the surrounding body panels and, if necessary, adjust the position of the tailgate hinges until satisfactory alignment is achieved.

Support strut

Removal

6 Open the tailgate, and support it in the open position using a wooden prop or similar tool.
7 Working at the lower end of the tailgate strut, undo the retaining screw and pull back the inner trim panel **(see illustrations)**.
8 Release the retaining clip and prise the lower end of the strut from the ball-stud fitting on the inner wing panel **(see illustration)**.
9 At the tailgate end, release the retaining clip and prise the top of the strut from the ball-stud fitting on the tailgate mounting bracket **(see illustration 14.3)**.

Refitting

10 Refitting is a reversal of removal.

---

15 Tailgate lock components – removal and refitting

Note: *Before removing any electrical connections, it is advisable to disconnect the battery negative lead, and position the lead away from the battery (also see 'Disconnecting the battery').*

Lock catch

Removal

1 Open the tailgate and unscrew the two lock securing bolts, and remove the lock out from the lower crossmember **(see illustrations)**.

Refitting

2 Refitting is a reversal of removal.

Lock button

Removal

3 Open the tailgate, and remove the lock catch as described in paragraph 1.
4 Remove the inner plastic trim panel, from the inside of the rear cross member **(see illustrations)**.
5 Remove the rear bumper as described in Section 6 of this Chapter.

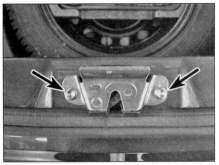

15.1a Undo the lock catch retaining bolts...

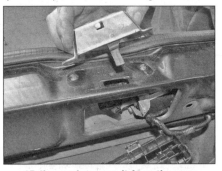

15.1b... and remove it from the rear crossmember

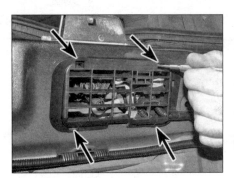

15.4a Release the retaining clips...

15.4b... and remove the inner trim panel

15.6a Undo the lock button retaining bolts...

15.6b... twist anti-clockwise...

15.6c... and remove the outer locking sleeve

6 Undo the two retaining bolts, and then rotate the outer sleeve anti-clockwise and remove it from the lock button (see illustrations).
7 Working inside the luggage compartment, withdraw the lock button, noting its fitted position in the lock actuator (see illustration).

Refitting

8 Refitting is a reversal of removal, bearing in mind the following points:
a) Make sure the lock button is firmly in place in the rear panel, and that the actuator lever (where applicable) is located correctly.
b) Check the operation of the lock mechanism before refitting the bumper.
c) Refit the rear bumper as described in Section 6.

Lock actuator

Removal

9 Open the tailgate, and remove the lock button as described previously in this Section.
10 Undo the two retaining bolts, and then remove the actuator from inside the luggage compartment (see illustrations).
11 Disconnect the wiring plug as the actuator is removed (see illustration).

Refitting

12 Refitting is a reversal of removal, but check the operation of the mechanism before refitting the bumper.

15.7 Withdraw the lock button, noting its location in the lock motor

15.10a Undo the lock motor retaining bolts...

15.10b... and remove it from inside the rear crossmember

15.11 Disconnect the wiring connector as it is removed

16 Central locking system components – removal and refitting

Note: Before removing any electrical connections, it is advisable to disconnect the battery negative lead, and position the lead away from the battery (also see 'Disconnecting the battery').

Door lock motor

1 The door lock motors are screwed to the lock assembly mounting bracket (see illustration). Removal and refitting is part of the door lock removal and refitting procedure in Section 12.

Door lock microswitch

2 The door lock microswitches (fitted to the

front doors) are an integral part of the lock assemblies. Removal and refitting is part of the door lock removal and refitting procedure in Section 12.

Door lock electronic control unit

3 The door lock control unit is fitted to the crossmember below the upper facia panel, behind the instrument cluster (see illustration).

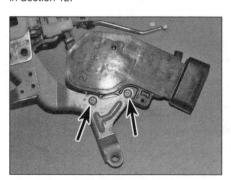

16.1 Lock motor retaining screws

16.3 Central door locking electronic control unit (ECU)

16.5a Disconnect the wiring plug...

16.5b... and unbolt the unit from the crossmember

16.9 Unbolt the relay block

16.10 Unbolt the receiver unit from the top of the crossmember

16.11 Disconnect the wiring plug as it is removed

4 Remove the upper section of the facia panel as described in Section 26 of this Chapter.

5 Disconnect the wiring plug, then unbolt and remove the unit from the crossmember **(see illustrations)**.

6 Refitting is a reversal of removal.

Remote locking receiver unit

7 The remote locking receiver unit is fitted to the crossmember below the upper facia panel, above the steering column.

8 Remove the upper section of the facia panel as described in Section 26 of this Chapter.

9 Undo the retaining bolt and remove the wiring/relay block from the top of the crossmember **(see illustration)**.

10 Undo the retaining bolt and remove the receiver unit, complete with mounting bracket, from below the wiring/relay block **(see illustration)**.

11 Disconnect the wiring plug, and if required, unbolt the receiver unit from the mounting bracket **(see illustration)**.

12 Refitting is a reversal of removal.

Remote control (key) battery

13 Remove the small screw from the key fob, and take off the key cover.

14 Lift out the battery case from the key, and prise off the case cover.

15 The battery is held in place (positive + side up) by retaining clips. Carefully prise the clips aside to release the battery, and slide it out of its holder.

16 Fit the new battery the same way up as the old one, and ensure it is held securely by the clips.

17 Reassemble the key fob, and test the operation (the key indicator light should come on when the key is pressed).

18 If the remote control does not work after the battery has been renewed, reprogramme it as described in the following paragraphs.

Reprogramming remote key

19 First make sure the ignition is switched off.

20 Switch the ignition back on.

21 Immediately press one of the remote control buttons, and hold it for a few seconds.

22 Then switch the ignition off again and remove the key from the ignition switch.

23 The remote control should now be working again. If the remote control continues to not work, see your local dealer to have the system checked.

17 Electric window components – removal and refitting

Window switches

1 Refer to Chapter 12, Section 4.

Window motors

2 The window motor is an integral part of the window regulator assembly, remove the regulator as described in Section 13.

18 Exterior mirrors – removal and refitting

Mirror

Removal

1 Open the front door and remove the trim panel from the inside of the door mirror by sliding it forwards **(see illustration)**.

2 Undo the two retaining screws and unclip the inner trim panel from the inside of the door frame **(see illustrations)**.

18.1 Slide the trim panel forwards

18.2a Undo the two retaining screws...

18.2b... and remove the trim panel from inside the door frame

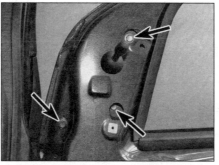

18.3a Undo the three retaining bolts...

18.3b... and remove the door mirror from outside the door frame

3 Support the mirror from the outside of the door and remove the three mirror mounting bolts, as the last is removed withdraw the mirror from the door **(see illustrations)**.

Refitting

4 Refitting is a reversal of removal, noting the following points:
a) *Check the condition of the mirror-to-body seal – any damage here could result in water entering the car.*
b) *Tighten the mirror mounting nuts securely.*

Mirror glass

 Warning: If the mirror glass is broken, wear gloves to protect your hands.

Removal

5 The mirror glass can be removed with the mirror in place if preferred.
6 Using a plastic trim tool, prise the top of the glass out to release the securing clips from the mounting plate **(see illustrations)**.

Refitting

7 Press firmly and evenly at the centre of the mirror glass to engage the retaining clips to the mounting plate **(see illustration)**. Use a piece of cloth to press against, taking care not to damage the mirror glass.

Mirror trim cover

Removal

8 Remove the mirror glass as described previously.
9 Working inside the mirror housing, release

the retaining clips and unclip the trim cover from the rear of the mirror **(see illustrations)**.

Refitting

10 Press the trim cover firmly onto the rear of the mirror housing, making sure the retaining clips are engaged securely.
11 Refit the mirror glass as described previously.

19 Windscreen, side and tailgate glass – general information

1 These areas of glass are secured by the tight fit of the weatherseal in the body aperture, and are bonded in position with a special adhesive. Renewal of such fixed glass is a difficult, messy and time-consuming

task, which is considered beyond the scope of the home mechanic. It is difficult, unless one has plenty of practice, to obtain a secure, waterproof fit. Furthermore, the task carries a high risk of breakage; this applies especially to the laminated glass windscreen. In view of this, owners are strongly advised to have this sort of work carried out by one of the many specialist windscreen fitters.

20 Sunroof – general information

1 Due to the complexity of the sunroof mechanism, considerable expertise is needed to repair, renew or adjust the sunroof components successfully. Removal of the roof first requires the headlining to be removed,

18.6a Prise the mirror glass off its mounting plate

18.6b Mirror glass removed, showing mounting plate and retaining clips

18.7 Press firmly until the retaining clips have engaged

18.9a Release the retaining clips...

18.9b... and remove the outer trim cover

21.3a Wheel arch trim securing clip

21.3b There are different types of clips securing the trims...

21.3c... and also some retaining bolts

21.4 Remove the inner wheel arch liner from under the wing panel

which is a complex and tedious operation, and not a task to be undertaken lightly. Therefore, any problems with the sunroof should be referred to a dealer.

2 On models with an electric sunroof, if the sunroof motor fails to operate, first check the relevant fuse. If the fault cannot be traced and rectified, the sunroof can usually be opened and closed manually using an Allen key to turn the motor spindle.

21 Body exterior fittings – removal and refitting

Bumpers

1 Refer to Section 6.

Scuttle cover panel

2 Refer to the windscreen wiper motor removal procedure in Chapter 12 Section 14.

Wheel arch liners

3 The wheel arch liners are secured by a combination of self-tapping screws and push-fit clips (see illustrations).
4 Remove the relevant wheel, and then with all the fasteners removed, pull the liner down from the arch and remove it (see illustration).

Body trim strips and badges

5 The various body trim strips and badges are held in position with a special adhesive. Removal requires the trim/badge to be heated, to soften the adhesive, and then cut away from the surface. Due to the high risk of damage to the paintwork during this operation, it is recommended that this task should be entrusted to a franchised dealer or bodyshop.

22 Seats – removal and refitting

Front seat

⚠️ **Warning: On models with side airbags, disconnect the battery negative lead (see 'Disconnecting the battery'), then wait for two minutes before proceeding. If this waiting period is not observed, there is danger of activating the airbag system.**

1 Slide the seat fully rearwards, and then unscrew the two front bolts securing the seat rails to the floor (see illustration).
2 Slide the seat fully forwards, and then unscrew the two rear bolts (see illustration).
3 Check under and around the seat for any wiring (typically, this will only be on models fitted with side airbags or a seat belt warning light), and disconnect it as necessary (see illustration).
4 Lift the seat, complete with mounting rails, and remove it from the car.
5 If required, undo the securing nuts from under the seat and remove the seat runners from the seat frame (see illustration).
6 To remove the seat lever from the side of the seat, unclip the centre cover, and then release the securing clips and withdraw the lever from the spindle (see illustrations).

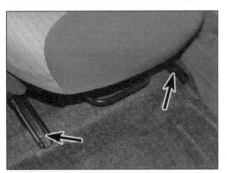

22.1 With the seat fully back, the front seat rail mounting bolts can be seen

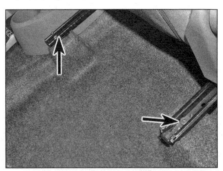

22.2 With the seat fully forwards, the back seat rail mounting bolts can be seen

22.3 Disconnect the wiring plugs under the seat

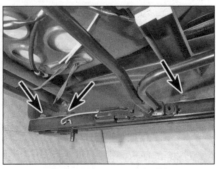

22.5 Retaining nuts securing the seat to the seat runners

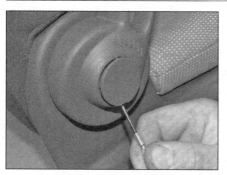

22.6a Unclip the centre cap...

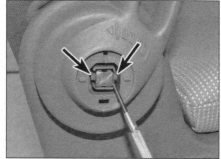

22.6b... release the securing clips each side...

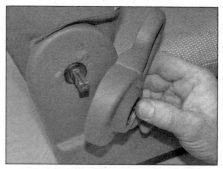

22.6c... and withdraw the seat lever

Note: *The seat lever centre cover locks the two retaining clips in place when it is refitted.*

7 Refitting is a reversal of removal, but tighten the seat mounting bolts, starting with the front two first, to the specified torque.

Rear seat

Split fold type

8 Pull the front of the seat base upwards to release the securing clips along the front edge of the seat cushion **(see illustration)**. Then slide the seat cushion forwards, and remove it from inside the passenger compartment.

9 Undo the two retaining bolts and remove the seat belt stalks from the centre of the rear seat brackets **(see illustration)**.

10 Undo the two retaining bolts from the rear seat brackets **(see illustration)**.

22.6d Note the centre cap keeps the securing clips locked in place

11 Undo the two retaining nuts from the centre rear seat brackets **(see illustration)**.

12 Pull the seat catch strap and tilt the seat back forward slightly, then undo the outer seat

22.8 Pull the seat base up to release the securing clips

bracket securing nut and bolt and remove from inside the passenger compartment **(see illustrations)**.

13 Undo the outer seat bracket securing

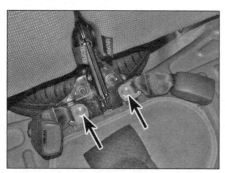

22.9 Seat belt stalk securing bolts

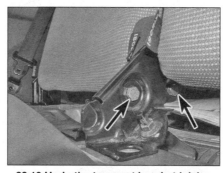

22.10 Undo the two seat bracket joining bolts...

22.11... and lower mounting nuts

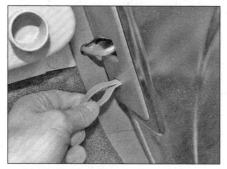

22.12a Release the catch on the seat back...

22.12b... undo the mounting bracket nut and bolt...

22.12c... and remove the seat back from inside the car

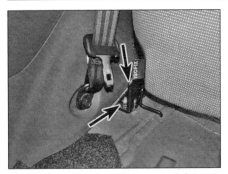

22.13 Undo the mounting bracket nut and bolt on the other side of the seat

nut and bolt on the remaining rear seat back, and remove from inside the passenger compartment **(see illustration)**.

14 Refitting is a reversal of removal, but tighten the seat mounting bolts to the specified torque.

Bench type

15 Pull the front of the seat base upwards to release the securing clips along the front edge of the seat cushion **(see illustration 22.8)**. Then slide the seat cushion forwards, and remove it from inside the passenger compartment.

16 Pull the seat catch strap and tilt the seat back forward slightly, then undo the outer seat bracket securing nuts and bolts from each side of the seat back. Remove the seat back from inside the passenger compartment.

17 Refitting is a reversal of removal, but tighten the seat mounting bolts to the specified torque.

23.2 Seat belt upper mounting bracket bolt

23 Seat belt components – removal and refitting

⚠️ **Warning: Disconnect the battery negative lead (see 'Disconnecting the battery'), then wait for two minutes before proceeding. If this waiting period is not observed, there is danger of activating the seat belt tensioner.**

Front belt

3-door models

1 Remove the rear trim panels as described in Section 24.

2 Unscrew the front seat belt upper anchorage bolt from the top of the B-pillar **(see illustration)**.

3 Disconnect the wiring plug for the seat belt pretensioner from the inertia reel by first lifting the (black) locking clip, then pulling off the yellow plug **(see illustrations)**.

4 Remove the two bolts securing the inertia reel **(see illustration)**, and then withdraw it from the bottom of the B-pillar.

5 Refitting is a reversal of removal, but tighten the seat belt bolts to the specified torque.

5-door models

6 Remove the B-pillar trim panels as described in Section 24.

7 Unscrew the front seat belt upper anchorage bolt from the top of the B-pillar **(see illustration)**.

8 Disconnect the wiring plug for the seat belt pretensioner from the inertia reel by first lifting the (black) locking clip, then pulling off the yellow plug **(see illustrations 23.3a and 23.3b)**.

9 Remove the two bolts securing the inertia reel **(see illustration 23.4)**, and then withdraw it from the bottom of the B-pillar.

10 Refitting is a reversal of removal, but tighten the seat belt bolts to the specified torque.

Front belt stalk

11 Slide the front seat fully forwards, to gain access to the wiring connector under the base of the seat. It may be easier to access the wiring if the seat is removed completely, as described in Section 22.

12 Disconnect the wiring connector (green) from under the seat and release it from its securing clips under the seat base **(see illustrations)**.

13 If the seat has not been removed completely,

23.3a Lift the locking clip...

23.3b... then pull off the pretensioner wiring plug

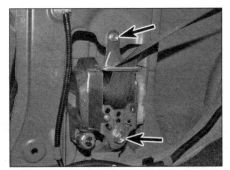

23.4 Front seat belt inertia reel mounting bolts

23.7 Unscrew the seat belt upper bolt

23.12a Disconnect the green wiring plug...

23.12b... and unclip the wiring loom from the seat

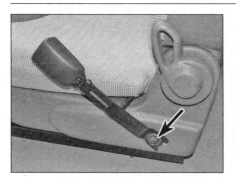

23.13 Seat belt stalk mounting bolt

23.17 Seat belt upper mounting bracket bolt

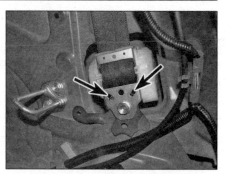

23.18 Locating pegs to position the inertia reel

slide if fully rearwards to gain access to the stalk mounting bolt **(see illustration)**.
14 Unscrew the bolt, and remove the stalk from the seat frame, carefully withdraw the wiring through the base of the seat cushion as the stalk is removed.
15 Refitting is a reversal of removal, bearing in mind the following points:
a) *Make sure that the stalk wiring is routed correctly under the seat.*
b) *Tighten the securing bolt to the specified torque.*

Rear inertia reel belt

3-door models

16 Remove the rear trim panels as described in Section 24.
17 Unscrew the rear seat belt upper anchorage bolt from the top of the C-pillar **(see illustration)**.
18 Remove the bolt securing the inertia reel **(see illustration)**. Withdraw the reel from the bottom of the C-pillar, noting the locating pegs on the mounting bracket.
19 Refitting is a reversal of removal, but tighten the seat belt bolts to the specified torque.

5-door models

20 Remove the C-pillar trim panels as described in Section 24.
21 Unscrew the rear seat belt upper anchorage bolt from the top of the C-pillar **(see illustration 23.17)**.
22 Remove the bolt securing the inertia reel **(see illustration 23.18)**. Withdraw the reel from the bottom of the C-pillar, noting the locating pegs on the mounting bracket.

23 Refitting is a reversal of removal, but tighten the seat belt bolts to the specified torque.

Rear belt buckles

24 Remove the rear seat base as described in Section 22.
25 The belt buckles are bolted to the rear seat back mounting brackets. Undo the retaining bolts and remove the belt buckles from the vehicle **(see illustration 22.9)**.
26 Refitting is a reversal of removal. Tighten the bolts to the specified torque.

24 Interior trim and fittings – removal and refitting

General

1 The interior trim panels are secured by

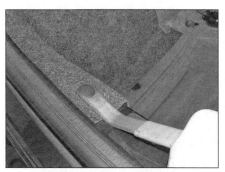

24.1a Prise out the securing clip...

24.1c... and remove the retaining screw

a combination of clips and screws, with easily broken plastic clips featuring heavily **(see illustrations)**. Removal and refitting is generally self-explanatory, noting that it may be necessary to remove or loosen surrounding panels to allow a particular panel to be removed. The following paragraphs describe the removal and refitting of the major panels in more detail.

Door inner trim panels

2 Refer to Section 11.

Steering column shrouds

3 Turn the steering wheel first the left and then to the right to access the two retaining screws, undo the two screws and unclip the upper shroud from around the instrument panel **(see illustrations)**.

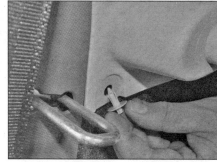

24.1b... release the retaining clip...

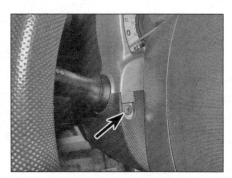

24.3a Turn the steering wheel to access the left-hand side screw...

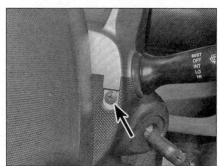

24.3b... and to access the right-hand side screw...

24.3c... and then withdraw the upper shroud from the instrument panel

24.4a Undo the retaining screw...

24.4b... and remove the lower shroud

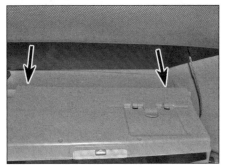

24.6a Open the glovebox lid and undo the two screws arrowed

24.6b Release the securing clip and remove the glovebox lid

24.8 Pull back the door seal from the lower trim

4 Undo the retaining screw and unclip the lower shroud from the steering column **(see illustrations)**.
5 Refitting is a reversal of removal.

Glovebox cover

6 Open the glovebox cover, and undo the two retaining screws from inside the glovebox, release the retaining clip on the lid stay.

Withdraw the lid from the facia, and remove it **(see illustrations)**.
7 Refitting is a reversal of removal.

Footwell side trim panels

8 Open the front door and pull the rubber door seal away from the front lower trim panel **(see illustration)**.
9 Carefully lever the trim panel to release the retaining clips, and then pull the trim rearwards to release it from the locating stud at the front of the trim panel **(see illustration)**.
10 Refitting is a reversal of removal. Align the panel on the bulkhead stud at the front, and then clip into place.

A-pillar trim panel

11 Open the door, and carefully prise the rubber door seal from the edge of the door aperture **(see illustration)**.
12 The A-pillar trim panels are clipped in place. Several clips are used, and some are quite stiff to release – start at the top of the panel, and pull the panel back as it is released **(see illustration)**. Check whether any of the clips pull out of the panel to be left on the car – transfer them back to the panel before refitting.
13 Refitting is a reversal of removal.

B-pillar trim panels

5-door models

14 Working your way around the front and rear door apertures, pull the rubber door seals away from the trims that require removing **(see illustration)**.

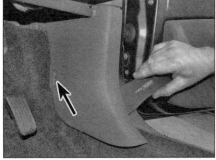

24.9 Unclip the trim panel and pull back to release from locating peg – arrowed

24.11 Pull back the door seal from along the trim panel

24.12 Unclip the trim panel from the A-pillar

24.14 Pull back the door seal from along the sill trim panel

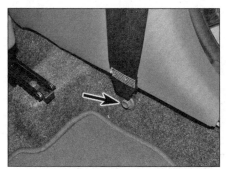

24.15 Undo the seat belt lower anchorage bolt

24.16 Unclip the sill trim panel

24.17a Unclip the B-pillar lower trim panel...

24.17b... and unclip it from the upper trim panel

24.18a Release the retaining clips from the B-pillar upper trim panel...

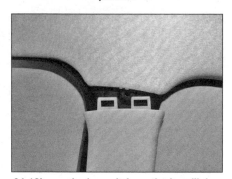

24.18b... and release it from the headlining

15 Unscrew the front seat belt lower anchorage bolt from the inner sill panel **(see illustration)**.
16 Disengage the rear sill trim from the lower B-pillar trim panel **(see illustration)**.
17 Unclip the B-pillar lower trim panel, and then disengage it from the upper trim panel **(see illustrations)**.
18 Unclip the B-pillar upper trim panel, and then disengage it from the headlining **(see illustrations)**.
19 Refitting is a reversal of removal.

C-pillar trim panel

5-door models

20 Remove the luggage compartment side carpet **(see illustration)**, as described later in this Section.
21 Unscrew the rear seat belt lower anchorage bolt from the rear wheel arch **(see illustration)**.
22 Disengage the rear sill trim from the lower B-pillar trim panel **(see illustration 24.16)**.
23 Unclip the lower trim panel from the rear wheel arch and rear seat catch bracket **(see illustration)**.
24 Unclip the C-pillar upper trim panel, and then disengage it from the headlining **(see illustration)**.
25 Refitting is a reversal of removal.

Rear trim panels

3-door models

26 Open the door and move the front seat as far forward as possible.

27 Working your way around the rear of the door aperture, pull the rubber door seal away from the trim that requires removing **(see illustration)**.

24.20 Remove the luggage compartment side carpet

24.21 Undo the seat belt lower anchorage bolt

24.23 Unclip the C-pillar lower trim panel

24.24 Unclip the C-pillar upper trim panel

28 Unscrew the front seat belt lower anchorage bolt from the inner sill panel **(see illustration)**.
29 Remove the rear parcel shelf and then

24.27 Pull back the door seal from along the trim panel

24.28 Undo the front seat belt lower anchorage bolt

24.30 Undo the rear seat belt lower anchorage bolt

24.31a Prise out the securing clips...

24.31b... and unclip the lower trim panel

24.32 Pull back the tailgate seal from along the trim panel

remove the rear seats as described in Section 22.

30 Unscrew the rear seat belt lower anchorage bolt from the inner wing panel **(see illustration)**.

31 Release the retaining clips and remove the lower part of the trim panel from inside the rear of the vehicle **(see illustrations)**.

32 Working your way around the tailgate aperture, pull the seal away from the trim that requires removing **(see illustration)**.

33 Undo the retaining screw and release the retaining clips from the lower edge of the upper trim panel **(see illustrations)**.

34 Unclip the upper part of the trim panel from the top of the window aperture, and guide the rear seat belt through the panel as it is removed **(see illustrations)**.

35 Refitting is a reversal of removal.

Luggage compartment carpets

36 Open the tailgate and lift out the carpet from the floor of the luggage compartment.

37 To remove the carpets from the side of the luggage compartment, remove the parcel shelf and tilt the rear seat back forwards.

24.33a Remove the retaining screw

24.33b... release the retaining clip...

24.33c... and prise out the securing clip

24.34a Unclip the upper trim panel...

24.34b... and guide the seat belt through the trim panel

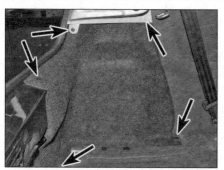

24.38a Remove the fasteners...

24.38b... and withdraw the luggage compartment side carpet

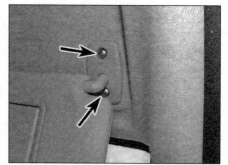

24.44a Undo the two retaining screws...

24.44b... and remove the sunvisor

24.45a Undo the retaining screw...

24.45b... and unclip the sunvisor securing clip

38 Undo the retaining screw and release the four retaining clips, and then remove the carpet trim from the side of the luggage compartment **(see illustrations)**.
39 Refitting is a reversal of removal.

Carpets

40 The passenger compartment floor carpet is in several pieces, and is secured along the edges by various types of clips.
41 Carpet removal and refitting is reasonably straightforward, but time-consuming, due to the fact that all adjoining trim panels must be released, and the seats and centre console must be removed.

Headlining

42 The headlining is clipped to the roof, and can be withdrawn only once all fittings

such as the grab handles, sunvisors, sunroof, front, centre and rear pillar trim panels, and associated components have been removed. The door, tailgate and sunroof aperture weatherseals will also have to be prised clear.
43 Note that headlining removal requires considerable skill and experience if it is to be carried out without damage, and is therefore best entrusted to an expert.

Sunvisors

44 Remove the two sunvisor hinge screws, and remove the sunvisor from the roof **(see illustrations)**.
45 To remove the holding clip, slacken the securing screw and withdraw the clip from the headlining **(see illustrations)**.
46 Refitting is a reversal of removal.

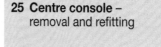

25 Centre console –
removal and refitting

Removal

1 Lift out the mat from the rearmost storage compartment in the console, and remove the bolt underneath **(see illustrations)**.

Manual transmission models

2 Using a plastic trim tool, carefully unclip the gear lever gaiter from the top of the centre console **(see illustrations)**.
3 Unscrew the gear knob and withdraw the gaiter from the gear lever **(see illustrations)**.

25.1a Lift out the small piece of carpet...

25.1b... and undo the retaining bolt

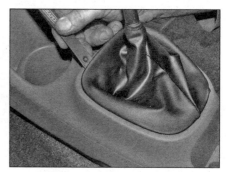

25.2a Using a plastic lever...

25.2b... to unclip the gear lever gaiter

25.3a Unscrew the gear knob...

25.3b... and withdraw the gaiter from the gear lever

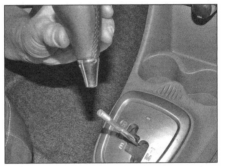

25.4 Unscrew the gear knob from the top of the lever

Multi-Mode transmission models

4 Unscrew the gear knob from the gear lever **(see illustration)**.

5 Using a plastic trim tool, carefully unclip the gear lever surround and remove it from the top of the centre console **(see illustration)**.

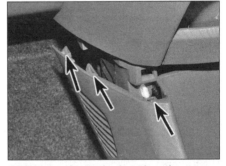

25.6b... to release the front locating pegs...

26.4a Undo the retaining bolt from the rev counter...

25.5 Unclip the trim panel from the centre console

All models

6 Lift the console up at the rear, and then pull the centre console away from the facia. This will release the locating clips on the front edge of the centre console **(see illustrations)**.

25.6c... and withdraw the centre console from over the gear lever

26.4b... and disconnect the wiring connector as it is removed

25.6a Pull the centre console...

Refitting

7 Refitting is a reversal of removal.

26 Facia assembly – removal and refitting

⚠️ **Warning: Disconnect the battery negative lead (see 'Disconnecting the battery'), then wait for two minutes before proceeding.**

Note: *The facia panel is in two sections (upper and lower), with a large metal crossmember underneath it. Depending on the other work being carried out, not all of the facia sections may need to be removed. It is strongly recommended that this Section be read through thoroughly before starting the procedure.*

Removal

Upper section

1 Disconnect the battery negative lead, with reference to 'Disconnecting the battery', then wait for two minutes before proceeding. If this waiting period is not observed, there is danger of activating the airbags.

2 Remove the driver's airbag, as described in Chapter 12 Section 22.

3 Remove the steering column shrouds as described in Section 24.

4 Where fitted, undo the retaining bolt and remove the rev counter from the top of the instrument panel. Disconnect the wiring connector as the rev counter is removed **(see illustrations)**.

26.7a Left-hand upper facia retaining nut

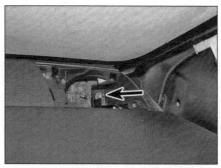

26.7b Right-hand upper facia retaining nut

26.8 Remove the heater control switch and undo the retaining screw

26.9 Unclip the radio/CD trim panel from the front of the facia

26.10 Undo the two upper facia retaining screws

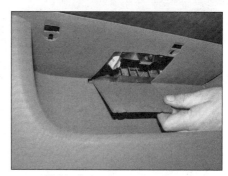

26.11a Open the access flap...

5 Remove the A-pillar trim panels as described in Section 24.

6 Remove the speakers from the top of the upper facia panel as described in Chapter 12 Section 18.

7 Slacken and remove the upper retaining nuts from inside the speaker aperture in the top of the facia **(see illustrations)**.

8 Carefully pull the heater control knob to release it from the bottom of the radio/CD trim panel, and undo the retaining screw **(see illustration)**.

9 Using a plastic trim tool, carefully lever the radio/CD unit trim panel from the facia **(see illustration)**. Disconnect the wiring connectors as it is removed.

10 Slacken and remove the two retaining screws from inside the radio/CD aperture in the centre of the facia **(see illustration)**.

11 Open the glovebox cover (where fitted), and unclip the access panel inside the facia. Disconnect the wiring connector for the passenger airbag and undo the airbag securing bolt **(see illustrations)**.

12 The upper section of the facia panel may now be removed, by carefully levering the front of the facia upwards to release the clips fitted along its front edge. Remove the panel from the car **(see illustrations)**.

Lower section

13 Remove the upper section of the facia, as described previously.

14 Remove the centre console, as described in Section 25.

15 Remove the instrument panel from the top of the steering column as described in Chapter 12.

16 Remove the footwell side trim panels **(see illustration)**, as described in Section 24.

17 Undo the four retaining bolts from

26.11b... disconnect the wiring connector...

26.11c... and undo the passenger airbag securing bolt

26.12a Carefully unclip the upper facia panel...

26.12b... and withdraw it from the top of the facia

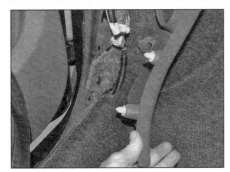

26.16 Unclip the lower front trim panels

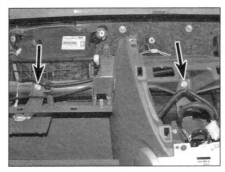

26.17a Undo the facia retaining bolts (arrowed)...

26.17b... from across the crossmember

26.18a Release the retaining clips...

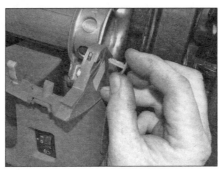

26.18b... from each end of the facia

21 Release the retaining clips and disconnect the diagnostic plug from the rear of the facia trim panel **(see illustration)**.

22 Slacken and remove the two retaining screws from the centre of the lower facia **(see illustration)**.

23 Slacken and remove the two retaining screws from each end of the lower facia **(see illustrations)**.

24 Working your way along the top of the lower facia, disconnect the wiring loom, cables and aerial lead from the retaining clips in the facia, noting their fitted position **(see illustrations)**.

25 Working up the back of the facia on the right- hand side, undo the lower retaining bolt from white plastic wiring/relay block **(see illustration)**.

26 Pull the right-hand side of the facia away from the crossmember and disconnect the

the top of the facia crossmember **(see illustrations)**.

18 Release the two retaining clips (one at each side) of the facia crossmember **(see illustrations)**.

19 Remove the heater control panel, as described in Chapter 3 Section 9.

20 Unclip the wiring loom from the bottom of the facia and disconnect the wiring plug from the rear of the cigar lighter **(see illustrations)**.

26.20a Unclip the wiring loom retaining clip...

26.20b... and disconnect the wiring connector on the cigar lighter

26.21 Unclip the diagnostic plug connector from the facia

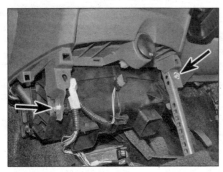

26.22 Undo the lower centre retaining bolts

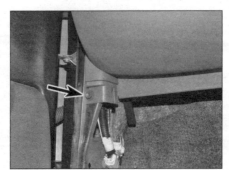

26.23a Left-hand lower facia retaining bolt

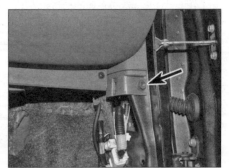

26.23b Right-hand lower facia retaining bolt

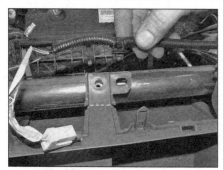

26.24a Unclip the upper wiring loom retaining clip...

26.24b... the aerial lead...

26.24c... and the lower wiring loom retaining clips

26.25 Undo the wiring block lower mounting bolt (pictured with facia removed)

26.26a Disconnect the wiring connectors from the ECU...

26.26b... the passenger airbag on/off switch...

wiring connectors from the steering ECU, passenger airbag on/off switch and headlight height adjuster (see illustrations).
27 Once all the wiring has been disconnected, make sure nothing else is attached to the lower facia and lift the panel from around the steering column and out of the car (see illustration).

Crossmember
28 Remove the upper and lower sections of the facia, as described previously.
29 Unbolt the steering column from under the crossmember (see illustration). There is no need to completely remove the steering column; secure the column to one side taking care not to damage the steering column joints (refer to Chapter 10 if necessary).
30 Undo the retaining bolt and remove

the wiring/relay block (white) from the right-hand side of the crossmember (see illustration).
31 Undo the retaining bolt and remove the

wiring/relay block (black) from the rear of the crossmember (see illustration).
32 Undo the retaining bolt from the top of the pedal bracket assembly (see illustration).

26.26c... and the headlight height adjustment switch

26.27 Check everything is detached from the lower facia and remove it from the vehicle

26.29 Undo the steering column mounting bolts

26.30 Undo the wiring block upper mounting bolt

26.31 Undo the relay block mounting bolt

26.32 Undo the mounting bolt from the pedal bracket

26.33 Undo the bolt from the upper brace

26.34 Undo the nut from the front brace

26.35a Unclip the wiring loom...

26.35b... from the top of the crossmember

26.36a Remove the crossmember mounting bolts at each end...

26.36b... and remove the crossmember from inside the vehicle

33 Undo the retaining bolt and disconnect the brace from the top of the crossmember **(see illustration)**.

34 Undo the retaining bolt and disconnect the brace from the front of the crossmember **(see illustration)**.

35 Working your way along the crossmember, disconnect the wiring harness and cable retaining clips from the crossmember, noting how it is routed and attached **(see illustrations)**.

36 Remove the four bolts (two each side) securing the crossmember in position, and then remove it from the car **(see illustrations)**.

Refitting

37 Refitting is a reversal of removal, bearing in mind the following points:
a) When the facia is being refitted, ensure that the battery is disconnected. It is dangerous, for example, to reconnect the airbag wiring with the battery connected.
b) Ensure that the wiring harness is securely reconnected to the facia crossmember, and is routed as before.
c) Tighten all bolts securely.

Chapter 12
Body electrical systems

Contents

Degrees of difficulty

Easy, suitable for novice with little experience		Fairly easy, suitable for beginner with some experience		Fairly difficult, suitable for competent DIY mechanic		Difficult, suitable for experienced DIY mechanic		Very difficult, suitable for expert DIY or professional	

Specifications

General

System type	12 volt, negative-earth	
Bulbs	Type	Wattage
Front direction indicator light	Bayonet-fit (amber)	21
Front direction indicator side repeater light	Push-fit (amber)	5
Sidelight	Push-fit	5
Headlight	H4	55/60
High-level brake light (4 x bulbs)	Push-fit	5
Interior light	Push-fit	5
Number plate light	Push-fit	5
Rear direction indicator light	Bayonet-fit	21
Rear foglight..	Bayonet-fit	21
Reversing light	Bayonet-fit	21
Brake/tail light	Bayonet-fit	21/5

Torque wrench settings

	Nm	lbf ft
Airbag control unit mounting bolts............................	10	7
Airbag sensor mounting bolts	10	7

1 General information and precautions

⚠️ *Warning: Before carrying out any work on the electrical system, read through the precautions given in Safety first! at the beginning of this manual, and in Chapter 5A.*

1 The electrical system is of 12 volt negative-earth type. Power for the lights and all electrical accessories is supplied by a lead-acid type battery, which is charged by the alternator.

2 This Chapter covers repair and service procedures for the various electrical components not associated with the engine. Information on the battery, alternator and starter motor can be found in Chapter 5A.

3 It should be noted that, prior to working on any component in the electrical system, the battery negative terminal should first be disconnected, to prevent the possibility of electrical short-circuits and/or fires.

Caution: Before disconnecting the battery, refer to 'Disconnecting the battery' in Reference.

2 Electrical fault finding – general information

Note: *Refer to the precautions given in 'Safety first!' and at the beginning of Chapter 5A before starting work. The following tests relate to testing of the main electrical circuits, and should not be used to test delicate electronic circuits (such as anti-lock braking systems), particularly where an electronic control module is used.*

General

1 A typical electrical circuit consists of an electrical component; any switches, relays, motors, fuses, fusible links or circuit breakers related to that component, and the wiring and connectors which link the component to both the battery and the chassis. To help to pinpoint a problem in an electrical circuit, wiring diagrams are included at the end of this Chapter.

2 Before attempting to diagnose an electrical fault, first study the appropriate wiring diagram, to obtain a more complete understanding of the components included in the particular circuit concerned. The possible sources of a fault can be narrowed down; this can be done by noting whether other components related to the circuit are operating properly. If several components or circuits fail at one time, the problem is likely to be related to a shared fuse or earth connection.

3 Electrical problems usually stem from simple causes, such as loose or corroded connections, a faulty earth connection, a blown fuse, a melted fusible link, or a faulty relay (refer to Section 3 for details of testing relays). Visually inspect the condition of all fuses, wires and connections in a problem circuit before testing the components. Use the wiring diagrams to determine which terminal connections will need to be checked, in order to pinpoint the trouble spot.

4 The basic tools required for electrical fault finding include a circuit tester or voltmeter (a 12 volt bulb with a set of test leads can also be used for certain tests); a self-powered test light (sometimes known as a continuity tester); an ohmmeter (to measure resistance); a battery and set of test leads; and a jumper wire, preferably with a circuit breaker or fuse incorporated, which can be used to bypass suspect wires or electrical components. Before attempting to locate a problem with test instruments, use the wiring diagram to determine where to make the connections.

5 To find the source of an intermittent wiring fault (usually due to a poor or dirty connection, or damaged wiring insulation), a 'wiggle' test can be performed on the wiring. This involves wiggling the wiring by hand, to see if the fault occurs as the wiring is moved. It should be possible to narrow down the source of the fault to a particular section of wiring. This method of testing can be used in conjunction with any of the tests described in the following sub-Sections.

6 Apart from problems due to poor connections, two basic types of fault can occur in an electrical circuit – open-circuit, or short-circuit.

7 Open-circuit faults are caused by a break somewhere in the circuit, which prevents current from flowing. An open-circuit fault will prevent a component from working, but will not cause the relevant circuit fuse to blow.

8 Short-circuit faults are caused by a 'short' somewhere in the circuit, which allows the current flowing in the circuit to 'escape' along an alternative route, usually to earth. Short-circuit faults are normally caused by a breakdown in wiring insulation which allows a feed wire to touch either another wire or an earthed component such as the bodyshell. A short-circuit fault will normally cause the relevant circuit fuse to blow.

Finding an open-circuit

9 To check for an open-circuit, connect one lead of a circuit tester or voltmeter to either the negative battery terminal or a known good earth.

10 Connect the other lead to a connector in the circuit being tested, preferably nearest to the battery or fuse.

11 Switch on the circuit, bearing in mind that some circuits are live only when the ignition switch is moved to a particular position.

12 If voltage is present (indicated either by the tester bulb lighting or a voltmeter reading, as applicable), this means that the section of the circuit between the relevant connector and the battery is problem-free.

13 Continue to check the remainder of the circuit in the same fashion.

14 When a point is reached at which no voltage is present, the problem must lie between that point and the previous test point with voltage. Most problems can be traced to a broken, corroded or loose connection.

Finding a short-circuit

15 To check for a short-circuit; first disconnect the load(s) from the circuit (loads are the components which draw current from a circuit, such as bulbs, motors, heating elements, etc).

16 Remove the relevant fuse from the circuit, and connect a circuit tester or voltmeter to the fuse connections.

17 Switch on the circuit, bearing in mind that some circuits are live only when the ignition switch is moved to a particular position.

18 If voltage is present (indicated either by the tester bulb lighting or a voltmeter reading, as applicable), this means that there is a short-circuit.

19 If no voltage is present, but the fuse still blows with the load(s) connected, this indicates an internal fault in the load(s).

Finding an earth fault

20 The battery negative terminal is connected to earth – the metal of the engine/transmission and the car body – and most systems are wired so that they only receive a positive feed, the current returning through the metal of the car body. This means that the component mounting and the body form part of that circuit. Loose or corroded mountings can therefore cause a range of electrical faults, ranging from total failure of a circuit, to a puzzling partial fault.

21 In particular, lights may shine dimly (especially when another circuit sharing the same earth point is in operation), motors (eg, wiper motors or the radiator cooling fan motor) may run slowly, and the operation of one circuit may have an apparently unrelated effect on another.

22 Note that on many vehicles, earth straps are used between certain components, such as the engine/transmission and the body, usually where there is no metal-to-metal contact between components, due to flexible rubber mountings, etc.

23 To check whether a component is properly earthed, disconnect the battery, and connect one lead of an ohmmeter to a known good earth point. Connect the other lead to the wire or earth connection being tested. The resistance reading should be zero; if not, check the connection as follows.

24 If an earth connection is thought to be faulty, dismantle the connection, and clean back to bare metal both the bodyshell and the wire terminal or the component earth connection mating surface. Be careful to remove all traces of dirt and corrosion, and then use a knife to trim away any paint, so that a clean metal-to-metal joint is made.

25 On reassembly, tighten the joint fasteners securely; if a wire terminal is being refitted, use serrated washers between the terminal and the bodyshell, to ensure a clean and secure connection.

26 When the connection is remade, prevent the onset of corrosion in the future by applying a coat of petroleum jelly or silicone-based grease, or by spraying on (at regular intervals) a proprietary ignition sealer.

3 Fuses and relays – general information

Fuses

1 Fuses are designed to break a circuit when a predetermined current is reached, in order to protect the components and wiring which could be damaged by excessive current flow. Any excessive current flow will be due to a fault in the circuit, usually a short-circuit (see Section 2).

2 The main fuses are located in the fusebox behind the instrument panel trim inside the passenger compartment. Remove the steering column upper shroud as described in Chapter 11, to access the fuses (see illustrations).

3 Additional fuses are located in a second fusebox in the engine compartment, behind the battery. Unclip the lid to access the fuses (see illustration).

4 A blown fuse can be recognised from its melted or broken wire.

5 To remove a fuse, first ensure that the relevant circuit is switched off. Taking out the ignition key is a start, but several circuits are live even with the ignition off – for maximum safety, disconnect the battery (see *Disconnecting the battery* in Reference).

6 Pull the fuse from its location, using the tool provided in the engine compartment fusebox (see illustrations). If the tool is not available, carefully remove the fuses using thin-nosed pliers.

7 Before renewing a blown fuse, trace and rectify the cause, and always use a fuse of the correct rating. Never substitute a fuse of a higher rating, or make temporary repairs using wire or metal foil; more serious damage, or even fire, could result.

8 Note that the fuses are colour-coded as follows. Refer to the wiring diagrams (or the vehicle handbook) for details of the circuits protected. Also note that these models use the later-type 'mini' fuses.

Colour	Rating
Brown	7.5A
Red	10A
Blue	15A
Yellow	20A
Clear or white	25A
Green	30A

9 Larger 'midi' fuses will also be found in the engine compartment fusebox and on the rear of the instrument panel (see illustrations).

3.2a Remove the upper shroud...

3.2c... and left-hand side of the instrument panel

Since many of these are rated in excess of 30 amps, if any of these is found to have blown, it indicates a serious wiring fault which should be investigated – just fitting a new fuse may cause further problems.

3.6a Using the tool provided...

3.9a Larger 'midi' fuses in the engine compartment fusebox...

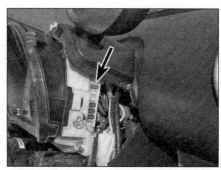
3.2b... to access the fuses on the right...

3.3 Additional fuses are located in the engine compartment fusebox

Relays

10 A relay is an electrically-operated switch, which is used for the following reasons:
a) A relay can switch a heavy current

3.6b... pull the fuse out from the fusebox

3.9b... and on the rear of the instrument panel

4.2a Disconnect the wiring plug from the immobiliser unit...

4.2b... then unclip it and slide it off the ignition switch

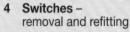
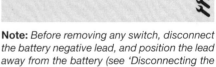

4 Switches – removal and refitting

Note: *Before removing any switch, disconnect the battery negative lead, and position the lead away from the battery (see 'Disconnecting the battery').*

Ignition switch/steering lock

1 Remove the steering column shrouds as described Chapter 11 Section 24.

2 Disconnect the wiring plug, then unclip and slide off the anti-theft immobiliser transceiver unit from the ignition switch/steering lock assembly **(see illustrations)**.

3 Disconnect the main wiring plug from the ignition switch **(see illustration)**.

4 The ignition switch/steering lock is held in place with a security bolt, called a 'shear bolt'. This is a bolt which has had its head snapped off when the bolt was tightened.

5 Using a junior hacksaw, cut a slot in the top of the bolt then, using a screwdriver, remove the bolt from below the ignition switch/steering lock **(see illustrations)**. A new security bolt will be required for refitting.

6 Insert the ignition key and turn it to position I, and then using a small screwdriver, depress the locking pin at the top of the lock housing, and pull out the lock cylinder using the key **(see illustrations)**.

7 Refitting is a reversal of removal noting the following points:

remotely from the circuit in which the current is flowing, allowing the use of lighter-gauge wiring and switch contacts.
b) *A relay can receive more than one control input, unlike a mechanical switch.*
c) *A relay can have a timer function – for example, the intermittent wiper relay.*

11 The relays are divided between the electrical wiring/relay block under the right-hand side of the facia and the engine compartment fusebox. Some models may feature a separate relay box under the upper facia panel above the steering column. Typically, the flasher relay and main power relay will be inside the car, with the rest under the bonnet. The central locking control unit is located under the upper section of the facia, mounted at the back of the crossmember – see Chapter 11.

12 If a circuit or system controlled by a relay develops a fault, and the relay is suspect, operate the system. If the relay is functioning, it should be possible to hear it 'click' as it is energised. If this is the case, the fault lies with the components or wiring of the system.

13 If the relay is not being energised, then either the relay is not receiving a main supply or a switching voltage, or the relay itself is faulty. Testing is by the substitution of a known good unit, but be careful – while some relays are identical in appearance and in operation, others look similar but perform different functions.

14 To remove a relay, first ensure that the relevant circuit is switched off. The relay can then simply be pulled out from the socket, and pushed back into position.

4.3 Disconnect the wiring plug from the ignition switch

4.5a Cut a slot in the head of the retaining bolt...

4.5b... then undo it using a screwdriver

4.6a With the key in position, press down on the locking peg...

4.6b... and withdraw the ignition switch

4.7a Fit a new security (shear) bolt...

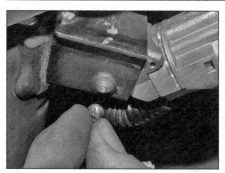

4.7b... and tighten until the head breaks off

4.9 Disconnect the wiring connectors

4.10a Release the retaining clip...

4.10b... and withdraw the switch

4.13a Release the locking clamp...

4.13b... to free the locating peg at the top of the column

a) *Make sure that ignition switch locking pin engages correctly.*
b) *Fit a new security bolt to hold the steering lock in position (see illustrations).*
c) *Make sure all wiring connections are secure.*
d) *Refit the steering column shrouds as described in Chapter 11 Section 24.*

Windscreen wiper switch

8 Remove the steering column shrouds as described in Chapter 11 Section 24.
9 Disconnect the wiring plug connectors from the base of the switch **(see illustration)**.
10 Use a small screwdriver to depress the release tab on the front of the switch, then withdraw the switch and remove it from the steering column **(see illustrations)**.
11 Refitting is a reversal of removal.

Lights/indicator switch

12 Remove the airbag rotary contact (clockspring), from the top of the steering column, as described in Section 22.
13 Release the retaining clamp from the rear of the switch assembly **(see illustrations)**. This holds a locating peg in the top of the steering column housing to prevent it from moving.
14 Withdraw the switch assembly from the top of the steering column, and disconnect the wiring connectors as it is removed **(see illustration)**.
15 Refitting is a reversal of removal.

Heated rear window switch

16 Remove the radio/CD player and trim panel as described in Section 17.

17 Release the retaining clips at the rear of the panel, and then withdraw the switch from the front of the trim panel **(see illustration)**.
18 Refitting is a reversal of removal.

Hazard warning light switch

19 Remove the radio/CD player and trim panel as described in Section 17.
20 Release the retaining clips at the rear of the panel, and then withdraw the switch from the front of the trim panel **(see illustration)**.
21 Refitting is a reversal of removal.

Air conditioning switch

22 Remove the radio/CD player and trim panel as described in Section 17.
23 Release the retaining clips at the

4.14 Remove the switch assembly from the steering column

4.17 Remove the heated rear window switch

4.20 Remove the hazard warning light switch

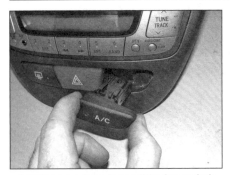

4.23 Remove the air conditioning switch

4.26a Release the retaining clips...

4.26b... and pull the switch from the control panel

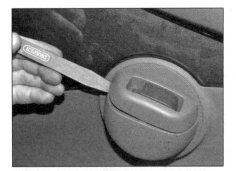

4.26b... and pull the switch from the control panel

4.29 Unclip the switch from the facia

removed as described in Chapter 3 Section 9.

26 Release the retaining clips at the rear of the panel, and then pull the switch to release it from the rear of the heater control panel **(see illustrations)**.

27 Refitting is a reversal of removal.

Headlight beam adjuster

28 Reach up behind the facia on the right-hand side, and push the switch to release it from the front of the facia panel.

29 Disconnect the wiring connector from the back of the switch, and withdraw the beam adjuster switch from the facia **(see illustration)**.

30 Refitting is a reversal of removal.

Electric window switches

31 Taking care not to mark the trim, prise out the switch panel from the door and disconnect the wiring connector **(see illustrations)**.

32 Release the retaining clips and pull the switch to remove it from the trim panel **(see illustration)**.

33 Refitting is a reversal of removal.

Door courtesy light switches

34 Open the relevant door. Remove the screw securing the switch to the door frame, and then prise the switch out of its location **(see illustrations)**.

35 Disconnect the wiring plug and remove the switch. Make sure that the wiring does not drop back into the aperture by using tape or string to secure it **(see illustration)**.

36 Refitting is a reversal of removal.

rear of the panel, and then withdraw the switch from the front of the trim panel **(see illustration)**.

24 Refitting is a reversal of removal.

Heater blower motor switch

25 The switch can only be removed from the back of the heater control panel, which is

4.31a Unclip the switch trim from the door panel...

4.31b... disconnect the wiring plug...

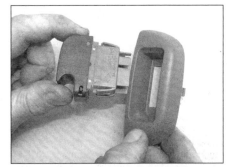

4.32... and unclip the switch from the outer trim

4.34a Undo the retaining screw...

4.34b... and remove the switch from the door pillar

4.35 Make sure the wiring connector does not drop inside the door pillar

5.2a Disconnect the wiring connector...

5.2b... and pull off the rubber cover for access to the headlight bulb

5.3a Unhook the wire clip at the top...

Handbrake-on warning switch

37 Refer to Chapter 9 Section 17.

Brake light switch

38 Refer to Chapter 9 Section 17.

5 Bulbs (exterior lights) – renewal

1 Whenever a bulb is renewed, note the following points:

a) *Disconnect the battery negative lead before starting work (see 'Disconnecting the battery' in Reference).*

b) *Remember that, if the light has just been in use, the bulb may be extremely hot.*

c) *Always check the bulb contacts and holder, ensuring that there is clean metal-to metal contact between the bulb and its live(s) and earth. Clean off any corrosion or dirt before fitting a new bulb.*

d) *Wherever bayonet-type bulbs are fitted (see Specifications), ensure that the live contact(s) bear firmly against the bulb contact.*

e) *Always ensure that the new bulb is of the correct rating, and that it is completely clean before fitting it; this applies particularly to headlight/fog light bulbs (see below).*

Headlight

Note: *Access to the headlight bulbholders*

5.3b... then hinge it down...

5.3c... and remove the bulb

is not great. On the passenger side, it may be helpful to remove the battery (Chapter 5A Section 4), or at least to remove the clamp and move it a little to improve access. Removing the headlight is quite involved (see Section 7) but may be the only option otherwise.

2 Disconnect the wiring connector from the rear of the bulb, then pull off the rubber cover **(see illustrations)**.

3 Release the bulb's wire retaining clip by unhooking it sideways at the top, then pivot the clip down. Withdraw the bulb **(see illustrations)**.

4 When handling the new bulb, use a tissue or clean cloth, to avoid touching the glass with the fingers; moisture and grease from the skin can cause blackening and rapid failure of this type of bulb. If the glass is accidentally touched, wipe it clean using methylated spirit.

5 Install the new bulb, ensuring that its locating tabs are correctly seated in the light cut-outs. Secure the bulb in position with the spring clip.

6 Refit the rubber cover, ensuring that a good seal is made to the back of the headlight. Reconnect the wiring connector.

Front sidelight

7 Refer to the note before paragraph 2 before starting. Disconnect the wiring plug from the bulbholder. Twist the bulbholder anti-clockwise, and pull it from the rear of the headlight **(see illustrations)**.

8 Pull out the wedge-base bulb from the holder, and fit a new one firmly into place **(see illustration)**.

9 Refit the bulbholder, twisting it firmly into place to secure it, and reconnect the wiring plug.

5.7a Disconnect the wiring connector...

5.7b... twist the sidelight bulbholder anti-clockwise...

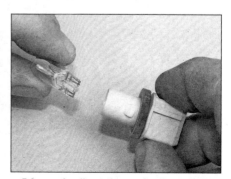

5.8... and pull out the wedge-base bulb

5.10a Disconnect the wiring connector...

5.10b... twist the indicator bulbholder anti-clockwise...

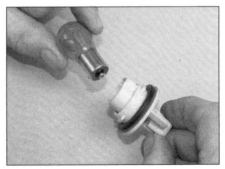

5.11... then push and twist out the bayonet bulb

Front direction indicator light

10 Refer to the note before paragraph 2 before starting. Disconnect the wiring plug from the bulbholder. Twist the bulbholder anti-clockwise, and pull it from the rear of the headlight **(see illustrations)**.
11 Depress and twist the bulb anti-clockwise to remove it from the holder, and fit a new one firmly into place **(see illustration)**.
12 Refit the bulbholder, twisting it firmly into place to secure it, and reconnect the wiring plug.

Indicator side repeater light

13 Slide the light unit to the front, against its internal spring clip. Hold the light against the spring tension, and unhook its rear edge **(see illustration)**.
14 Withdraw the light unit, and disconnect

the wiring plug, using a small screwdriver if necessary **(see illustration)**. To avoid the possibility of the wiring and plug disappearing back inside the hole in the wing, tape it temporarily in place.
15 The side repeater is a sealed unit and is sold as a complete unit with the bulb. We found if the lens was carefully cut away from the base, the wedge-base bulb could be pulled out from the holder and renewed. The lens will need to be re-sealed to the base on completion **(see illustrations)**.
16 Refitting is a reversal of removal.

Front fog lights

17 Remove the wheel arch liner as described in Chapter 11, Section 21
18 Reach behind the front bumper and disconnect the wiring connector from the rear of the fog light unit **(see illustration)**.

19 Twist the bulb holder and remove the bulb complete with holder from the fog light unit **(see illustration)**. Note the bulb is part of the holder.
20 Refitting is a reversal of removal.

Daytime running lights – Later models

21 On later models, there are daytime running lights fitted to the front bumper. These are fitted with LED lights and have to be changed as a complete unit if they are faulty, see Section 7.

Rear lights – C1 and 107 models

22 Open the tailgate, and undo the two retaining screws from inside the tailgate aperture **(see illustration)**.
23 Working at the front edge of the light unit, carefully lever the light unit away from the body to release it from the two locating pegs

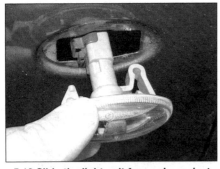

5.13 Slide the light unit forwards against the spring, and unhook it at the back

5.14 Disconnect the wiring connector

5.15a The side repeater can be split in two to renew the wedge-base bulb

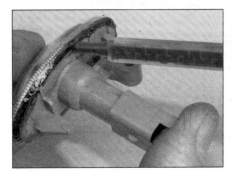

5.15b The side repeater will need to be resealed

5.18 Disconnect the wiring connector

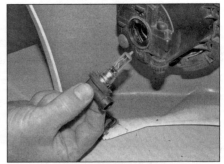

5.19 Remove bulb and holder

5.22 Undo the two retaining screws

5.23a Using a wide lever, carefully unclip...

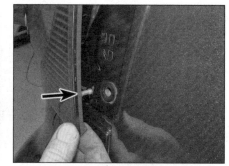

5.23b... the lower locating peg...

at the top and bottom of the light unit **(see illustrations)**.

24 As the light unit is removed, disconnect the wiring plug from the rear of the light unit **(see illustration)**.

25 Release the retaining clips, and withdraw the bulbholder from the rear of the light unit **(see illustrations)**.

26 Any of the bayonet-fitting bulbs can now be removed by pressing and turning them anti-clockwise **(see illustration)**.

27 Fit the new bulb(s), and then clip the bulbholder back onto the light unit. Reconnect the wiring plug and refit the light unit, making sure the locating pegs are correctly fitted.

Rear lights – Aygo models

28 Open the tailgate, then release the retaining clips and remove the carpet trim from the side of the luggage compartment **(see illustration)**.

5.23c... and the upper locating peg

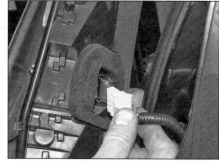

5.24 Disconnect the wiring connector

29 Working up under the plastic side trim panel disconnect the wiring connector and undo the securing nut from the rear of the light unit **(see illustrations)**. If required, to

make access easier, undo the screw and release the clips from the plastic trim panel and remove it from the side of the luggage compartment.

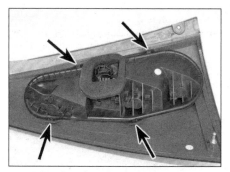

5.25a Release the retaining clips...

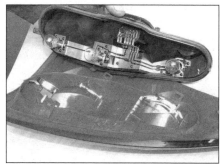

5.25b... and unclip the bulbholder

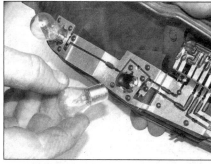

5.26 Push and twist out the bayonet bulb

5.28 Remove the inner carpet trim panel

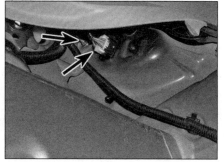

5.29a Undo the securing nut and disconnect the wiring connector...

5.29b... seen with the upper plastic trim removed for clarity

5.30 Carefully withdraw the light unit from the vehicle

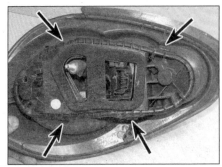

5.31a Release the retaining clips...

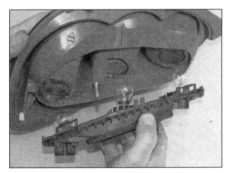

5.31b... and unclip the bulbholder

5.32 Push and twist out the bayonet bulb

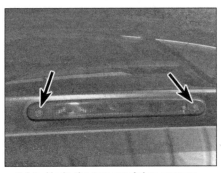

5.34a Undo the two retaining screws...

5.34b... and withdraw the high-level brake light

30 Carefully lever the light unit away from the body to release it from the locating pegs **(see illustration)**.
31 Release the retaining clips, and withdraw the bulbholder from the rear of the light unit **(see illustrations)**.
32 Any of the bayonet-fitting bulbs can now be removed by pressing and turning them anti-clockwise **(see illustration)**.
33 Fit the new bulb(s), and then clip the bulbholder back onto the light unit. Refit the light unit, aligning the locating pegs into the vehicle body. Reconnect the wiring plug and tighten the securing nut on the rear of the light unit.

High-level brake light
34 Undo the two retaining screws and unclip the light unit from the rear of the roof panel **(see illustrations)**.
35 Disconnect the wiring connector and the rear washer pipe from the rear of the light unit **(see illustrations)**.
36 Release the retaining clips, and withdraw the bulbholder from the rear of the light unit **(see illustration)**.
37 Pull out the wedge-base bulb from the holder, and fit a new one firmly into place **(see illustration)**.
38 Refitting is a reversal of removal.

Number plate light – C1 and 107 models
39 Reaching up behind the bumper, release the retaining clips and unclip the number plate light from the bumper **(see illustrations)**.

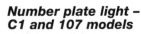

5.35a Disconnect the wiring connector...

5.35b... and the rear screen washer pipe

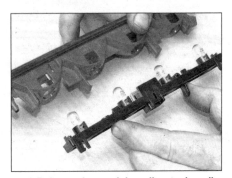

5.36 Release the retaining clips and unclip the bulbholder

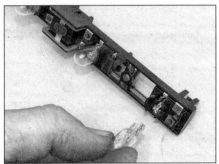

5.37 Pull out the wedge-base bulbs

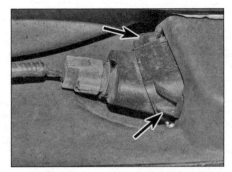

5.39a Release the retaining clips...

5.39b... and withdraw the number plate light unit

5.40 Twist and remove the bulbholder...

5.41... and the pull out the wedge-base bulb

5.43 Unclip the number plate light unit...

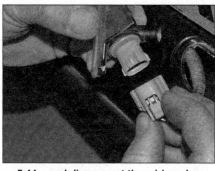

5.44... and disconnect the wiring plug

5.45 Twist and remove the bulbholder...

40 Twist the bulbholder anti-clockwise from the light **(see illustration)**.
41 Pull out the wedge-base bulb, and press a new one into place **(see illustration)**.
42 Refitting is a reversal of removal.

Number plate light – Aygo models

43 Using a thin screwdriver, release the retaining clips and unclip the number plate light from the bumper **(see illustration)**.
44 Disconnect the wiring connector from the rear of the light unit as it is removed **(see illustration)**.
45 Twist the bulbholder anti-clockwise to remove it from the light **(see illustration)**.
46 Pull out the wedge-base bulb, and press a new one into place **(see illustration)**.
47 Refitting is a reversal of removal.

6 Bulbs (interior lights) – renewal

General

1 Refer to Section 5, paragraph 1.

Interior and map reading lights

2 Carefully prise the light unit lens down at the side, using a small screwdriver and disconnect the wiring connector as it is removed **(see illustrations)**.

3 Squeeze the retaining clips together and withdraw the bulbholder from the light unit **(see illustration)**.

4 Pull out the wedge-base bulb, and press a new one into place **(see illustration)**.
5 Refitting is a reversal of removal.

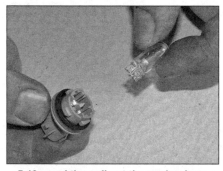

5.46... and the pull out the wedge-base bulb

6.2a Carefully prise out the interior light unit...

6.2b... and disconnect the wiring connector

6.3 Release the retaining clips and remove the bulbholder

6.4 Pull out the wedge-base bulb

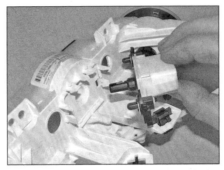

6.8 Unclip the heater blower switch

6.9 Pull out the small wedge-base bulb

Instrument panel illumination

6 The instrument panel is a sealed unit and can only be renewed as a complete unit. Remove the instrument panel, as described in Section 11 of this Chapter.

Switch illumination

7 The bulbs are integral with the switches, and cannot be renewed separately.

Heater control illumination

8 Remove the heater blower motor switch **(see illustration)**, as described in Section 4 of this Chapter.
9 Pull out the wedge-base bulb, and press a new one into place **(see illustration)**.
10 Refit the heater blower motor switch, as described in Section 4 of this Chapter.

7.2a Remove the two upper mounting bolts...

7.2b.. and lower mounting bolt

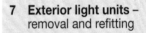

**7 Exterior light units –
removal and refitting**

Note: *Before removing any wiring connections, disconnect the battery negative lead, and position the lead away from the battery (see 'Disconnecting the battery').*

Headlight

1 Remove the front bumper as described in Chapter 11 Section 6.
2 Remove the two securing bolts on the top of the headlight unit, and the one at the lower outer corner of the headlight unit **(see illustrations)**.
3 Pull the unit forwards slightly, and then disconnect the four wiring connectors from the back of the headlight – one adjustment motor, three bulb holders – and remove it **(see illustrations)**.
4 Refitting is a reversal of removal.

Front direction indicator light

5 The front indicator is integral with the headlight.

Indicator side repeater light

6 The procedure is described as part of the bulb renewal procedure in Section 5 of this Chapter.

7.3a Disconnect the adjuster motor wiring connector...

7.3b...and the bulb wiring connectors

Front fog lights

7 Release the fixings and pull back the front of the wheel arch liner.
8 Disconnect the wiring connector from the rear of the fog light unit.
9 Undo the retaining screw and withdraw the light unit from the rear of the front bumper **(see illustrations)**.
10 Refitting is a reversal of removal.

7.9a Undo the retaining screw...

7.9b...and remove the light unit

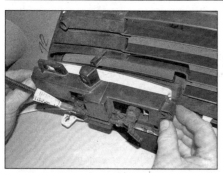

7.12a Remove the light unit...

7.12b... undo the retaining screw...

7.12c... disconnect the wiring connector

Daytime running lights – Later models

11 Release the fixings and pull back the front of the wheel arch liner.

12 On Aygo models, undo the retaining screws and remove the complete light unit and mounting bracket from the rear of the bumper. Undo the retaining screw from the front of the light unit and withdraw it from the mounting bracket. disconnect the wiring connector as the light unit is removed **(see illustrations)**.

13 On C1 and 107 models, disconnect the wiring connector from the rear of the light unit. Undo the retaining screws and remove the light unit from the rear of the bumper **(see illustrations)**.

14 Refitting is a reversal of removal.

Rear lights

15 The procedure is described as part of the bulb renewal procedure in Section 5 of this Chapter.

Rear number plate light

16 The procedure is described as part of the bulb renewal procedure in Section 5 of this Chapter.

High-level brake light

17 The procedure is described as part of the bulb renewal procedure in Section 5 of this Chapter.

7.13a Disconnect the wiring connector...

7.13b... and remove the light unit

8 Headlight adjuster components – removal and refitting

1 All models are equipped with an electrical vertical beam adjuster unit – this can be used to adjust the headlight beam to compensate for the load which the car is carrying.

2 A manual adjuster switch is provided on the right-hand side of the facia which has four positions. This needs to be set at the correct level to prevent dazzling other road users.

a) *0 – Driver only or driver and front passenger.*
b) *1 – Driver and all passengers.*
c) *2 – Driver, all passengers and full luggage compartment.*
d) *3 – Driver only and full luggage at the rear of the vehicle.*

Adjuster switch

3 Refer to Section 4.

Adjuster motor

4 The motor is fitted to the rear of the headlight unit. First remove the headlight unit from the vehicle, as described in Section 7 of this Chapter

5 Release the securing clip and twist the motor, and withdraw it from the rear of the light unit. Unclip the balljoint from the slot inside the headlight unit reflector to remove completely **(see illustrations)**.

6 Refitting is a reversal of removal. Making

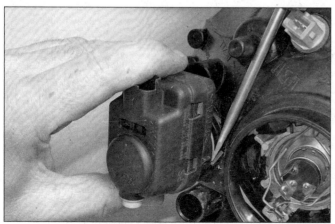

8.5a Release the securing clip...

8.5b... and disengage the balljoint from the slot in the reflector

9.2 Headlight manual adjuster screws

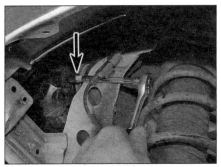

9.3 Turning outer headlight adjuster – Aygo models

11 Instrument panel – removal and refitting

Removal

1 Remove the rev counter, as described in the previous Section. On models without rev counter fitted, remove the steering column upper shroud, as described in Chapter 11 Section 24.
2 Undo the retaining bolts at the bottom of the instrument panel, and then withdraw it up from the top of the steering column (see illustrations).
3 As the instrument panel is moved forwards, disconnect the fourteen wiring block connectors from the rear of the instrument panel and remove it from the facia (see illustration). Note: These connections are all different sizes, shapes and colours, so should not need to be labelled for refitting.

Refitting

4 Refitting is a reversal of removal.

12 Horn – removal and refitting

Removal

1 The horn is positioned behind the front bumper, and in front of the radiator, to the left-hand side of the vehicle. Remove the front bumper, as described in Chapter 11 Section 6.

sure the balljoint is located in the slot in the headlight reflector and the motor is secured in position with the retaining clip.

9 Headlight beam alignment – general information

1 Accurate adjustment of the headlight beam is only possible using optical beam-setting equipment, and this work should therefore be carried out by a franchised dealer or suitably-equipped workshop.
2 For reference, the headlights can be finely adjusted by rotating the adjuster screws fitted to the rear of each light unit (see illustration).
3 On Aygo models, remove the wheel arch liner and access the outer adjuster from under the wheel arch (see illustration).

10 Rev counter – removal and refitting

Removal

1 Disconnect the battery negative lead, and position the lead away from the battery (see *Disconnecting the battery*).
2 Remove the steering column upper shroud (see illustration), as described in Chapter 11 Section 24.
3 Undo the retaining bolt on the top of the instrument panel, and then withdraw the rev counter, disconnecting the wiring connector as it is removed (see illustrations).

Refitting

4 Refitting is a reversal of removal.

10.2 Remove the instrument panel upper shroud

10.3a Undo the rev counter mounting bolt...

10.3b... and disconnect the wiring plug as it is removed

11.2a Undo the retaining bolts...

11.2b... and lift the instrument panel upwards

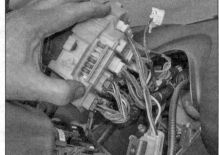

11.3 Disconnect the wiring block connectors

2 Disconnect the wiring plug from the bottom of the horn **(see illustration)**.

3 Unscrew the single horn mounting bolt, and withdraw the horn from its mounting **(see Illustration)**.

Refitting

4 Refitting is a reversal of removal.

13 Wiper arms – removal and refitting

Removal

1 Operate the wiper motor, then switch it off so that the wiper arm returns to the 'park' position. If required, use a piece of tape on the screen, to mark the position of the blade for refitting.

Front wiper arm

2 Prise off the wiper arm spindle nut cover, then slacken and remove the spindle nut **(see illustrations)**.

3 Lift the blade off the glass, and pull the wiper arm off its spindle. Note that on some models, the wiper arms may be very tight on the spindle splines – it may be necessary to use a small puller to release the wiper arm from the spindle **(see illustrations)**.

Rear wiper arm

4 Unclip the wiper arm spindle nut cover, then slacken and remove the spindle nut **(see illustrations)**.

5 Lift the blade off the glass, and pull the

12.2 Disconnect the wiring connector...

12.3... and unbolt the horn from the front panel

13.2a Prise off the windscreen wiper arm nut cover...

13.2b... then unscrew and remove the nut

wiper arm off its spindle. Note that on some models, the wiper arm may be very tight on the spindle splines – it may be necessary to use a small puller to release the wiper arm from the spindle **(see illustrations)**.

Refitting

6 Ensure that the wiper arm and spindle splines are clean and dry, and then refit the arm to the spindle. Where applicable,

13.3a Using a puller to remove the windscreen wiper arm...

13.3b... off the splines and unclip the support linkage

13.4a Unclip the tailgate wiper arm cover up, or off completely...

13.4b... and unscrew the securing nut

13.5a Using a puller to release...

13.5b... the wiper arm off the splines

14.2 Disconnect the windscreen washer pipe

14.3a Remove the securing clips...

14.3b... and remove the trim covers from the scuttle panel

14.4a Remove the wiper motor assembly mounting bolts...

14.4b... lift out the wiper motor and linkage...

14.4c... and disconnect the wiring plug from the wiper motor

align the wiper blade with the tape fitted on removal.

7 Refit the spindle nut, tightening it securely, and clip the nut cover back into position.

14 Windscreen wiper motor and linkage – removal and refitting

Removal

1 Remove the front wiper arm as described in Section 13.

2 Open the bonnet and disconnect the windscreen washer pipe from the driver's side of the scuttle panel trim cover **(see illustration)**.

3 Prise out the various retaining clips from the two trim covers, and then unclip and remove them as one complete piece **(see illustrations)**.

4 Remove the two bolts, and then lift the wiper motor and linkage out from below the windscreen. Disconnect the wiring plug from the motor as it is removed **(see illustrations)**.

Refitting

5 Refitting is a reversal of removal, bearing in mind the following points:
a) Ensure that the motor spindle is in the 'parked' position, then refit the washer and tighten the nut.
b) Tighten all fasteners securely.
c) Refit the wiper arms with reference to Section 13.

15 Tailgate wiper motor – removal and refitting

Removal

1 Remove the rear wiper arm as described in Section 13.

2 Open the tailgate, and remove the inner trim panel which is clipped in place over the wiper motor **(see illustration)**.

3 Disconnect the wiper motor wiring plug **(see illustration)**.

4 Unclip the wiper arm spindle nut cover, then slacken and remove the spindle nut, and remove the lower plastic spacer/washer **(see illustrations)**.

15.2 Unclip the trim cover

15.3 Disconnect the wiper motor wiring plug

15.4a Unclip the plastic cover...

5 Remove the inner motor mounting bolt, and remove the motor from the inside of the tailgate **(see illustrations)**. If the grommet/spacer on the tailgate glass is loose, remove it for safekeeping until the wiper motor is refitted.

Refitting

6 Refitting is a reversal of removal. Tighten the mounting bolts securely.

16 Windscreen/tailgate washer system components – removal and refitting

Washer fluid reservoir

Removal

1 Remove the front bumper (see Chapter 11 Section 6).
2 Remove the driver's side headlight as described in Section 7.
3 Anticipate some spillage of washer fluid (have a suitable container ready), and then disconnect the washer hoses, noting their fitted locations **(see illustration)**.
4 Disconnect the wiring plug from the washer pump **(see illustration)**.
5 Remove the reservoir mounting bolts, then lift the reservoir to disengage the mounting pegs on the inner wing and manoeuvre it out from its location **(see illustrations)**.

Refitting

6 Refitting is a reversal of removal. Make sure the washer hoses are securely reconnected to their original positions.

Washer fluid pump

Removal

7 Proceed as described in paragraphs 1 to 4.
8 Prise the pump from the reservoir, and recover the rubber sealing grommet.

Refitting

9 Examine the rubber sealing grommet, and renew if necessary.
10 Refitting is a reversal of removal, but take care not to push the grommet into the reservoir when refitting the pump. Make sure that the pump is securely fitted in its sealing grommet, and make sure that the fluid hose(s) are securely reconnected.

Windscreen washer jet

Removal

11 The windscreen washer jets are located in the plastic trim covers, just below the windscreen. Remove the trim covers as described in Section 14, paragraphs 2 and 3.
12 Carefully prise the washer jet from the plastic trim covers, disconnect the washer hose from the jet, and remove the jet completely.

15.4b... remove the securing nut...

15.4c... and remove the lower spacer/washer

15.5a Remove the mounting bolt...

15.5b... and withdraw the wiper motor

Refitting

13 Refitting is a reversal of removal, but make sure that the washer hose connections are securely remade before refitting the trim panels.

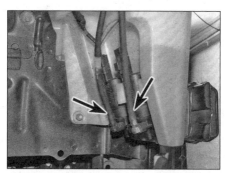
16.3 Disconnect the washer fluid hoses

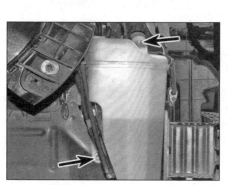
16.5a Undo the washer reservoir mounting bolts...

Tailgate washer jet

Removal

14 The tailgate washer jet is located in the

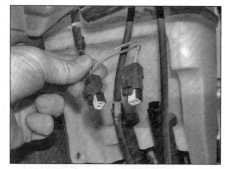
16.4 Disconnect the wiring plugs from the washer pumps

16.5b... and remove the reservoir from the vehicle

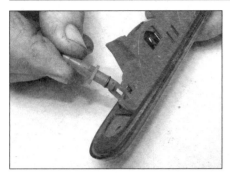

16.15 Unclip the washer jet from the
high-level brake light unit

high-level brake light. Remove the high-level
brake light as described in Section 7.
15 Release the retaining clips and pull the
washer jet from the rear of the high-level

brake light **(see illustration)**. When releasing
the retaining clips take great care, as they are
easily broken.

Refitting

16 Refitting is a reversal of removal, but make
sure that the fluid hose connection is securely
remade.

17 Radio/CD unit –
removal and refitting

Removal

1 Carefully pull the heater control knob to
release it from the bottom of the radio/CD
trim panel, and undo the retaining screw **(see
illustration)**.
2 Using a plastic trim tool, carefully lever the

radio/CD unit complete with trim panel from
the facia **(see illustration)**.
3 As the unit is removed, disconnect the
wiring connectors and aerial lead from the
rear of the radio/CD **(see illustration)**.
4 Also disconnect the wiring connectors from
the switches on the lower part of the trim
panel **(see illustration)**.
5 Release the radio/CD securing clips at each
side, also release the securing clips at the top
and bottom, and then slide the radio/CD out
from the trim panel **(see illustrations)**.

Refitting

6 Refitting is a reversal of removal.

18 Speakers –
removal and refitting

Door speaker

1 Remove the door trim panel as described in
Chapter 11 Section 11.
2 Disconnect the speaker wiring plug **(see
illustration)**.
3 The door speakers are secured to the door
trim panel by retaining bolts and nuts **(see
illustration)**. Note: The amount of bolts may
vary between two or four bolts, depending on
type of speaker fitted.
4 Refitting is a reversal of removal.

Facia speaker

5 Taking care not to damage the facia,
first prise up the front of the speaker cover,

17.1 Unclip the heater blower switch and
undo the retaining screw

17.2 Unclip the radio/CD trim panel from
the facia

17.5a Release the radio/CD securing clips
on the side...

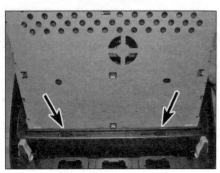

17.3 Disconnect the wiring and aerial lead
from the radio/CD

17.4 Disconnect the wiring connectors
from the switches

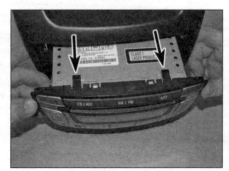

17.5b... at the bottom...

17.5c... and the top to withdraw the radio/
CD from the panel

18.2 Disconnect the wiring plug from the
door speaker

and then pull it rearwards to release it **(see illustration)**.

6 Undo the two speaker mounting bolts **(see illustration)**

7 Lift the speaker out of its location, disconnect its wiring plug, and remove it from the facia **(see illustration)**.

8 Refitting is a reversal of removal.

19 Radio aerial – removal and refitting

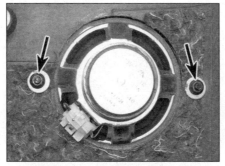

18.3 This speaker is secured by two securing nuts

18.5 Unclip the speaker grille cover

Removal

1 If only the aerial mast is to be removed, this can be unscrewed from the aerial base on the roof of the vehicle.

2 Remove the interior/map reading light from the front of the headlining, as described in Section 6 of this Chapter.

3 To remove the aerial mast complete with base, undo the retaining nut and remove the aerial base and mast from the roof of the vehicle **(see illustration)**.

4 To remove the aerial lead, first remove the radio unit as described in Section 17 of this Chapter and remove the upper section of the facia, for access to the aerial lead, as described in Chapter 11.

5 The aerial lead goes from the back of the radio/CD and runs across the top of the facia crossmember. From there, it runs up the passenger A-pillar **(see illustrations)**, and across under the headlining to the base of the aerial, where it is secured by a nut.

Refitting

6 Refitting is a reversal of removal.

20 Anti-theft immobiliser – general information

1 An engine immobiliser system is fitted as standard to all models, and the system is operated automatically every time the ignition key is inserted/removed.

2 The immobiliser system ensures that the car can only be started using the original keys supplied with the car when new. Each

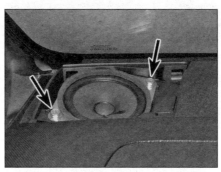

18.6 Undo the speaker retaining bolts

18.7 Lift out and disconnect the wiring connector from the speaker

key contains an electric chip (transponder), which is programmed with a code. When the key is inserted into the ignition switch, it uses the current present in the sensor coil (which is fitted to the switch housing) to send a signal to the immobiliser electronic control unit (ECU). The ECU checks this code every time the ignition on. If the key code does not match the ECU code, the ECU will disable the fuel pump and ignition circuits to prevent the engine being started.

3 The security indicator light on the facia panel indicates when the system is active. Should the light continue to flash once the ignition key has been inserted, the engine will not start – the most likely reason for this being the use of an uncoded key.

4 If the ignition key is lost, a new one can be obtained from a franchised dealer. They have access to the correct key code for the

immobiliser system of your car, and will be able to supply a new coded key.

5 If you have any spare keys cut, if they are not coded correctly, they will only open the doors, etc, and will not be capable of starting the engine. For this reason, it may be best to have any spare keys supplied by your franchised dealer.

6 If the battery in the key requires changing, refer to Chapter 11 Section 16.

21 Airbag system – general information, precautions and system de-activation

General information

1 Driver's and front seat passenger's airbags are fitted as standard equipment on

19.3 Aerial base/lead retaining nut

19.5a The aerial lead is routed along the crossmember...

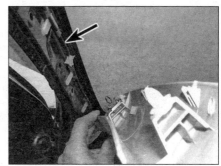

19.5b... and up the passenger side A-pillar

22.2a Driver's airbag Torx screw location –
early models

22.2b On later models, unclip the plastic
covers...

22.2c...and undo the retaining screws

most models. The driver's airbag is fitted to the steering wheel centre pad, while the passenger's unit is fitted to the top of the facia. These airbags are intended to deploy in the event of a head-on collision.

2 Later models may also have side airbags, which fire from modules built into the front seats. The side airbags are only supposed to be triggered in the event of a lateral impact.

3 The system is armed only when the ignition is switched on. However, a reserve power source maintains a power supply to the system in the event of a break in the main electrical supply. The system is activated by 'g' sensors (deceleration sensors), incorporated in the electronic control unit. All models have separate sensors, in the B-pillars (and in the front doors on 3-door models). Note that the electronic control unit also controls the front seat belt tensioners, fitted to all models.

4 The airbags are inflated by gas generators, which force the bags out from their locations. Although these are safety items, their deployment is violently rapid, and this may cause injury if they are triggered unintentionally.

Precautions

⚠ Warning: The following precautions must be observed when working on vehicles equipped with an airbag system, to prevent the possibility of personal injury.

General precautions

5 The following precautions must be observed when carrying out work on a vehicle equipped with an airbag:

a) Do not disconnect the battery with the engine running.
b) Before carrying out any work in the vicinity of the airbag, removal of any of the airbag components, or any welding work on the car, de-activate the system as described in the following sub-Section.
c) Do not attempt to test any of the airbag system circuits using test meters or any other test equipment.
d) If the airbag warning light comes on, or any fault in the system is suspected, consult a franchised dealer without delay. Do not attempt to carry out fault diagnosis, or any dismantling of the components.

When handling an airbag

a) Transport the airbag by itself, bag upwards.
b) Do not put your arms around the airbag.
c) Carry the airbag close to the body, bag outwards.
d) Do not drop the airbag or expose it to impacts.
e) Do not attempt to dismantle the airbag unit.
f) Do not connect any form of electrical equipment to any part of the airbag circuit.

When storing an airbag unit

a) Store the unit in a cupboard with the airbag upwards.
b) Do not expose the airbag to temperatures above 80°C.
c) Do not expose the airbag to flames.
d) Do not attempt to dispose of the airbag – consult a franchised dealer.

e) Never refit an airbag that is known to be faulty or damaged.

De-activation of airbag system

6 The system must be de-activated as follows, before carrying out any work on the airbag components or surrounding area.
a) Switch off the ignition.
b) Remove the ignition key.
c) Switch off all electrical equipment.
d) Disconnect the battery negative lead (see 'Disconnecting the battery' in Reference).
e) Insulate the battery negative terminal and the end of the battery negative lead to prevent any possibility of contact.
f) Wait for at least two minutes before carrying out any further work.

22 Airbag system components – removal and refitting

⚠ Warning: Refer to the precautions given in Section 21 before attempting to carry out work on the airbag components.

Driver's airbag

Removal

1 De-activate the airbag system as described in Section 21. The airbag unit is an integral part of the steering wheel centre pad.

2 The airbag's two Torx screws are fitted to the back of the steering wheel centre pad. On early models, there is a small recess to access the retaining screws. On later models, unclip the plastic trim to access the retaining screws (see illustrations). The screws cannot be removed completely – when the screw head is flush with the back of the wheel pad, it has been released.

3 If required, to free the airbag unit completely, carefully pull away the back section of the wheel boss each side – this will pull the airbag screws out a fraction, and allow the airbag to be released (see illustration).

4 Lift the unit from the wheel slightly, and disconnect the wiring plug connectors. Prise up the small yellow retaining clip on the back of the plug, then disconnect the plug from the airbag (see illustrations).

22.3 Withdraw the airbag from the steering
wheel

22.4a Release the locking clip...

22.4b... and disconnect the airbag wiring plug

22.5 Disconnect the earth wire for the airbag

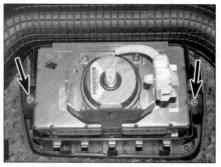

22.9 Passenger airbag retaining nuts

5 Disconnect the earth wire **(see illustration)** and remove the airbag from the steering wheel. Store the airbag in a safe place, with reference to the precautions in Section 21.

Refitting

6 Refitting is a reversal of removal, noting the following points:
a) *The battery must still be disconnected when reconnecting the airbag wiring.*
b) *Ensure that the airbag wiring connectors are securely reconnected.*
c) *Tighten the airbag Torx screws securely.*

Passenger's airbag

Removal

7 De-activate the airbag system as described in Section 21.
8 Remove the upper section of the facia panel as described in Chapter 11 Section 26.
9 Turn the facia panel over, and remove the two airbag retaining nuts **(see illustration)**.
10 Carefully prise up the clips round the edge of the airbag, and release the unit from the facia.

Refitting

11 Refitting is a reversal of removal, bearing in mind the following points:
a) *The battery must still be disconnected when reconnecting the airbag wiring.*
b) *Make sure that the wiring harness is routed as noted before removal, and that the connectors are reconnected to their original positions.*
c) *Make sure that the wiring connectors are securely reconnected.*
d) *Tighten the airbag mounting nuts securely.*

Airbag rotary contact (clockspring)

Removal

12 Remove the driver's airbag unit as described previously in this Section.
13 Remove the steering wheel as described in Chapter 10 Section 14.
14 Remove the steering column shrouds as described in Chapter 11 Section 24.
15 If the clockspring will be off the car for any length of time, secure it using tape so that it is not turned **(see illustrations)**. Note the alignment arrowhead at the bottom of the rotary contact.

16 Noting their positions for refitting, disconnect the wiring plug connectors from the bottom of the rotary contact **(see illustration)**.
17 Release the clips at the back of the unit (one each side, one at the top), then withdraw the rotary contact unit from the column – take care not to turn it as it is removed **(see illustration)**.

Refitting

18 Refitting is a reversal of removal.
19 If the steering column or the rotary contact has not been moved since removal, refit the steering wheel as described in Chapter 10 Section 14.
20 If the steering column or rotary contact has been moved, the rotary contact unit will need to be centralised. First, turn the rotary contact anti-clockwise gently, until resistance is felt. Now turn the

rotary contact about two and a half turns clockwise, until the arrowhead markings on the front face and outer cover are aligned **(see illustration 22.15b)**. **Note:** *It is not enough to simply align the marks – the unit must be centralised first, with the marks as confirmation. There should be approximately two and a half turns to the right and to the left from the central position.*
21 When you are sure the rotary contact is central, refit the steering wheel as described in Chapter 10 Section 14.

Side airbags

22 The side airbags are located internally within the front seat backrest, and no attempt should be made to remove them. Any suspected problems with the side airbag system should be referred to a franchised dealer. Remove the seats as described in Chapter 11 Section 22.

22.15a Tape the rotary contact to prevent it from turning...

22.15b... making sure the arrows are aligned

22.16 Disconnect the two wiring connectors...

22.17... and unclip the rotary contact 'clockspring' from the steering column

22.24 Withdraw the airbag on/off switch
from the facia

22.27a Remove the carpet retaining clip...

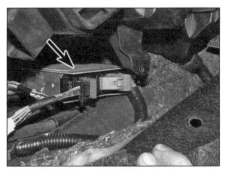

22.27b... and pull back the carpet to
access the control unit

22.28 Release the wiring connector locking
clips – arrowed

22.29 Remove the carpet retaining clip

22.30 Airbag control unit mounting bolts

Passenger airbag on/off switch

Removal

23 Reach up behind the facia on the right-hand side, and push the switch to release it from the front of the facia panel.

24 Disconnect the wiring connector from the back of the switch, and withdraw the airbag on/off switch from the facia **(see illustration)**.

Refitting

25 Refitting is a reversal of removal.

Airbag control unit

Removal

26 The airbag control unit is located behind the carpet trim panel in front of the centre console. Before removing the control unit, de-activate the airbag system as described in Section 21.

27 Working in the driver's side footwell, prise out the trim clip from the side of the carpet

trim, then pull the carpet down to access the control unit **(see illustrations)**.

28 Release the locking clips and then disconnect the wiring plugs from the side of the control unit **(see illustration)**. If there is any chance of incorrectly refitting them, mark them for position first.

29 Working in the passenger front footwell, prise out the trim clip from the side of the carpet trim, then pull the carpet down to access the mounting bolts for the control unit **(see illustration)**.

30 Remove the three retaining bolts used to secure the control unit, and remove it from the floor **(see illustration)**.

Refitting

31 Refitting is a reversal of removal, bearing in mind the following points:

a)   The battery must still be disconnected when reconnecting the airbag wiring.

b)   Make sure that the wiring connectors are securely reconnected.

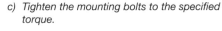

c)   Tighten the mounting bolts to the specified torque.

Side impact sensors

Removal

32 The sensors are located in the B-pillars, above the seat belt inertia reel on 5-door models and at the bottom of the front doors on 3-door models **(see illustrations)**. Before removing the sensors, de-activate the airbag system as described in Section 21.

33 On 5-door models, remove the B-pillar trim panel and front seat belt, as described in Chapter 11.

34 On 3-door models, remove the door trim panel, as described in Chapter 11 Section 11.

35 Disconnect the sensor wiring plug by squeezing the sides of the outer sleeve and separating the connector halves.

36 Unscrew the sensor mounting, and withdraw the sensor **(see illustrations)**.

22.32a Impact sensor location
(5-door models)

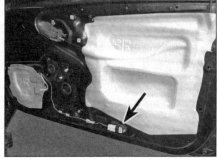

22.32b Impact sensor location
(3-door models)

22.36a Impact sensor securing nut
(5-door models)

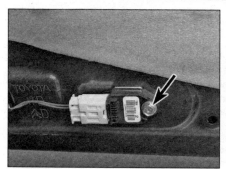

22.36b Impact sensor securing bolt
(3-door models)

23.2 Disconnect the wiring connectors
from the control unit

23.3 Steering motor electronic control unit
mounting bolts

Refitting

37 Refitting is a reversal of removal, bearing in mind the following points:
a) *The battery must still be disconnected when reconnecting the wiring.*
b) *Make sure that the wiring connectors are securely reconnected.*
c) *Tighten the mounting bolts to the specified torque.*

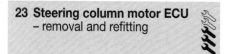

23 Steering column motor ECU – removal and refitting

Note: *Disconnect the battery negative lead*

(see ' *Disconnecting the battery'*). *Insulate the battery negative terminal and the end of the battery negative lead to prevent any possibility of contact. Wait for at least two minutes before carrying out any further work.*

Removal

1 The steering column motor electronic control unit is located behind the facia on the lower right-hand side, just below the headlight adjustment switch. Before removing the control unit, disconnect the battery negative lead (see *Disconnecting the battery*) and de-activate the airbag system as described in Section 21.
2 Working in the driver's side footwell,

disconnect the four wiring plugs from the lower part of the control unit **(see illustration)**. If there is any chance of incorrectly refitting them, mark them for position first.
3 Remove the two retaining bolts used to secure the control unit, and remove it from the floor **(see illustration)**.

Refitting

4 Refitting is a reversal of removal, bearing in mind the following points:
a) *The battery must still be disconnected when reconnecting the wiring connectors.*
b) *Make sure that the wiring connectors are securely reconnected.*
c) *Tighten the mounting bolts securely.*

Toyota Aygo wiring diagrams (typical)

Diagram 1

 WARNING: This vehicle is fitted with a supplemental restraint system (SRS) consisting of a combination of driver (and passenger) airbag(s), side impact protection airbags and seatbelt pre-tensioners. The use of electrical test equipment on any SRS wiring systems may cause the seatbelt pre-tensioners to abruptly retract and airbags to explosively deploy, resulting in potentially severe personal injury. Extreme care should be taken to correctly identify any circuits to be tested to avoid choosing any of the SRS wiring in error.
For further information see airbag system precautions in body electrical systems chapter.
Note: The SRS wiring harness can normally be identified by yellow and/or orange harness or harness connectors.

Key to symbols

Solenoid actuator		Bulb		Wire splice, soldered joint, or unspecified connector	
Earth point and location	E7	Switch		Connecting wires	
		Fuse	F26	Diode	
Wire colour (Blue/Yellow)	L/Y	Maxifuse fusible link	FL	Light-emitting diode	
		Resistor		Item number	12
Dashed outline denotes part of a larger item, containing in this case an electronic or solid state device. Connector number 3D, pins 16 & 17	3D 16 17 (K)	Variable resistor		Motor/pump	M
		Variable resistor		Heating element	

Engine fusebox 4

Fuse	Rating	Circuit protected
F1	50A	Automatic transmission, fan (Diesel)
F2	10A	Sidelights, dip and main beam
	20A	Daytime running lights
F3	30A	ABS/ESP
F4	30A	Ignition switch supply
F5	10A	Hazard warning lights, instrument cluster warning lights, direction indicators
F6	10A	Sidelights, dip and main beam
F7	15A	Interior light, speedometer, audio equipment, instrument cluster, tachometer
F8	15A	Engine management control unit (petrol)
	25A	Engine management control unit (Diesel)
F9	10A	Horn
F10	30A	Engine cooling fan (petrol)
F11	50A	ABS/ESP
F12	50A	Power steering

Motor fuse/relay board 1 5

Fuse	Rating	Circuit protected
F13	7.5A	Starter
F14	7.5A	Engine management control unit
R1		Starter relay

Motor fuse/relay board 2 15

Fuse	Rating	Circuit protected
F15	15A	Engine management control unit
F16	10A	RH main beam
F17	10A	LH main beam (control unit)
F18	10A	RH dipped beam
F19	10A	LH dipped beam (control unit)
F20	10A	Engine management control unit
R2		Air conditioning relay

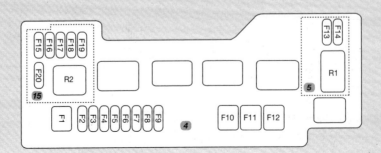

H47297

Wire colours

W	White	O	Orange
L	Blue	R	Red
BE	Beige	P	Pink
GR	Grey	G	Green
Y	Yellow	V	Violet
BR	Brown	SB	Sky blue
B	Black	LG	Light green

Key to items

1 Battery
2 Starter motor
3 Alternator
4 Engine fusebox
  R1 = engine cooling fan relay
  R2 = horn relay
6 Ignition switch
7 Instrument cluster
  a = alternator warning light
9 Horn
10 Steering rotary connector
11 Horn switch
12 Interior relay plate
13 Engine cooling fan
14 Engine coolant temperature sensor

Diagram 2

H47298

Instrument cluster fusebox ⑦

Fuse	Rating	Circuit protected
F1	10A	Stop lights, ABS, automatic gearbox
F2	25A	Central locking
F3	20A	Heated rear window
F4	7.5A	Rear lights, number plate lights, instrument cluster
F5	7.5A	Diagnostic connector
F6	7.5A	Rear foglights, instrument cluster, automatic gearbox
F7	-	Spare
F8	7.5A	ABS, power steering, air conditioning blower motor
F9	10A	Rear lights, central locking, electric windows, heated rear window, speedometer, air conditioning, heating and ventilation, tachometer
F10	20A	Front and rear wipers
F11	15A	Audio, immobiliser, accessory socket
F12	7.5A	Heated rear window, ABS, heater blower, front and rear wipers, power steering, central locking, air conditioning, electric windows, speedometer, tachometer
F13	15A	Airbag, engine management, immobiliser, automatic transmission, instrument cluster
F14	7.5A	Air conditioning
F15	40A	Accessories, heated rear window, ABS
F16	30A	Electric windows
F17	40A	Air conditioning

Earth locations

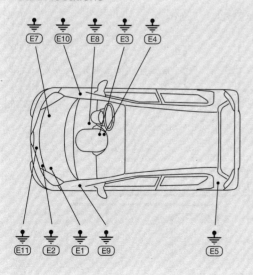

Starting & charging

Horn

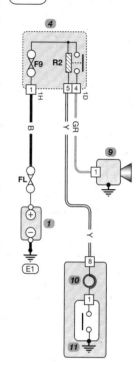

Engine cooling fan

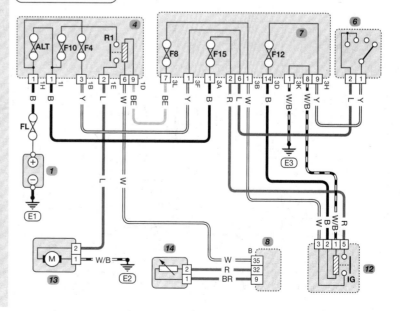

Wire colours

W	White	O	Orange
L	Blue	R	Red
BE	Beige	P	Pink
GR	Grey	G	Green
Y	Yellow	V	Violet
BR	Brown	SB	Sky blue
B	Black	LG	Light green

Key to items

1 Battery
4 Engine fusebox
6 Ignition switch
7 Instrument cluster
  b = power steering warning light
  c = illumination
  d = dipped beam warning light
  e = main beam warning light
8 Engine management control unit
12 Interior relay plate
17 ABS control unit
18 Diagnostic connector

19 Power steering control unit
20 Power steering torque sensor
21 Power steering motor
22 LH rear light unit
  a = stop light
  b = reversing light
  c = tail light
23 RH rear light unit
  (as above)
24 Stop light switch
25 Reversing light switch
26 High level stop light

27 LH front light unit
  a = sidelight
  b = dipped beam
  c = main beam
  d = headlight levelling actuator
28 RH front light unit
  (as above)
29 Number plate light
30 Light switch
31 Headlight levelling adjuster

Diagram 3

H47299

Power steering

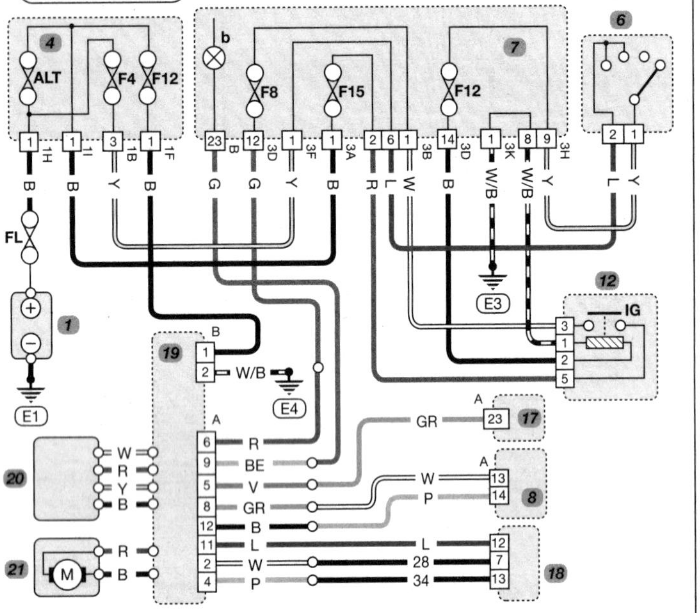

Side, tail and number plate lights

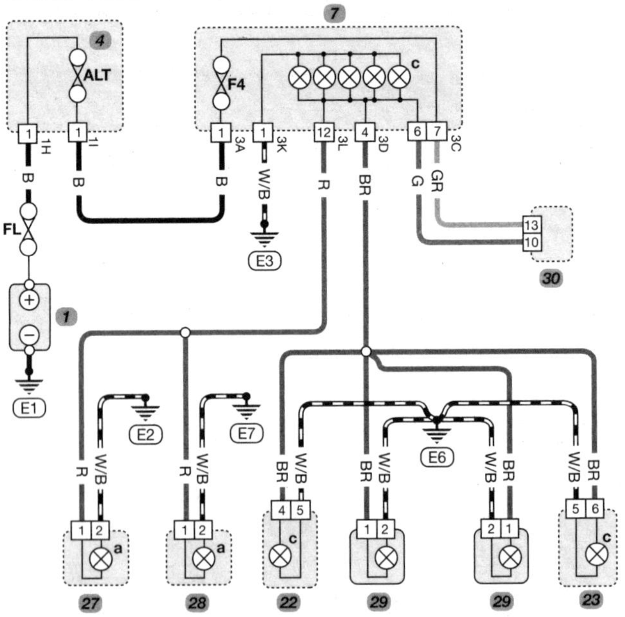

Stop and reversing lights

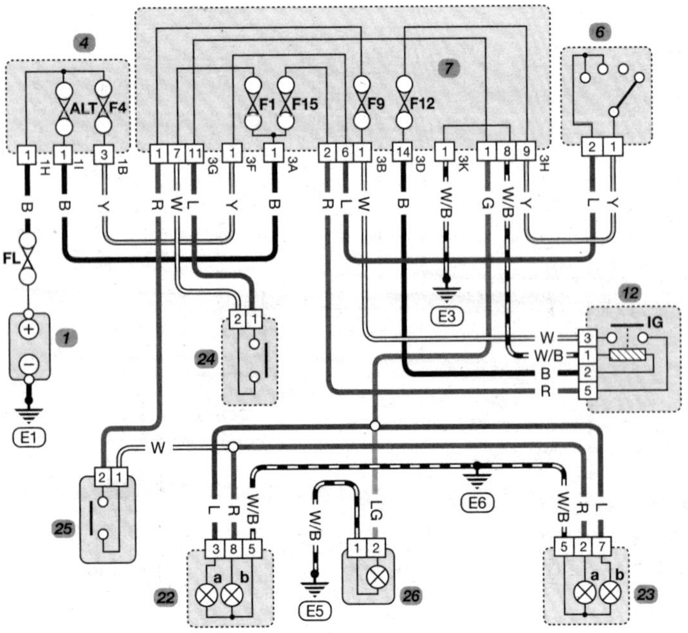

Headlights and headlight levelling

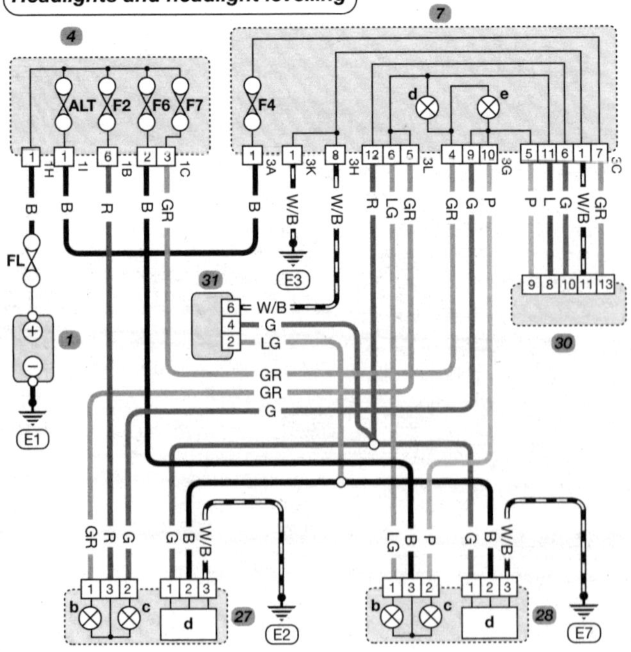

Wire colours

W	White	O	Orange
L	Blue	R	Red
BE	Beige	P	Pink
GR	Grey	G	Green
Y	Yellow	V	Violet
BR	Brown	SB	Sky blue
B	Black	LG	Light green

Key to items

1 Battery
4 Engine fusebox
6 Ignition switch
7 Instrument cluster
  f = foglight warning light
  g = LH indicator warning light
  h = RH indicator warning light
12 Interior relay plate
22 LH rear light unit
  d = foglight
  e = direction indicator

23 RH rear light unit
  (as above)
27 LH front light unit
  e = direction indicator
28 RH front light unit
  (as above)
30 Light switch
35 Hazard warning light switch
36 LH indicator side repeater
37 RH indicator side repeater
38 Interior light

39 Interior light door switch
40 Audio unit
41 LH speaker
42 RH speaker

Diagram 4

H47300

Fog lights

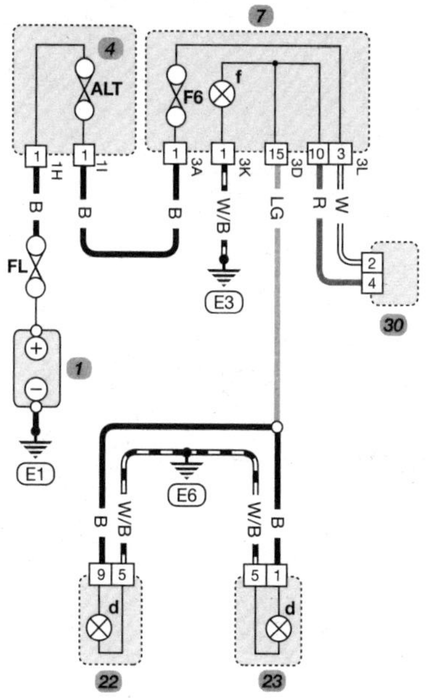

Direction indicators and hazard warning lights

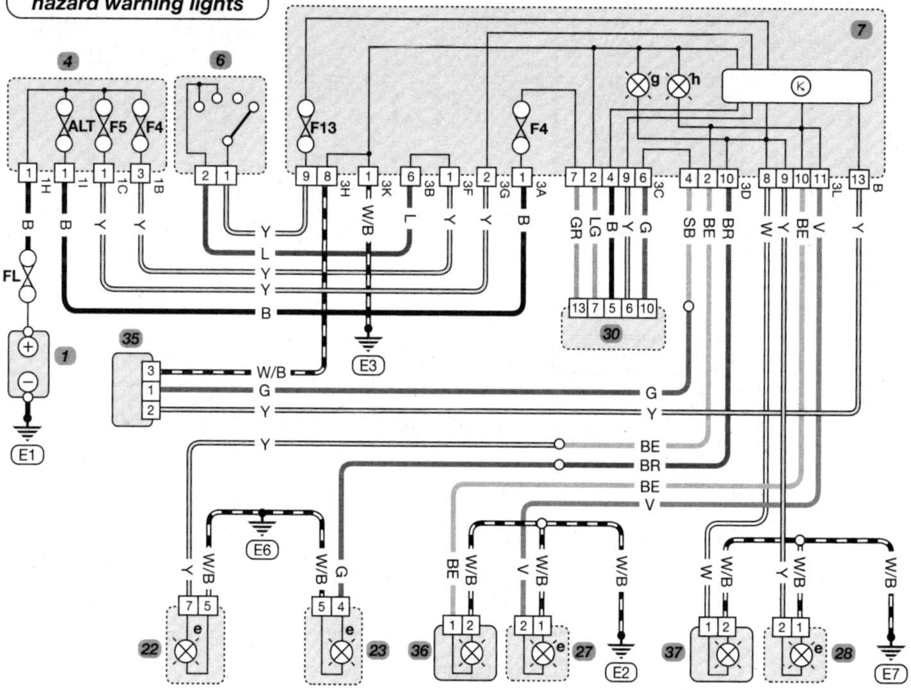

Interior lighting

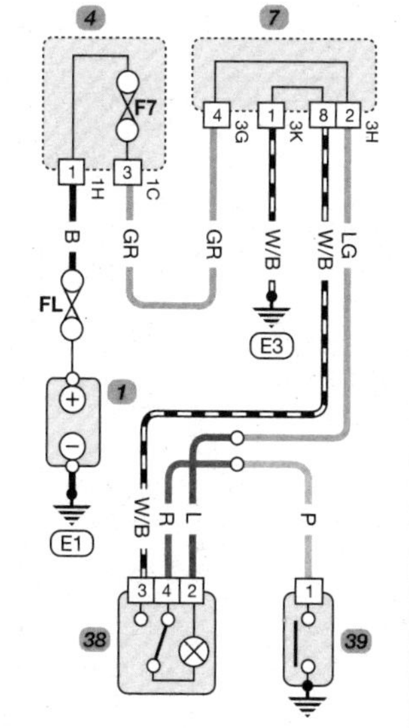

Audio system

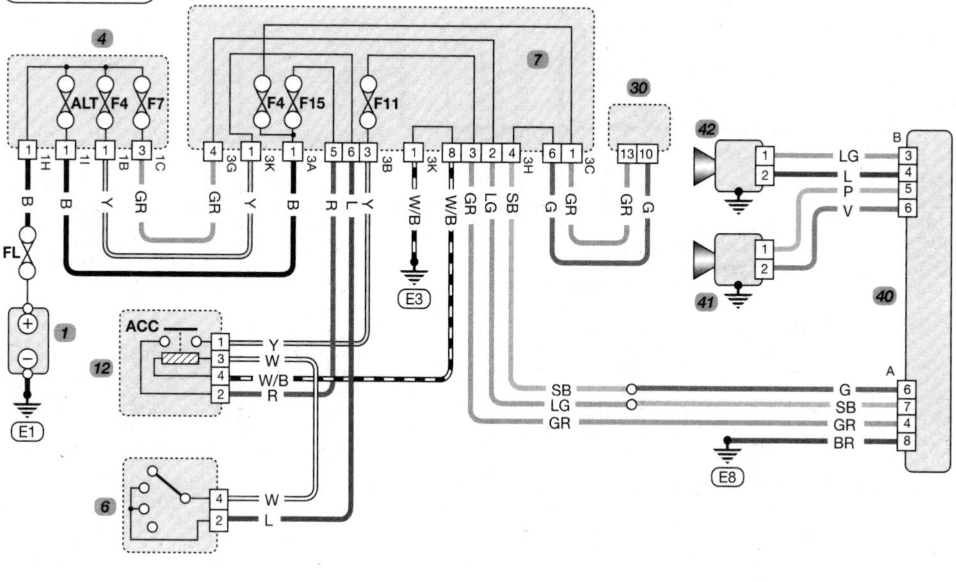

Wire colours

W	White	**O**	Orange
L	Blue	**R**	Red
BE	Beige	**P**	Pink
GR	Grey	**G**	Green
Y	Yellow	**V**	Violet
BR	Brown	**SB**	Sky blue
B	Black	**LG**	Light green

Key to items

1 Battery
4 Engine fusebox
6 Ignition switch
7 Instrument cluster
12 Interior relay plate
30 Light switch
45 Heater blower motor
46 Heater blower resistor pack
47 Heater blower speed control
48 Wash/wipe switch
49 Friont wiper motor
50 Rear wiper motor
51 Front washer pump
52 Rear washer pump

Diagram 5

H47301

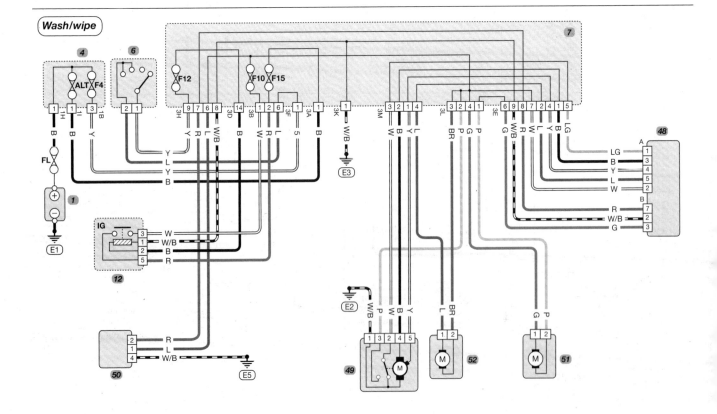

Heater blower

Wash/wipe

Wire colours

W	White	O	Orange
L	Blue	R	Red
BE	Beige	P	Pink
GR	Grey	G	Green
Y	Yellow	V	Violet
BR	Brown	SB	Sky blue
B	Black	LG	Light green

Key to items

1 Battery
4 Engine fusebox
6 Ignition switch
7 Instrument cluster
  i = brake fluid/handbrake warning light
8 Engine management control unit
12 Interior relay plate
14 Engine coolant temperature sensor
17 ABS control unit
30 Light switch
35 Hazard warning light switch
39 Interior light door switch
56 Electric window relay
57 LH window switch
58 RH window switch
59 LH window motor
60 RH window motor
61 Common connecting point 3
62 Central locking control unit
63 LH front door lock
64 LH rear door lock
65 RH front door lock
66 RH rear door lock
67 Tailgate lock
68 Tachometer
69 Handbrake switch
70 Low brake fluid switch
71 Fuel pump/fuel gauge sender unit

Diagram 6

H47302

Electric windows

Central locking

**Instrument cluster –
warning lights and gauges**

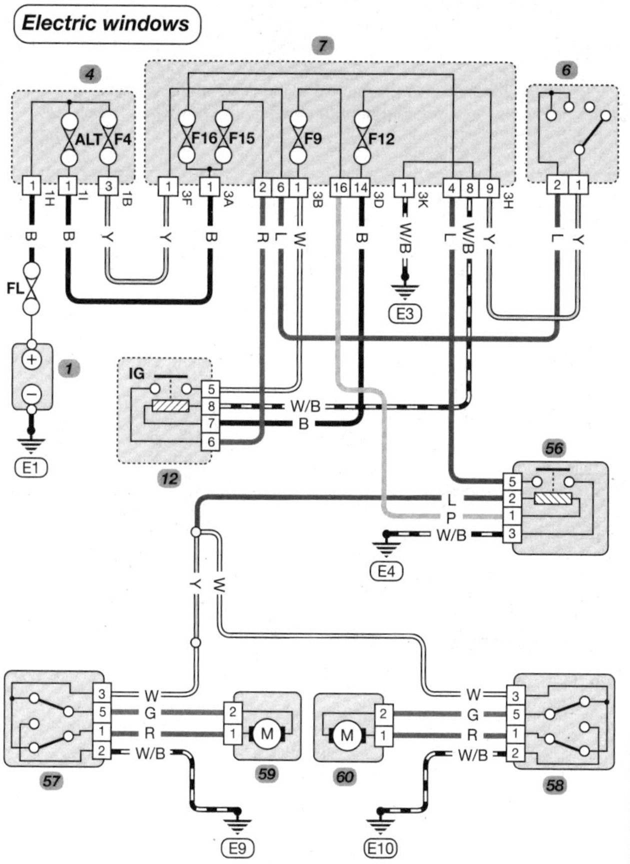

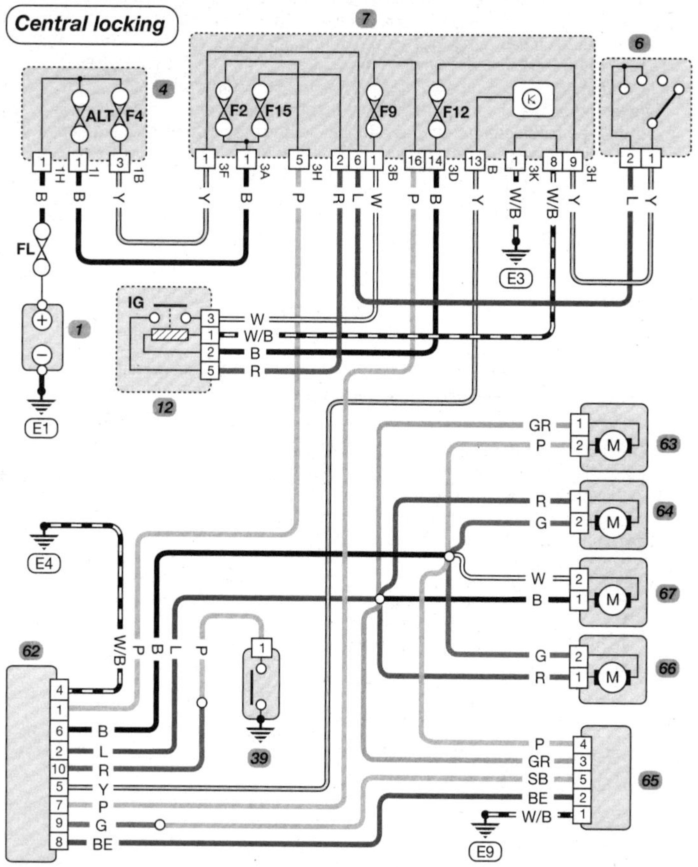

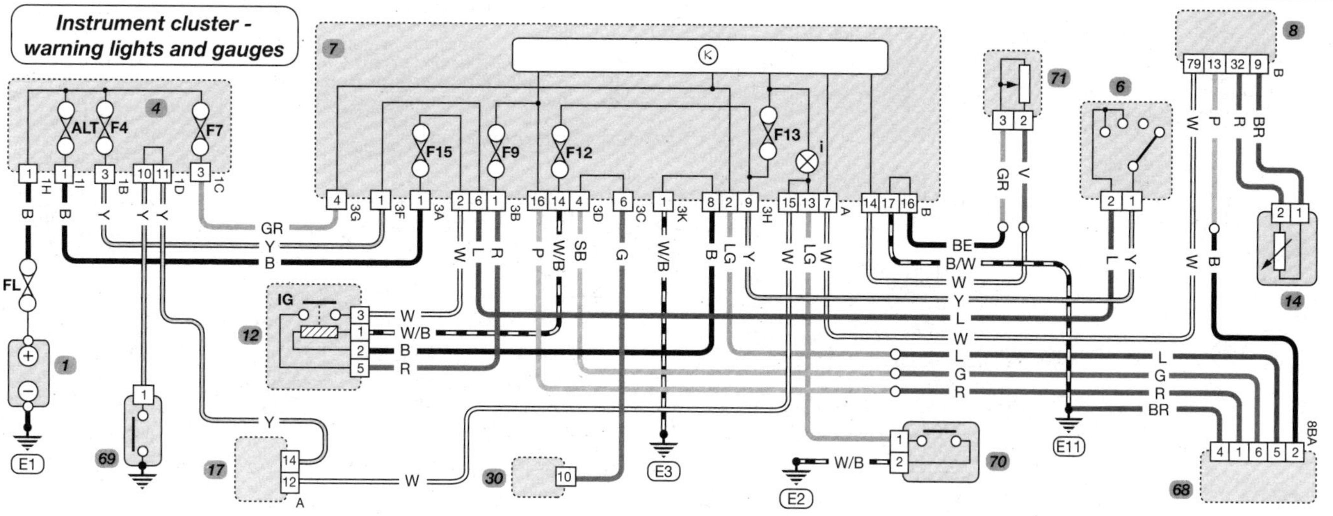

Peugeot 107 and Citroen C1 wiring diagrams (typical)

Diagram 1

WARNING: This vehicle is fitted with a supplemental restraint system (SRS) consisting of a combination of driver (and passenger) airbag(s), side impact protection airbags and seatbelt pre-tensioners. The use of electrical test equipment on any SRS wiring systems may cause the seatbelt pre-tensioners to abruptly retract and airbags to explosively deploy, resulting in potentially severe personal injury. Extreme care should be taken to correctly identify any circuits to be tested to avoid choosing any of the SRS wiring in error.
For further information see airbag system precautions in body electrical systems chapter.
Note: The SRS wiring harness can normally be identified by yellow and/or orange harness or harness connectors.

The prime method of wire identification is by the number code printed on each wire. Additionally, the wires can be identified by using the terminal pin numbers (moulded into each component or connector and shown in the diagrams).
To relate each diagram to the vehicle wiring, locate the relevant component or connector illustrated and find the wire(s) connected to the terminal pin(s) as shown in the diagram.
Caution: Whilst a number (indicating the function of that wire) may be printed on each wire, this is not always the case, and in such instances, this is reflected by the absence of such wire numbering on our diagrams. Similarly, numbering of the connector/component terminal pins is not always available from the manufacturers' source information and may also be missing from our diagrams.

Key to symbols

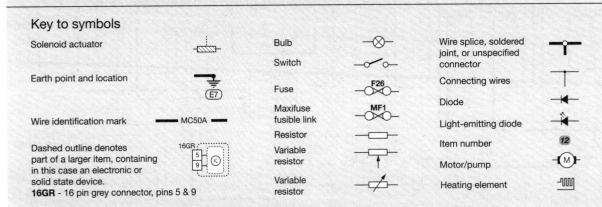

Solenoid actuator

Earth point and location — E7

Wire identification mark — MC50A

Dashed outline denotes part of a larger item, containing in this case an electronic or solid state device.
16GR - 16 pin grey connector, pins 5 & 9

Bulb

Switch

Fuse — F26

Maxifuse fusible link — MF1

Resistor

Variable resistor

Variable resistor

Wire splice, soldered joint, or unspecified connector

Connecting wires

Diode

Light-emitting diode

Item number — 12

Motor/pump — M

Heating element

Engine fusebox 4

Fuse	Rating	Circuit protected
F1	50A	Automatic transmission, fan (Diesel)
F2	10A	Sidelights, dip and main beam
	20A	Daytime running lights
F3	30A	ABS/ESP
F4	30A	Ignition switch supply
F5	10A	Hazard warning lights, instrument cluster warning lights, direction indicators
F6	10A	Sidelights, dip and main beam
F7	15A	Interior light, speedometer, audio equipment, instrument cluster, tachometer
F8	15A	Engine management control unit (petrol)
	25A	Engine management control unit (Diesel)
F9	10A	Horn
F10	30A	Engine cooling fan (petrol)
F11	50A	ABS/ESP
F12	50A	Power steering

Motor fuse/relay board 1 5

Fuse	Rating	Circuit protected
F13	7.5A	Starter
F14	7.5A	Engine management control unit
R1		Starter relay

Motor fuse/relay board 2 15

Fuse	Rating	Circuit protected
F15	15A	Engine management control unit
F16	10A	RH main beam
F17	10A	LH main beam (control unit)
F18	10A	RH dipped beam
F19	10A	LH dipped beam (control unit)
F20	10A	Engine management control unit
R2		Air conditioning relay

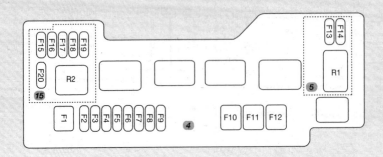

H47291

Colour codes

BA	White	**OR**	Orange
BE	Blue	**RG**	Red
BG	Beige	**RS**	Pink
GR	Grey	**VE**	Green
JN	Yellow	**VI**	Mauve
MR	Brown		
NR	Black		

Key to items

1 Battery
2 Starter motor
3 Alternator
4 Engine fusebox
  R1 = engine cooling fan relay
  R2 = horn relay
5 Motor fuse/relay board 1
  R1 = starter relay
6 Ignition switch
7 Instrument cluster
  a = alternator warning light
8 Engine management control unit
9 Horn
10 Steering rotary connector
11 Horn switch
12 Interior relay plate
13 Engine cooling fan
14 Engine coolant temperature sensor

Diagram 2

H47292

Instrument cluster fusebox ⑦

Fuse	Rating	Circuit protected
F1	10A	Stop lights, ABS, automatic gearbox
F2	25A	Central locking
F3	20A	Heated rear window
F4	7.5A	Rear lights, number plate lights, instrument cluster
F5	7.5A	Diagnostic connector
F6	7.5A	Rear foglights, instrument cluster, automatic gearbox
F7	-	Spare
F8	7.5A	ABS, power steering, air conditioning blower motor
F9	10A	Rear lights, central locking, electric windows, heated rear window, speedometer, air conditioning, heating and ventilation, tachometer
F10	20A	Front and rear wipers
F11	15A	Audio, immobiliser, accessory socket
F12	7.5A	Heated rear window, ABS, heater blower, front and rear wipers, power steering, central locking, air conditioning, electric windows, speedometer, tachometer
F13	15A	Airbag, engine management, immobiliser, automatic transmission, instrument cluster
F14	7.5A	Air conditioning
F15	40A	Accessories, heated rear window, ABS
F16	30A	Electric windows
F17	40A	Air conditioning

Earth locations

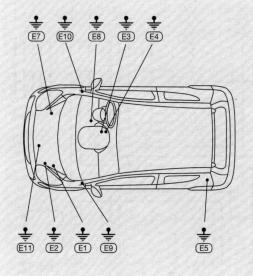

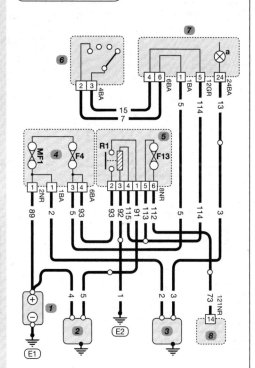

Starting & charging

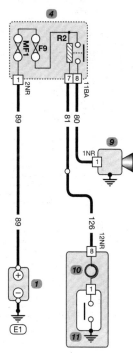

Horn

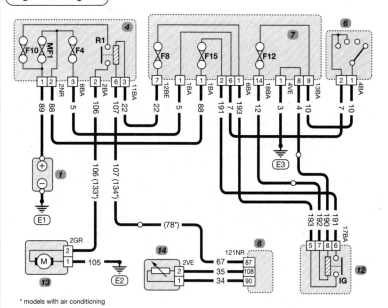

Engine cooling fan

* models with air conditioning

Colour codes

BA	White	**OR**	Orange
BE	Blue	**RG**	Red
BG	Beige	**RS**	Pink
GR	Grey	**VE**	Green
JN	Yellow	**VI**	Mauve
MR	Brown	**VJ**	Green/
NR	Black		Yellow

Key to items

1 Battery
4 Engine fusebox
6 Ignition switch
7 Instrument cluster
  b = power steering warning light
  c = illumination
  d = dipped beam warning light
  e = main beam warning light
8 Engine management control unit
12 Interior relay plate
17 ABS control unit
18 Diagnostic connector

19 Power steering control unit
20 Power steering torque sensor
21 Power steering motor
22 LH rear light unit
  a = stop light
  b = reversing light
  c = tail light
23 RH rear light unit
  (as above)
24 Stop light switch
25 Reversing light switch
26 High level stop light

27 LH front light unit
  a = sidelight
  b = dipped beam
  c = main beam
  d = headlight levelling actuator
28 RH front light unit
  (as above)
29 Number plate light
30 Light switch
31 Headlight levelling adjuster

Diagram 3

H47293

Power steering

Side, tail and number plate lights

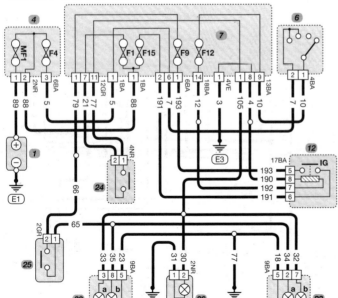

Stop and reversing lights

Headlights and headlight levelling

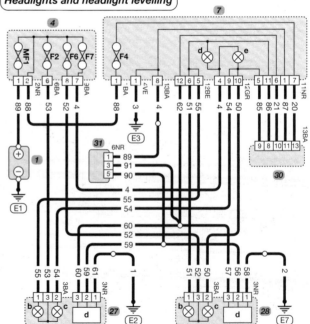

Colour codes

BA	White	OR	Orange
BE	Blue	RG	Red
BG	Beige	RS	Pink
GR	Grey	VE	Green
JN	Yellow	VI	Mauve
MR	Brown	VJ	Green/
NR	Black		Yellow

Key to items

1 Battery
4 Engine fusebox
6 Ignition switch
7 Instrument cluster
  f = foglight warning light
  g = LH indicator warning light
  h = RH indicator warning light
12 Interior relay plate
22 LH rear light unit
  d = foglight
  e = direction indicator

23 RH rear light unit
  (as above)
27 LH front light unit
  e = direction indicator
28 RH front light unit
  (as above)
30 Light switch
35 Hazard warning light switch
36 LH indicator side repeater
37 RH indicator side repeater
38 Interior light

39 Interior light door switch
40 Audio unit
41 LH speaker
42 RH speaker
43 Common connecting point 1

Diagram 4

H47294

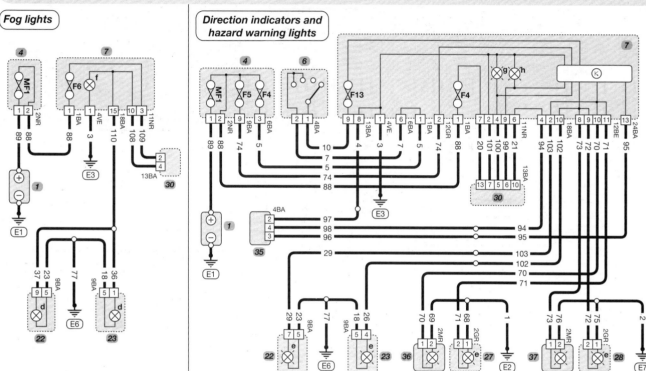

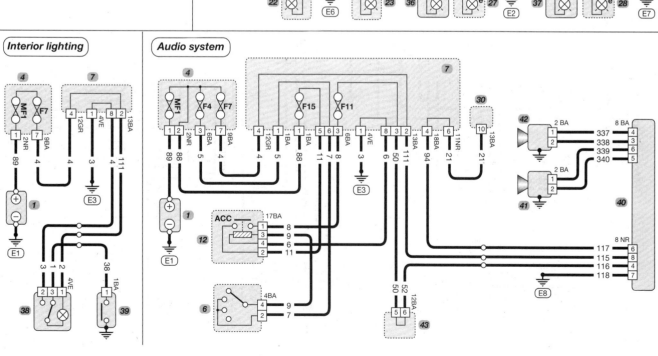

Colour codes

BA	White	**OR**	Orange
BE	Blue	**RG**	Red
BG	Beige	**RS**	Pink
GR	Grey	**VE**	Green
JN	Yellow	**VI**	Mauve
MR	Brown	**VJ**	Green/
NR	Black		Yellow

Key to items

1 Battery
4 Engine fusebox
6 Ignition switch
7 Instrument cluster
12 Interior relay plate
30 Light switch
45 Heater blower motor
46 Heater blower resistor pack
47 Heater blower speed control
48 Wash/wipe switch
49 Friont wiper motor
50 Rear wiper motor
51 Front washer pump
52 Rear washer pump

Diagram 5

H47295

Heater blower

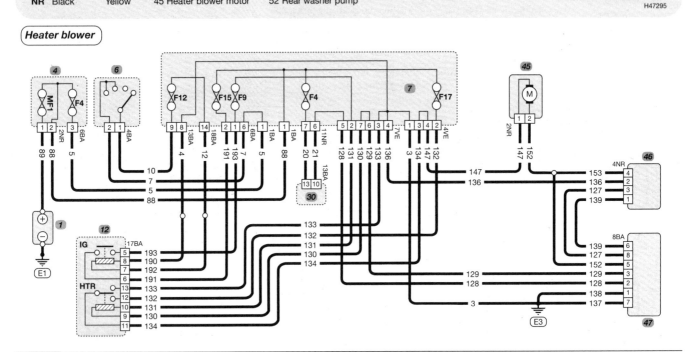

Wash/wipe

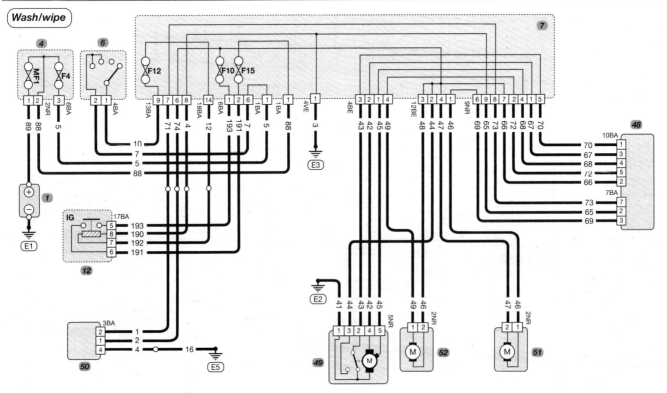

Colour codes

BA	White	OR	Orange
BE	Blue	RG	Red
BG	Beige	RS	Pink
GR	Grey	VE	Green
JN	Yellow	VI	Mauve
MR	Brown	VJ	Green/
NR	Black		Yellow

Key to items

1 Battery
4 Engine fusebox
6 Ignition switch
7 Instrument cluster
  i = brake fluid/handbrake warning light
8 Engine management control unit
12 Interior relay plate
14 Engine coolant temperature sensor
17 ABS control unit
30 Light switch

35 Hazard warning light switch
39 Interior light door switch
43 Common connecting point 1
55 Common connecting point 2
56 Electric window relay
57 LH window switch
58 RH window switch
59 LH window motor
60 RH window motor
61 Common connecting point 3

62 Central locking control unit
63 LH front door lock
64 LH rear door lock
65 RH front door lock
66 RH rear door lock
67 Tailgate lock
68 Tachometer
69 Handbrake switch
70 Low brake fluid switch
71 Fuel pump/fuel gauge sender unit

Diagram 6

H47296

Electric windows

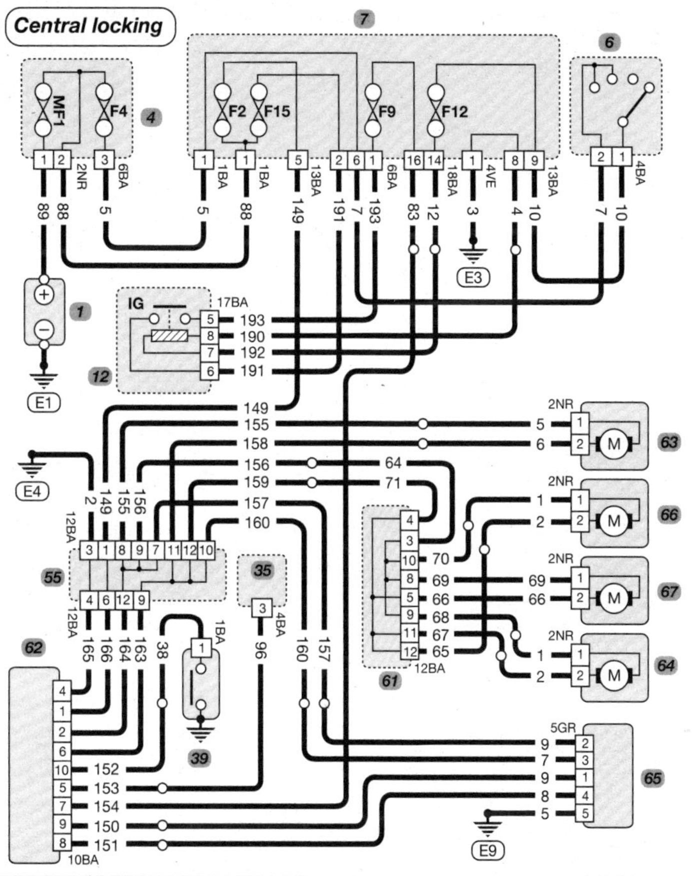

Central locking

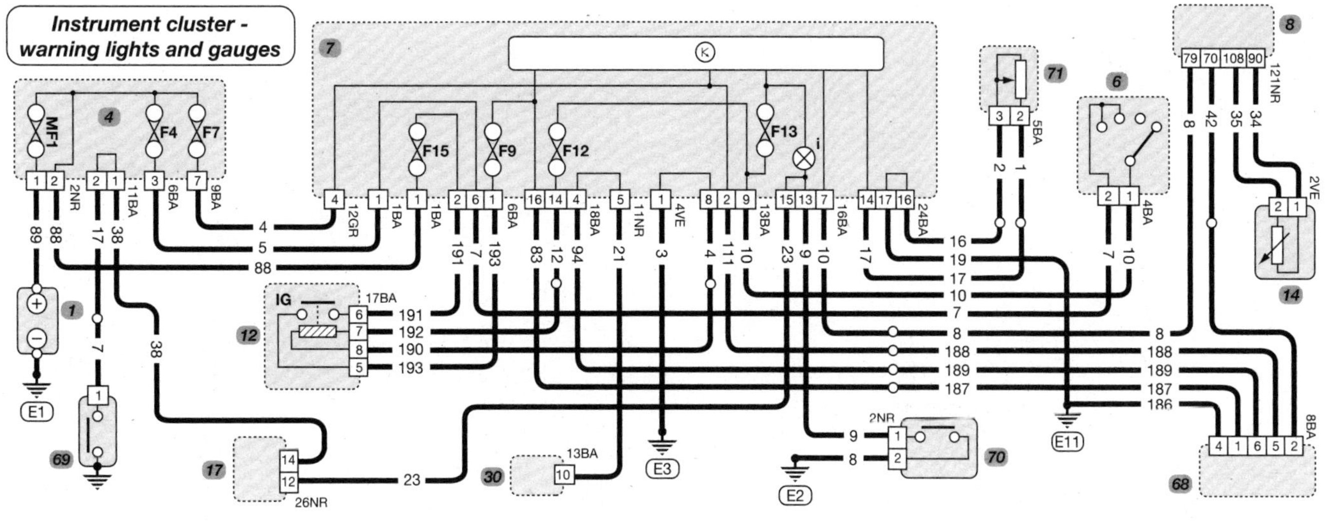

Instrument cluster - warning lights and gauges

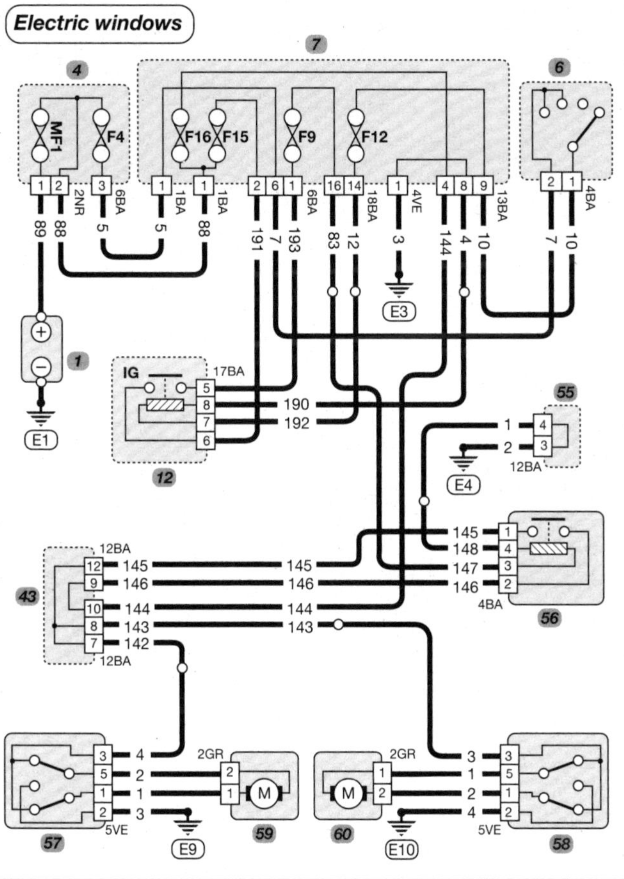

Reference REF•1

Dimensions and weights . . . . **REF•1**
Conversion factors. . . . . **REF•2**
Buying spare parts . . . . **REF•3**
Vehicle identification. **REF•3**
General repair procedures . . . . **REF•4**
Jacking and vehicle support . . . . **REF•5**
Disconnecting the battery . . . . **REF•5**
Tools and working facilities . . . . **REF•6**
MOT test checks . . . . **REF•8**
Fault finding . . . . **REF•12**
Index. . . . . **REF•20**

Dimensions and weights

Note: *All figures are approximate, and may vary according to model. Refer to manufacturer's data for exact figures.*

Dimensions

Overall length . . . . 3415 to 3435 mm
Overall width:
   Including mirrors. . . . . 1840 to 1855 mm
   Not including mirrors . . . . 1615 to 1630 mm
Overall height (unladen) . . . . 1465 mm
Wheelbase . . . . 2340 mm

Weights

Kerb weight:
   Manual transmission models . . . . 790 to 850 kg
   Multi-Mode Transmission (MMT) models . . . . 825 to 915 kg
Maximum gross vehicle weight . . . . 1160 to 1190 kg
Maximum weight on roof bars . . . . 50 kg

Length (distance)

Inches (in)	x 25.4	= Millimetres (mm)	x 0.0394	=	Inches (in)
Feet (ft)	x 0.305	= Metres (m)	x 3.281	=	Feet (ft)
Miles	x 1.609	= Kilometres (km)	x 0.621	=	Miles

Volume (capacity)

Cubic inches (cu in; in^3)	x 16.387	= Cubic centimetres (cc; cm^3)	x 0.061	=	Cubic inches (cu in; in^3)
Imperial pints (Imp pt)	x 0.568	= Litres (l)	x 1.76	=	Imperial pints (Imp pt)
Imperial quarts (Imp qt)	x 1.137	= Litres (l)	x 0.88	=	Imperial quarts (Imp qt)
Imperial quarts (Imp qt)	x 1.201	= US quarts (US qt)	x 0.833	=	Imperial quarts (Imp qt)
US quarts (US qt)	x 0.946	= Litres (l)	x 1.057	=	US quarts (US qt)
Imperial gallons (Imp gal)	x 4.546	= Litres (l)	x 0.22	=	Imperial gallons (Imp gal)
Imperial gallons (Imp gal)	x 1.201	= US gallons (US gal)	x 0.833	=	Imperial gallons (Imp gal)
US gallons (US gal)	x 3.785	= Litres (l)	x 0.264	=	US gallons (US gal)

Mass (weight)

Ounces (oz)	x 28.35	= Grams (g)	x 0.035	=	Ounces (oz)
Pounds (lb)	x 0.454	= Kilograms (kg)	x 2.205	=	Pounds (lb)

Force

Ounces-force (ozf; oz)	x 0.278	= Newtons (N)	x 3.6	=	Ounces-force (ozf; oz)
Pounds-force (lbf; lb)	x 4.448	= Newtons (N)	x 0.225	=	Pounds-force (lbf; lb)
Newtons (N)	x 0.1	= Kilograms-force (kgf; kg)	x 9.81	=	Newtons (N)

Pressure

Pounds-force per square inch (psi; lbf/in^2; lb/in^2)	x 0.070	= Kilograms-force per square centimetre (kgf/cm^2; kg/cm^2)	x 14.223	=	Pounds-force per square inch (psi; lbf/in^2; lb/in^2)
Pounds-force per square inch (psi; lbf/in^2; lb/in^2)	x 0.068	= Atmospheres (atm)	x 14.696	=	Pounds-force per square inch (psi; lbf/in^2; lb/in^2)
Pounds-force per square inch (psi; lbf/in^2; lb/in^2)	x 0.069	= Bars	x 14.5	=	Pounds-force per square inch (psi; lbf/in^2; lb/in^2)
Pounds-force per square inch (psi; lbf/in^2; lb/in^2)	x 6.895	= Kilopascals (kPa)	x 0.145	=	Pounds-force per square inch (psi; lbf/in^2; lb/in^2)
Kilopascals (kPa)	x 0.01	= Kilograms-force per square centimetre (kgf/cm^2; kg/cm^2)	x 98.1	=	Kilopascals (kPa)
Millibar (mbar)	x 100	= Pascals (Pa)	x 0.01	=	Millibar (mbar)
Millibar (mbar)	x 0.0145	= Pounds-force per square inch (psi; lbf/in^2; lb/in^2)	x 68.947	=	Millibar (mbar)
Millibar (mbar)	x 0.75	= Millimetres of mercury (mmHg)	x 1.333	=	Millibar (mbar)
Millibar (mbar)	x 0.401	= Inches of water (inH$_2$O)	x 2.491	=	Millibar (mbar)
Millimetres of mercury (mmHg)	x 0.535	= Inches of water (inH$_2$O)	x 1.868	=	Millimetres of mercury (mmHg)
Inches of water (inH$_2$O)	x 0.036	= Pounds-force per square inch (psi; lbf/in^2; lb/in^2)	x 27.68	=	Inches of water (inH$_2$O)

Torque (moment of force)

Pounds-force inches (lbf in; lb in)	x 1.152	= Kilograms-force centimetre (kgf cm; kg cm)	x 0.868	=	Pounds-force inches (lbf in; lb in)
Pounds-force inches (lbf in; lb in)	x 0.113	= Newton metres (Nm)	x 8.85	=	Pounds-force inches (lbf in; lb in)
Pounds-force inches (lbf in; lb in)	x 0.083	= Pounds-force feet (lbf ft; lb ft)	x 12	=	Pounds-force inches (lbf in; lb in)
Pounds-force feet (lbf ft; lb ft)	x 0.138	= Kilograms-force metres (kgf m; kg m)	x 7.233	=	Pounds-force feet (lbf ft; lb ft)
Pounds-force feet (lbf ft; lb ft)	x 1.356	= Newton metres (Nm)	x 0.738	=	Pounds-force feet (lbf ft; lb ft)
Newton metres (Nm)	x 0.102	= Kilograms-force metres (kgf m; kg m)	x 9.804	=	Newton metres (Nm)

Power

Horsepower (hp)	x 745.7	= Watts (W)	x 0.0013	=	Horsepower (hp)

Velocity (speed)

Miles per hour (miles/hr; mph)	x 1.609	= Kilometres per hour (km/hr; kph)	x 0.621	=	Miles per hour (miles/hr; mph)

Fuel consumption*

Miles per gallon, Imperial (mpg)	x 0.354	= Kilometres per litre (km/l)	x 2.825	=	Miles per gallon, Imperial (mpg)
Miles per gallon, US (mpg)	x 0.425	= Kilometres per litre (km/l)	x 2.352	=	Miles per gallon, US (mpg)

Temperature

Degrees Fahrenheit = (°C x 1.8) + 32   Degrees Celsius (Degrees Centigrade; °C) = (°F - 32) x 0.56

It is common practice to convert from miles per gallon (mpg) to litres/100 kilometres (l/100km), where mpg x l/100 km = 282

Spare parts are available from many sources, including maker's appointed garages, accessory shops, and motor factors. To be sure of obtaining the correct parts, it will sometimes be necessary to quote the vehicle identification number. If possible, it can also be useful to take the old parts along for positive identification. Items such as starter motors and alternators may be available under a service exchange scheme – any parts returned should be clean.

Our advice regarding spare parts is as follows.

Officially appointed garages

This is the best source of parts which are peculiar to your car, and which are not otherwise generally available (eg, badges, interior trim, certain body panels, etc). It is also the only place at which you should buy parts if the car is still under warranty.

Accessory shops

These are very good places to buy materials and components needed for the maintenance of your car (oil, air and fuel filters, light bulbs, drivebelts, greases, brake pads, touch-up paint, etc). Components of this nature sold by a reputable shop are usually of the same standard as those used by the car manufacturer.

Besides components, these shops also sell tools and general accessories, usually have convenient opening hours, charge lower prices, and can often be found close to home. Some accessory shops have parts counters where components needed for almost any repair job can be purchased or ordered.

Motor factors

Good factors will stock all the more important components which wear out comparatively quickly, and can sometimes supply individual components needed for the overhaul of a larger assembly (eg, brake seals and hydraulic parts, bearing shells, pistons, valves). They may also handle work such as cylinder block reboring, crankshaft regrinding, etc.

Engine reconditioners

These specialise in engine overhaul and can also supply components. It is recommended that the establishment is a member of the Federation of Engine Re-Manufacturers, or a similar society.

Tyre and exhaust specialists

These outlets may be independent, or members of a local or national chain. They frequently offer competitive prices when compared with a main dealer or local garage, but it will pay to obtain several quotes before making a decision. When researching prices, also ask what extras may be added – for instance fitting a new valve, balancing the wheel and tyre disposal all both commonly charged on top of the price of a new tyre.

Other sources

Beware of parts or materials obtained from market stalls, car boot sales, on-line auctions or similar outlets. Such items are not invariably sub-standard, but there is little chance of compensation if they do prove unsatisfactory. In the case of safety-critical components such as brake pads, there is the risk not only of financial loss, but also of an accident causing injury or death.

Second-hand components or assemblies obtained from a car breaker can be a good buy in some circumstances, but this sort of purchase is best made by the experienced DIY mechanic.

Vehicle identification

Modifications are a continuing and unpublicised process in vehicle manufacture, quite apart from major model changes. Spare parts manuals and lists are compiled upon a numerical basis, the individual vehicle identification numbers being essential to correct identification of the component concerned.

When ordering spare parts, always give as much information as possible. Quote the car model; year of manufacture, body and engine numbers as appropriate.

The vehicle identification plate is located on the driver's side B-pillar or C-pillar (see illustrations), depending on model. In addition to many other details, it carries the Vehicle Identification Number (VIN), maximum vehicle weight information, and codes for interior trim and body colours.

The Vehicle Identification Number (VIN) is stamped into the floor crossmember, below the driver's seat – an access slit in the carpet is provided (see illustration).

The engine number is stamped on the transmission end of the cylinder block, at the front (see illustration).

3.3a There is a vehicle identification plate located on the B-pillar...

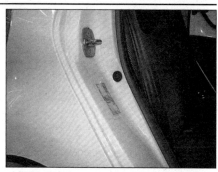

3.3b...or C-pillar, depending on model

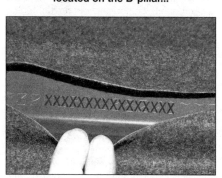

3.4 The VIN also appears on the floor crossmember under the driver's seat

3.5 Engine number location

Whenever servicing, repair or overhaul work is carried out on the car or its components, observe the following procedures and instructions. This will assist in carrying out the operation efficiently and to a professional standard of workmanship.

Joint mating faces and gaskets

When separating components at their mating faces, never insert screwdrivers or similar implements into the joint between the faces in order to prise them apart. This can cause severe damage which results in oil leaks, coolant leaks, etc upon reassembly. Separation is usually achieved by tapping along the joint with a soft-faced hammer in order to break the seal. However, note that this method may not be suitable where dowels are used for component location.

Where a gasket is used between the mating faces of two components, a new one must be fitted on reassembly; fit it dry unless otherwise stated in the repair procedure. Make sure that the mating faces are clean and dry, with all traces of old gasket removed. When cleaning a joint face, use a tool which is unlikely to score or damage the face, and remove any burrs or nicks with an oilstone or fine file.

Make sure that tapped holes are cleaned with a pipe cleaner, and keep them free of jointing compound, if this is being used, unless specifically instructed otherwise.

Ensure that all orifices, channels or pipes are clear, and blow through them, preferably using compressed air.

Oil seals

Oil seals can be removed by levering them out with a wide flat-bladed screwdriver or similar implement. Alternatively, a number of self-tapping screws may be screwed into the seal, and these used as a purchase for pliers or some similar device in order to pull the seal free.

Whenever an oil seal is removed from its working location, either individually or as part of an assembly, it should be renewed.

The very fine sealing lip of the seal is easily damaged, and will not seal if the surface it contacts is not completely clean and free from scratches, nicks or grooves. If the original sealing surface of the component cannot be restored, and the manufacturer has not made provision for slight relocation of the seal relative to the sealing surface, the component should be renewed.

Protect the lips of the seal from any surface which may damage them in the course of fitting. Use tape or a conical sleeve where possible. Where indicated, lubricate the seal lips with oil before fitting and, on dual-lipped seals, fill the space between the lips with grease.

Unless otherwise stated, oil seals must be fitted with their sealing lips toward the lubricant to be sealed.

Use a tubular drift or block of wood of the appropriate size to install the seal and, if the seal housing is shouldered, drive the seal down to the shoulder. If the seal housing is unshouldered, the seal should be fitted with its face flush with the housing top face (unless otherwise instructed).

Screw threads and fastenings

Seized nuts, bolts and screws are quite a common occurrence where corrosion has set in, and the use of penetrating oil or releasing fluid will often overcome this problem if the offending item is soaked for a while before attempting to release it. The use of an impact driver may also provide a means of releasing such stubborn fastening devices, when used in conjunction with the appropriate screwdriver bit or socket. If none of these methods works, it may be necessary to resort to the careful application of heat, or the use of a hacksaw or nut splitter device. Before resorting to extreme methods, check that you are not dealing with a left-hand thread!

Studs are usually removed by locking two nuts together on the threaded part, and then using a spanner on the lower nut to unscrew the stud. Studs or bolts which have broken off below the surface of the component in which they are mounted can sometimes be removed using a stud extractor.

Always ensure that a blind tapped hole is completely free from oil, grease, water or other fluid before installing the bolt or stud. Failure to do this could cause the housing to crack due to the hydraulic action of the bolt or stud as it is screwed in.

For some screw fastenings, notably cylinder head bolts or nuts, torque wrench settings are no longer specified for the latter stages of tightening, "angle-tightening" being called up instead. Typically, a fairly low torque wrench setting will be applied to the bolts/nuts in the correct sequence, followed by one or more stages of tightening through specified angles.

When checking or retightening a nut or bolt to a specified torque setting, slacken the nut or bolt by a quarter of a turn, and then retighten to the specified setting. However, this should not be attempted where angular tightening has been used.

Locknuts, locktabs and washers

Any fastening which will rotate against a component or housing during tightening should always have a washer between it and the relevant component or housing.

Spring or split washers should always be renewed when they are used to lock a critical component such as a big-end bearing retaining bolt or nut. Locktabs which are folded over to retain a nut or bolt should always be renewed.

Self-locking nuts can be re-used in non-critical areas, providing resistance can be felt when the locking portion passes over the bolt or stud thread. However, it should be noted that self-locking stiffnuts tend to lose their effectiveness after long periods of use, and should then be renewed as a matter of course.

Split pins must always be replaced with new ones of the correct size for the hole.

When thread-locking compound is found on the threads of a fastener which is to be re-used, it should be cleaned off with a wire brush and solvent, and fresh compound applied on reassembly.

Special tools

Some repair procedures in this manual entail the use of special tools such as a press, two or three-legged pullers, spring compressors, etc. Wherever possible, suitable readily-available alternatives to the manufacturer's special tools are described, and are shown in use. In some instances, where no alternative is possible, it has been necessary to resort to the use of a manufacturer's tool, and this has been done for reasons of safety as well as the efficient completion of the repair operation. Unless you are highly-skilled and have a thorough understanding of the procedures described, never attempt to bypass the use of any special tool when the procedure described specifies its use. Not only is there a very great risk of personal injury, but expensive damage could be caused to the components involved.

Environmental considerations

When disposing of used engine oil, brake fluid, antifreeze, etc, give due consideration to any detrimental environmental effects. Do not, for instance, pour any of the above liquids down drains into the general sewage system, or onto the ground to soak away, as this is likely to pollute your local environment. Many local council refuse tips provide a facility for waste oil disposal, as do some garages. You can find your nearest disposal point by calling the Environment Agency on 03708 506 506 or by visiting www.oilbankline.org.uk.

Note: It is illegal and anti-social to dump oil down the drain. To find the location of your local oil recycling bank, call 03708 506 506 or visit www.oilbankline.org.uk.

The jack supplied with the car's tool kit should only be used for changing the roadwheels – see *Wheel changing* at the front of this book. When carrying out any other kind of work, raise the car using a hydraulic (or 'trolley') jack, and always supplement the jack with axle stands positioned under the jacking/support points. If the roadwheels do not have to be removed, consider using wheel ramps – if wished, these can be placed under the wheels once the car has been raised using a hydraulic jack, and then lowered onto the ramps so that it is resting on its wheels.

Only ever jack the car up on a solid, level surface. If there is even a slight slope, take great care that the car cannot move as the wheels are lifted off the ground. Jacking up on an uneven or gravelled surface is not recommended, as the weight of the car will not be evenly distributed, and the jack may slip as the car is raised.

As far as possible, do not leave the car unattended once it has been raised, particularly if children are playing nearby.

Before jacking up the front of the car, ensure that the handbrake is firmly applied. When jacking up the rear of the car, place wooden chocks in front of the front wheels, and engage first gear **(see illustration)**.

To raise the front and/or rear of the car, use the jacking/support points at the front and rear ends of the door sills, which are located between two notches in the sill's lower flange **(see illustration)**. Supplement the jack with axle stands positioned as close as possible to the jacking points.

When using a hydraulic jack or axle stands, always try to position the jack head or axle stand head under one of the relevant jacking points.

Providing care is taken (and a block of wood is used to spread the load), the centre of the front subframe, and the protrusion just inside the rear bumper lower edge, may be used as support points **(see illustration)**. It may be safe to use the reinforced areas of the floor pan ('chassis legs') as support points, particularly those in the region of suspension mountings – consult a specialist for advice before using anything other than the approved jacking points, however.

Do not jack the car under any other part of the sill, sump, floorpan, or directly under any of the steering or suspension components, including the rear axle. Avoid trapping cables, fuel pipes and brake pipes, and do not compress the suspension.

Never work under, around, or near a raised vehicle, unless it is adequately supported on stands. Do not rely on a jack alone, as even a hydraulic jack could fail under load.

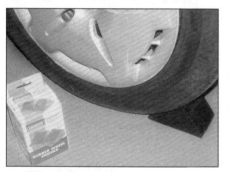

5.4 Wheel chocks should be used in front of the front wheels when jacking the rear of the car

5.5 Jacking points are located between the two notches on the sill flange

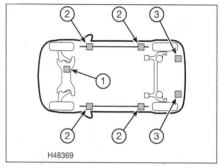

H48369

5.7 Vehicle jacking and support points

1 *Centre of front subframe*
2 *Door sill front and rear jacking points*
3 *Reinforced pad inside of rear bumper*

Disconnecting the battery

Several of the systems require battery power to be available at all times (permanent live). This is either to ensure their continued operation (such as the clock), or to maintain electronic memory settings, which would otherwise be erased. Whenever the battery is to be disconnected, first note the following points, to ensure there are no unforeseen consequences:

a) *Firstly, on any vehicle with central door locking, it is a wise precaution to remove the key from the ignition, and to keep it with you. This avoids the possibility of the key being locked inside the car, should the central locking engage when the battery is reconnected.*

b) *If a security-coded audio unit is fitted, and the unit and/or the battery is disconnected, the unit will not function until the correct security code has been entered. Therefore, if you do not know the correct security code for the radio/CD unit, do not disconnect either of the battery terminals, or remove the radio/CD unit from the vehicle. Where applicable, details for entering the code appear in the vehicle handbook. Should the code*

have been misplaced or forgotten, on production of proof of ownership, a franchised dealer or in-car entertainment specialist may be able to help.

c) *The engine management system ECU is of the 'self-learning' type, meaning that, as it operates, it adapts to changes in operating conditions, and stores the optimum settings found (this is especially true for idle speed settings). When the battery is disconnected, these 'learned' settings are lost, and the ECU reverts to the base factory settings. When the engine is restarted, it may idle and run roughly until the ECU has 'relearned' the best settings. To further this 'learning' process, take the car for a road test of at least 15 minutes' duration, covering as many engine speeds and loads as possible, and concentrating on the 2000 to 4000 rpm range.*

d) *On completion, let the engine idle for at least 10 minutes, turning the steering wheel occasionally and switching on high-current-draw equipment such as the heater fan or heated rear window. If the engine does not regain its normal*

performance, have the system checked for faults by a franchised dealer.

e) *On vehicles equipped with an anti-theft alarm system, before disconnecting the battery, de-activate the alarm system; otherwise the alarm will be triggered.*

Devices known as 'memory-savers' or 'code-savers' can be used to avoid some of the above problems. Precise details of use vary according to the device used. Typically, it is plugged into the cigarette lighter socket, and is connected by its own wiring to a spare battery; the vehicle battery is then disconnected from the electrical system, leaving the memory-saver to pass sufficient current to maintain audio unit security codes, and other memory values, and also to run permanently-live circuits such as the clock.

⚠ **Warning: Some of these devices allow a considerable amount of current to pass, which can mean that many of the vehicle's systems are still operational when the main battery is disconnected. If a memory-saver is used, ensure that the circuit concerned is actually 'dead' before carrying out any work on it.**

Introduction

A selection of good tools is a fundamental requirement for anyone contemplating the maintenance and repair of a motor vehicle. For the owner who does not possess any, their purchase will prove a considerable expense, offsetting some of the savings made by doing-it-yourself. However, provided that the tools purchased meet the relevant national safety standards and are of good quality, they will last for many years and prove an extremely worthwhile investment.

To help the average owner to decide which tools are needed to carry out the various tasks detailed in this manual, we have compiled three lists of tools under the following headings: *Maintenance and minor repair, Repair and overhaul*, and *Special*. Newcomers to practical mechanics should start off with the *Maintenance and minor repair* tool kit, and confine themselves to the simpler jobs around the vehicle. Then, as confidence and experience grow, more difficult tasks can be undertaken, with extra tools being purchased as, and when, they are needed. In this way, a *Maintenance and minor repair* tool kit can be built up into a *Repair and overhaul* tool kit over a considerable period of time, without any major cash outlays. The experienced do-it-yourselfer will have a tool kit good enough for most repair and overhaul procedures, and will add tools from the *Special* category when it is felt that the expense is justified by the amount of use to which these tools will be put.

Maintenance and minor repair tool kit

The tools given in this list should be considered as a minimum requirement if routine maintenance, servicing and minor repair operations are to be undertaken. We recommend the purchase of combination spanners (ring one end, open-ended the other); although more expensive than open-ended ones, they do give the advantages of both types of spanner.

☐ Combination spanners:
 Metric - 8 to 19 mm inclusive
☐ Adjustable spanner - 35 mm jaw (approx.)
☐ Spark plug spanner (with rubber insert) - petrol models
☐ Spark plug gap adjustment tool - petrol models
☐ Set of feeler gauges
☐ Brake bleed nipple spanner
☐ Screwdrivers:
 Flat blade - 100 mm long x 6 mm dia
 Cross blade - 100 mm long x 6 mm dia
 Torx - various sizes (not all vehicles)
☐ Combination pliers
☐ Hacksaw (junior)
☐ Tyre pump
☐ Tyre pressure gauge
☐ Oil can
☐ Oil filter removal tool (if applicable)
☐ Fine emery cloth
☐ Wire brush (small)
☐ Funnel (medium size)
☐ Sump drain plug key (not all vehicles)

Repair and overhaul tool kit

These tools are virtually essential for anyone undertaking any major repairs to a motor vehicle, and are additional to those given in the *Maintenance and minor repair* list. Included in this list is a comprehensive set of sockets. Although these are expensive, they will be found invaluable as they are so versatile - particularly if various drives are included in the set. We recommend the half-inch square-drive type, as this can be used with most proprietary torque wrenches.

The tools in this list will sometimes need to be supplemented by tools from the *Special* list:

☐ Sockets to cover range in previous list (including Torx sockets)
☐ Reversible ratchet drive (for use with sockets)
☐ Extension piece, 250 mm (for use with sockets)
☐ Universal joint (for use with sockets)
☐ Flexible handle or sliding T "breaker bar" (for use with sockets)
☐ Torque wrench (for use with sockets)
☐ Self-locking grips
☐ Ball pein hammer
☐ Soft-faced mallet (plastic or rubber)
☐ Screwdrivers:
 Flat blade - long & sturdy, short (chubby), and narrow (electrician's) types
 Cross blade - long & sturdy, and short (chubby) types
☐ Pliers:
 Long-nosed
 Side cutters (electrician's)
 Circlip (internal and external)
☐ Cold chisel - 25 mm
☐ Scriber
☐ Scraper
☐ Centre-punch
☐ Pin punch
☐ Hacksaw
☐ Brake hose clamp
☐ Brake/clutch bleeding kit
☐ Selection of twist drills
☐ Steel rule/straight-edge
☐ Allen keys (inc. splined/Torx type)
☐ Selection of files
☐ Wire brush
☐ Axle stands
☐ Jack (strong trolley or hydraulic type)
☐ Light with extension lead
☐ Universal electrical multi-meter

Brake bleeding kit

Sockets and reversible ratchet drive

Torx key, socket and bit

Hose clamp

Angular-tightening gauge

Special tools

The tools in this list are those which are not used regularly, are expensive to buy, or which need to be used in accordance with their manufacturers' instructions. Unless relatively difficult mechanical jobs are undertaken frequently, it will not be economic to buy many of these tools. Where this is the case, you could consider clubbing together with friends (or joining a motorists' club) to make a joint purchase, or borrowing the tools against a deposit from a local garage or tool hire specialist.

The following list contains only those tools and instruments freely available to the public, and not those special tools produced by the vehicle manufacturer specifically for its dealer network. You will find occasional references to these manufacturers' special tools in the text of this manual. Generally, an alternative method of doing the job without the vehicle manufacturers' special tool is given. However, sometimes there is no alternative to using them. Where this is the case and the relevant tool cannot be bought or borrowed, you will have to entrust the work to a dealer.

☐ Angular-tightening gauge
☐ Valve spring compressor
☐ Valve grinding tool
☐ Piston ring compressor
☐ Piston ring removal/installation tool
☐ Cylinder bore hone
☐ Balljoint separator
☐ Coil spring compressors (where applicable)
☐ Two/three-legged hub and bearing puller
☐ Impact screwdriver
☐ Micrometer and/or vernier calipers
☐ Dial gauge
☐ Tachometer
☐ Fault code reader
☐ Cylinder compression gauge
☐ Hand-operated vacuum pump and gauge
☐ Clutch plate alignment set
☐ Brake shoe steady spring cup removal tool
☐ Bush and bearing removal/installation set
☐ Stud extractors
☐ Tap and die set
☐ Lifting tackle

Buying tools

Reputable motor accessory shops and superstores often offer excellent quality tools at discount prices, so it pays to shop around.

Remember, you don't have to buy the most expensive items on the shelf, but it is always advisable to steer clear of the very cheap tools. Beware of 'bargains' offered on market stalls, on-line or at car boot sales. There are plenty of good tools around at reasonable prices, but always aim to purchase items which meet the relevant national safety standards. If in doubt, ask the proprietor or manager of the shop for advice before making a purchase.

Care and maintenance of tools

Having purchased a reasonable tool kit, it is necessary to keep the tools in a clean and serviceable condition. After use, always wipe off any dirt, grease and metal particles using a clean, dry cloth, before putting the tools away. Never leave them lying around after they have been used. A simple tool rack on the garage or workshop wall for items such as screwdrivers and pliers is a good idea. Store all normal spanners and sockets in a metal box. Any measuring instruments, gauges, meters, etc, must be carefully stored where they cannot be damaged or become rusty.

Take a little care when tools are used. Hammer heads inevitably become marked, and screwdrivers lose the keen edge on their blades from time to time. A little timely attention with emery cloth or a file will soon restore items like this to a good finish.

Working facilities

Not to be forgotten when discussing tools is the workshop itself. If anything more than routine maintenance is to be carried out, a suitable working area becomes essential.

It is appreciated that many an owner-mechanic is forced by circumstances to remove an engine or similar item without the benefit of a garage or workshop. Having done this, any repairs should always be done under the cover of a roof.

Wherever possible, any dismantling should be done on a clean, flat workbench or table at a suitable working height.

Any workbench needs a vice; one with a jaw opening of 100 mm is suitable for most jobs. As mentioned previously, some clean dry storage space is also required for tools, as well as for any lubricants, cleaning fluids, touch-up paints etc, which become necessary.

Another item which may be required, and which has a much more general usage, is an electric drill with a chuck capacity of at least 8 mm. This, together with a good range of twist drills, is virtually essential for fitting accessories.

Last, but not least, always keep a supply of old newspapers and clean, lint-free rags available, and try to keep any working area as clean as possible.

Micrometers

Dial test indicator ("dial gauge")

Oil filter removal tool (strap wrench type)

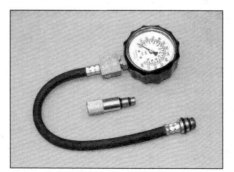

Compression tester

Bearing puller

This is a guide to getting your vehicle through the MOT test. Obviously it will not be possible to examine the vehicle to the same standard as the professional MOT tester. However, working through the following checks will enable you to identify any problem areas before submitting the vehicle for the test.

It has only been possible to summarise the test requirements here, based on the regulations in force at the time of printing. Test standards are becoming increasingly stringent, although there are some exemptions for older vehicles.

An assistant will be needed to help carry out some of these checks.

The checks have been sub-divided into four categories, as follows:

1 Checks carried out **FROM THE DRIVER'S SEAT**

2 Checks carried out **WITH THE VEHICLE ON THE GROUND**

3 Checks carried out **WITH THE VEHICLE RAISED AND THE WHEELS FREE TO TURN**

4 Checks carried out on **YOUR VEHICLE'S EXHAUST EMISSION SYSTEM**

---

1 Checks carried out **FROM THE DRIVER'S SEAT**

Handbrake (parking brake)

☐ Test the operation of the handbrake. Excessive travel (too many clicks) indicates incorrect brake or cable adjustment.
☐ Check that the handbrake cannot be released by tapping the lever sideways. Check the security of the lever mountings.

☐ If the parking brake is foot-operated, check that the pedal is secure and without excessive travel, and that the release mechanism operates correctly.
☐ Where applicable, test the operation of the electronic handbrake. The brake should engage and disengage without excessive delay. If the warning light does not extinguish when the brake is disengaged, this could indicate a fault which will need further investigation.

Footbrake

☐ Depress the brake pedal and check that it does not creep down to the floor, indicating a master cylinder fault. Release the pedal,

wait a few seconds, then depress it again. If the pedal travels nearly to the floor before firm resistance is felt, brake adjustment or repair is necessary. If the pedal feels spongy, there is air in the hydraulic system which must be removed by bleeding.

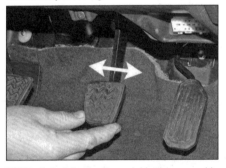

☐ Check that the brake pedal is secure and in good condition. Check also for signs of fluid leaks on the pedal, floor or carpets, which would indicate failed seals in the brake master cylinder.
☐ Check the servo unit (when applicable) by operating the brake pedal several times, then keeping the pedal depressed and starting the engine. As the engine starts, the pedal will move down slightly. If not, the vacuum hose or the servo itself may be faulty.

Steering wheel and column

☐ Examine the steering wheel for fractures or looseness of the hub, spokes or rim.
☐ Move the steering wheel from side to side and then up and down. Check that the steering wheel is not loose on the column, indicating wear or a loose retaining nut. Continue moving the steering wheel as before, but also turn it slightly from left to right.

☐ Check that the steering wheel is not loose on the column, and that there is no abnormal movement of the steering wheel, indicating wear in the column support bearings or couplings.
☐ Check that the ignition lock (where fitted) engages and disengages correctly.
☐ Steering column adjustment mechanisms (where fitted) must be able to lock the column securely in place with no play evident.

Windscreen, mirrors and sunvisor

☐ The windscreen must be free of cracks or other significant damage within the driver's field of view. (Small stone chips are acceptable.) Rear view mirrors must be secure, intact, and capable of being adjusted.

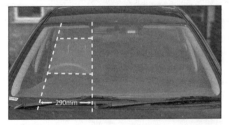

☐ The driver's sunvisor must be capable of being stored in the "up" position.

Seat belts and seats

Note: *The following checks are applicable to all seat belts, front and rear.*

☐ Examine the webbing of all the belts (including rear belts if fitted) for cuts, serious fraying or deterioration. Fasten and unfasten each belt to check the buckles. If applicable, check the retracting mechanism. Check the security of all seat belt mountings accessible from inside the vehicle, ensuring any height adjustable mountings lock securely in place.

☐ Seat belts with pre-tensioners, once activated, have a "flag" or similar showing on the seat belt stalk. This, in itself, is not a reason for test failure.

☐ The front seats themselves must be securely attached and the backrests must lock in the upright position.

Doors

☐ Both front doors must be able to be opened and closed from outside and inside, and must latch securely when closed.

Bonnet and boot/tailgate

☐ The bonnet and boot/tailgate must latch securely when closed.

2 Checks carried out WITH THE VEHICLE ON THE GROUND

Vehicle identification

☐ Number plates must be in good condition, secure and legible, with letters and numbers correctly spaced – spacing at (A) should be 33 mm and at (B) 11 mm. At the front, digits must be black on a white background and at the rear black on a yellow background. Other background designs (such as honeycomb) are not permitted.

☐ The VIN plate and/or homologation plate must be permanently displayed and legible.

Electrical equipment

☐ Switch on the ignition and check the operation of the horn.

☐ Check the windscreen washers and wipers, examining the wiper blades; renew damaged or perished blades. Also check the operation of the stop-lights.

☐ Check the operation of the sidelights and number plate lights. The lenses and reflectors must be secure, clean and undamaged.

☐ Check the operation and alignment of the headlights. The headlight reflectors must not be tarnished and the lenses must be undamaged.

☐ Switch on the ignition and check the operation of the direction indicators (including the instrument panel tell-tale) and the hazard warning lights. Operation of the sidelights and stop-lights must not affect the indicators - if it does, the cause is usually a bad earth at the rear light cluster. Indicators should flash at a rate of between 60 and 120 times per minute – faster or slower than this could indicate a fault with the flasher unit or a bad earth at one of the light units.

☐ Check the operation of the rear foglight(s), including the warning light on the instrument panel or in the switch.

☐ The warning lights must illuminate in accordance with the manufacturer's design. For most vehicles, the ABS and other warning lights should illuminate when the ignition is switched on, and (if the system is operating properly) extinguish after a few seconds. Refer to the owner's handbook.

Footbrake

☐ Examine the master cylinder, brake pipes and servo unit for leaks, loose mountings, corrosion or other damage. If ABS is fitted, this unit should also be examined for signs of leaks or corrosion.

☐ The fluid reservoir must be secure and the fluid level must be between the upper (**A**) and lower (**B**) markings.

☐ Inspect both front brake flexible hoses for cracks or deterioration of the rubber. Turn the steering from lock to lock, and ensure that the hoses do not contact the wheel, tyre, or any part of the steering or suspension mechanism. With the brake pedal firmly depressed, check the hoses for bulges or leaks under pressure.

Steering and suspension

☐ Have your assistant turn the steering wheel from side to side slightly, up to the point where the steering gear just begins to transmit this movement to the roadwheels. Check for excessive free play between the steering wheel and the steering gear, indicating wear or insecurity of the steering column joints, the column-to-steering gear coupling, or the steering gear itself.

☐ Have your assistant turn the steering wheel more vigorously in each direction, so that the roadwheels just begin to turn. As this is done, examine all the steering joints, linkages, fittings and attachments. Renew any component that shows signs of wear or damage. On vehicles with power steering, check the security and condition of the steering pump, drivebelt and hoses.

☐ Check that the vehicle is standing level, and at approximately the correct ride height.

Shock absorbers

☐ Depress each corner of the vehicle in turn, then release it. The vehicle should rise and then settle in its normal position. If the vehicle continues to rise and fall, the shock absorber is defective. A shock absorber which has seized will also cause the vehicle to fail.

Exhaust system

☐ Start the engine. With your assistant holding a rag over the tailpipe, check the entire system for leaks. Repair or renew leaking sections.

3 Checks carried out **WITH THE VEHICLE RAISED AND THE WHEELS FREE TO TURN**

Jack up the front and rear of the vehicle, and securely support it on axle stands. Position the stands clear of the suspension assemblies. Ensure that the wheels are clear of the ground and that the steering can be turned from lock to lock.

Steering mechanism

☐ Have your assistant turn the steering from lock to lock. Check that the steering turns smoothly, and that no part of the steering mechanism, including a wheel or tyre, fouls any brake hose or pipe or any part of the body structure.
☐ Examine the steering rack rubber gaiters for damage or insecurity of the retaining clips. If power steering is fitted, check for signs of damage or leakage of the fluid hoses, pipes or connections. Also check for excessive stiffness or binding of the steering, a missing split pin or locking device, or severe corrosion of the body structure within 30 cm of any steering component attachment point.

Front and rear suspension and wheel bearings

☐ Starting at the front right-hand side, grasp the roadwheel at the 3 o'clock and 9 o'clock positions and rock gently but firmly. Check for free play or insecurity at the wheel bearings, suspension balljoints, or suspension mount-ings, pivots and attachments.
☐ Now grasp the wheel at the 12 o'clock and 6 o'clock positions and repeat the previous inspection. Spin the wheel, and check for roughness or tightness of the front wheel bearing.

☐ If excess free play is suspected at a component pivot point, this can be confirmed by using a large screwdriver or similar tool and levering between the mounting and the component attachment. This will confirm whether the wear is in the pivot bush, its retaining bolt, or in the mounting itself (the bolt holes can often become elongated).

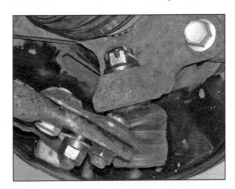

☐ Carry out all the above checks at the other front wheel, and then at both rear wheels.

Springs and shock absorbers

☐ Examine the suspension struts (when applicable) for serious fluid leakage, corrosion, or damage to the casing. Also check the security of the mounting points.
☐ If coil springs are fitted, check that the spring ends locate in their seats, and that the spring is not corroded, cracked or broken.
☐ If leaf springs are fitted, check that all leaves are intact, that the axle is securely attached to each spring, and that there is no deterioration of the spring eye mountings, bushes, and shackles.

☐ The same general checks apply to vehicles fitted with other suspension types, such as torsion bars, hydraulic displacer units, etc. Ensure that all mountings and attachments are secure, that there are no signs of excessive wear, corrosion or damage, and (on hydraulic types) that there are no fluid leaks or damaged pipes.
☐ Inspect the shock absorbers for signs of serious fluid leakage. Check for wear of the mounting bushes or attachments, or damage to the body of the unit.

Driveshafts (fwd vehicles only)

☐ Rotate each front wheel in turn and inspect the constant velocity joint gaiters for splits or damage. Also check that each driveshaft is straight and undamaged.

Braking system

☐ If possible without dismantling, check brake pad wear and disc condition. Ensure that the friction lining material has not worn excessively, (A) and that the discs are not fractured, pitted, scored or badly worn (B).

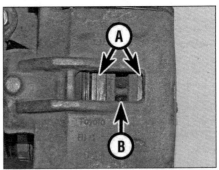

☐ Examine all the rigid brake pipes underneath the vehicle, and the flexible hose(s) at the rear. Look for corrosion, chafing or insecurity of the pipes, and for signs of bulging under pressure, chafing, splits or deterioration of the flexible hoses.
☐ Look for signs of fluid leaks at the brake calipers or on the brake backplates. Repair or renew leaking components.
☐ Slowly spin each wheel, while your assistant depresses and releases the footbrake. Ensure that each brake is operating and does not bind when the pedal is released.

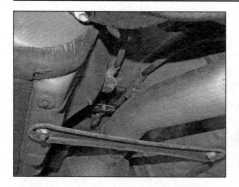

☐ Examine the handbrake mechanism, checking for frayed or broken cables, excessive corrosion, or wear or insecurity of the linkage. Check that the mechanism works on each relevant wheel, and releases fully, without binding.

☐ It is not possible to test brake efficiency without special equipment, but a road test can be carried out later to check that the vehicle pulls up in a straight line.

Fuel and exhaust systems

☐ Inspect the fuel tank (including the filler cap), fuel pipes, hoses and unions. All components must be secure and free from leaks. Locking fuel caps must lock securely and the key must be provided for the MOT test.

☐ Examine the exhaust system over its entire length, checking for any damaged, broken or missing mountings, security of the retaining clamps and rust or corrosion.

Wheels and tyres

☐ Examine the sidewalls and tread area of each tyre in turn. Check for cuts, tears, lumps, bulges, separation of the tread, and exposure of the ply or cord due to wear or damage. Check that the tyre bead is correctly seated on the wheel rim, that the valve is sound and properly seated, and that the wheel is not distorted or damaged.

☐ Check that the tyres are of the correct size for the vehicle, that they are of the same size and type on each axle, and that the pressures are correct.

☐ Check the tyre tread depth. The legal minimum at the time of writing is 1.6 mm over the central three-quarters of the tread width. Abnormal tread wear may indicate incorrect front wheel alignment or wear in steering or suspension components.

☐ If the spare wheel is fitted externally or in a separate carrier beneath the vehicle, check that mountings are secure and free of excessive corrosion.

Body corrosion

☐ Check the condition of the entire vehicle structure for signs of corrosion in load-bearing areas. (These include chassis box sections, side sills, cross-members, pillars, and all suspension, steering, braking system and seat belt mountings and anchorages.) Any corrosion which has seriously reduced the thickness of a load-bearing area (or is within 30 cm of safety-related components such as steering or suspension) is likely to cause the vehicle to fail. In this case professional repairs are likely to be needed.

☐ Damage or corrosion which causes sharp or otherwise dangerous edges to be exposed will also cause the vehicle to fail.

Towbars

☐ Check the condition of mounting points (both beneath the vehicle and within boot/hatchback areas) for signs of corrosion, ensuring that all fixings are secure and not worn or damaged. There must be no excessive play in detachable tow ball arms or quick-release mechanisms.

4 Checks carried out on YOUR VEHICLE'S EXHAUST EMISSION SYSTEM

Petrol models

☐ The engine should be warmed up, and running well (ignition system in good order, air filter element clean, etc).

☐ Before testing, run the engine at around 2500 rpm for 20 seconds. Let the engine drop to idle, and watch for smoke from the exhaust. If the idle speed is too high, or if dense blue or black smoke emerges for more than 5 seconds, the vehicle will fail. Typically, blue smoke signifies oil burning (engine wear); black smoke means unburnt fuel (dirty air cleaner element, or other fuel system fault).

☐ An exhaust gas analyser for measuring carbon monoxide (CO) and hydrocarbons (HC) is now needed. If one cannot be hired or borrowed, have a local garage perform the check.

CO emissions (mixture)

☐ The MOT tester has access to the CO limits for all vehicles. The CO level is measured at idle speed, and at 'fast idle' (2500 to 3000 rpm). The following limits are given as a general guide:

  At idle speed – Less than 0.5% CO
  At 'fast idle' – Less than 0.3% CO
  Lambda reading – 0.97 to 1.03

☐ If the CO level is too high, this may point to poor maintenance, a fuel injection system problem, faulty lambda (oxygen) sensor or catalytic converter. Try an injector cleaning treatment, and check the vehicle's ECU for fault codes.

HC emissions

☐ The MOT tester has access to HC limits for all vehicles. The HC level is measured at 'fast idle' (2500 to 3000 rpm). The following limits are given as a general guide:

  At 'fast idle' – Less then 200 ppm

☐ Excessive HC emissions are typically caused by oil being burnt (worn engine), or by a blocked crankcase ventilation system ('breather'). If the engine oil is old and thin, an oil change may help. If the engine is running badly, check the vehicle's ECU for fault codes.

Diesel models

☐ The only emission test for diesel engines is measuring exhaust smoke density, using a calibrated smoke meter. The test involves accelerating the engine at least 3 times to its maximum unloaded speed.

Note: *On engines with a timing belt, it is VITAL that the belt is in good condition before the test is carried out.*

☐ With the engine warmed up, it is first purged by running at around 2500 rpm for 20 seconds. A governor check is then carried out, by slowly accelerating the engine to its maximum speed. After this, the smoke meter is connected, and the engine is accelerated quickly to maximum speed three times. If the smoke density is less than the limits given below, the vehicle will pass:

  Non-turbo vehicles: 2.5m-1
  Turbocharged vehicles: 3.0m-1

☐ If excess smoke is produced, try fitting a new air cleaner element, or using an injector cleaning treatment. If the engine is running badly, where applicable, check the vehicle's ECU for fault codes. Also check the vehicle's EGR system, where applicable. At high mileages, the injectors may require professional attention.

Engine

- [ ] Engine fails to rotate when attempting to start
- [ ] Engine rotates, but will not start
- [ ] Engine difficult to start when cold
- [ ] Engine difficult to start when hot
- [ ] Starter motor noisy or excessively-rough in engagement
- [ ] Engine starts, but stops immediately
- [ ] Engine misfires, or idles unevenly
- [ ] Engine stalls, or lacks power
- [ ] Engine backfires
- [ ] Engine noises
- [ ] Oil consumption excessive
- [ ] Oil pressure warning light illuminated with engine running

Cooling system

- [ ] Overheating
- [ ] Overcooling
- [ ] External coolant leakage
- [ ] Internal coolant leakage
- [ ] Corrosion

Fuel and exhaust systems

- [ ] Fuel consumption excessive
- [ ] Fuel leakage and/or fuel odour
- [ ] Black smoke in exhaust
- [ ] Blue or white smoke in exhaust
- [ ] Excessive noise or fumes from exhaust system

Clutch

- [ ] Pedal travels to floor – no pressure or very little resistance
- [ ] Clutch fails to disengage (unable to select gears)
- [ ] Clutch slips (engine speed increases, with no increase in vehicle speed)
- [ ] Judder as clutch is engaged
- [ ] Noise when depressing or releasing clutch pedal

Manual transmission

- [ ] Noisy in neutral with engine running
- [ ] Noisy in one particular gear
- [ ] Difficulty engaging gears
- [ ] Jumps out of gear
- [ ] Vibration
- [ ] Lubricant leaks

Multi-Mode transmission

- [ ] Noisy in neutral with engine running
- [ ] Noisy in one particular gear
- [ ] Difficulty engaging gears
- [ ] Jumps out of gear
- [ ] Vibration
- [ ] Lubricant leaks
- [ ] General gear selection problems
- [ ] Engine will not start in any gear, or starts in gears other than Park or Neutral

Driveshafts

- [ ] Vibration when accelerating or decelerating
- [ ] Clicking or knocking noise on turns (at slow speed on full-lock)

Braking system

- [ ] Car pulls to one side under braking
- [ ] Noise (grinding or high-pitched squeal) when brakes applied
- [ ] Excessive brake pedal travel
- [ ] Brake pedal feels spongy when depressed
- [ ] Excessive brake pedal effort required to stop vehicle
- [ ] Judder felt through brake pedal or steering wheel when braking
- [ ] Brakes binding
- [ ] Rear wheels locking under normal braking

Suspension and steering

- [ ] Car pulls to one side
- [ ] Wheel wobble and vibration
- [ ] Excessive pitching and/or rolling around corners, or during braking
- [ ] Wandering or general instability
- [ ] Excessively-stiff steering
- [ ] Excessive play in steering
- [ ] Lack of power assistance
- [ ] Tyre wear excessive

Electrical system

- [ ] Battery will only hold a charge for a few days
- [ ] Ignition (no-charge) warning light remains illuminated with engine running
- [ ] Ignition (no-charge) warning light fails to come on
- [ ] Lights inoperative
- [ ] Instrument readings inaccurate or erratic
- [ ] Horn faults
- [ ] Windscreen/tailgate wiper faults
- [ ] Windscreen/tailgate washer faults
- [ ] Electric window faults
- [ ] Central locking system faults

Introduction

The car owner who does his or her own maintenance according to the recommended service schedules should not have to use this section of the manual very often. Modern component reliability is such that, provided those items subject to wear or deterioration are inspected or renewed at the specified intervals, sudden failure is comparatively rare. Faults do not usually just happen as a result of sudden failure, but develop over a period of time. Major mechanical failures in particular are usually preceded by characteristic symptoms over hundreds or even thousands of miles. Those components, which do occasionally fail without warning, are often small and easily carried in the car.

With any fault finding, the first step is to decide where to begin investigations. Sometimes this is obvious, but on other occasions, a little detective work will be necessary. The owner who makes half a dozen haphazard adjustments or replacements may be successful in curing a fault (or its symptoms), but will be none the wiser if the fault recurs, and ultimately may have spent more time and money than was necessary. A calm and logical approach will be found to be more satisfactory in the long run. Always take into account any warning signs or abnormalities that may have been noticed in the period preceding the fault – power loss, high or low gauge readings,

unusual smells, etc – and remember that failure of components such as fuses may only be pointers to some underlying fault.

The pages, which follow, provide an easy reference guide to the more common problems that may occur during the operation of the car. These problems and their possible causes are grouped under headings denoting various components or systems, such as Engine, Cooling system, etc. The Chapter and/or Section which deals with the problem is also shown in brackets. Whatever the fault, certain basic principles apply. These are as follows:

Verify the fault. This is simply a matter of being sure that you know what the symptoms are before starting work. This is particularly important if you are investigating a fault for someone else, who may not have described it very accurately.

Don't overlook the obvious. For example if the car won't start, is there fuel in the tank? (Don't take anyone else's word on this particular point, and don't trust the fuel gauge either!) If an electrical fault is indicated, look for loose or broken wires before using the test gear.

Cure the disease, not the symptom. Substituting a flat battery with a fully charged one will get you off the hard shoulder, but if the underlying cause is not attended to, the new battery will go the same way.

Don't take anything for granted. Particularly, don't forget that a 'new' component may itself be defective (especially if it's been rattling around in the boot for months), and don't leave components out of a fault diagnosis sequence just because they are new or recently fitted. When you do finally diagnose a difficult fault, you'll probably realise that all the evidence was there from the start.

Consider what work, if any, has recently been carried out. Many faults arise through careless or hurried work. For instance, if any work has been performed under the bonnet, could some of the wiring have been dislodged or incorrectly routed, or a hose trapped? Have all the fasteners been properly tightened? Were new, genuine parts and new gaskets used? There is often a certain amount of detective work to be done in this case, as an apparently unrelated task can have far-reaching consequences.

Engine

Engine fails to rotate when attempting to start

- [ ] Battery terminal connections loose or corroded (*Weekly checks*).
- [ ] Battery discharged or faulty (Chapter 5A).
- [ ] Broken, loose or disconnected wiring in the starting circuit (Chapter 5A).
- [ ] Defective starter solenoid or ignition switch (Chapter 5A or 12).
- [ ] Defective starter motor (Chapter 5A).
- [ ] Flywheel ring gear or starter pinion teeth loose or broken (Chapter 2A or 5A).
- [ ] Engine earth strap broken or disconnected.
- [ ] Engine suffering 'hydraulic lock' (eg, from water taken in after traversing flooded roads, or from a serious internal coolant leak) – consult a dealer for advice.
- [ ] Multi-Mode transmission shift lock fault, footbrake not depressed, or faulty brake light switch (Chapter 7B or 9).

Engine rotates, but will not start

- [ ] Fuel tank empty.
- [ ] Battery discharged or inadequate capacity (engine rotates slowly) (Chapter 5A).
- [ ] Battery terminal connections loose or corroded (*Weekly checks*).
- [ ] Ignition components damp or damaged (Chapter 1 or 5B).
- [ ] Worn, faulty or incorrectly-gapped spark plugs (Chapter 1).
- [ ] Immobiliser faulty or incorrectly used, or 'uncoded' ignition key being used (Chapter 12).
- [ ] Crankshaft sensor, or other engine management system sensor, fault (Chapter 4A)
- [ ] Air filter element dirty or clogged (Chapter 1).
- [ ] Blockage in exhaust system (Chapter 4B).
- [ ] Low cylinder compressions (Chapter 2A)
- [ ] Valve timing incorrect, possibly through a poorly-fitted timing chain (Chapter 2A).
- [ ] Major mechanical failure (eg, camshaft drive) (Chapter 2A).

Engine difficult to start when cold

- [ ] Battery discharged (Chapter 5A).
- [ ] Battery terminal connections loose or corroded (see *Weekly checks*).
- [ ] Worn, faulty or incorrectly-gapped spark plugs (Chapter 1).
- [ ] Other ignition system fault (Chapter 5B).

- [ ] Fuel system fault (Chapter 4A).
- [ ] Wrong grade of engine oil used (*Weekly checks* or Chapter 1).
- [ ] Low cylinder compressions (Chapter 2A)

Engine difficult to start when hot

- [ ] Air filter element dirty or clogged (Chapter 1).
- [ ] Fuel system fault (Chapter 4A).
- [ ] Low cylinder compressions (Chapter 2A).

Starter motor noisy or excessively rough

- [ ] Starter pinion or flywheel ring gear teeth loose or broken (Chapter 2A or 5A).
- [ ] Starter motor mounting bolts loose or missing (Chapter 5A).
- [ ] Starter motor internal components worn or damaged (Chapter 5A).

Engine starts, but stops immediately

- [ ] Loose or faulty electrical connections in the ignition circuit (Chapter 1 or 5B).
- [ ] Vacuum leak at the throttle body, inlet manifold or associated hoses (Chapter 4A).
- [ ] Blocked injectors/fuel system fault (Chapter 4A).
- [ ] Fuel very low in tank.
- [ ] Restriction in fuel feed.
- [ ] Air cleaner dirty, or blockage in air intake system (Chapter 1 or 4A).
- [ ] Blockage in exhaust system (Chapter 4B).

Engine misfires, or idles unevenly

- [ ] Air cleaner dirty or blockage in air intake system (Chapter 1 or 4A).
- [ ] Vacuum leak at the throttle body, inlet manifold or associated hoses (Chapter 4A).
- [ ] Worn, faulty or incorrectly-gapped spark plugs (Chapter 1).
- [ ] Valve clearances incorrect (Chapter 2A).
- [ ] Uneven or low cylinder compressions (Chapter 2A).
- [ ] Camshaft lobes worn (Chapter 2A).
- [ ] Timing chain incorrectly fitted (Chapter 2A).
- [ ] Blocked injectors/fuel injection system fault (Chapter 4A).
- [ ] Valve(s) sticking, valve spring(s) weak or broken, or poor compressions (Chapter 2A).
- [ ] Overheating (Chapter 3).
- [ ] Cylinder head gasket blown (Chapter 2A).

Engine (continued)

Engine stalls, or lacks power

☐ Fuel filter choked (Chapter 4A).
☐ Fuel pump faulty, or delivery pressure low (Chapter 4A).
☐ Valve clearances incorrect (Chapter 2A).
☐ Vacuum leak at the throttle body, inlet manifold or associated hoses (Chapter 4A).
☐ Worn, faulty or incorrectly-gapped spark plugs (Chapter 1).
☐ Faulty ignition coils (Chapter 5B).
☐ Uneven or low cylinder compressions (Chapter 2A).
☐ Blocked injector/fuel system fault (Chapter 4A).
☐ Blocked catalytic converter (Chapter 4B).
☐ Engine overheating (Chapter 3).
☐ Air filter element blocked (Chapter 1).
☐ Accelerator cable problem (Chapter 4A).
☐ Throttle position sensor fault (Chapter 4A).
☐ Engine management warning light on (fault code in system) (Chapter 4A).
☐ Timing chain worn, or incorrectly fitted (Chapter 2A).
☐ Brakes binding (Chapter 1 or 9).
☐ Clutch slipping (Chapter 6).

Engine backfires

☐ Timing chain incorrectly fitted (Chapter 2A).
☐ Vacuum leak at the throttle body, inlet manifold or associated hoses (Chapter 4A).
☐ Blocked catalytic converter (Chapter 4B).
☐ Ignition coil(s) faulty (Chapter 5B).

Engine noises

Pre-ignition (pinking) or knocking during acceleration or under load

☐ Ignition system fault (Chapter 1 or 5B).
☐ Incorrect grade of spark plug (Chapter 1).
☐ Incorrect grade (or type) of fuel used (Chapter 4A).
☐ Vacuum leak at the throttle body, inlet manifold or associated hoses (Chapter 4A).
☐ Excessive carbon build up in cylinder head/pistons (Chapter 2A or 2B).
☐ Blocked injector/fuel injection system fault (Chapter 4A).

Whistling or wheezing noises

☐ Leaking inlet manifold or throttle body gasket (Chapter 4A).

☐ Leaking exhaust manifold gasket, or pipe-to-manifold joint (Chapter 4B).
☐ Leaking vacuum hose (Chapter 4B or 9).
☐ Blowing cylinder head gasket (Chapter 2A).
☐ Partially blocked or leaking crankcase ventilation system (Chapter 4B).

Tapping or rattling noises

☐ Worn camshaft(s) (Chapter 2A)
☐ Ancillary component fault (coolant pump, alternator, etc) (Chapter 3, 5A, etc).
☐ Valve clearances incorrect (Chapter 2A).

Knocking or thumping noises

☐ Worn big-end bearings (regular heavy knocking, perhaps less under load) (Chapter 2B).
☐ Worn main bearings (rumbling and knocking, perhaps worsening under load) (Chapter 2B).
☐ Piston slap – most noticeable when cold, caused by piston/bore wear (Chapter 2B).
☐ Ancillary component fault (coolant pump, alternator, etc) (Chapter 3, 5A, etc).
☐ Engine mountings worn or defective (Chapter 2A).
☐ Front suspension or steering components worn (Chapter 10).

Oil consumption excessive

☐ External leakage (standing or running) – eg, timing chain cover, crankshaft oil seals (Chapter 2A).
☐ New engine not yet run-in.
☐ Engine oil incorrect grade/poor quality, or oil level too high (*Weekly checks*).
☐ Crankcase ventilation system obstructed (Chapter 1 or 4B).
☐ Burning oil due to general engine wear – pistons and/or bores, valve stem oil seals, etc (Chapter 2B).

Oil pressure warning light illuminated with engine running

☐ Low oil level or incorrect oil grade (*Weekly checks*).
☐ Engine oil and filter change overdue (Chapter 1).
☐ Faulty oil pressure warning light switch (Chapter 2A).
☐ Worn engine bearings and/or oil pump (Chapter 2A or 2B).
☐ High engine operating temperature (Chapter 3).
☐ Oil pick-up strainer clogged – remove sump to check (Chapter 2A).

Cooling system

Overheating

☐ Insufficient coolant in system (*Weekly checks*).
☐ Thermostat faulty (Chapter 3).
☐ Radiator core blocked or grille restricted (Chapter 3).
☐ Radiator electric cooling fan or coolant temperature sensor faulty (Chapter 3).
☐ Pressure cap faulty (Chapter 3).
☐ Inaccurate coolant temperature gauge sender (Chapter 3).
☐ Airlock in cooling system (Chapter 1).
☐ Engine management system fault (Chapter 4A).
☐ Blockage in exhaust system (Chapter 4B).
☐ Cylinder head gasket blown (Chapter 2A).

Overcooling

☐ Thermostat faulty (Chapter 3).
☐ Inaccurate coolant temperature gauge sender (Chapter 3).

External coolant leakage

☐ Deteriorated or damaged hoses or hose clips (Chapter 1).
☐ Radiator core or heater matrix leaking (Chapter 3).
☐ Pressure cap faulty (Chapter 1).
☐ Water pump or thermostat housing leaking (Chapter 3).
☐ Boiling due to overheating (Chapter 3).
☐ Core plug leaking (Chapter 2B).

Internal coolant leakage

☐ Leaking cylinder head gasket (Chapter 2A).
☐ Cracked cylinder head or cylinder bore (Chapter 2A or 2B).

Corrosion

☐ Infrequent draining and flushing (Chapter 1).
☐ Incorrect antifreeze mixture, or inappropriate antifreeze type (*Weekly checks* and Chapter 1).

Fuel and exhaust systems

Fuel consumption excessive

- [ ] New engine not yet run-in.
- [ ] Air cleaner element dirty, or blockage in air intake system (Chapter 1 or 4A).
- [ ] Fuel system fault (Chapter 4A).
- [ ] Crankcase ventilation system blocked (Chapter 4B).
- [ ] Unsympathetic driving style, or adverse conditions.
- [ ] Tyres underinflated (see *Weekly checks*).
- [ ] Brakes binding (Chapter 1 or 9).
- [ ] Fuel leak, causing apparent high consumption (Chapter 1 or 4A).
- [ ] Valve timing incorrect, possibly through a poorly-fitted timing chain (Chapter 2A).

Fuel leakage and/or fuel odour

- [ ] Damaged or corroded fuel tank, pipes or connections (Chapter 1).
- [ ] Evaporative emissions system fault (Chapter 4B).

Black smoke in exhaust

- [ ] Air cleaner element dirty, or blockage in air intake system (Chapter 1 or 4A).
- [ ] Fuel system fault (Chapter 4A).

Blue or white smoke in exhaust

- [ ] Engine oil incorrect grade or poor quality, or fuel passing into sump (worn piston rings/bores).
- [ ] Air cleaner element dirty, or blockage in air intake system (Chapter 1 or 4A).
- [ ] Injector(s) faulty (Chapter 4A).
- [ ] Blocked or damaged emissions system hoses or components (Chapter 4B).
- [ ] General engine wear – pistons and/or bores, valve stem oil seals, etc (Chapter 2B).
- [ ] Cylinder head gasket blown – white smoke (Chapter 2A).

Excessive noise or fumes from exhaust system

- [ ] Leaking exhaust system or manifold joints (Chapter 1 or 4B).
- [ ] Leaking, corroded or damaged silencers or pipe (Chapter 1 or 4B).
- [ ] Oxygen sensors loose or damaged (Chapter 4B).
- [ ] Broken mountings, causing body or suspension contact (Chapter 1 or 4B).

Clutch

Pedal travels to floor – no pressure or very little resistance

- [ ] Faulty cable/electric release system (Chapter 6).
- [ ] Clutch pedal return spring detached or broken (Chapter 6).
- [ ] Broken clutch release bearing or fork (Chapter 6).
- [ ] Broken diaphragm spring in clutch pressure plate (Chapter 6).

Clutch fails to disengage (unable to select gears)

- [ ] Faulty cable/electric release system (Chapter 6).
- [ ] Clutch disc sticking on transmission input shaft splines (Chapter 6).
- [ ] Clutch disc sticking to flywheel or pressure plate (Chapter 6).
- [ ] Faulty pressure plate assembly (Chapter 6).
- [ ] Clutch release mechanism worn or incorrectly assembled (Chapter 6).

Clutch slips (engine speed increases, with no increase in vehicle speed)

- [ ] Faulty cable/electric release system (Chapter 6).

- [ ] Clutch disc linings excessively worn (Chapter 6).
- [ ] Clutch disc linings contaminated with oil or grease (Chapter 6).
- [ ] Faulty pressure plate or weak diaphragm spring (Chapter 6).

Judder as clutch is engaged

- [ ] Clutch disc linings contaminated with oil or grease (Chapter 6).
- [ ] Clutch disc linings excessively worn (Chapter 6).
- [ ] Faulty or distorted pressure plate or diaphragm spring (Chapter 6).
- [ ] Worn or loose engine/transmission mountings (Chapter 2A).
- [ ] Clutch disc hub or transmission input shaft splines worn (Chapter 6 or 7).

Noise when depressing or releasing clutch pedal

- [ ] Worn clutch release bearing (Chapter 6).
- [ ] Worn or dry clutch pedal bushes (Chapter 6).
- [ ] Faulty pressure plate assembly (Chapter 6).
- [ ] Pressure plate diaphragm spring broken (Chapter 6).
- [ ] Broken clutch disc cushioning springs (Chapter 6).

Manual transmission

Noisy in neutral with engine running

- [ ] Lack of oil (Chapter 1).
- [ ] Input shaft bearings worn (noise apparent with clutch pedal released, but not when depressed) (Chapter 7A).*
- [ ] Clutch release bearing worn (noise apparent with clutch pedal depressed, possibly less when released) (Chapter 6).

Noisy in one particular gear

- [ ] Worn, damaged or chipped gear teeth (Chapter 7A).*

Difficulty engaging gears

- [ ] Clutch fault (Chapter 6).
- [ ] Worn or damaged gear cables (Chapter 7A).
- [ ] Worn synchroniser assemblies (Chapter 7A).*

Jumps out of gear

- [ ] Worn or damaged gear cables (Chapter 7A).

- [ ] Worn synchroniser assemblies (Chapter 7A).*
- [ ] Worn selector forks (Chapter 7A).*

Vibration

- [ ] Lack of oil (Chapter 1).
- [ ] Worn bearings (Chapter 7A).*

Lubricant leaks

- [ ] Leaking differential side gear oil seal (Chapter 7A).
- [ ] Leaking housing joint (Chapter 7A).*
- [ ] Leaking input shaft oil seal (Chapter 7A).*
- [ ] Leaking selector shaft oil seal (Chapter 7A).*

* Although the corrective action necessary to remedy the symptoms described is beyond the scope of the home mechanic, the above information should be helpful in isolating the cause of the condition, so that the owner can communicate clearly with a professional mechanic.

Multi-Mode Transmission

Note: *The Multi-Mode Transmission system consists of a manual transmission (as seen in Chapter 7A), a self-adjusting clutch pressure plate (see Chapter 6), a transmission ECU, actuators, sensors and switches. This allows the manual transmission to be electro-mechanically controlled. For problems other than the following, see manual transmissions previously. Do not be too hasty in removing the transmission if a fault is suspected, as most of the testing is carried out with the unit still fitted.*

General gear selection problems

☐ Chapter 7B deals with the gear change actuators and solenoids.

Engine will not start in any gear, or starts in gears other than Neutral

☐ Shift lock system faulty (Chapter 7B).
☐ Selector wiring faulty (Chapter 7B).

Driveshafts

Vibration when accelerating or decelerating

☐ Worn inner constant velocity joint (Chapter 1 or 8).
☐ Bent or distorted driveshaft (Chapter 8).
☐ Loose or damaged driveshaft nut (Chapter 1 or 8).

Clicking or knocking noise on turns (at slow speed on full-lock)

☐ Lack of constant velocity joint lubricant (Chapter 8).
☐ Worn outer constant velocity joint (Chapter 1 or 8).
☐ Loose or damaged driveshaft nut (Chapter 1 or 8).

Braking system

Note: *Before assuming that a brake problem exists, make sure that the tyres are in good condition and correctly inflated, that the front wheel alignment is correct, and that the car is not loaded with weight in an unequal manner. Apart from checking the condition of all pipe and hose connections, any faults occurring on the Anti-lock Braking System (ABS) should be referred to a dealer for diagnosis.*

Car pulls to one side under braking

☐ Worn, defective, damaged or contaminated front or rear brake pads/shoes on one side (Chapter 1).
☐ Seized or partially-seized front caliper, or leaking rear wheel cylinder (Chapter 9).
☐ A mixture of brake pad/shoe lining materials fitted between sides (Chapter 1).
☐ Brake caliper mounting bolts loose (Chapter 9).
☐ Rear hub/brake backplate mounting bolts loose (Chapter 9).
☐ Worn or damaged steering or suspension components (Chapter 10).

Noise (grinding or high-pitched squeal) when brakes applied

☐ Brake pad or shoe friction lining material worn down to metal backing Chapter 1).
☐ Excessive corrosion of brake disc or drum (may be apparent after the car has been standing for some time) (Chapter 1).

Excessive brake pedal travel

☐ Inoperative rear brake self-adjust mechanism (Chapter 9).
☐ Rear wheel cylinders leaking (Chapter 9).
☐ Faulty master cylinder (Chapter 9).
☐ Air in hydraulic system (Chapter 9).

Brake pedal feels spongy when depressed

☐ Air in hydraulic system (Chapter 9).

☐ Rear wheel cylinders leaking (Chapter 9).
☐ Deteriorated flexible rubber brake hoses (Chapter 9).
☐ Master cylinder mounting nuts loose (Chapter 9).
☐ Faulty master cylinder (Chapter 9).

Excessive brake pedal effort required to stop car

☐ Faulty vacuum servo unit (Chapter 9).
☐ Disconnected, damaged or insecure brake servo vacuum hoses (Chapter 9).
☐ Primary or secondary hydraulic circuit failure (Chapter 9).
☐ Seized brake caliper or wheel cylinder piston(s) (Chapter 9).
☐ Brake pads or brake shoes incorrectly fitted (Chapter 9).
☐ Incorrect grade of brake pads or brake shoes fitted (Chapter 1).
☐ Brake pads or brake shoe linings contaminated (Chapter 1).

Judder felt through brake pedal or steering wheel when braking

☐ Excessive run-out or distortion of front discs or rear discs/drums (Chapter 9).
☐ Brake pad or brake shoe linings worn (Chapter 1).
☐ Brake caliper or rear brake backplate mounting bolts loose (Chapter 9).
☐ Wear in suspension or steering components or mountings (Chapter 10).

Brakes binding

☐ Seized brake caliper or wheel cylinder piston(s) (Chapter 9).
☐ Faulty handbrake mechanism (Chapter 9).
☐ Faulty master cylinder (Chapter 9).

Rear wheels locking under normal braking

☐ Rear brake pad/shoe linings contaminated (Chapter 1).
☐ Faulty brake pressure regulator valves, or ABS unit (Chapter 9).

Suspension and steering

Note: *Before diagnosing suspension or steering faults, be sure that the trouble is not due to incorrect tyre pressures, mixtures of tyre types, or binding brakes.*

Car pulls to one side

- [ ] Defective tyre (Chapter 1).
- [ ] Excessively wear in suspension or steering components (Chapter 10)
- [ ] Incorrect front wheel alignment (Chapter 10).
- [ ] Accident damage to steering or suspension components (Chapter 10).

Wheel wobble and vibration

- [ ] Front roadwheels out of balance (vibration felt mainly through the steering wheel) (Chapter 1).
- [ ] Rear roadwheels out of balance (vibration felt throughout the car) (Chapter 1).
- [ ] Roadwheels damaged or distorted (Chapter 1).
- [ ] Faulty or damaged tyre (*Weekly checks*).
- [ ] Worn steering or suspension joints, bushes or components (Chapter 10).
- [ ] Roadwheel nuts loose (Chapter 1).
- [ ] Wear in driveshaft joint, or loose driveshaft nut (vibration worst when under load) (Chapter 1 or 8).

Excessive pitching and/or rolling around corners, or during braking

- [ ] Defective shock absorbers (Chapter 10).
- [ ] Broken or weak coil spring and/or suspension components (Chapter 10).
- [ ] Worn or damaged anti-roll bar or mountings (Chapter 10).

Wandering or general instability

- [ ] Incorrect front wheel alignment (Chapter 10).
- [ ] Worn steering or suspension joints, bushes or components (Chapter 10).
- [ ] Tyres out of balance (*Weekly checks*).
- [ ] Faulty or damaged tyre (*Weekly checks*).
- [ ] Roadwheel nuts loose (Chapter 1).
- [ ] Defective shock absorbers (Chapter 10).

Excessively-stiff steering

- [ ] Lack of steering gear lubricant (Chapter 10).

- [ ] Seized track rod end balljoint or suspension balljoint (Chapter 10).
- [ ] Faulty electric steering motor, blown fuse, or damaged wiring (electric power steering) (Chapter 10).
- [ ] Incorrect front wheel alignment (Chapter 10).
- [ ] Steering rack or column bent or damaged (Chapter 10).

Excessive play in steering

- [ ] Worn steering column universal joint (Chapter 10).
- [ ] Worn steering track rod end balljoints (Chapter 10).
- [ ] Worn rack-and-pinion steering gear (Chapter 10).
- [ ] Worn steering or suspension joints, bushes or components (Chapter 10).

Lack of power assistance

- [ ] Broken or slipping auxiliary drivebelt (hydraulic power steering) (Chapter 1).
- [ ] Faulty power steering motor, blown fuse, or damaged wiring (electric power steering) (Chapter 10).
- [ ] Faulty rack-and-pinion steering gear (Chapter 10).

Tyre wear excessive

Tyres worn on inside or outside edges

- [ ] Tyres under-inflated (wear on both edges) (*Weekly checks*).
- [ ] Incorrect camber or castor angles (wear on one edge only) (Chapter 10).
- [ ] Worn steering or suspension joints, bushes or components (Chapter 10).
- [ ] Excessively-hard cornering.
- [ ] Accident damage.

Tyre treads exhibit feathered edges

- [ ] Incorrect toe setting (Chapter 10).

Tyres worn in centre of tread

- [ ] Tyres over-inflated (*Weekly checks*).

Tyres worn on inside and outside edges

- [ ] Tyres under-inflated (*Weekly checks*).

Tyres worn unevenly

- [ ] Tyres out of balance (*Weekly checks*).
- [ ] Excessive wheel or tyre run-out (Chapter 1).
- [ ] Worn shock absorbers (Chapter 10).
- [ ] Faulty tyre (*Weekly checks*).

Electrical system

Note: *For problems associated with the starting system, refer to the faults listed under Engine earlier in this Section.*

Battery will only hold a charge for a few days

- [ ] Battery defective internally (Chapter 5A).
- [ ] Battery electrolyte level low (Chapter 5A).
- [ ] Battery terminal connections loose or corroded (*Weekly checks*).
- [ ] Auxiliary drivebelt worn or slipping (Chapter 1).
- [ ] Alternator not charging at correct output (Chapter 5A).
- [ ] Alternator or voltage regulator faulty (Chapter 5A).
- [ ] Short-circuit causing continual battery drain (Chapters 5A and 12).

Ignition (no-charge) warning light remains illuminated with engine running

- [ ] Auxiliary drivebelt broken, worn, or slipping (Chapter 1).
- [ ] Alternator brushes worn, sticking, or dirty (Chapter 5A).
- [ ] Alternator brush springs weak or broken (Chapter 5A).

- [ ] Internal fault in alternator or voltage regulator (Chapter 5A).
- [ ] Disconnected or loose wiring in charging circuit (Chapter 5A).

Ignition (no-charge) warning light fails to come on

- [ ] Warning light bulb blown (Chapter 12).
- [ ] Broken, disconnected, or loose wiring in warning light circuit (Chapters 5A and 12).
- [ ] Alternator faulty (Chapter 5A).

Lights inoperative

- [ ] Bulb blown (Chapter 12).
- [ ] Corrosion of bulb or bulbholder contacts (Chapter 12).
- [ ] Blown fuse (Chapter 12).
- [ ] Faulty relay (Chapter 12).
- [ ] Broken, loose, or disconnected wiring (Chapter 12).
- [ ] Faulty switch (Chapter 12).

Electrical system (continued)

Instrument readings inaccurate or erratic

Gauges give no reading

- ☐ Faulty gauge sender unit (Chapter 3 or 4A).
- ☐ Wiring open-circuit (Chapter 12).
- ☐ Faulty gauge (Chapter 12).

Gauges give continuous maximum reading

- ☐ Faulty gauge sender unit (Chapter 3 or 4A).
- ☐ Wiring short-circuit (Chapter 12).
- ☐ Faulty gauge (Chapter 12).

Horn faults

Horn fails to operate

- ☐ Blown fuse (Chapter 12).
- ☐ Cable or cable connections loose or disconnected (Chapter 12).
- ☐ Faulty switch (Chapter 12).
- ☐ Faulty horn (Chapter 12).

Horn emits intermittent or unsatisfactory sound

- ☐ Cable connections loose (Chapter 12).
- ☐ Horn mountings loose (Chapter 12).
- ☐ Faulty horn (Chapter 12).

Horn operates all the time

- ☐ Horn push either earthed or stuck down (Chapter 12).
- ☐ Horn cable to horn push earthed (Chapter 12).

Windscreen/tailgate wiper faults

Wipers fail to operate, or operate very slowly

- ☐ Wiper blades stuck to screen, or linkage seized (Chapter 12).
- ☐ Blown fuse (Chapter 12).
- ☐ Cable or cable connections loose or disconnected (Chapter 12).
- ☐ Faulty switch (Chapter 12).
- ☐ Faulty relay (Chapter 12).
- ☐ Faulty wiper motor (Chapter 12).

Wiper blades sweep over the wrong area of glass

- ☐ Wiper arms incorrectly-positioned on spindles (Chapter 12).
- ☐ Excessive wear of wiper linkage (Chapter 12).
- ☐ Wiper motor or linkage mountings loose or insecure (Chapter 12).

Wiper blades fail to clean the glass effectively

- ☐ Wiper blade rubbers worn or perished (Weekly checks).
- ☐ Wiper arm tension springs broken, or arm pivot seized (Chapter 12).
- ☐ Insufficient windscreen washer additive to adequately remove road film (Weekly checks).

Windscreen/tailgate washer faults

One or more washer jets inoperative

- ☐ Blocked washer jet (Weekly checks or Chapter 12).
- ☐ Disconnected, kinked or restricted fluid hose (Chapter 12).
- ☐ Insufficient fluid in washer reservoir (Weekly checks).

Washer pump fails to operate

- ☐ Broken or disconnected wiring or connections (Chapter 12).
- ☐ Blown fuse (Chapter 12).
- ☐ Faulty washer switch (Chapter 12).
- ☐ Faulty washer pump (Chapter 12).

Washer pump runs for some time before fluid is emitted from jets

- ☐ Faulty one-way valve in fluid supply hose (Chapter 12).

Electric window faults

Window glass will only move in one direction

- ☐ Faulty switch (Chapter 12).

Window glass slow to move

- ☐ Regulator seized or damaged, or lack of lubrication (Chapter 11).
- ☐ Door internal components or trim fouling regulator (Chapter 11).
- ☐ Faulty motor (Chapter 12).

Window glass fails to move

- ☐ Blown fuse (Chapter 12).
- ☐ Faulty relay (Chapter 12).
- ☐ Broken or disconnected wiring or connections (Chapter 12).
- ☐ Faulty motor (Chapter 12).

Central locking system faults

Complete system failure

- ☐ Blown fuse (Chapter 12).
- ☐ Faulty control unit or relay (Chapter 11).
- ☐ Broken or disconnected wiring or connections (Chapter 12).

Latch locks but will not unlock, or unlocks but will not lock

- ☐ Faulty master switch (Chapter 12).
- ☐ Faulty lock (Chapter 11).
- ☐ Faulty relay (Chapter 12).

One lock motor fails to operate

- ☐ Broken or disconnected wiring or connections (Chapter 12).
- ☐ Faulty lock motor (Chapter 11).
- ☐ Fault in door latch (Chapter 11).

Note: *References throughout this index are in the form "**Chapter number**" • "**Page number**". So, for example, 2C•15 refers to page 15 of Chapter 2C.*

Index REF•21

Note: *References throughout this index are in the form* "**Chapter number**" • "**Page number**". *So, for example, 2C•15 refers to page 15 of Chapter 2C.*

Flywheel – 2A•20
Front anti-roll bar and links – 10•7
Front brake caliper – 9•4
Front brake disc – 9•5
Front brake pads – 1•10, 9•2
Front hub bearings – 10•4
Front lower arm – 10•8
   balljoint – 10•9
Front strut – 10•5
Front subframe – 10•9
Front swivel hub – 10•2
Fuel and exhaust system fault finding – REF•15
Fuel injection system – 4A•8
Fuel lines and fittings – 4A•3
Fuel pump/fuel gauge sender unit – 4A•6
Fuel pump/fuel pressure – 4A•5
Fuel system – 4A•1 *et seq*
   depressurisation – 4A•2
Fuel tank – 4A•5
Fuses and relays – 12•3

G

Gear lever and gearchange cables – 7A•3

H

Handbrake – 1•9
   cables – 9•16
   lever – 9•15
   warning light switch – 9•17
Headlight adjuster components – 12•13
Headlight beam alignment – 12•14
Heater blower motor – 3•9
Heater matrix – 3•9
Heater unit – 3•10
Heating and ventilation – 3•7
Horn – 12•14

I

Ignition coils – 5B•2
Ignition system – 5B•1 *et seq*
   sensors – 5B•3
   timing – 5B•3
Inlet manifold – 4A•13
Instrument panel – 12•14
Interior trim and fittings – 11•21
Introduction – 0•4

J

Jacking and vehicle support – REF•5
Jump starting – 0•7

L

Leaks – 0•9, 1•7
Light units – 12•12
Lubricants and fluids – 0•16

M

Main and big-end bearings – 2B•11
Manual transmission – 7A•1 *et seq*
   fault finding – REF•15
MOT test checks – REF•8
Multi-Mode transmission – 7B•1 *et seq*
   electrical components – 7B•3
   fault finding – REF•16

O

Oil pressure switch – 2A•17
Oil pump – 2A•17
Oil seals – REF•4
Oxygen sensors – 4B•2

P

Piston/connecting rod assemblies – 2B•8, 2B•9, 2B•12
Pollen filter – 1•7

R

Radiator – 3•2
   cooling fan – 3•5
Radio/CD unit – 12•18
   aerial – 12•19
Rear axle assembly – 10•11
Rear axle pivot bushes – 10•13
Rear brake drum – 9•5
Rear brake shoes – 1•14, 9•6
Rear hub and bearings – 10•10
Rear shock absorber – 10•10
Rear spring – 10•11
Rear wheel cylinder – 9•8
Rev counter – 12•14
Reversing light switch – 7A•4, 7B•5
Road test – 1•12
Routine maintenance and servicing – 1•1 *et seq*

Note: *References throughout this index are in the form "**Chapter number**" • "**Page number**". So, for example, 2C•15 refers to page 15 of Chapter 2C.*

Preserving Our Motoring Heritage

< *The Model J Duesenberg Derham Tourster. Only eight of these magnificent cars were ever built – this is the only example to be found outside the United States of America*

Almost every car you've ever loved, loathed or desired is gathered under one roof at the Haynes Motor Museum. Over 300 immaculately presented cars and motorbikes represent every aspect of our motoring heritage, from elegant reminders of bygone days, such as the superb Model J Duesenberg to curiosities like the bug-eyed BMW Isetta. There are also many old friends and flames. Perhaps you remember the 1959 Ford Popular that you did your courting in? The magnificent 'Red Collection' is a spectacle of classic sports cars including AC, Alfa Romeo, Austin Healey, Ferrari, Lamborghini, Maserati, MG, Riley, Porsche and Triumph.

A Perfect Day Out

Each and every vehicle at the Haynes Motor Museum has played its part in the history and culture of Motoring. Today, they make a wonderful spectacle and a great day out for all the family. Bring the kids, bring Mum and Dad, but above all bring your camera to capture those golden memories for ever. You will also find an impressive array of motoring memorabilia, a comfortable 70 seat video cinema and one of the most extensive transport book shops in Britain. The Pit Stop Cafe serves everything from a cup of tea to wholesome, home-made meals or, if you prefer, you can enjoy the large picnic area nestled in the beautiful rural surroundings of Somerset.

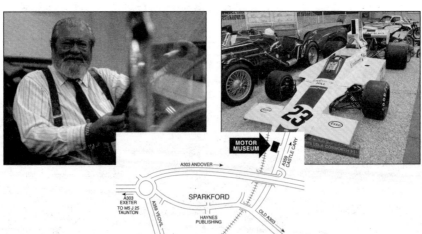

> *John Haynes O.B.E., Founder and Chairman of the museum at the wheel of a Haynes Light 12.*

< *Graham Hill's Lola Cosworth Formula 1 car next to a 1934 Riley Sports.*

The Museum is situated on the A359 Yeovil to Frome road at Sparkford, just off the A303 in Somerset. It is about 40 miles south of Bristol, and 25 minutes drive from the M5 intersection at Taunton.
Open 9.30am - 5.30pm (10.00am - 4.00pm Winter) 7 days a week, *except Christmas Day, Boxing Day and New Years Day*
Special rates available for schools, coach parties and outings Charitable Trust No. 292048